MARTHA WASHINGTON'S
BOOKE OF COOKERY

MARTHA WASHINGTON'S
BOOKE OF COOKERY

*and Booke of Sweetmeats: being a Family Manuscript, curiously
copied by an unknown Hand sometime in the seventeenth century,
which was in her Keeping from 1749, the time of her Marriage
to Daniel Custis, to 1799, at which time she gave it to
Eleanor Parke Custis, her grandaughter, on the occasion of her
Marriage to Lawrence Lewis*

TRANSCRIBED BY

KAREN HESS

WITH HISTORICAL NOTES
AND COPIOUS ANNOTATIONS

COLUMBIA UNIVERSITY PRESS
NEW YORK

The author and publisher gratefully acknowledge the generosity of The Historical Society of Pennsylvania in providing access to the manuscript and use of reproductions.

Library of Congress Cataloging in Publication Data

Main entry under title:

Martha Washington's Booke of cookery.

Transcription of A booke of cookery and A booke of sweetmeats, a ms. owned by Martha Washington.
Bibliography: p.
Includes index.
1. Cookery, English—Early works to 1800.
2. Cookery, American—Virginia—Early works to 1800.   3. Washington, Martha Dandridge Custis, 1731–1802.   I. Hess, Karen.   II. Title: Booke of cookery.   III. Title: Booke of sweetmeats.
TX705.M368   641.5941   80-18257
ISBN 0-231-04930-7
10 9 8 7 6 5

Columbia University Press
New York and Guildford, Surrey

Copyright © 1981 Columbia University Press
All rights reserved
Printed in the United States of America

FOR JOHN,
who held my hand all the way

ACKNOWLEDGMENTS

In the belief that we cannot understand our cookery without going to its sources, I offer the text of this seventeenth-century English recipe manuscript which was in the possession of Martha Washington for fifty years. I thank the Historical Society of Pennsylvania and James Mooney, director, for their graciousness in permitting me to study the manuscript.

And I thank Columbia University Press and Bernard Gronert, my editor, for giving *Martha Washington's Booke of Cookery* a good home with a grateful nod to Maria Caliandro.

Among the many individuals whose encouragement and assistance made this work possible, I am indebted to Elizabeth David for her enthusiastic interest in the manuscript, her erudition, and her overwhelming generosity.

I am also deeply indebted to Daniel Okrent, my former editor, whose faith in my work sustained me through a difficult period. It was he who helped me whip a mass of papers into a book, and the present shape and organization are essentially as he proposed.

Also, Frank Anderson, Honorary Curator of Rare Books and Manuscripts of the New York Botanical Garden Library, has been an ever present help in matters concerning medieval medicine.

Among other institutions who opened their facilities to me, I start with Oxford University, where various scholars could not have been more kind. I single out Margaret Crum of Western Manuscripts, who initiated me into membership of the Bodleian Library, and R. E. Alton of St. Edmund Hall, whose contributions are attributed. Waverly Winfree, Curator of Manuscripts, Virginia Historical Society, Richmond; Edmund Berkeley, Jr., Curator of Manuscripts, Alderman Library, University of Virginia, Charlottesville; Edward Riley, Colonial Williamsburg Foundation; and H.M.G. Baillie, Royal Commission of Historical Manuscripts, London, were all unfailingly helpful, as were the staff members of the following libraries: New York Academy of Medicine Library, Rare Book Room; New York Public Library, particularly the rare book, manuscript, and genealogical departments; and Guildhall Library, London.

In addition, Barbara Scott, Amparo Chamberlain, and Rudolf Grewe elucidated difficult points or were otherwise helpful. And to those who aided me in other ways, I thank them, one and all.

Karen Hess
New York City, 1980

CONTENTS

PART I

INTRODUCTION TO
A BOOKE OF COOKERY

This beguiling manuscript, comprising *A Booke of Cookery* and *A Booke of Sweetmeats*, was in the keeping of Martha Washington from 1749, the year of her marriage to Daniel Custis, until 1799, when she presented it to Nelly Custis, her granddaughter. In light of the Washington association, it is indeed curious that so little serious attention has been drawn to this historic document. Its pages are pages from the living past, a treasure trove of culinary secrets set down by mothers and grandmothers of some of our earliest colonists, part of our American heritage from England. It is also a delightful cookbook.

Few scholars are cooks—and fewer cooks scholars. Perhaps this accounts for the fact that no other aspect of human endeavor has been so neglected by historians as home cooking. I cannot help but feel that this neglect is also related to the ageless depreciation of the work of women. Yet since time immemorial—when not searching for food, making baskets and pottery, tilling the soil and tending livestock, spinning and weaving, and bearing and rearing children, of course—women have been inventing and perfecting the art of cooking. The importance of agriculture and the significance of the spice routes were always well understood by the historians, and the actual cooking pots, if ancient enough, might be displayed in museums. But the homely art of the hearth has never been deemed worthy of the same study as are other disciplines. Until fairly recently, most English scholars who worked with ancient cookery manuscripts did so only because of their interest in social customs, manners, and especially language, all of which is reasonable enough. If the editors had been as versed in cookery as in Middle English, there would have been yet another dimension to their work. A large body of invaluable culinary documents has been published in England, with exemplary attention to faithful transcription, and thus made available to those who would study them.

We have not been so fortunate in America. We do not have the long and rich bibliography of the English, to be sure, but this is all the more reason to cherish what we do have, and it is

3

not inconsiderable. Most of the works that have purported to present our culinary heritage have been ludicrously bowdlerized. Recipes are "modernized" beyond recognition, and it is rare that anyone so much as bothers to give a source.* (To be sure, it is not only American source material that receives such cavalier treatment.) It is difficult to know where to lay the blame. It is not lack of interest; we are endlessly fascinated with the Americans of 1776 in their fine satin waistcoats and powdered wigs, sipping their possets and syllabubs. Too many of us, perhaps, are content to accept picture-book versions of history; we leave the perusal of primary sources to the scholars, little dreaming that it is they who are having all the fun, and that we are the poorer for having allowed ourselves to be cheated of the pleasures of glimpsing for ourselves bits of life from the fascinating past.

And private documents, such as family manuscripts, are the most fascinating and revealing of all. The recipes they contain were recorded partly through filial piety and duty, to be sure, but mostly as a reminder to oneself and to one's daughter of the best way *To Souse a pigg of 3 or 4 shillings price* (C 35),† or *To make A Frykecy* (C 2) with a golden silken sauce without curdling. Because the writers had no thought of impressing publishers or dazzling readers, we catch intimate glimpses from a time when it was entirely reasonable to have in the household a feather bed "where one lyeth continually," and the cherries were to be kept warm, yet "neere noe fire" (see C 153). Methods of keeping cherries may have been improved—I am not entirely convinced—but we learn in a few lines a great deal about the vagaries of sixteenth- and seventeenth-century heating systems, and something of family attitudes towards the care of their aged. And all charmingly expressed.

But let no one think that the recipes of this manuscript are too archaic to be used today. A certain number of them will be of mainly historical interest, it is true, but the seventeenth century was the golden age of the English kitchen. Medieval excesses were being sloughed off; the heavy *standing pottages* (stews thickened with cereals) were largely being replaced by more bracing soups, at least among the wealthy; spices were being used rather more discreetly, except for the ubiquitous nutmeg; the use of fresh herbs was becoming more skilled; and *the sauces were never cheapened with flour.* (The *roux*, under the name of *fried flour*, seems to have made its appearance sometime after mid-seventeenth century, but it did not become popular until sometime in the eighteenth cen-

---

* There are a few exceptions. See bibliography for details.

† Recipe number 35 in *A Booke of Cookery.* Just so, all recipes from *A Booke of Sweetmeats* are designated with an *S.*

tury, judging by manuscripts and cookbooks.) The wheat starch liaison of Roman cookery and, less commonly, of medieval cookery, seems not to have survived the fifteenth century in England. Our manuscript is especially interesting in this regard because the recipes span the Elizabethan and Jacobean eras, or from mid-sixteenth century to about 1625. More important, the recipes are of outstanding quality, with few exceptions; the art of liaison is handled with skill and perception and modern cooks would do well to learn the secrets of cookery that were confided to the pages of this manuscript.

In these notes, I deal with the sixteenth- and seventeenth-century English cookery presented in the Washington manuscript and its relationship with early American cookery, particularly that of Virginia, along with the products of the mother country and of the New World. The role of medieval dietary practice in this cuisine is discussed in my introduction to *A Booke of Sweetmeats*, beginning page 205, where I also explain my reasons for using the *Oxford English Dictionary* as my source for scientific nomenclature. In Appendices 1 and 2, I sketch the historical background of the English home recipe manuscript in general, and of this manuscript in particular. Readers interested in problems of transcription and in certain orthographical and philological details (the altered runic thorn in *y*, for example, so that it is pronounced *the*) are referred to Appendix 3.

AMERICAN COOKERY
American cookery is a tapestry of extraordinarily complex design, reflecting our rich and varied ethnic origins (including the unique American Indian and African contributions), our New World produce, and our frontier history. Still, the warp of our cooking is English, much as common law remains the basis of our law. Even Louisiana cuisine was not exempt, as evidenced by the oyster loaf of New Orleans, which was, however, long commonplace in English cookbooks.

So to understand American cooking it is necessary to start with some acquaintance with English cookery, particularly that of the seventeenth century, the cuisine that was brought over by the early settlers. The dissident Puritans, who with great perseverance wrested a living from the stormy seas and stony soil of New England, in spite of rigorous winters; the equally industrious Quakers who chose to settle in the richer lands of Pennsylvania; and the gentry (largely younger sons of younger sons whose families had run out of land in England) and assorted ne'er-do-wells who came to the lush tidelands of Virginia and who early turned to the slave traders to supply them with working hands, being ill-prepared to earn a living with their own hands—all brought essentially the same cuisine with them. They seem all to have used pretty much the same cookbooks, for example, and those family manuscripts with which I am acquainted show great similarity, whether they belonged to William Penn of Pennsylvania, Katherine Pirrott of Connecticut, or Martha Washington of Virginia. Yet the differences in climate, soil, and social conditions early produced distinct regional differences. Eighteenth-century writers make it clear that this differentiation was well developed by that time, and when American cookbooks finally started appearing at the end of that century, we have clear documentation in the form of recipes. Amelia Simmons in *American Cookery*, 1796, and Lydia Maria Child in *The American Frugal Housewife*, 1832, both New Englanders, give us recipes for baked beans, chowders, soft gingerbreads, pumpkin pies, turkey with *cramberry-sauce*, and boiled and baked Indian puddings. Mary Randolph in *The Virginia Housewife*, 1824, gives us recipes for *shoat* (young pig), *homony*, beaten biscuit, a number of *à la daube* dishes (reflecting the French Huguenot presence), a number of Spanish dishes (not Creole), some fourteen recipes calling for tomatoes (tomatoes were in common use in Virginia during the last quarter of the eighteenth century, but this seems to be their first appearance in a cookbook written by an American), recipes calling for eggplant and okra and an inordinate number of fine recipes for ice cream. It is altogether a sumptuous and sophisticated cuisine and thoroughly American withal, with fascinating traces of black influence, as well there might be since black women traditionally did most of the cooking.* Mrs. Randolph's heyday was in the 1790s and there is reason to believe that the cuisine she records dates from that time. So that within a very short period, both the New England and Virginia cuisines had assumed their definitive character. While the family relationship between them and the mother cuisine is evident, the differences among the three at the turn of that century are striking. (The cuisine presented by Eliza Leslie in *Directions for Cookery*, 1837,

---

* Okra, to name but one product, is native to West Africa. Helen Mendes, in *The African Heritage Cookbook*, 1971, claims that blacks were cooking with tomatoes in Africa by the seventeenth century; if so, it would have been due to the influence of the Portuguese, who had been in West Africa since the fifteenth century, and who early and enthusiastically took to the tomato. The tomato is, of course, native to Mexico; it is amusing to think that black slaves may indeed have brought the tomato to Virginia. It was used there perhaps half a century earlier and with more flair and abandon than elsewhere in the United States. They brought blackeyed peas or cowpeas, benne or sesame seeds, and quite likely eggplant, the two latter products having been brought to Africa by the Arab slave traders.

Philadelphia, is curiously less regional in scope or rather, perhaps, more inclusively American.)

What place does the Washington manuscript occupy in the history of Virginia cuisine? In the larger sense, it was simply one more manifestation of the mother cuisine, and this role is discussed in the annotations. Specifically, it is harder to say and necessarily involves some speculation. I believe that our manuscript (or possibly the manuscript of which ours is a copy) came to Virginia in mid-seventeenth century. (Problems of dating and tracing lines of ownership are discussed in the Appendices.) The little volume shows considerable evidence of kitchen wear. Aside from certain damage by fire along the lower edges, there are grease splatterings and water stains. More interesting, although inconclusive, there is an undecipherable system of markings (mostly crosses, but slashes also appear) both before and after many recipe titles, and also in the index. I believe that as many as four different hands were involved in this checking off. There is no way of knowing when the various markings, presumably indicating that the recipes had been tried, were made. However, in three recipes that have no such markings, there are emendments made in another hand, so clearly the lack of a mark does not mean that a particular recipe was never tried. I believe that all of the marks and comments were made before the death of Frances Custis in 1715, and for the most part, in the preceding century.

By the time the manuscript came into the hands of Martha Custis in 1749, I think that it had long since become a family heirloom and that it had not served as a working kitchen manual since the beginning of the century, perhaps earlier. Many of the recipes must have seemed old-fashioned to Martha, and they became increasingly so as time went on; the cuisine of the manuscript is that of Elizabethan and Jacobean England. But Virginia cuisine had already assumed its definitive characteristics by mid-eighteenth century; the basis was the same cuisine so brilliantly presented in our manuscript, the cuisine of a privileged master class, wealthy enough to make prodigal use of imported almonds, oranges, and wines, for instance, who evidently cared for the good life and had the leisure to enjoy it—a cuisine predicated on having a large staff of servants. In the development of this cuisine, our manuscript, or others like it, played a decisive role.

In 1747, there appeared in England *The Art of Cookery* by Hannah Glasse, which was to become the most popular cookbook in England and in the Colonies for the rest of the century and beyond. The cuisine of Hannah Glasse seems very modern compared to that of our manuscript, although the younger is clearly the child of the elder. She gives, for example, an early recipe for

7

ice cream (1751) and one calling for love apples or tomatoes (1758), and potatoes (white) have become commonplace. More important, the medieval combinations of meat with fruits, sugar, and spices, traces of which are so strong in our manuscript, have been relegated to the dessert section in the form of the vestigial mince pie. Spicing of meat dishes is largely limited to pepper, with occasional fillips of other spices. That is perhaps oversimplified, because an *English Catchup* of mushrooms (1755) and various pickles, all well spiced, are used as condiments and seasoning. There is also an early recipe *To make A Currey the Indian Way*, calling for turmeric, ginger, and black pepper, as spices. Mrs. Glasse has a penchant for Indian recipes and they are of better quality than many of those that were to follow.

Clearly, it was a book whose time had come. The first cookbook to be printed in America, *The Compleat Housewife* by E. Smith, 1742 (differing little from the 1727 English edition), looks backward to a different era. While much of Mrs. Glasse's book seems old-fashioned to us, much of Mrs. Smith's book is quaint. Still, whole areas of cookery had changed little or not at all from the cuisine of our manuscript. Roasting was still properly conducted before the fire, and the usual sauce for a roast was still the natural roasting juices heightened with a few drops of lemon juice, a bit of anchovy, or the new ketchup (made at home with vinegar, mushrooms or oysters, and spices, not so different from the pickled oysters used in our manuscript); bread was still baked from the same recipes in brick ovens; and the rather stodgy puddings continued to be popular. The coarse pastries, the *coffins*, seem to have given way for the most part to finer ones, and cakes had become increasingly sweet (as main dishes became less so) and rich, often depending on eggs as leavening rather than yeast, reflecting the use of increasingly efficient whisks. Marchpane was no longer made at home (Mrs. Smith still gave a recipe for it), but most of the other favorites continued relatively unchanged.

The same changes were also taking place in Virginia cookery, since they were using English cookbooks. But whether it was the peculiar contributing influences noted earlier, or the perceptiveness of Mary Randolph as a cook, Virginia cookery as presented by her in *The Virginia Housewife*, 1824, is finer and more imaginative than that of Hannah Glasse, even as it shows the imprint of the older work.

Let us now turn to the actual cuisine represented in our manuscript. In my annotations I have attempted to explain such terms and practices as might not be familiar to the modern reader, and to give a brief background of dishes and products that I have considered to be useful or interesting in some way. Still, there are some general points that may be made.

The most striking characteristic is doubtless the lavishness of the kitchen. Butter and cream, in particular, are used in prodigal amounts. Some sources explain this by saying that they were cheap, but according to the records of Ingatestone Hall of 1561,* on the occasion of a visit by Queen Elizabeth, cream cost 8 pence the gallon and butter 7 pence the dish. (Most sources fix this measure between 1 ½ and 2 ½ pounds. However, I find this hopelessly wrong in recipes of the period, where a pound is more than generous, even allowing for the over-richness characteristic of many dishes of the time.) The same list shows that a chicken was to be had for as little as 2 ½ pence, a dozen eggs for 3 pence, a goose for 5 pence, an entire steer for £4, and Seville oranges at the rate of 10 for a penny. In proportion, I find neither cream nor butter cheap.

Cooking with butter was characteristic of Tudor cookery, largely replacing the earlier lard and olive oil (being expensive, the latter came to be reserved for salads), but never altogether replacing beef suet and marrow among the wealthy. Butter was frequently overused, and some of our recipes illustrate this unfortunate tendency.

Fresh or sweet butter, so often specified in our recipes, is butter that has been neither salted nor clarified for long keeping. Clarified butter keeps remarkably well (it is the milk solids that are so subject to turning rancid) and serves very well for frying, and is indeed then far easier to handle. For many purposes, salt butter was well washed before use to remove the salt. While it then never has quite the flavor and charm of fresh butter, it was surely in no worse condition than most of the butter we are able to buy today, which has little character to begin with and has sojourned in cold storage for months. Ultra-pasteurized cream cannot be described in polite society.

In the earliest English manuscripts, recipes calling for almond milk outnumber those calling for cow's milk. It was originally

* *Tudor Food and Pastimes* by F. G. Emmison, 1964. Ingatestone Hall, in Essex, was the estate of Sir William Petre, who served successively as secretary to Henry VIII, Edward VI, Mary, and Elizabeth, an extraordinary feat in those troubled days. The household records of the Hall, as excerpted and commented on by Emmison, illuminate many areas of daily life among the wealthy in Tudor England. Such prices as are given antedate the period represented by perhaps the major portion of our manuscript, but I believe that the proportions hold fairly true well into Stuart times, and that in spite of the social and political turmoil of the period, the actual day-by-day life in the kitchen did not materially change.

the Saracen influence, but almond milk proved convenient for the observance of innumerable fast days (in letter, if not in spirit), when "white meats" (dairy products) were proscribed along with other meats. Anne Wilson cites L. F. Salzman's *English Trade in the Middle Ages* to the effect that the royal household consumed "no less than 28,500 pounds" of almonds in 1286, not an extraordinary year, apparently. Even a relatively small household bought 40 pounds in 1418-19. Fasting regulations gradually became less stringent with the growth of Protestantism and by the seventeenth century, almond milk was pretty much relegated to sweet dishes, except for *white broth*, and that was rapidly changing (see C 113 and 203). The use of almond milk lingers in a number of our recipes, and among the sweet dishes, the use of almonds can only be described as prodigal.

Many other exotic luxuries were lavishly called for in our manuscript. Raisins, currants, pomegranates, rose water, dates, ginger, musk, ambergris, and a great array of spices from the East had been known and used by the wealthy since the time of the Crusades, or earlier; all except pomegranates are used in generous amounts in these recipes. Citing Salzman again, we learn that 15 lemons and 7 oranges, together with 230 pomegranates and dried fruits, were bought from a Spanish ship at Portsmouth in 1289 for Eleanor of Castile, the queen of Edward I; 39 lemons were bought on another occasion. These were not routine imports, to be sure, but they continued and trade swelled. Lemons and Seville oranges seem not to have entered cookery except in preserving until the time of Elizabeth, when they begin to be used somewhat as *verjuice* was (see C 4), and continued to be for some time. The advantages of lemon juice as a taste enhancer gradually became appreciated. Recipes calling for lemon juice or diced pulp are frequent and there is a dish of stewed mutton with oranges (C 14).

The use of rose water somewhat parallels that of almonds, but it persisted far longer in meat cookery, as evidenced by our manuscript. So far as the use of spices is concerned, the older recipes show strong medieval traces, while the newer one have become somewhat more subtle, except for the ubiquitous nutmeg. (In all instances, I suggest a light hand with nutmeg unless you love its muskiness.) Ginger is still very much used, particularly in the older recipes; green ginger is frequently specified and it is often used in an almost Chinese fashion, particularly in the fish recipes. Saffron is another holdover from medieval cookery. It was grown in England from the fourteenth century until well past the time of our manuscript, giving its name to the town of Saffron Walden in Essex. It was used in both meat cookery and sweets, and it persisted in various regional cakes long after its use pretty much disappeared in other dishes. Mustard also came to be grown in England, and was extremely popular as a condiment, rarely entering recipes. A number of other aromatic herbs that originated elsewhere were also naturalized in England, such as coriander seeds from the Levant. The use of musk and ambergris was another characteristic of sixteenth- and seventeenth-century cooking, although it is difficult to be sure how long their use actually continued; I suspect that recipes called for these substances long after they were no longer much used (see S20, 113, and C76). For the use of the imported anchovy, see C 1.

The amount of sugar used in early English cookery is a vexing problem, but it cannot have been so great as is sometimes thought. According to Anne Wilson, the amount used in Elizabethan England averaged one pound per person per year. Practically speaking, all of that went to the very wealthy, and most of that must have gone into preserving fruits, various sweets such as marchpane and comfits, and medicinal preparations. According to Wilson, the cost of a pound was "at least a shilling [12 pence], which was a day's wage for an Elizabethan craftsman." At that price, honey remained the only sweetening for ordinary people; the exclusive use of sugar in our manuscript (except in *Honey of Roses* and the gingerbreads) is yet another sign of the wealth of the household in which it originated. (By sometime in the latter part of the seventeenth century, well past the time of our manuscript, consumption had quadrupled in spite of import duties; this must reflect use by the newly affluent, the burgeoning merchant class, rather than increased individual consumption.)

The source of sugar for England varied with the period. The specification of Brazil (S 8) and Barbary sugar (S 53), for example, would seem to indicate that the recipes originated before the time when England acquired her own sugar colonies—that is, well before mid-seventeenth century, and most likely earlier.

Sugar finally came to the sixteenth- and seventeenth-century consumer in blocks or cones, in varying degrees of refinement. This accounts for the elaborate directions for clarifying sugar, and the reiterated instructions to *searce* (sift) or powder it. (Powdered sugar was only finely sifted sugar, *not* confectioners' sugar.) Block sugar also accounts for the strewing of *scraped* sugar that made for a charming textural and taste contrast that we have all but forgotten.

The presence of sugar in so many of our meat recipes, almost invariably in conjunction with fruits and spices (and occasionally, almond milk), is part of our heritage from medieval cooking which, in turn, had come from the Arabs. It is virtually impossible to give precise amounts of sugar required, but I believe

11

that in most dishes, it was added in a quantity comparable to that of the spices, in a manner to highlight the spices rather than to actually sweeten a dish. In a recipe for *Chekyns in sauce* from *A Noble Boke off Cookry* (mid-fifteenth century), in a rare example of precision of proportion, we find among the spices "an unce of sugar [2 tablespoons]," followed by "an unce of cannelles [about 4 tablespoons of cinnamon]," and "a litille veniger," to an unspecified amount of wine sauce that required, however, the yolks of 40 eggs to enrich and thicken it, perhaps 20 cups of sauce. (It is interesting to note that this sauce is called a *ceryp*, a not uncommon designation, from which we are permitted to deduce, I believe, that either it was considered sweet, or that the consistency of the sauce was runny, or both.) Certain dishes were indeed quite sweet (mincemeat, for example), but I have the impression that this tends to emphasize a restrained hand elsewhere. The soursweet dishes pose an interesting problem. In the fifteenth-century Laud MS. 553, in a recipe for *Egredoucet*, we find: "vynegre & ye thrudde p[er]ty sug[ar]," or one-third as much sugar as vinegar. To be sure, we do not know how widespread these practices were nor how long they continued. However, in Part II of *The Good Huswives Jewell* by Thomas Dawson there is a recipe *To boyle a capon in white broth* that directs us to add "halfe a quartern of sugar [and] five spoonefull of verdjuice" to perhaps a cup or so of the richest part of the broth. The sugar amounts to 2 ounces or 4 tablespoons; if the spoon held a good ounce of verjuice, the proportions held well into our period.

Any excitement in the sixteenth and seventeenth centuries over the strange products from the New World shows little trace in our document. Turkey, for instance, is mentioned but once, although elaborate recipes for it appear as early as 1586, and turkey seems to have been served when Elizabeth visited Ingatestone Hall in 1561 (see C 24). Kidney beans are mentioned, but, they must have been considered simply as another strain of beans they already knew. Pumpkins are not mentioned, but edible "gourds" that were cooked and used in soups much as pumpkin had been known for centuries and are not mentioned either. Not surprisingly, there is no mention of tomatoes. Although Gerard described them in 1597, all but giving actual Spanish recipes for them, the English did not commonly eat them until after mid-eighteenth century, judging by the cookbooks. Nor is there mention of chocolate, which became enormously popular towards the mid-seventeenth century. Pepys, in 1664, stopped at the *coffee-house* for a cup of *jocolatte*, which he pronounced "very good," and recipes for it proliferated in manuscript cookery books during the final quarter of that century. According to Wilson, vanilla (along with tomatoes and chocolate also from Mexico) was used to flavor chocolate in England during the same period; I have not found it in the cook-books, however, and it appears infrequently even in the eighteenth century. The 1805 American edition of Hannah Glasse's *The Art of Cookery* calls for *vanelas* to flavor chocolate, and the first American recipe that I know that features vanilla on its own is one for vanilla ice cream in Mary Randolph's *The Virginia Housewife*, 1824; similar recipes had, however, been appearing in France, and Jefferson brought back one in 1784, showing once again how the printed word lags behind usage. (Tea from the Far East and coffee from the Arabs were also introduced into England around the middle of the seventeenth century; in due course, they came to America.)

Among meats, mutton was the most popular, not too sur-prising in a great wool-producing society; lamb was more rarely sacrificed. Veal was also common, as is to be expected in a land of milk cows. (Heifers are spared, but bull calves are supernu-merary in dairy herds.) Many recipes for veal appear in *The Forme of Cury*, about 1390, and other medieval manuscripts; those who write that veal did not appear on the English medieval table are in error. With all meats, fine cuts were roasted on the spit and coarser cuts were stewed or baked in a crust with aromatics and vegetables. The running juices of roast mutton, so often called for in our manuscript, were a prime resource of the English cook, being used to season and give substance to all manner of dishes.

It may seem curious that there is no recipe for roast beef in our manuscript. It must be remarked that all roasting recipes are concerned only with stuffings or other special treatment; the roasting procedure is nowhere described. In fact, roasting direc-tions are rare in English cookbooks until the eighteenth century.* But the absence of recipes for roast beef in earlier cookbooks has caused certain writers to assume that the English did not have beef fit for roasting until the eighteenth century. Now it is true that in medieval cookery, while beef was frequently chopped for use in

---

* It should not be necessary to refute the oft-told tale that roasts did not grace the English table until after the general acceptance of the individual table fork, usually placed around mid-seventeenth century, although Ben Jonson, for one, knew of the use of "your silver fork" in polite society by 1605 (*Volpone*) and the use of carving forks and even specialized serving forks antedated that by perhaps centuries. Too much is made of the use of a fork as an instrument of civilized eating; the lack of it never prevented the enjoyment of roast meat of all kinds by the English and other Europeans, as the slightest acquaintance of literature or period art would show, to say nothing of the peoples of the Middle, Near, and Far East, who have managed to enjoy opulent feasts with exquisite man-ners without the help of a fork. Specifically, English medieval menus and instruction manuals make it clear that roast meats were carved and served with nicety.

various baked combinations, stewed, or "powdered" with salt for long keeping and then boiled, it was less often roasted; the menus make it clear that venison, mutton, hare, and all manner of fowl were more highly regarded as roasts than was beef, so special meat strains would seem to have been a later development. By Tudor times, however, we find *Roosted beyfe* on a menu in *A Proper Newe Booke of Cokerye*, 1545 (?), although no recipe is given for it. And at a Twelfth Day dinner, 1552, at Ingatestone Hall, six pieces of *rosting beiffe* were served, part of a princely array of other meats, roasted, boiled, and baked. Markham, in the *Dayrie worke* section of *The English Hus-wife*, 1615, discusses the choice of *Kine*: her shape "must a little differ from the Butchers rule," and goes into considerable detail. He lists eight different breeds of milk cow that exceeded all others; evidently, careful breeding had been going on for quite some time in both meat and dairy strains. The quality of English pasturage was legendary, so the quality of all meat and dairy products must have been very fine indeed.

The quality of English game, furred and feathered, has always been splendid; its fame has survived into modern times. Venison, a prerogative of the crown, was perhaps the most highly regarded of all meats; this extended to the *umbles* (innards), which were most often baked in a crust, the name of which was later corrupted into the homonymic *humble pie* (C 64). Making beef taste like red deer was a common conceit—or deceit, rather—of the late sixteenth and early seventeenth centuries (C 48).

For the rest, pork, hare, rabbits, capon, chicken, goose, pigeon, duck, teal, turkey (possibly including guinea fowl), partridge, pheasant, woodcock, plover, curlew, and sparrows, are all represented in our manuscript. There is a beautiful fricassee recipe (C 2), one for roast capon with oysters, and a number of delectable and interesting recipes for pigeon. Not one of the sauces is sludged up with a grain of flour.

The fish recipes are of exceptional interest. You may not be tempted to try the virtually medieval way *to boyle A Carpe in its Blood* (C 187), but you surely will not be able to resist reading about it. Most of the recipes are perfectly suitable for today, or would be if one could but find the fish. It is not so much the problem of the varieties available. It is true that we have neither true sole nor turbot, and that our oysters are quite different, but that is hardly serious compared to the problem of quality. Some of the finest fish of the great Atlantic swam within sight of English shores and, for the rest the English were intrepid seafarers, and fishing boats were often equipped with ingenious sea water flow-through "keeps." There were fine streams everywhere and all estates had large ponds where lake fish were kept. It beat refrigeration. What fish had to be kept was pickled (there are delightful recipes in our manuscript), dried, or salted. Again, it beat refrigeration. And there was no pollution to speak of—no oil spills, no insecticides, no chemical wastes, no atomic fallout. All salt and fresh water creatures must have had a fine clean taste that none of us has ever tasted, nor ever shall.

It has been frequently written that little attention was paid to vegetables in the sixteenth and seventeenth centuries. Those who so say cannot have read the sources. In our manuscript alone, there are recipes and gardening hints concerning: asparagus, artichokes, cucumbers, carrots, turnips, parsnips, skirrets, kidney beans, peas, purslane, onions, garlic, potatoes (sweets imported from Spain), lettuce, rocket, sorrel, spinach, and cabbage, besides more than a score of aromatic and medicinal herbs. In *The English Hus-wife*, 1615, Markham says that the first step in attaining skill in cookery is "to have knowledge of all sorts of hearbes belonging to the Kitchin, whether they bee for the pot, for sallets; for sauces, for servings, or for any other seasoning or adorning." Without repeating any of the above vegetables, he gives gardening instructions for radishes, chives, coleworts (kale), chervil, gourds, cresses, several varieties of lettuce, basil, leeks, scallions, fennel, coriander, *Mellons*, *bleets* (chard), and *Apples of Love* (tomatoes, for curiosity, I suppose, although much is made of the fact that this is a kitchen garden). Lawson's *The Country House-wives Garden*, 1637, includes *pumpeons* (pumpkins) and saffron in addition to most of the above. In *Husbandry*, a gardening manuscript of about 1651, we have directions for: *Muske melons*, *Colliflower*, rocket, several varieties of peas and beans, beets, and rhubarb (probably medicinal, S 231), in addition to most of the vegetables listed above, and a much expanded list of herbs. (For the month of March, there is a reminder: "Buy Capers Leimons Olives Oranges Rice Sampire.") Strawberries, gooseberries, currants, and raspberries were normally included in the kitchen garden, as well as a number of what we now consider purely ornamental plants such as roses, marigolds, and violets, which entered into cooking and preserving. (I do not mention hops, cereals, or other such crops.) Not one of these manuals, or others from the period, so much as mentions potatoes, not even the latest and most extensive one of 1651.

There is no recipe for green salad in our manuscript. For those who think that simply dressed mixed green salads are a relatively modern development, I give this delightful recipe from *The Forme of Cury*, 1390, for *Salat*: "Take parsley, sage, garlic, chives, onions, leeks, borage, mint, maiden's leek, cress, fennel, rue, rosemary, purslane; wash them clean, pluck them small with thine hand and mix them well with raw [olive] oil. Lay on vinegar and salt, and serve it forth." (I have transcribed this into modern terms. K.H.) And to show that it was a continuing tradition, Gerard in 1597 discusses the eating of raw salads under numerous headings, including raw artichokes, usually dressed only with olive oil and salt. Markham gives three pages to salads in 1615 and John Evelyn, the diarist, devoted to the subject an entire book, *Acetaria: A Discourse of Sallets*, 1699, where he lovingly discusses the choice and quality of olive oil (best Lucca), vinegar, and even salt (brightest bay salt), in addition to the choice and most felicitous combinations of greens and herbs according to season. Since our manuscript gives a recipe for pickled lettuce stalks (C 163), it seems reasonable to suppose that green salads were eaten in the household.

The sixteenth and seventeenth centuries saw an explosion of interest in horticulture, and a great deal of fine work was done in grafting and otherwise improving fruit trees. In *Husbandry* and *Soyle for an Orchard*, companion private manuscripts, both about 1650, we find that apples, pears, cherries, *Aprecocks*, plums (including the incomparable damsons), *Nectarines*, peaches, *Figgs* (with careful explanations for winter protection), grapes, quinces, mulberries, medlars, walnuts, hazel nuts, and chestnuts, were all grown (near Oxford, apparently), most of them in several varieties. There is knowledgeable discussion of proper soil, good stocks, grafting, propagating, mulching, pruning, and control of pests and diseases. Better known printed horticultural manuals might be dismissed as having been written by professionals (a number of whom were French and Italian and worked for the Court), but these working manuscripts are precious indications of actual practice. Interestingly, "pomum Amoris, love apples," are listed among flowers in *Soyle for an Orchard*.

I cannot offhand think of an important fruit that is not represented in our own manuscript except for bananas, cranberries (but barberries are comparable), and pineapple (there is *pinapple* in our manuscript but it refers to pine nuts). I should also except sweet oranges and grapefruit, a much later development, but Seville oranges and lemons were imported in surprising quantity and figure importantly in our manuscript. They also used a number of fruits now considered old-fashioned and so rather difficult to come by, such as gooseberries and red currants, or quince, for that matter. And where are the damsons of yesteryear?

Surprisingly large quantities of wine were consumed as a matter of course by the wealthy in Tudor England. According to the records of Ingatestone Hall, December 6, 1551, there were in the cellar 584 gallons of wine: Gascon (see S 275), *French*, Rhenish (German white), sack (sherry), and malmsey (S 289). Other inventories make it clear that claret was normally on hand in this cellar (see C 22); *French wines* is an unhelpful designation, but it may refer to white French wines as opposed to the German whites. When prices are listed in 1561, they range from a little under 10 pence for a gallon of Gascon wine to 20 pence the gallon for Rhenish wine or sack. It is difficult to estimate just how much wine was used; not all the purchases are listed, but they were not infrequent. Sir William did considerable entertaining, to be sure, but he also spent weeks on end at Court, often accompanied by Lady Petre, during which time no wine would be drunk; servants drank no wine. A great deal of wine went into cooking, as can be seen from the recipes in our manuscript and other sixteenth- and seventeenth-century cookbooks.

The same 1551 figures give three hogsheads of verjuice (189 gallons) and one of perry (S 267). Emmison explains that the verjuice was "a sort of sharp cider," and it may well have been, but unless it was so specified it could just as well have been unripe grape juice (C 4) when one reads that wine grapes were also cultivated on the estate.

Although Ingatestone Hall had a piped supply of "sweet" spring water inside the house, ale and beer seem to have been the main beverage for the entire household, especially for the servants. Brewing was done on the premises, once a fortnight, and Emmison figures that the per capita daily consumption was one gallon. This was "small beer" of low alcoholic content, but it still seems a fair amount of liquid. Ale was brewed on malt and water; beer came to denote the brew preserved and flavored with the slightly bitter hops, which were introduced into England around 1525, according to Emmison. The brewing of ale and beer was the province of the housewife, whatever her station; in great houses, a brewer was brought in to do the actual work. Home brewing explains the use of *barm* (S 151) as leavening in many of our recipes and the use of brewing equipment in others. Ale also enters into a certain number of recipes.

BREAD

Bread was still the staff of life in Tudor and Stuart England, more so among the poor than the rich, to be sure. Its importance was such that the *Assizes of Bread*, dating from 1266, took upon itself overseeing and policing of the bakers. The price of the loaf was fixed; the weight was permitted to fluctuate in compliance with an official table that took into account the price of wheat and the extent of bolting (C 85). The finest regular loaf was the *penny white*, next the *penny wheaten*, corresponding perhaps to 85 percent extraction rate, and the *household penny*, which was, in effect, 100 percent whole wheat, or nearly. This last loaf was about twice the weight of white bread, so that the less affluent got not only far more nutritious bread—and so recognized—but more of it for a penny.

The wealthy ate white bread. While it was golden, not the chalky lifeless bread made possible by industrialized milling in the nineteenth century, it was whiter and finer than most writers would have us believe; bolting methods were not all that primitive. It may have corresponded to 80 percent extraction rate. Elizabeth David tells me that even in times of famine, "the finest part of the wheat flour was still reserved for the rich and the religious houses," while the bran was mixed with "flour" made from beans or peas.

These patterns hold true in such records as I have seen from wealthy households. Three grades of bread were baked at Ingatestone Hall, usually listed as *manchet* (C 95), the finest, *yeoman's bread*, and *carter's bread*, from which only the coarsest bran had been extracted, and which was generally considered "agreeable enough for labourers," as quoted by Emmison in *Tudor Foods and Pastimes*. (There was hierarchy among servants, as well.) He says that only wheat flour was used there; *maslin*, a mixture of grains (most often wheat and rye planted together) was not uncommon among the coarser breads, particularly in the countryside. The popular "thirded" bread of the American colonists, made of wheat, rye, and *Indian* (corn meal), was a variation that persisted into the twentieth century; early recipes for Boston Brown Bread are but steamed versions.

These coarser breads were usually leavened with sour dough, alone or in conjunction with ale yeast. Markham describes the making of *cheate bread*, which was made with about 85 percent flour: the "sowre leaven . . . saved from a former batch" is broken into bits in warm water, strained, mixed with flour into a sponge "as thicke as pancake batter," let sit all night, mixed with a little more water, *barme* (S 151), "salt to season it," enough flour to make it "stiffe, and firme," then kneaded and turned into loaves. The same method may be used for any "compound graine as wheat and rie, or wheat, rie and barley," as well as for wheat alone, as here. This is a most excellent basic method. "Browne bread, or bread for your hinde servants, which is the coursest bread for mans use," includes barley, peas, wheat or rye, malt, and sour dough.

A word on traditional wheat flours. Major English millers nowadays blend native English strains, which are soft, with Manitoba hard wheat (*strong* flour) for more impressive volume, but this is historically recent. Above all, the flour of the day was neither bleached nor "enriched" nor otherwise "improved" with loathesome chemicals; that is, such additions were rightly considered as adulteration when uncovered. I buy my flour from a mill that has been turning since 1710. The house offers natural stone-gound flours in 100 percent whole wheat and unbleached white versions in both hard and soft varieties. As I explain in C 92 and 95, I add a small proportion of sifted whole wheat flour to the unbleached in order to approximate the somewhat less efficient bolting of the day, increasing the amount somewhat to approximate 85 percent extraction rate. This also improves the flavor. I prefer the flavor of soft flours but these are very soft indeed, so I blend them with hard flours with results that may be compared to those from native English 81 percent and 85 percent flours from traditional mills. The aroma and taste are subtly different, but the doughs handle not too differently and the textures are surprisingly similar. Sources for natural flours are given on page 28.

The English predilection for pastries is well illustrated in our manuscript; anything that could conceivably be baked in a pie was. It may be news to some, but cheesecakes, heralded by a leading food writer as an American invention, were popular in England, and elsewhere for that matter, centuries before the first colonist set foot on American soil; there are a number of recipes in our manuscript (C 106).

Baking was done in a brick oven. Large ovens were located in outbuildings, but smaller ovens were often built in conjunction with the kitchen hearth. (Home ovens were a sign of wealth, even station.) When it was hot enough—a tricky moment—and the bread was ready, the ashes were swept out, the bread placed directly on the floor of the oven, and the cumbersome oven door tightly closed. The art of baking bread evolved with the peculiar characteristics of this ancient oven: the highly heated floor and vaulted chamber of the oven and the principle of the "falling oven" (slowly diminishing temperature) and gradual dissipation of the initial steaminess generated by the dough itself, resulting in a loaf with a wonderful crunchy crust and a springy crumb with a good "bite." Modern home ovens have none of these qualities; steel simply does not have the heat-retentive traits of brick, and the requisite initial humidity never has a chance to build up sufficiently to properly form the crust. The methods proposed by writers of today to approximate the ancient oven—tiles, large shallow pans of boiling water, even super-heated axe heads—are unwieldy and inefficient, not to say wildly dangerous.

If you are going to try the bread and pastry recipes, it will be worth your while to approximate the conditions of the brick oven, be it by so little. I laid a thick slab of soapstone, 16 × 22 inches, directly on the floor of my capacious oven, thus increasing the heat-retentive qualities enormously. (It must be placed so as not to interfere with any vents.) If this is not feasible, a pizza stone of 16-inch diameter will do nicely and is easy to handle. In addition, a terra cotta flower pot (or outsize casserole) of about 14 inches across the top and 8 inches in depth is necessary—stop the hole with a wad of foil. Stone and pot are to be thoroughly preheated with the oven to about 500° F. When it is time to cast your bread, slide the lightly floured loaf onto a wooden peel (the paddle that comes with many pizza stones is ideal, but a shingle will do), lightly slash the top of the loaf with the time honored cross (done with a razor at a 30° angle, not too deeply), and slide the loaf onto the hot stone with a confident flick of the wrist. Clap the preheated pot over the bread, effectively creating a tiny terra cotta oven that works on ancient principles. To simulate the falling oven, I turn the thermostat down to 350° F, but each oven has its idiosyncracies, to say nothing of faulty thermostats, so you must be prepared to be resourceful and act on your own, keeping in mind the basic precepts outlined above.

Pastries bake ever so much better on the stone, as well. The ancient oven retained heat for an astonishingly long time. Pastries were usually put in after the bread was drawn, but were also baked in a falling oven; in my oven, I preheat the stone (without the flower pot) and the oven to only 425° F, turning it down to 350° as with the bread.

A WORD OF CAUTION. Be sure that your forearms are well covered and that your hands are adequately protected against the superheated terra cotta. And practice the logistics involved beforehand in a cool oven.

Anyone at all interested in the baking of bread should consult the already classic *English Bread and Yeast Cookery* by Elizabeth David, a history of milling and baking, including some 200 traditional recipes, a work to which I am indebted beyond telling. (See Bibliography.)

COOKING METHODS

Most cooking was done by the open fireplace. While it is back-breaking toil, the entire art of cookery was invented and perfected by women working over such a fire. Indeed the fireplace, a historically recent development, had been a great step forward in convenience; it channeled the smoke up the chimney, and permitted the installation of a number of cunning contrivances such as the swinging crane, which enabled the cook to move a massive cauldron full of simmering broth farther from or nearer to the fire, giving more flexibility in heat control than we moderns might imagine; various ratchetted devices permitted additional control.

All manner of footed pots and pans, most often with long handles, were part of any well-equipped kitchen and some are mentioned in our manuscript, the *posnet*, for example. Braising dishes (from French *braise*, ember) ingeniously designed with concave lids into which embers could be heaped, would be nestled in the hot ashes to one side of the hearth in such a way that the savory stews contained therein could sit for hours at an imperceptible simmer, virtually untended. (The design survives in the French *daubière*.) And then all sorts of foods were cooked directly in the ashes, such as the roasted eggs called for in our manuscript a number of times; when indicated, foods were wrapped in fragrant leaves or clay for protection. There were also various double unglazed earthenware vessels, fitting tightly together so that they could be buried in the ashes (still current in certain regions of France as *diables*) making them wonderful for cooking such things as chestnuts and, later, potatoes. (They are making a reappearance, but are far more suited to use with ashes than with modern fuels.) The turnspit, often run by elaborate and handsome clockwork thermodynamic systems, was another labor-saving device. Earlier turnspits were run by servants, often mere children, although there are accounts of harnassing dogs to this work.

This may be the place to discuss roasting methods. To this day, the English retain the important distinction between roasting and baking of meats. Baking meat in a closed compartment such as an oven inevitably generates a certain amount of vapor; some meats may support this moist cooking—indeed require it— but it is not roasting. The characteristic of roasted meat is the formation of a lightly caramelized crust on the outer surfaces. This crust, of an intense meaty flavor, seals in the juices and there is a wonderful contrast in both texture and flavor between the crust and the succulent rare interior. (The creation of such delightful contrasts is the art of cookery and the simpler they are in concept, the more successful, usually. The grey sodden mass palmed off on us as "roast" by the home economists is a prime example of the homogenization and debasement of taste and texture of modern food—this, in spite of our noble tradition in roasting.) If the heat be insufficient, the juices will ooze out, leaving the meat dry and tasteless; if the heat be too intense, the meat will char before it is done. The timing and gauging of the heat in relation to the size, shape, and nature of the meat, is the art of roasting. The roast must be kept turning so that all surfaces are evenly cooked; "done to a turn" had literal meaning. Doing the meat in front of the fire (instead of over the fire as we are wont to do in our patio barbecue pits) assures that the juices will not drip into the fire (causing flare-ups and giving the meat the taste of burnt fat) but will fall instead into a dripping pan placed under the turning meat, where they cannot be scorched. These precious drippings are used to baste the roast, contributing to the formation of the crust and, suitably seasoned, serve as the perfect sauce to the meat, mingling with the juices from carving. English roasting methods were grudgingly admired even by the French, it must be noted, who were also envious of the quality of English beef.

Fireplace cookery gives other qualities to the food. The fragrance of burning wood, vine cuttings, and fruit and nut tree woods are considered especially choice in this regard. Hams and sausages were usually hung from the rafters to slowly cure; many Tudor chimneys had special recesses for this purpose, according to Dorothy Hartley. Nor was it only roasted and smoked meats that benefitted; just as the flavor of bread baked in a brick oven fired with aromatic woods tastes different from that baked in the fumes of a gas oven, so also does the flavor of an omelet subtly vary with the nature of the fuel.

We now come to the *chafing dish of coles* so frequently specified in our manuscript. The recorded use of a chafing dish goes back to antiquity. Cicero described it as "a kind of sauce pan of Corinthian brass . . . made with such art that its contents cook instantly and almost without fire. This simple and ingenious vessel possessed a double bottom, the uppermost one holds the light delicacies destined for the dessert and the fire is underneath." And Seneca wrote that "Daintiness gave birth to this useful invention in order that no viand should be chilled and that everything should be hot enough to please the most pampered palate. The kitchen follows the supper."*

The elaborate chafing dishes mentioned above were probably borrowed from the Greeks. But cooks must have very early found that for conducting fussy bits of cooking, a vessel containing a few embers or brightly burning sticks of charcoal (depending on the required temperature) in a small container at table height was infinitely more efficient and convenient than working by the sort of fire necessary for roasting, for example; braziers of one kind or another must be nearly as ancient as cooking pots. Early mentions of these contraptions in English are forms of French *chauffer*, to heat; they appear to have been applied indifferently to both the vessel holding the embers and that holding the food to be heated. In sixteenth- and seventeenth-century cookbooks, however, *chafing dish* designated the vessel holding the coals. Undoubtedly, elaborate chafers were used in princely halls to keep foods warm and to finish the presentation of *salmis* and similar dishes; the chafing

* *One Hundred Recipes for the Chafing Dish* by H. M. Kinsley.

dish was a more workaday utensil, a portable grate or brazier mounted on a tripod. The recipe for *A Stewd dish* (C 15) illustrates perfectly the use of the *chafing dish*; both the gentle stewing of the meat and the fragile egg liaison are accomplished over the gentle heat of embers in the brazier; the making of such a delicate sauce would not be feasible at the great heat of the fireplace. The making of syrups and preserves was also carried out over the chafing dish.

The use of the chafing dish is also to be understood in the common instruction to cook "twixt 2 dishes," cooking ware, to be sure. As late as the 1796 edition of Hannah Glasse's *Art of Cookery,* we find this technique spelled out in her recipe for *A Pretty Way of stewing Chickens*: the reader is to place pieces of parboiled chicken in a dish, "cover it with another dish; set it over a stove, or chafing-dish of coals," and send to table "in the same dish they were stewed in." (The *stove* would have been a rather more structured sort of chafing dish, involving cooking in a tightly closed chamber; *stoved* dishes we would call *smothered*. In our manuscript, *stoving* refers more to a drying than a cooking process, as in S 68. The application of *stove* to the modern cooking range is American; the English call it a *cooker*.)

Chafing dishes came to colonial America. Kinsley cites records from 1720 showing that a well-off American ordered from England "a truly elegant outfit" which included "6 small brass Chafing Dishes, 4 shillings apiece," as a wedding present for his daughter. And as late as the 1860 edition of *The Virginia Housewife* (1824), Mary Randolph lists "a large chafing dish, with long legs for the convenience of moving it to any part of the room," as desirable equipment for the kitchen, particularly for preserving.

Such were the cooking methods brought to the New World by the English; they were to change surprisingly little during the next two centuries. The equipment of the earliest years and of the frontier must have been considerably more primitive, but once the community became well established, the fireplace, with all its paraphernalia, and the brick oven appeared. Sometime around mid-nineteenth century, use of the iron range came to be fairly general and the kitchen fireplace was doomed. The new iron ovens neither roasted properly nor baked bread properly, but the top of the stove was a great advance for certain kinds of cooking. Modern ranges are wonderfully convenient, it must be said, but the culinary problems posed by the early ranges have yet to be solved.

The stony soil of New England was not very hospitable (see page 5), but in Virginia there was an abundance of magnificent produce, and aside from certain curious indigenous additions, it was essentially the same kind of produce. The colonists brought with them English fruit strains and English vegetable

seeds. They brought English wheat. They brought English milk
cows, pigs, and chickens. The game and fish were not so different
as to preclude using their old recipes. (The North American wild
turkey did not strike them as being so different from the domesticated turkey brought to England in the sixteenth century, for
example.) Even the strange Indian meal (corn meal) did not defy
adaptation to English recipes, as in "thirded bread" and Indian
pudding.

William Byrd, naturalist and fellow of the Royal Society
(then headed by Sir Isaac Newton), founder of Richmond, and a
brother-in-law of Frances Parke Custis, called Virginia the "Garden
of Eden." In his *Natural History of Virginia*, 1737, he wrote that
every kind of European fruit and vegetable had long been cultivated in the colony: artichokes, "beautiful cauliflower . . . very
large and long asparagus of splendid flavor . . . watermelons and
fragrant melons," as well as all manner of pumpkins, squashes,
and cucumbers. He was ecstatic over the fruits, listing 24 kinds of
apples, explaining that he "wanted only to describe the best species
of them." All common fruits grew in profusion and even almonds,
pomegranates, coffee, and tea, grew in the gardens of "fanciers
of beautiful fruits," he said. He also claimed that the beef, veal,
mutton, and pork were "always as good as the best European can
be, since the pastures in this country are very fine."

Robert Beverley, a contemporary of Byrd's, in *History of
the Present State of Virginia*, 1705, writes: "As for Fish, both of Fresh
and Salt-Water, of Shell-Fish, and others, no Country can boast of
more Variety, greater Plenty, or of better in their several Kinds."
He mentions herring, shad, lamprey, flounder, whiting, bass,
crabs, oysters, mussels, cockles, shrimp, eels, conger, perch, and
catfish, among others. There were ducks, snipe, woodcock, larks,
pheasant, partridge, "Wild Turkeys of a incridible Bigness" (up to
40 pounds, he claims), deer, hare, squirrel, and wild pigs. The pigs
had been brought from England by the earliest settlers and Beverley reports that "hogs swarm like Vermine upon the Earth," and
that estates often did not bother to list them in their inventories.
These lean pigs foraged on acorns and other fallen fruits and nuts,
and must have made wonderful eating. This, then, was the beginning of the justly famous Virginia ham.

Nor was the produce limited to that raised in Virginia.
The wealthy aid not deprive themselves of all manner of spices,
wine, oranges, almonds, raisins, dates, sugar, Lisbon salt, tea, and
other exotic luxuries. This is evidenced not only by frequent allusions in letters and diaries of the day, especially those of Byrd
and, later, of Thomas Jefferson, but by earliest American cookbooks. I have not studied lading statistics so I cannot say what part

of that trade was with England. However, in 1685, William Byrd, father, ordered from merchants in *Barbadoes* the following: "4 Negroes, 2 men and 2 women, not to exceed 25 years old and to bee likely. About 1200 Gallons of Rum. 3000 lbs. Muscovado Sugar [partially refined]. 1 Barrell of White S[ugar] about 2 cwt. 3 Tun of Molasses. 1 Caske Limejuice and 2 cwt. Ginger."* (The cwt. was, by definition, 100 pounds, but the British cwt. now amounts to 112.)

The cooks in Virginia had the gifts of Paradise for raw material; they had slave hands in the kitchen and in the fields; they had the stimulation of working with many wondrous strange products, which they handled with elan; they learned from both Indians and their black cooks tricks of working with this new produce; they learned from the French Huguenots, perhaps even from the hoitytoity French cuisine brought to their midst by Thomas Jefferson— Mary Randolph was a contemporary of Jefferson and of the same social milieu. But to compare her *Virginia Housewife*, 1824, and the pages of our manuscript is to learn about the source and formation of Virginia cooking. The palate and the hands of a fine Virginia cook like Mrs. Randolph had been shaped and trained in the continuing tradition of Elizabethan and Jacobean cooking. Recipe after recipe comes from the same cultural pool: *Shrewsbury Cakes, Jumbals, A Marrow Pudding, Gooseberry Fool, Syllabub, A Curd Pudding, To Pickle Oysters, To Collar a Flank of Beef, To Make Souse,* and scores of other titles from the Randolph book also appear in our manuscript, with little or no change in technique; the greatest change is in the language. A number of recipes had simply disappeared. Sugar has been purged from all meat preparations; not even her version of Virginia baked ham has a grain of sugar. Perhaps the biggest change in the English recipes is the appearance of demon flour in a few of the sauces, a debasement that had already shown up in eighteenth-century cookbooks. Mrs. Randolph handled flour with an exceptionally light hand: what amounts to a *beurre manié* has but 1 teaspoon of flour to 4 tablespoons of butter, whereas the usual proportions call for equal amounts by volume. She brought her personal flair to everything she did, but she had been trained to give meticulous attention to detail in the best traditions of the English kitchen, so beautifully exemplified in our manuscript; in so doing, she, in turn, helped to shape Virginia cuisine.

I should say, perhaps, that while I have attempted to explain the old measures and techniques found in our manuscript, I did not modernize the recipes. It was quite beyond the scope of this work and alien to the spirit of our manuscript to present fool-

---

* *The Virginia Historical Register*, Vol. II, edited by William Maxwell. Richmond, 1849.

proof directions, complete to the last ⅛ teaspoon of pepper, for the benefit of beginning cooks. (I might say, however, that there is more precision in our recipes than was customary in sixteenth- and seventeenth-century cookbooks.) I have had to assume some flair in the kitchen, some measure of intellectual curiosity, a willingness to *fit your pallate*, on the part of those who would try the recipes. Certain techniques that I found especially perceptive, questionable, or otherwise interesting, I lingered over; others I took for granted.

The recipes are grouped in sections, at least in principle. I have tried to observe these divisions, making general observations on the characterizing elements and techniques along with the opening recipe in each section. There is, however, a certain amount of overlapping and confusion, so that in some cases it seemed more logical to discuss a procedure when referred to in a later recipe. No recipe stands alone; very often, what seems to be a particularly puzzling procedure will be clarified by instructions in a later recipe. I have provided numerous cross references, particularly when a recipe is entered out of category, but they too can be exasperating to the reader. Archaic terms pose similar problems, but they may be more easily looked up in the index.

Of the 531 recipes represented in the manuscript proper, a few are, I fear, impracticable in today's kitchen, but they make fascinating reading. (The 23 additional recipes entered later in the inner pages are curiously devoid of interest; the only exceptions are the "prescription," the facsimile of which may be found page 458, and a pasted-in recipe addressed to Mrs. Custis, following S 261.) The medicinal recipes are strictly for the pleasure of learning about our past; aside from the skin lotions, possibly, I urge abstinence. But most of the recipes need no modernization whatsoever, and your only problem will be to find decent produce.

On the question of special ingredients. Some of the simplest will be the most difficult: really thick beautiful cream, good milk, "new layd eggs," real chicken, mature mutton, tree-ripened fruit, dewy fresh vegetables, and flapping fresh fish. What can I say? Search out serious tradesmen, encourage and patronize farmers' markets, cajole all suppliers, making sure that they understand that they are to do their best. But know that all manner of food, whether it be fruit, grain, vegetable, flesh, fish, or fowl, was more flavorful then than now.

If you enjoy gardening, you are in luck. Even if you live in a city apartment, try growing the herbs that interest you; many of them thrive surprisingly well in a sunny window. Fancy food departments and health food stores carry a fair number of dried herbs. Shops specializing in Middle Eastern products are perhaps the best source for herbs and spices; they also carry rose water and rose petals. Pharmacies often carry an array of dried herbs and flowers. Finding green ginger can be difficult if you live far from a Chinese community; appeal to the good graces of a Chinese restaurateur. Really good ginger positively gleams with freshness; if you must, peel it, place it in a glass jar and cover it with sherry; it will remain usable for some time, and you can use the liquid for seasoning, as well. I have not had brilliant luck freezing it.

The possession of musk, I understand, is illegal in the United States; various synthetic substitutes are meant only for perfumery and are *not* to be ingested. (Also, be sure that such items as rose water, rose petals and other flowers, are intended for consumption and not for cosmetic purposes, particularly if you get them from a pharmacy.) Pharmacists occasionally carry ambergris—at a price. Do not fret over musk and ambergris; I think that they were omitted as often as not. Some writers suggest a vanilla bean, but it is not authentic and does not harmonize well with rose water. Lemon or orange zest makes an attractive alternative to some of the more exotic flavorings, if need be, and is justifiable historically.

SOURCES FOR FLOUR

The mills listed below offer naturally grown, traditionally milled flours:

ARROWHEAD MILLS, OLDE MILL FLOURS, Box 866, Hereford, Texas 79045

ELAM MILLS, 2625 Gardner Road, Broadview, Ill. 60153.

EL MOLINO, 345 North Baldwin Park Blvd., City of Industry, Calif. 91746.

EREWHON TRADING CO., 33 Farnsworth Street, Boston, Mass. 02210
     and 8003 Beverley Blvd., Los Angeles, Calif. 90048.

GREAT VALLEY MILLS, P.O. Box 260, Quakertown, Pa. 18951.

SHILOH FARMS, Sulphur Springs, Ark. 72768.

WALNUT ACRES, Penn's Creek, Pa. 17862.

With the exception of Great Valley Mills, who ship promptly, the products of the above houses are to be found at health food and fancy food shops; the same sources are suggested for preservative-free yeast, sea salt, and Demerara sugar (which is likely to resemble the sugar of the time).

APHRODISIA PRODUCTS, 28 Carmine Street, New York City 10014, carries a large selection of dried herbs and flowers; they will send a catalogue on request.

THE INDEX

* Surely the signature of Frances Parke (see facsimile, page 30).

* I excised a repeated *ueale*.
† I excised a letter *f*; the *e* in *steakes* is a blot.

* Recipes for *cracknells* and puff paste, while numbered correctly, were inadvertently transposed by the scribe.

* N° 177, number and recipe, was omitted.
† Written *lub*.

* This recipe does not appear in the scribe's index.

A BOOKE OF COOKERY

A Booke of Cookery

How to stew A neck or loyne of muton

1. Take A neck of muton & cut it 2 ribbs together, boil
or chopp it. y bones must be broaken, then season it w
nutmegg, pepper, & salt, w must be well rubd in, then
set them in 2 dishes with as much water as will couer
them, & when y meat is haffe roady put into y water as
much wine vinegar as will season it, some leamond pill, some
large mace, & one anchouis, y turne y meat & stir y sauce
& when it is enough serue it in w sippots, & a little butter.

To make A Frykecy

2. Take 2 Chicken, or a hare, kill & flaw them hot, take out
theyr intrills & wipe them within, cut them in pieces & break
theyr bones with they A pestle, y put haffe a pound of but
ter into y frying pan, & fry it till it be browne, y put in
y Chicken & giue it a walme or two, y put in haffe a pinte
of faire water, well seasoned with pepper, & salt, & a little after
put in a handfull of parsley, & time, & an ounion, shread all small
fry all these together till they be enough, & when is ready to be
dished up put into y pan y yonlks of 5 or 6 eggs, well beaten
& mixed with A little wine vinegar or iuice of leamons, stir them
well together least it curdle, y dish it up without any more
frying ~ ~ ~ ~ ~ ~ ~ ~ ~ ~ ~ ~ ~ ~ ~ ~ ~

To make A Fryplacy of Chikin
lamb veale or rabbits

3. After y chicken are cut in small pieces season them with clo
mace nutmegg, & pepper; boil small together & some salt
then fry them a little in sweet butter, y beat 3 or 4 eggs
yonlks with a little white wine, & sweet hearbs minced small
into y eggs & wine, y take out y meat & mix y herbs & eggs in
y pan, & giue y another fry together, & put into y A little titing
broth, some gr mie, a little angelust, a slice of lemon minced,
together y dish it up, garnish y dish

1   HOW TO STEW A NECK OR LOYNE OF
     MUTON

Take A neck of muton & cut it 2 ribbs together. bea[t]
or Chopp it. ye bones must be broaken. then season it
wth nutmegg, pepper, & salt, wch must be well rub'd
in. then set them in 2 dishes with as much water as will
cover them, & when y^r meat is halfe ready, put into y^e
water as much wine vinegar as will season it, some
leamond pill, some large mace, & one anchovis. y^n
turne y^r meat & stir ye sauce, & when it is enough,
serve it in wth sippets, & a little butter.

Our *Booke of Cookery* could hardly open with a more appropriate
recipe; the use of nutmeg, lemon peel, anchovy, and wine vinegar
to season stewed mutton, with butter stirred in at the end as the
only liaison, makes this dish a fine example of English cookery in
the opening years of the seventeenth century. (This is one of the
more "modern" recipes in our manuscript.) The breaking up of
the bones to facilitate the release of flavor is characteristic of older
cookery methods and is a technique that might well be revived.
If the final liquor really is too thin, lift out the meat when done
and reduce the liquid as seems necessary. Then, off the fire and
after letting it stand a minute or so, whip in the butter little by
little; the result will be a light shimmering liaison. (A tablespoon
or two of butter for each pound of meat is usually sufficient.) The
technique is that of *faire monter au beurre*, of course, long associated
with finest French culinary practice (but also practiced by the English) and recently made popular by the early proponents of the so-
called *nouvelle cuisine*.

   In American butchery, the *neck of muton* cut in this way
would correspond to rib chops from the mature sheep, if only it
were available. Even what passes for mutton today is rarely more
than a pale memory of the real thing. A strong homemade beef
broth will lend a bit of the intense meaty flavor associated with
mutton, but know that it is a far cry.

   The English took to *nutmegg* early on; Chaucer, for instance, mentions it several times, and it is rare to find a recipe
without it well into the seventeenth century, when it came to be
abused. At the risk of lessening authenticity, I counsel using it
with discretion; I personally find its muskiness overpowering. (For
further notes on use, see C 6; also S 271.)

Cooking *between 2 dishes* refers to the use of well fitted pans over a *chafing dish of coles* (see C 15). In modern terms, one is simply to cook in a tightly covered pan over very gentle heat.

Leamond and *leamon* were both current forms of lemon. The word comes to us by way of Arabic *laimūn* from Persian *līmūn* (*OED*) and the fruit by the same path. The use of *pill* for peel is invariable by our scribe. *Pill* was being displaced by the modern form in the seventeenth century but the *English Dialect Dictionary* notes that it survived in dialect in the Midland counties.

Anchouis, anchovy, a small Mediterranean fish related to the sprat and sardine, is usually pickled and salted for long keeping. The word seems not to have appeared in either French or English until the sixteenth century; the process, however, and the use of similar pickle in cooking, dates from time immemorial. (The *garum* of the Romans, for example, came from Liguria and while it may have been ranker than the cured anchovy that still characterizes the cooking of Nice today, the principle remains the same.) It should be noted that anchovy is an important ingredient of most bottled sauces that are heavily used in both English and American kitchens.

Sippet is the diminutive of *sop,* a piece of bread which is toasted, fried, or well dried, and used to sop the liquid. (*Sop* appeared in Old English and is related to Old French *sope,* of the same meaning, which became *soupe,* finally often referring to the liquid to be imbibed rather than the bread; the presence of bread is still implied, however, especially in French.) Properly done sippets are crisp and retain textural interest even when they are sopped; they have nothing to do with the limp toast points (the customary translation) that too often adorn fancy dishes. (See C 4.)

---

2   TO MAKE A FRYKECY

Take 2 Chicken, or a hare, kill & flaw them hot. take out theyr intrills & wipe them within, cut them in pieces & break theyr bones with A pestle. y^n put halfe a pound of butter into ye frying pan, & fry it till it be browne, y^n put in ye Chiken & give it a walme or two. y^n put in halfe a pinte of faire water well seasoned with pepper, & salt, & a little after put in a handfull of parsley, & time, & an ounion shread all smal[l]. fry all these together till they be enough, & when it is ready

to be dished up, put into ye pan ye youlks of 5 or 6
eggs, well beaten & mixed wth A little wine vinegar or
juice of leamons. stir thes[e] well together least it
Curdle, y^n dish it up without any more frying.

This is a fine recipe presented by a thoughtful cook; a number of
excellent ones throughout the manuscript are also hers, I believe.
The butter should be allowed to turn no darker than a golden
brown; customarily, fricassee was—and often is—cooked *à blanc*,
without coloring. Because chicken nowadays has little discernible
flavor, I suggest using homemade chicken or veal stock in place
of water. Also, eggs were smaller then; I suggest 2 yolks for
each cup of cooking juices for a beautifully light silken sauce. I find
that a tablespoon of fresh lemon juice enhances the flavor and cuts
the richness perfectly, but you may increase this if you please. It
is prudent to add some of the hot liquid to the egg mixture, stirring,
before adding it to the pan, off the fire and always stirring. The
dish does not tolerate reheating so arrange any leftover chicken
on a platter and spoon the sauce over; it will jell to a delightful
chaud-froid of finer flavor and texture than any flour-based one. If
you add the chopped parsley at the end you will have a prettier
dish.

The earliest mention of the dish seems to be in the first
printed edition of *Le Viandier*, 1490, as *Friquassée*. (The usual explanation of the name is that it is formed of *frire*, to fry, and *casser*,
to break.) The recipe calls for the chicken to be dismembered raw,
fried in lard with chopped onion, then simmered in beef broth
with seasonings of ginger and verjuice. The technique was by no
means new, however. In the Sion manuscript from about 1300
(earliest known version of *Le Viandier*), we find numerous similar
recipes under different names. A recipe for *Hochepot de poullaile*
calls for dismembering fowl, frying in lard, then simmering beef
broth with toasted bread and the livers mashed with wine; the
seasonings are ginger, cinnamon, grains of Paradise, and verjuice.
Other recipes specify veal, hare, or rabbit; some sauces are given
body with pounded almonds, some with "egg yolks well beaten."
I speak only of those recipes that have the peculiar characteristics
of a fricassee: the braising of small cracked joints or pieces of meat
that have been previously fried; the liaisons are varied, as are the
seasonings, but the tartness of vinegar or verjuice is invariable.
(The *minutal* of Apicius, often translated as fricassee, is more properly a hash; the meat is minced and the principle of succeeding
operations is absent. Some of the recipes under *ofellae* might qualify
as fricassees, however.)

In England also there were early recipes bearing the hallmark of the fricassee long before the name appeared. (The first citing in *OED* is 1568, not in a recipe.) A representative one in Harleian MS. 279 (N° 42), about 1430, calls for hacking into pieces rabbit, hen, or duck, frying it in lard, then simmering it with onions in broth, which is then thickened with bread; the seasonings are mace, clove, pepper, cinnamon, ginger, vinegar, and salt.

In *The Good Huswifes Jewell, Part I*, 1586, Thomas Dawson tells us how *To frie Chickins*. The recipe is interesting in that it illustrates the evolving English techniques of succeeding frying and stewing procedures, which were occasionally reversed. (Just so, women of the Perigord fry cooked soup vegetables in an operation called *fricasser*.) The chickens are simmered in broth before being fried in butter, "but you must not let them be browne with frying." They are then finished with a light liaison of broth and egg yolk; the seasonings are verjuice, nutmeg, cinnamon, ginger, and pepper. In *Part II*, 1587, he gives three less typical recipes for *fricacies* of : *a lambes head and purtenance, tripes,* and *Neates feete.*

A Booke of Cookrye by A. W., 1591, gives a group of fricassee recipes, the most interesting of which is *A Fricace of Goose giblets or Hennes, or Capons.* This is *la petite oye* (giblets, neck, feet, etc., of a goose) of ancient French cookery. In *Le Ménagier*, about 1390, *la petite oé* is simmered, then fried, and served with a *potage* thickened with egg yolk; elaborate instructions are given so as to assure smoothness. *Bref*, a fricassee. These fricassees of giblets remain an important aspect of regional cuisine in France, particularly south of the Loire; in some of the more remote areas, the ancient name of *petite oie* survives to this day.

Let us consider for a moment giblets, pettitoes, *pepitoria*, and such *garbage*. An archaic meaning of giblets is "the portions of a goose that are taken out or cut off before cooking, the liver, gizzard, etc., with the pinions and feet" (*OED*). Or, *la petite oye*. This is confirmed by Palsgrave, in 1530, when he translates "Garbage of a foule [as] *petitoye*." (In *A Noble Boke off Cookry*, mid-fifteenth century, we find a recipe for making a *Garbage*. Again, *la petite oye*.) In 1611, Cotgrave says that *la petite oye* applies to the *intralls* not only of the goose but "of other edible creatures." In a citation from 1555, we hear of a *Pygges Pettytoe* (*OED*). It is not clear whether the term applies to the corresponding offal of the pig or only the feet. In a recipe from 1591, A. W. instructs: "Take your Pigs feet and the Liver and Lightes." But in 1586, immediately preceding the *fricacies* noted above, Dawson gives a recipe, *For a Goose gibluts and pigges petitoes* (also a fricassee); here, *petitoes* specifically refers to feet. The English forgot the French meaning and thought in terms of *petty toes*; eventually the term applied only to pigs' feet. Curiously, *OED* offers little or no illumination here. It is of interest to note that Percivall, in 1591, translates the Spanish "*Pepitoria* [as] the giblets of a goose, or anie bird" (*OED*). Properly speaking, it is *petitoria*, from *petit oye*, according to Corominas, but here again, popular etymology prevailed. The ancient liaison of pounded almonds, so common in medieval cuisine, lingered in Spain centuries after it languished in France and England and was typically employed in this fricassee called *pepitoria*; the confusion lay in the word *pepita*, kernel or pip. Nowadays, *pepitoria* is more likely to be a fricassee of chicken—pounded almonds are still characteristic—but *la petite oye* lives on in the figurative meaning of medley or olio.

In the seventeenth century, the *Fricase* took a fanciful turn. Markham, in *The English Hus-wife*, 1615, has a section called *Of Fricases and quelque-choses* (which came to be *kickshaws*) in which they are defined as "dishes of manie compositions . . . all beeing prepared and made ready in a frying panne." There are *Collops and egges*, tansies, fritters, pancakes, *veale tosts*, and *panperdy* (C 72). In *A New Booke of Cookerie*, 1615, J. Murrell gives a recipe for *A Fregesey of Egges* that is very like our *apple tansie* in C 150. *A True Gentlewomans Delight*, 1653, by the Countess of Kent, stays closer to tradition, but Robert May in *The Accomplisht Cook*, 1671, gives a recipe for an *Other Fricase or Quelque-shose* that is remarkably like the Murrell recipe and one for *A rare Fricase* that is an olio of pigeons, *chicken-peepers*, "head and all on," lambstones, sweetbreads, asparagus, oysters, and marrow bone.

In the eighteenth century, the dish settled back into more traditional patterns, but writers began to introduce small amounts of flour as a stabilizing element to the delicate egg yolk liaisons characteristic of English fricassees, so admirably illustrated in our manuscript. In the 1755 edition of *The Art of Cookery*, Hannah Glasse adds "a little Piece of Butter rolled in Flour" in addition to 2 egg yolks to bind a copious sauce composed of the cooking broth, white wine, and cream. Other fricassees still depend only on enriching ingredients for body. The first American edition of Susannah Carter's *The Frugal Housewife*, 1772, has an entire chapter of 25 fine fricassee recipes, but American writers have not understood the fricassee. The singularly poor recipe given by Fannie Farmer in *The Boston Cooking-School Cook Book*, 1896, documents the decline of this once noble dish: boiled chicken is dredged with flour, fried, and arranged on toast; one is then to "Pour around White or Brown Sauce."

Chicken appears in Old English as *cicen* and *ciken*. In southwest England, *chicken* was treated as plural, as *ox* and *oxen* (*OED*). The usage lingers in our manuscript.

Flaw is an old form of *flay*, to skin the beast. *Walme* is an old Jute word—it appears in *Beowulf*, for example—meaning bubble. *Faire* means clean or pure. *Ounion (Alium cepa)* comes from Old French *ougnon*; it was an archaic form by the seventeenth century. For *time*, thyme, see S 246.

Frying means the boiling of liquid, an exceedingly rare usage. Indeed, the only such citations given in *OED* are poetic: "Ye might have seene frothy billowes fry Vnder the ship" (Spenser, *The Faerie Queene*, 1590). It occurs in the following recipe and again in C 27.

---

3   TO MAKE A FRYKACY OF CHIKIN LAMB UEALE OR RABBITS

After y^r chicken are cut in small pieces, season them wth clove, mace, nutmegg, & pepper beat small together, & some salt. then fry them a little in sweet butter. y^n beat 3 or 4 egge youlks wth a little white wine, & sweet hearbs minced small p[ut] into ye eggs & wine. y^n take out ye meat & mix ye herbs & eggs in ye pan, & give y^m another fry together. & put into y^m A little strong broth, some gravie, a little vinegar, a slice of lemon minced. give all a [fry] together, y^n dish it up. garnish y^r dish with grapes [or] barberies. put in a [?].

The last line of this recipe is badly damaged; several words are wanting. But the use of spices, as well as herbs, and the garnish of grapes or barberries (most likely pickled, as in C 168 and 169), mark this recipe for fricassee as coming from an earlier era than the previous one. While the flavors are not as well balanced, this recipe is not without interest. You court disaster if you allow it to *fry* again, and yet again, as directed, after adding the egg yolks; you will do well to follow the procedure suggested in C 2.

Sweet hearbs would be what the French call *fines herbes* except that the English rarely used tarragon and the term was not nearly so arbitrary. Besides parsley and chervil, it also included thyme and other aromatic herbs as well. (Also, see C 30.)

Grauie, gravy, always refers to the natural cooking juices of meat, usually mutton, and especially those that flow when the roasted meat is cut (C 41). The practice is additional proof that red meats were roasted very rare; the procedure is often described. These juices were never cheapened with flour, as can be seen by

44

perusing the pages of this manuscript. The word appeared in Middle English as *gravé*, which apparently had been a scribal error for Old French *grané*, referring to that which is being cooked. *Gravé* appears in the Sion MS. of *Le Viandier*, before 1300, was repeated in later manuscripts, and again in *Le Ménagier*, about 1390, so that it was well established in French, contrary to what certain writers have claimed. (The word was later replaced by *jus*.)

---

4   TO MAKE SCOTCH COLLOPS

> Take a legg of muton or veale or fresh beefe, cut them in thin slyces, & lay them on a table. beat them with ye back of your knife, y^n steep y^m in vinegar or verges. after, lay y^m in a frying pan, put to y^m a pint of strong broth, & halfe a pinte of faire water, & put into it a bunch of time, sweete marjerum, & winter savory, & an ounion, & let them boyle till y^r meat be tender. then pour out y^r liquor into a dish & put to it a little manchet cut like dice, anchovis, Capers or oysters, & leamon minced, & a piece of fresh butter. when they are boyld enough, take y^r sops & fry y^m in fresh butter till they are crisp. y^n lay y^m in y^r dish & pour on y^r sause. serve y^m up wth sippets, & garnish y^r dish with leam[on]s & capers.

This is an interesting recipe from a historical point of view. The beating, or *scotching*, and the marinade are to tenderize the meat. I urge braising it in good homemade beef broth further enriched with veal broth (in order to nourish the meat and not the other way about) and cooked at an imperceptible simmer. The slightly puzzling procedure that follows has to do with working on the brazier. It is much simpler to lift out the meat to a warm serving dish, and then reduce and finish your sauce in the cooking pan. The oysters are surely pickled (C 173); the diced fresh lemon is a lovely touch. I suggest adding the butter to the sauce just before serving, off the fire, stirring it in so that you get a light emulsion, as in C 1.

    The sops are to be done just before finishing the sauce with butter. You will do well to follow the scribe's advice on fixing all *sops* and *sippets*; she understood very well that they must be crisp. What she could not have foreseen is that it would be necessary to caution on the quality of the bread. Stale homemade bread is what is wanted (see C 92 and 95). Clarified butter is best for the frying. (If you prefer, they may be dried to a crisp in a slow oven.)

Scotch collops are scotched, scored or beaten, not Scottish. I respectfully submit that the recorded use of *scotch* in cookery antedates by more than a century its recorded use as a contracted form for Scottish, which was not until 1570, according to *OED*. Harleian MS. 4016, about 1450, directs us to "skoche [the pike] in two or iij placys in the bak, but not thorgh," and Shakespeare, in *Coriolanus*, says: "He scotchd him and notchd him like a Carbinado." (A *carbonade* is a *collop* to be broiled.) The explicit instructions in our recipe leave little room for doubt.

A *collop* is a slice of meat; it appears in *Promptorium parvulorum*, 1440, as *Colloppe*. On derivation, *OED* suggests various Teutonic forms, such as Swedish *kollops* and German *klops*, without much conviction and speculates on a connection with *coal*, citing *carbonella*. Perhaps. But it does seem curious that French *escalope* and Italian *scaloppine*, with parallel meanings, are not so much as mentioned. Given the French and Italian influence in European cuisines down through the centuries, it would seem less tortuous to consider Robert's proposal of Old French *eschalope*, shell; the connection between the edible muscle of the *scallop* (which *OED* describes as an aphetic form of *escalope*) and a slice of raw meat, particularly from veal tenderloin, is one that would occur to any cook. (For another aspect of *collop*, see S 195.)

Verges is verjuice, the juice of unripe grapes or crab apples. The word comes from Old French *verjus*, green juice. *Uerges* is a sixteenth-century form (*OED*) and is nearly invariable throughout the manuscript. Some writers claim that in England it was made only with apples, but Cotgrave, in 1611, describes it as "especially that which is made of sowre, and unripe grapes" (See C 156). In the Harleian MS. cited above, in a recipe for stewed mutton, we find "a litull vynegre or vergeous" called for; while they are different, clearly cooks used one for the other with little ado, and so may you.

Manchet is best white bread (see C 95). Neither *boyl* nor *boyle* were current forms after the sixteenth century. The word comes from Old French *boillir*, to form bubbles. *Sause* is sauce, from popular Latin *salsa*, meaning salted, by way of Old French *sausse*, which came to mean that which adds savor. (*Souse*, a related word, is discussed in C 35.) *Ueale* is Old French *veal*; *beefe* is from Old French *boef*; both forms used in the manuscript are sixteenth century (*OED*).

5   TO STEW A BREST OF VEALE

> Put y^r breast of veale into a stewing pan with water;
> put in whole mace, a bundle of sweet hearbs, & a little
> salt. stir y^m together, & put to them a little white wine.
> after it bee stewed enough, thiken it with youlks of
> eggs, put in some oysters, slyces of leamon, & some
> barbaries, & garnish y^r dish with ye same, & soe serve
> it up.

This is a *blanquette* with practically medieval touches. I suggest 2
egg yolks to each cup of cooking liquor for a golden liaison. Read
directions for *Frykecy*, C 2. Both the oysters (C 173) and the barberries (C 168 and 169) are surely pickled.

6   HOW TO STUFF A LEGG OF VEALE

> Take a legg of veale & stuff it all in ye insyde wth sweet
> hearbs shread small. put to y^r hearbs egg youlks, mace,
> & A few bread crums, a little nutmegg, & salt, & a little
> lemon pill, shread small, an anchovis or pickld oysters,
> & a few capers. mix all these together & stuff y^r legg
> wth it & lard ye right sid of y^r veale with backon. y^n
> make for y^r sauce, white wine vinegar, a little leamon
> pill, a little slyc'd nutmegg, & butter. beat up all these
> together till it be thick, y^n poure it all over the meat. &
> garnish ye dish with hard eggs shread with hearbs and
> salt.

This is an elaborate but carelessly presented recipe; no directions
for cooking the meat are given, for example. Its position among
other recipes indicates poaching but there is no good reason why
roasting or baking would not be equally successful. Actually, the
needs of veal are well understood: heightening of the flavor, which
can be bland, and providing fat for the cooking flesh, which has
a tendency to dryness if not well handled. The sauce melting over
the meat and the contrasting stuffing sounds delicious. The formula may easily be adapted for a smaller piece of veal, say a rolled
roast; the baronial appearance would be lost, but the recipe would
become more useful.

Lard (from Old French *lard*, unsmoked bacon) nowadays means to draw strips of fat through the meat. At the time, however, it also meant to wrap or daub the meat with fat, and this is borne out by the text. (What we call larding was less frequently called for, and the operation was usually detailed when required I think.) Modern bacon is so full of preservatives that I prefer to use sheets of fresh pork flare specially cut for barding. *Backon* comes from Frankish *bakko* by way of Old French *bacon*, meaning haunch; the word is cognate with *back*. *Bakon* (the *c* was inserted as an after-thought) was a fifteenth-century form (*OED*).

It is difficult to slice nutmeg without splintering but it can be managed by using a razor blade. Markham, in 1615, calls for "a Nutmegge slic't into four quarters," *to be removed before serving*. This gives a subtle dimension to a sauce because only the aroma remains. But do take care; the splinters are quite unpleasant to come upon. Of course, a scrap of freshly grated nutmeg is ever so much simpler and will do nicely.

Sid (there was ample space), a fourteenth-century form and *insyde*, a twelfth- to sixteenth-century form were archaic long before our scribe made this copy of the manuscript.

---

7   A HASH OF VEALE

Cut it thin & set it on ye fire wth an ounion, a few

capers, liquor & all, a little claret, some gravie, &

butter. when it is stewd, serve it up wth sippet[s].

Hash comes from French *hache* which Cotgrave, in 1611, translates as hacked, sliced, or hewn in pieces. The modern meaning of eking out minced leftover meat, with the figurative and perjorative con-notations of mishmash, has obscured the older meaning and this braised dish of *sliced* meat will surprise many. The main culinary problem here is a tendency to dryness; I suggest fortifying the running juices of roast meat (*grauie*, C 3) with a little rich veal broth, as well as the butter. The liquor here is the pickling liquid from the capers, but exercise judgment. For *claret*, see C 22.

Capers are the flower buds of *Capparis spinosa*, native to the Mediterranean, which are usually preserved for use by pickling or salting (*OED*). They have been known to the English since 1382, at least, when Wycliff mentioned the *erbe caperis* in his translation of the Bible. Gerard reports that they were used by the Greeks, and that they "stir up an appetite to meat, are good for a moist stomacke . . . clensing away the flegme . . . [and] open the stop-pings of the liver" (see S 296).

48

8   A HASH OF MUTON

Take a boyled legg of muton & mince both fat & lean
together, & break ye bone to ly in ye dish. stew it
betwixt 2 dishes wth water & good store of capers.
when it is enough, put in as much salt & vergis as will
season it, & a piece o[f] butter, If you please, with an
anchovis, & soe serve it up.

We have here a recipe that would seem to conform more to our
idea of hash than do recipes C 7 and 9.
    For the braising liquid, I propose the poaching broth, en-
riched with a little veal broth. For stewing *betwixt 2 dishes*, see C
1. This recipe could be carried out using a smaller cut of mutton.

---

9   A HASH OF MUTON OR VEALE

Cut y^r meat very thin, & set it on ye fire. put to it a few
capers & liquor, 2 or 3 ounions, a little spinnage,
min[t], or what other hearbs you please; put in a little
vinegar, water, gravie, & some butter. soe let it stew 2
houres before you serve it up.

This is another early recipe for hash, in reality a little ragout. The
combination of spinach and mint, along with other seasonings
such as capers and vinegar, is what gives this dish its unmistakable
late Elizabethan air; that, and the blessed lack of flour. There is an
inherent flaw in the construction, however, in that sliced meat
cooked in this fashion tends to be dry; I suggest excellent strong
broth, well fortified with veal, as the braising liquid. (See recipes
C 7 and 8.)
    Spinnage—spinach, *Spinacia oleracea*. Corominas states that
espinaca comes from Spanish Arabic *'ispināh* and Persian *ispānāh*,
which seems more reasonable than the usual proposal of Latin
spina, thorn, as the source. The case for Arabic origin is strengthened by Cotgrave's 1611 citation of *Herbe d'Espaigne* for *spinage*,
which would be the expected path. *OED* prudently claims an obscure origin, but seems to have missed the word's appearance in
The Forme of Cury, about 1390, as *Spynoch* in a perfectly straightforward recipe. This oversight has confounded certain food historians, who place its introduction into English cookery in the
sixteenth century. There are also several recipes for *espinoches* in

Le Viandier, about 1375, and *Le Ménagier*, about 1390; it would be curious if such an easy growing potherb had not reached England. It is true that we hear less of it in the fifteenth century, but by the time of Henry VIII it was in broad use again, appearing in herbals, gardening manuals, and cookbooks. Gerard discusses it, saying that it is cold and moist and that it "is used in sallads when it is yong and tender."

---

10   TO BOYLE A BREAST OF MUTON

Take parsley, time, burrage, pot marjerum, nutmegg, & caper[s], & put into y^r muton when it is allmoste boyled, first takeing out part of ye liquor. ye hearbs must be shread, & If you please, put in a piece of butter, & serve up ye meat with the broth.

You will have tastier mutton if you conduct the cooking as you would braising, using a good homemade broth, and following the suggestions in my notes for C 1. Or, if you simmer the breast as indicated, reduce the poaching broth to concentrate the goodness.

Parsley (*Petroselinum sativum*), the commonest and most widespread of all aromatic herbs, is an umbelliferous biennial. The name comes from Greek by way of French *persil*. It is mentioned in a Saxon manuscript, about 1000, as *petersilie* (*OED*). It is appropriate that the word should have taken just that form because in both Greek and Latin the word means rock herb, and Peter is the Anglicized form of *petrus*, meaning rock. Parsley enters into virtually all the recipes from early English manuscripts on cookery, and remains the most popular. Gerard says that it is hot and dry in the third degree, and so is good for combatting phlegm and other cold and clammy diseases.

Time, garden thyme (*Thymus vulgaris*), is from the Mediterranean. The name comes from the Greek, where it means to burn sacrifice (*OED*). It has a particularly attractive aroma in cooking and is one herb that survives drying reasonably well. It was thought to have all the virtues of other hot and dry herbs and, according to Gerard, "is good against the Sciatica, . . . against the winde in the side and belly, and is profitable also for such as are fearefull, melancholicke, and troubled in minde" (see S 246).

Pot marierum is sweet marjoram (*Origanum majorana*). Gerard notes that "Sweet Marjerome is a remedy against cold diseases of the braine and head . . . [and] it easeth the tooth-ache being chewed in the mouth" (see S 139).

11   TO STEW A LEGG OF MUTON
OR ROSTE IT

Take time, rosemary, marjerum, hard eggs; chope all
these together & stuff y^r muton. roste it whole or stew
it. for sau[se], take currans, barberies, & hearbs, &
boyle them in verges, put in some suger, & soe serve it
up.

To roast is to roast on the spit before the fire. (For many of us,
oven roasting will just have to do, but the English maintain to this
day the distinction made in this manuscript between roasting and
baking of meats. See page 21. The word comes from Old French
rostir; roste is a fourteenth- and fifteenth-century form (*OED*) and
is nearly invariable in our manuscript. If you choose the alternative
stewing method, I suggest braising it in good broth, as in
recipe C 1.

The sweet-sour sauce that accompanies this roast mutton
is not all that different in concept from the medieval *egurdouce*
(from Old French *egre*, sour, and *douce*, sweet), a remarkable recipe
for which is given in *The Forme of Cury*, about 1390. It too is characterized by *raysons of Corance*, raisins of Corinth (through French).
For that matter, currants or raisins characterize a sweet-sour sauce
still frequently served with tongue or ham. (For more on these
egurdouce sauces, see page 12; for pickled barberries, see C 168 or
169.)

Currans are the dried fruit of a dwarf grape from the Levant, associated historically with Corinth, although Gerard says that
they grow on the "Vine of Alexandria." The name became shortened to currants, with many variants. They quite likely became
familiar to the English at the time of the Crusades. They early
became extremely popular in upperclass English cookery and remain to this day the characterizing note of scores of cakes and
buns. (See S 151, for example.) They have an intensity of flavor
unmatched by that of raisins, which are no substitute.

12   TO BOYLE A NECK OF MUTON

Take a neck of muton & cut away ye worst; joint it &
boyle it in water & salt; put to it a good handfull of
parsley & a whole mace or 2. & when it is boyled,
shread ye parsley & put to it a little verges & sugar, & a

piece of butter, & a little of ye bro[th]; set it on ye fire &
stir it till be thick, y^n take ye muton up & lay it in a
dish, & poure all ye sauce upon it, & so serve it up.

Trim the meat and joint it, or have it cut in chops by the butcher.
(In American mutton butchery, the ribs correspond to the neck.)
The technique of cooking a great deal of parsley and then chopping
it is an ancient practice; it still is called for in sixteenth-century
recipes, but rarely later. As for the butter, I propose a quarter of
a pound, as suggested by C 15. I think that the verjuice and sugar
were added in small amounts here, a spoonful or two.

---

13   TO FORSE A LEGG OF LAMBE
        OR [MUTON]

Take one of ye bigest leggs of lamb you can get &
fatest; stuff it all in ye but end with sweet hearbs,
shread small, & some of the best of ye kell shread
amongst it, with an anchovis, & a few capers allsoe
shread, & a little leamon pill, & a little peper & salt,
mixed alltogether. when you have stufd it, crush ye top
of ye shank end upward, & lay it in a pudding pie pot;
y^n put to it a little white wine, a little salt, & a little
nutmegg mixed together, with which wash ye legg all
over with a feather. y^n set it in ye oven with other
meat; an hour will serve it. you must have in a
readyness some sweet breads of veale or lamb, sheeps
kidneys, & lambs stones, against y^r legg of lamb is
baked. fry them in sweet butter with saussages, & lay
about y^r legg when it is dished up. for ye sauce, take
some strong broth & gravie of roste meat, an anchovie
or 2, & a little pickle of oysters. give them all a boyle
together. y^n beat an egg youlk or two together, & when
ye sauce is boyled, put in y^r eggs, & stir them, but let it
not boyle after least it curdle. y^n poure y^r sauce on y^r
meat being layd in a large dish; stick in sippits &
garnish y^r dish with hearbs, & hard eggs, shread small
together.

This is an impressive dish with a good deal more finesse in the concept and handling of details than one might appreciate at first glance. The seasoning is well balanced, and please note that the meat is baked for only one hour. Even if the animals were somewhat smaller then, as perhaps they were, this means delightfully rosy lamb or properly rare mutton, as the case may be. The baking of the meat, in contradistinction to roasting, with the brushing of white wine, is interesting. If you cannot find caul, you may substitute a little beef suet or marrow, or fresh pork fat (chopped and lightly rendered). And, "against y^r legg of lamb is baked," you are to set about preparing the garnish. There is a fine sausage recipe farther on, C 25. The oyster pickle for the sauce is more difficult, although there are instructions given in C 173. I suggest using good broth to deglaze the pan juices from the roast, assuming you took care not to let them scorch. I refer you to recipe C 2 for instructions on dealing with egg liaison. With this velvety sauce, I find the chopped egg texturally distracting and quite unnecessary from any point of view.

Forse, or force, an obsolete word for stuff. *Force* is actually an alteration of *farce,* from Old French *farcir* (to stuff), by confusion with a meaning of *force,* to violate a woman (*OED*). (To further confuse things, *force,* as used in fifteenth-century cookery, could mean *afforce,* or *reinforce,* particularly with regard to seasoning or enrichments.)

The *kell,* or caul, is the lacy, fatty membrane investing the intestines. *Kell* is, and was, long since obsolete except in north of England dialect (*OED*). *Kell* could also be the archaic form of kale, or almost any cabbage, but there is no question of that in this recipe.

Lambs stones are the testicles.

---

[1]4 TO STEW A NECK OF MUTON WITH ORRINGES

Take and cut a neck of mutton ribb by ribb; season it
with pepper, salt, & a little nutmegg; lay it in a dish
wth a spoonfull or 2 of verges, some raysons of ye sun,
ye pith of 4 or 5 orringes, & If you please, a little butter;
cover them close and soe let them stew till they are
enough.

I cannot recall an example of the use of oranges in English cookery (aside from confectionery and medicine) before the sixteenth century (see S 28). Nor was I able to find any such recipes in the first edition of *Le Viandier*, 1490 (nor in earlier manuscripts) but did find several recipes in *Le Ménagier de Paris*, about 1390, that call for orange with fish, chicken, or partridge. We know that oranges were known in England by the fourteenth century and quite likely much earlier. Its absence in early manuscripts is inconclusive, especially since many of them are incomplete, but it is curious nevertheless.

In any event, oranges are very much present in Elizabethan cookery, and this is an interesting example. The dish is not so cloying as one might think because the oranges are the bitter Seville variety, for which the English have always had a predilection. Cotgrave, in 1611, gives "a civile Orange" as an illustration of *Aigre-douce*, and this dish is indeed another *Egurdouce*. If you cannot find bitter oranges, you might try including a proportion of fresh lemon and grapefruit juice, or diced pulp, as well as some orange zest. In any case, lemon juice would be the best substitute for the verjuice in this sort of recipe. The fruit is the only liquid and it burns easily; great care is necessary.

According to *OED*, the pith of an orange is the white inner membrane, but manifestly, it must refer to the juicy pulp in this context. Perhaps the more basic meaning of the word, vital essence, obtained at the time with regard to oranges. In many recipes, considerable pains were taken to discard the unpleasant membrane.

Raysons of ye sun are sun-dried grapes. Gradually, *raisin* came to be applied only to the dried fruit but the memory of the Old French word *raizin*, meaning grape, lingered for some time. The fresh fruit took the name of Old French *grape*, meaning bunch.

For the meat, mutton rib chops are wanted.

---

15   A STEWD DISH

Take what meat you please, slice it not too thick, put in some water, some wine, and a little salt, & a few capers, & a little leamon pill; let it stew well upon a chafing dish of coles, & when it is enough, take out some of ye liquor and let it coole a little; y^n take 5 or 6 youlks of beaten eggs & put to ye liquor you took out to coole; y^n take ye rest of ye meat out of ye other liquor, & put it in a cleane dish, wth sippets; y^n put a quarter of a pound of butter into ye liquor you took y^r meat

from, stir it till it is melted, & y^n mingle ye liquor y^t has
ye eggs in it with ye other; & stir it well y^t ye eggs flake
not; then poure it upon ye meat & put in some
barbaries, & garnish ye dish with capers, slyced
leamon, & barbaries.

This recipe differs little from some of the other stewed dishes; they
are all versions of a *blanquette*. The instructions for managing a
liaison of egg yolks are well understood but awkwardly expressed;
the basic idea is to temper the yolks before subjecting them to the
enriched hot liquid and, of course, not allowing them to *flake*, or
decompose.

The *chafing dish of coles*, a charcoal brazier, was used wher-
ever a steady gentle heat was wanted. (For further discussion, see
page 22.)

16　　TO BOYLE CHICKEN

Pull & draw them, then put parsley & [　in their]
bellies; boyle y^m with water, & salt, & [　] butter,
vinegar, & some of y^e [　] in; beat y^m together, y^n cut
[　] If you can get goosberies [　] put in a little
suger, & [　]

This incomplete recipe is clear enough in its basic structure: the
bird is stuffed with parsley, poached, then served with a sauce
composed of the parsley, which is chopped and mixed with butter,
vinegar, and some of the broth. It is unclear whether the sweetened
gooseberries are to be added to the sauce or used as a garnish; I
would opt for adding them to the sauce.

17　　TO BOY[LE CHICKIN ANOTHER WAY]

After they are ki[lled　] a little salt in theyr
be[llies　] boyle y^m together, y[　] boyled put in y^e
liq[uor　] & boyle y^m in wate[r　] other sauce in
wit[h　] & grapes on ye top　]

Recipe N° 17, *To boyle Chickin another way* (taken from the index),
is too heavily damaged to permit even a sketchy reconstruction.
The only noteworthy characteristic remaining is a garnish of
grapes.

18   TO BOYLE PIGEONS

Take pigeons & tie them together & perboyle y^m; then take strong broth & put it & ye pigeons in a pipkin wth roottes. after they boyle & are scummed clean, put in whole mace, cloves, & pepper, beaten small, & salt, chopt parsley, & a piece of fresh butter. boyle all together; y^n have some capers & pine apple seeds boyled in another pipkin with strong broth & butter to lay on ye pigeons; y^n serve them up with sippets & lay y^m in a large dish.

This is an interesting and feasible recipe, and a very old one, I believe. *Perboyle* means to cook through (C 52), but I feel that it is unnecessary and suggest braising the pigeons in a good chicken or veal stock. I would also lift out the pigeons when done and use the braising liquor for the sauce, reducing it before whipping in the butter just before serving for a lovely light liaison. For four pigeons, I propose a tablespoon or so of capers and a handful of pignola.

Roottes are root vegetables such as carrots, parsnips, turnips, and skirrets (C 53). Young turnips would be nice here.

Pine apple seeds are pine nuts, or *pignola*. Gerard, in 1597, says that the fruit of the pine tree is called "Pineapple, Clog, and Cone," and among its virtues he notes that "it increaseth milke and seed, and therefore it also provoketh fleshly lust." *OED* cites a Tolem manuscript from 1398: "pinea, the pineappel, is the frute of the pine tre." It also appears in a Saxon manuscript of about 1000 as *pinhnyte*.

It is instructive to note that *Ananassa sativa*, which is what we now call pineapple and is native to tropical America, gradually took over the name because of its fancied resemblance to the pine cone. This seems to have started after the mid-seventeenth century, not long after the fruit was first brought to England. There can be no question of anything but pine nuts in this recipe; it is a very old one and the context permits nothing else. (The appearance of *ananas* in a pretentious and costly volume of putative medieval cookery should have alerted even those without specialized knowledge. Nor was it the only anomaly.) By the seventeenth century, the use of pine nuts seems to have very nearly disappeared from English cookery, although they lingered in confectionery for some time.

19 TO STEW SPARROWS

Boyle them in water and salt, with a little rosemary &
sweet margerum; y^n take a pinte of white wine & halfe
[a pin]t of muton or veale broth; y^n break in little pieces
[cinnam]on, whole mace, a handfull of currans, & a
quarter [ounce of ?] sugar, & 2 or 3 dates, some whole
pieces of [   ] together to a pinte; y^n put in y^e
spar[rows] [   ] on a soft fire, y^n serve y^m up.

There is little mystery about the missing parts of this recipe; cinnamon was traditional with sparrows, and it could hardly be anything else. The quarter ounce of sugar (½ tablespoon) seems about
right; and, on a wild guess, I suggest ginger as the missing ingredient—it fits the instruction and is likely. Then, boil the liquids
down to a pint, finish simmering the sparrows in this fragrant
broth, and serve them up. Thomas Cogan, in 1584, says that sparrows "are very hotte, and stirre up Venus, especially the cocke
sparowes." He allowed that, "Being boyled in a brothe, they are
restorative, and good for weake and aged persons."

This ancient recipe was obsolete when it was last copied
sometime in the seventeenth century; the eating of sparrows by
the English seems not to have survived Elizabeth. Markham, an
almost exact contemporary of Shakespeare, in *The English Hus-wife*,
1615, mentions sparrows only once; significantly, it is in *Olepotrige*,
a recipe of some 47 ingredients from *Spaine*. Elsewhere, he gives
several lengthy lists of birds, discussing their mode of preparation;
sparrows are not so much as mentioned. This does not mean that
one cannot find seventeenth-century recipes for sparrows, perhaps; it does mean that Markham thought that they were old-
fashioned, and since his was the most popular cookbook of the
day, he was quite likely right.

[20] [TO MAKE] PULLPEACHES

[   ] loyne of porke & beat [   ] of marrow to it, or
for [   ] beat it together till [g]ood many sweet
hearbs [sea]son it wth pepper & salt
[c]arrawayes, y^n mingle [   ]in what fashion you
[pu]t them in a dish w^{th} [   ]ce, & strew some
[y]ou please.

The name of this dish posed a delightful puzzle. The scanty clues gleaned from the mutilated recipe (more than half of which had been destroyed), combined with a merry etymological chase, lead me to conclude that *pullpeach* is a dialectal corruption of one of a whole family of words, all derived, finally, from Latin *pulpa*, for pulp: *polpette* in Italian, *poupe* and *paupiette* in French, and *poupeton* and *poupette* in English. Curiously, it is not until we get to much later forms of *poupette* in *OED* that we find *poupic* and *poupick*. Perhaps they were errors as *OED* suggests, but I believe that they were regional variants of older words and if one introduces—or reintroduces—an *l* as in the Italian, we have *poulpick*. The one common characteristic of all these dishes is meat pounded to a pulp, shaped into a dumpling, and often wrapped in a thin slice of meat, as are veal birds and *paupiettes*. What little remains of the recipe bears out my construction. There are a number of similar conceits in Elizabethan cookery, one of which is a recipe *To make Peares to be boiled in meate*, given by Thomas Dawson in *The Good Hus-wives Jewell, Part II*, 1587, in which the pounded meat is shaped like pears, complete with stems of sage, before being simmered in broth.

It would be folly to attempt a complete reconstruction, but it is clear that the pork is beaten to a mass, seasoned, shaped in what fashion you please, put into a pan with broth and a blade of mace, and gently simmered till done. I think that before serving, butter was stirred in "if you please."

---

21 TO BOYLE PIGEONS W[th] PUDDINGS

When y[r] Pigeons are clean dres'd, boyle y[m] in water & salt. y[n] take for y[e] pudding some grated bread, a little flower, 3 or 4 eggs, & a little creame. take marrow or beefe suet, shread small, mace, nutmegg, & cinnamon to your taste, & a little sack; for hearbs take a little sweete margerum, tarragon, & sorrell. mix all these together pritty stiff, adding a few currans. y[n] take cloaths, wet y[m] & flower them, & tie y[e] pudding meat in severall partitions about y[e] biggness of an egge, & boyle y[m] wth y[r] pigeons. when they are boyled make this sauce: a little white wine & butter, a little verges & suger, y[n] put in 2 youlks of eggs well beaten. when you dish y[m] up, set a sprigg of roasmary in y[e] breast of

each pigeon & betwixt every pigeon, a pudding. poure
on ye sauce & soe serve y^m up.

This is an interesting recipe, if a bit mannered. It is not perfectly
clear, but I believe that the pigeons are to be simmered till tender,
and the little wrapped puddings added part way through. (The
poaching broth will make the base of a splendid lentil soup.) There
are no instructions given for the sauce. I would say to heat about
a cup of white wine with a little verjuice (or excellent wine vinegar),
a teaspoon or so of sugar, and 2 or 3 tablespoons of butter. Add
a little of the hot liquid to the egg yolks, and proceed as in C 2.
(For suggestions on making the puddings, see C 80; for the boiling
of them, see C 76.)

In sixteenth- and seventeenth-century England, *sack* was
a general name for a class of wines imported chiefly from Spain
and the Canaries. It is most often considered to have been dry
sherry, and that is what I suggest, but it seems to have been more
complicated than that. It is thought that the name comes from *vin
sec* (dry wine), but some think it comes from *vin de sac* (*OED*). See
Falstaffe on *Sherris-Sack*, S 303.

Tarragon (*Artemisia dracunculus*) is often cited in Arab
texts as *tarkhōn* but it is thought, nevertheless, to be from Greek
sources (*OED*). Tarragon, so dear to the French, rarely enters English cookery, and this manuscript is typical. Gerard says that it is
hot and dry in the third degree, "and not to be eaten alone in
sallades, but joyned with other herbs, as Lettuce, [and] Purslain
. . . that it may also temper the coldnesse of them." Note that it
is here joined with sorrel, which was considered to be chilling (see
S 278).

---

22   TO MAKE CAPON SAUCE

Take oysters with theyr liquor, & ale, & set y^m on y^e
fire. y^n put into y^m a little clarret, & some whole
ma[ce], & shread in a little ounio[n], a little leamon pill,
& a little salt. when it [is] stewd a little while, thicken it
wth a little grated bread, & put in a piece of fresh
butte[r] but let it not boyle after.

Later English bread sauces became very stodgy indeed; I believe
that very little bread is called for here, if for no other reason than
that farinaceous thickening of any kind was so rare. The combination of ale (not beer) and wine was common in sixteenth-century

recipes, particularly those involving sea food (see C 186). I wonder, however, whether *ale* might not be a scribal error for *all*; "liquor & all" is a typical culinary turn of phrase (see C 7) So add ale, or not, as you see fit. In most of our recipes, pickled oysters (C 173) are called for but here it surely is fresh ones that are wanted. I counsel adding them just before the bread crumbs, as they toughen on cooking. Add salt and freshly gound pepper to taste and stir in the butter just before serving.

Clarret, a sixteenth-century form, comes from Old French *claret*, meaning clear, to be sure, but also light or bright. Until about 1600, according to *OED*, it was a term applied to light red wines to distinguish them from both deeper reds and whites, a meaning that *clairet* still has in French; *clairette*, a specific wine, has such a color. (This is not the pink hue of *rosé*.) About that time, *claret* began to assume its present usage, designating red wines from Bordeaux. (Until then, Bordeaux wines had usually been indifferently classed among *Gascoyne* wines in England. See S 275.) Not surprisingly, *claret*, the color, also changed from a pale red with yellowish undertones to the deep red of the typical Bordeaux (*OED*). Sixteenth-century sources, however, show that certain pale wines that we would classify as white may have been called claret; the golden glints may have been the determining factor, and the whites of the southwest of France are often golden, especially compared to the wines of the Rhine. Since our manuscript spans just this period of flux in nomenclature, it is difficult to know with certainty which wine is indicated by the term claret. In general, I suggest a light red wine; as here, however, the color of white wine would often be more appetizing. Also, see C 58 and C 198.

---

23   TO MAKE HEN SAUCE

Take ye gravie of muton & a hard roasted egg, or 2, minced smal[l], a little mustard wth the juice of leamon, if you have it; If not, a little white wine vinegar. soe heat them together.

Eggs were roasted in hot ashes; hard boiled will do as well in this case. The gravy, one must remember, is the running juice of roast meat, of an intense meaty flavor, nothing to do with our floury pallid mixtures (see C 3). This sauce would provide a zesty accent for boiled fowl.

24   TO MAKE SAUSE FOR FOULE

For turkeys, Capons, partridge, phesants, woodcock,
tele, duck, plover, curlues, & quailes. take gravie &
strong broth & leamon, minc'd, & grated bread, a
spoonefull or 2 of claret wine & a little butter. & If you
have an anchovie. give all a boyle together.

Two quite different birds have been known as turkey in English.
First was the guinea fowl, *Numida*, native to Africa and known
to Aristotle and Pliny as *Meleagris*; curiously, it seems not to have
been known in England until early in the sixteenth century. OED
explains the name of turkey by its importation into England
through "Turkish dominions." (Just so, maize was called *Turkey
corn*.) Then, in 1518, the Conquistadores found in Mexico what we
now call the turkey, already domesticated by the Aztecs. It was
introduced into Europe, where it quickly gained favor, but was
immediately confused with the guinea fowl and also called turkey.
Linnaeus later compounded the confusion by giving the ancient
name *Meleagris* to the usurper, the American turkey (*OED*). Sixteenth-century citations of turkey can be maddeningly frustrating;
it is often difficult to know with certainty which bird is meant and
I suspect that it frequently meant either, reflecting popular mis-
conception. In *Food and Drink in Britain*, C. Anne Wilson tells us
that by 1555, the sale of turkeys was such that their price in the
London market was officially fixed, along with those of other
poultry; a turkey-cock cost six shillings that year, which seems to
me a very high price. (For other prices, see page 9 and C 35.)
As always, cookbooks lagged behind usage. But in 1586, Thomas
Dawson gives us an elaborate recipe for turkey that involves de-
boning it. By 1615, when Markham published *The English Hus-wife*,
turkey is mentioned very nearly as frequently as chicken, and has
its own recipes and sauces. So that for the Pilgrims, the turkey
(albeit a different strain) had long been a familiar bird and must
have been a welcome sight in that strange land that was America.
The teal, *Querquedula*, is the smallest of the ducks. *Tele*
appears in Middle English and was current until the sixteenth
century. The plover is a common name for any of the family Char-
adriidae. The name comes from Old French *plovier*, rain-bird
(*OED*). In France, at least, it is roasted undrawn, like woodcock.
Woodcock, *Scolopax rusticula*, is a migratory bird much esteemed
by gastronomes. It is interesting to note that one Middle English
form was *wide cok* (tree cock) with parallel forms in Old French,
one of which has survived in Norman patois as *videcoq*.

The curlew, *Numenius*, is a grallatorial bird, which simply means that it walks on stilts. It has delightful names in Britain, such as *whaup* and *whimbrel* (*OED*). Curlew (the *u* in the manuscript is unclear—it may be *carlues*) was still eaten in early sixteenth-century England; in household accounts that Pegge appended to *The Forme of Cury*, we find that they were purchased for a great feast in 1526 at a price of 16 pence, the same price as that of a pheasant in the list. But in 1615 Markham does not so much as mention curlew in several comprehensive lists of birds and earlier books indicate a gradual decline in favor, along with heron, crane, and swan, to say nothing of peacock. Evidently, the tastier guinea fowl and turkey gradually displaced them all.

The list of fowl is interesting. This is the only mention of turkey in the manuscript, and from the absence of the popular guinea fowl, I think it possible, at the time of original entry, that turkey applied indifferently to either bird, as noted above. The sauce is less interesting, but not untypical. I would omit the optional anchovy, whose pervasive flavor I find jarring and unnecessary with these birds, but the minced fresh lemon is a lovely touch. The birds were roasted on the spit before the fire and the juices from the dripping pan were quite likely added to the little sauce. (If you oven roast, be sure that the pan juices are not scorched.) By preference, I would use veal or chicken broth, but stronger broths, along with the customary juices of rare roast mutton (*grauie*, C 3), would be more typical. The butter is whipped in just before serving.

---

25 TO MAKE OXFORD KATES SAUSAGES

Take ye leane of a legg of porke, or veale, & 4 pound of beef suet, or butter, & shread y^m together very fine. y^n season y^m with 3 quarter of an ounce of pepper & halfe as much cloves & mace, a good handfull of sage, shread small, & what salt fits y^r pallate. mingle these together, y^n take 10 eggs, all but 3 whites, & temper alltogether with y^r hands. & when you use y^m, roule y^m out about ye length & biggness of y^r finger. you may roule y^m up in flower, If you like it, but it is better without. when you fry y^m, ye butter must boil in ye pan before you put y^m in. when they are pritty browne, take y^m up. theyr sauce is mustard.

This is a splendid sausage recipe. Leaving out some of the whites is a perceptive note, as is the advice not to roll the sausage in flour; "they are nicer without." Equally wise is the instruction to have the butter hot enough; unlike link sausages, these must be seized, as the French put it, not allowed to ooze.

The amount of actual meat on a fresh ham runs from 10 to 12 pounds, according to my butcher. Pigs may have been slightly smaller then; I suggest a proportion of twice as much lean meat, or more, to suet or butter. You will have a more attractive texture if you chop the meat with a knife; for a small batch, it is little more trouble than setting up and cleaning the grinder. (The French food processor does it all in seconds; do it in small batches and use the on-off technique so that the meat is chopped, not mashed.) One tablespoon of peppercorns weighs about a ¼ ounce; grind them fresh. Start with 1 teaspoon of sea salt per pound of mixture; fry a tiny patty to taste for seasoning. This sausage does not keep. Once you have tasted homemade sausages, you will never again be happy with those you buy.

The Oxford Sausage, 1764, with a frontispiece "portrait" of a "Mrs. Dorothy Spreadbury, Inventress of the Oxford Sausage," is a university lampoon. It may have spread the fame of the home-town sausage, but the sausage was entirely figurative and it was the poetry that was "happily blended . . . [and] highly seasoned."

I believe this to be a very early recipe for Oxford sausages. I have come across early seventeenth-century recipes for other dishes attributed to the *Tavern at Oxford Gates*; this may have come from there, as well. (The *k* in *kates* is pristine.) One eighteenth-century recipe for *Oxford Sausage* from a charming family manu-script inherited by Mrs. Christine Robertson of Oxford is not so different from our own. It calls for pork and veal mixed, an element for which there is a harbinger above. Hannah Glasse gives a recipe in *The Art of Cookery*, 1796, which substitutes ½ a pound of grated bread for eggs, with 1 pound each of veal, pork, and suet. But the characterizing features are a mixture of pork and veal, a binding of eggs, and the fashioning into finger-shaped sausages without casings.

---

26   TO MAKE SAUSSAGES

Take ye leane of a sweete bone of porke y^t is without strings, & to y^r leane take a double quantety of fat. chopp y^m small together. y^n beat y^m in a mortar very well. y^n season y^m with cloves & mace, & as much pepper as y^m both, & what salt you please. & put in or leave out what hearbs you fancy. y^n stamp y^m well & fill y^m, but not too full. they will keepe good to fry or broyle a moneth. y^r guts must be thin scoured.

This is a straightforward country sausage recipe, mercifully free of the cereals that later came to characterize sausages in England. The proportion of fat to lean is exceedingly high; most sausage recipes call for the inverse proportion, or twice as much lean as fat. (However, in *The Compleat Housewife*, American edition, 1742, E. Smith gives a recipe calling for the same proportions, so it would appear not to be an error.) When the writer says that they will keep a month, she assumes that they be hung, not touching, from the rafters in a dry, cool, and airy place, as I have so often seen in rural France. Unless you have such facilities and are experienced in sausage making, I do not recommend this procedure. Since the extra fat assists in preservation, I suggest reverting to the more customary proportions, particularly since our lean meat is probably more fatty nowadays. See the previous recipe for notes on chopping and seasoning. *Thin scoured guts* have been purged and "thinned" of extraneous and viscous matter.

---

27   TO MAKE BROTH COLLOPS

Cut a raw legg of muton in thin pieces. beat y^m a little, y^n fry them a little wth water & salt y^t ye gravie may be in y^m. then put them in a dish & stew y^m in ye same liquor. putting in some wh[ite] wine & leamon & an anchovis. & when they are enough, serve them up in ye broth.

The ingredients are not surprising; what is interesting is the technique of sealing in the juices of the meat by dipping the collops in boiling salted water. (If you want to favor the broth, you put the meat into cool unsalted water and gradually bring it to an imperceptible simmer.) This can most expeditiously be done with a fry basket; have plenty of well-salted water at a full boil, and take care not to put in too much meat at a time or the juices will leach into the water, a bit of technique that the cook understood very well. (The French still cook certain cuts of meat in this fashion.) I understand less well why the meat is stewed thereafter. I suggest rich beef broth, fortified with veal, for the braising liquid. (For *collops*, see C 4; for the use of *fry* for boil, see C 2.)

28   TO MAKE FRENCH POTTAGE

Four hours before you goe to dinner or supper, hang
ove[r] ye fire a good pot of water, with a pritty piece of
bee[f] & let it boyle an houre. y^n put in a marrow bone
or 2 & let it boyle an houre longer, y^n put in ye cragg
end of a neck of muton or veale, & an hour before
dinner put in a little bacon, some sorrell & spinnage, &
cabbedg leaves, green pease, what salt you like. when
you serve it up, set a dish over some coles with a good
many sippets, & put some of this broth in it, & when
ye bread is well soaked, y^n fill ye dish up with y^e
thickest y^t is in ye pot, & in ye middle lay ye marrow
bones. & have some 3 youlks of eggs, beaten wth some
of ye broth, to poure on ye dish when it is served up.

Pottage came into Middle English as *potage*, unchanged from Old
French; gradually the accent shifted to the first syllable and the
spelling changed to reflect this (*OED*). The ancient *standing* pottage
was very heavy with cereal, so that this is indeed a fancied-up
version showing the influence of the French *soupe*, whose principal
characteristic was the soaking of the sops (see C 1) over gentle
heat, a process called *mittoner*. (In France, a modern *potage* is a
strained soup, considered to be more elegant than the rustic *soupe*,
which still, at least in principle, contains soaked bread. Amusingly,
potage has been reintroduced into English as a high-flown term for
an elegant soup.)
The *cragg end*, or scrag end, refers in American butchery
to the neck. A *pretty* piece is one of a pretty good size. Among the
older meanings of *bacon* is a haunch of pork (see C 6), or simply
pork. In any event, I think that modern smoked bacon would be
out of place and I propose something like the shank end of a fresh
ham to be put in from the beginning.
One of the first things one notices about these old soups
is that they were often so very green. The egg yolk liaison is a
sumptuous touch. (See C 2 for directions.) It cannot be reheated,
so thicken only as much broth as you expect to serve.

29 TO MAKE FRENCH POTTAGE

Take 3 ducks & halfe roste y^m. then put y^m in a pipkin with strong broth, streyned. put in 3 or 4 carrets & as much cabbage as a penny loaf, & a little whole mace. when y^r cabbage is tende[r], take up y^r rootes & cut y^m dice wayes, & put y^m in againe. y^n p[ut] to y^m some strong gravie, a little white wine, & an anchovy* or 2, shread small, If you please,† you may stew y^r ducks in another pipkin in part of y^r broth till they are enough. then lay them on y^r dish & poure ye cabbage & broth upon y^m, & garnish y^r dish with fryde parsley & salt.

This is a great flavorsome soup. The technique of dicing the carrots after cooking is an ancient one (it occurs in Apicius, for example) related to that of chopping parsley after cooking, which also appears in our manuscript. I would omit the anchovy, but that is perhaps personal. American ducks are often fatty, and while partial roasting (a technique that adds immeasurably to flavor) leaches off a good deal of fat, you will most likely want to skim the soup before serving. The garnish of fried parsley and salt is a sophisticated touch. The *grauie* is most likely of mutton (C 3) and the strong broth may be of beef, mutton, or chicken.

Carret (*Daucus carota*) is a sixteenth-century form; *carrot* appeared by 1597, in Gerard. The name comes from Greek *karoton*. According to Gerard, the Greeks knew it as *Daucus*, often qualifying it further with *pastinaca*, usually translated as parsnip. Apicius gave recipes for *caroetae seu pastinacae* (carrots or parsnips), and Pliny, among others, described carrots. About 1390, *Le Ménagier* reported that *garroittes* (*carottes*), described as *racines rouges* (red roots) were sold in Les Halles. So it is curious that the first citation of the word by *OED* is in 1533, as "Parsnepes and carettes" from Elyot's *The Castel of Helth*. However, Turner in 1548 treats them familiarly, saying that "Carettes growe in al countreis in plentie," carefully distinguishing them from wild carrots, so that those who claim that the carrot was not introduced into England until the time of Elizabeth, and even later, are in error. (Anne Wilson thinks that the Romans may have introduced garden carrots in the first century.) It is true that I do not find carrots called for

---

* Following the y, there is an indecipherable stroke that does not appear to be an *s*.
† There was punctuation neither before nor after this phrase.

by name in earlier cookbooks; this must be due to the historical association—not to say confusion—between carrots and parsnips. Gerard, for example, says that there were red as well as yellow carrots—parsnips are treated separately—so that the indifferent grouping of these roots under one name becomes somewhat more understandable. Whatever their earlier history in England was, the turn of the century marked the beginning of a new popularity for carrots. In 1603, Richard Gardiner gives them disproportionate space in *Instructions for Kitchin Gardens*, praising them with evangelical fervor; they rapidly displaced skirrets (C 53) early in the seventeenth century, as may be seen in succeeding editions of Markham's *The English Hus-wife*, 1615, 1623, 1637, and 1660. Carrots are mentioned only three times on our manuscript.

A *pipkin* is an earthenware cooking pot, usually described as being small, but clearly it came in larger sizes as well. It was usually used on the *chafing dish of coles* (C 15). The size of a *penny loaf* varied considerably (C 85); I suggest a small to medium cabbage.

---

30   TO MAKE FRENCH BROTH

Take a leane piece of beefe, a piece of veale or muton, & a hen, & boyle y^m in a pot, & scum y^m. put in some large mace, & halfe a cabbage If a little one,* some sweet hearbs, as letice & spinnage. & boyle y^m well till all ye goodness be out. y^n put in ye bottom of a houshould lofe. toward ye end, roste a leane piece of bee[f] & cut it often for gravie. drawe y^r broth clear from ye bottom & boyle some pigeons in salt & water. & save a piece of cabbedg to put in ye middle of y^r dish. Let it stand on coles after ye pigeons, gravie & broth is in.

This is an imposing soup, a proper *soupe* in the French sense (see C 28). The roasting of the beef solely for its *grauie* is prodigal; while the meat was surely thrown into the stock pot, it is clear that there was never any thought of economy in this household. As to the cabbage, either half a large one or a small one is wanted. Calling lettuce and spinach *sweet hearbs* shows how elastic the term was;

* I suggest that it should read: *or* a little one. There was punctuation neither before nor after this phrase.

their presence is part of the slightly archaic flavor of the soup, as is the nuttiness and textural interest of the wholemeal bread.

A *houshould lofe* was the sort of bread from which trenchers were cut for medieval place settings. The *Northumberland Household Book* decrees that it "be made of the meal as it cometh from the mill" (100 percent whole wheat flour) and this held true into the eighteenth century. Whether for trenchers or sops, the bread was easier to handle and functioned better when 4 days old. The presence of a horizontal slice of bread in this soup permits one to speculate that trenchers were still being cut in this household at the time of original entry. (*Houshould* is a fourteenth- to seventeenth-century form; *lofe* is from the fifteenth.) For further discussion, see *bread*, page 17, C 92, and 95.

---

31   T O M A K E P E A S E P O R R A G E O F O L D
P E A S E

Take 2 quarts of white pease, pick & wash y^m cleane, y^n set them on in 3 gallons of water. keepe y^m boyling & as ye water wastes, fill it up wth cold water to break ye husks. & as ye husks rise, [after] it is filled up wth cold water, scum them of into a cullender into a dish to save ye liquor & pease to put into ye pot againe. then t[ake] up all ye pease & posh y^m wth a spoone; y^n put y^m in againe. & when they have boyled a while, put in 2 cloves of garlick, halfe an ounce of corriander seeds beaten, some sifted pepper & some salt, an ounce of powder of dryed spearmint. all these must be put in at ye second boyling. shread in 2 ounions & a handfull of parsley very small, & put in halfe a pound of fresh butter. y^n let all boyle together for a quarter of an houre. y^n serve y^m up with bread & bits of fresh butter put into y^m. & If you love it, put in a little ellder vinegar.

This is an excellent, well-balanced recipe; the problem of brightening the rather mealy taste and texture of the peas is well thought out. The lavish use of butter instead of the commoner fat pork is a further example of the lavishness which characterizes the kitchen of this household. The recipe will work fine with split yellow or green peas, nor will you have difficulty with husks.

White pease may simply be mature dried garden peas (*Pisum sativum*), but Gerard says that they are of a different strain, white or gray when mature with very tough skins, that he calls *pisum Romanum*. (Sources are contradictory.) It is of interest to note that *pease* was originally singular in form (plural, *peasen*). Thus, Turner in 1548 uses *pease* in the singular while Gerard uses it in the plural as well. Of their virtues, Gerard says: "The Pease, as *Hippocrates* saith, is lesse windie than Beans," but agrees with Galen that they should nevertheless be eaten with prudence. Coriander seeds, with their warm spicy fragrance, are delicious in all legume dishes; along with the other herbs and spices, also considered to be hot and dry, they were thought to temper the cold and windy effects of peas. Even garlic, rare in English cookery, was called upon (C 41).

Porrage, porridge, is considered by *OED* to be an altered form of *pottage* (C 28), possibly influenced by *porrey*, the medieval soup. *Porrey* is thought by some to be derived from Old French *porreau*, leek, but others prefer Old French *porée*, a word designating the white ribs of chard, cardoons, and even spinach. In about 1393, *Le Ménagier* devotes an entire section to *porées*, variously using leeks, chard, spinach, cabbage shoots, or cress as the characterizing vegetable and some using meats, pureed peas, or almond milk as well. Clearly, both *porreau* and *porée* were formative, but I feel that early forms of *purée* (Du Cange cites Latin *porea* from 1231) were nearly as important, particularly in England. In various fourteenth- and fifteenth-century manuscripts we find *Perrey of Peson*, *Porry of white Pese*, *Blanche porrey* (with leeks), as well as a curious *Porry Chapeleyn* calling for onions, olive oil, and almond milk, with a pasta garnish. Recipes based on peas are significantly more numerous than those with leeks, and those involving chard or other leafy vegetables are rare if at all; the one constant factor was increasingly that of having been forced though a sieve. The English had forgotten *poireaux* and *porée*, but *purée* still had meaning. (Also, see Austin in *Two Fifteenth-Century Cook-Books*, listed under Harleian MS. in the bibliography.) *Porridge* eventually came to be more often applied to boiled grain although *pease porridge* survives, at least in folklore.

Posh appears to be a variation of *pash*, a long obsolete word meaning to mash, to reduce to a pulp (*OED*). Elder vinegar was much liked. Gerard says that "The vinegar in which the dried floures [of elder] are steeped is wholesome for the stomacke." (For elder, see S 254.)

32 TO MAKE GREEN PEASE, PORRAGE

Take of ye youngest pease you can get, what quantety
you please, & put y^m in a little more faire water then
will cover them. boyle y^m till they be tender. y^n take
new milke & make them of what thickness you please.
Let y^m boyle well together, y^n take a little flower and
wet it with milke enough to thicken it, & put it in with
some spearmint & marrigoulds shread small. when it is
boyled enough, put in a good piece of fresh butter, a
little salt, & some pepper, If you please, & soe dish [it]
up.

This recipe is unique in the manuscript in that it uses flour as a
binding agent. It is true that young peas will give little consistency;
fine French cooks solve this problem by adding a few mature peas
to provide a liaison. The use of flour here is a vestige of medieval
practices. In Laud MS. 553, about 1450, there is a recipe for *Peys
de almayne* that calls for peas, brayed small, tempered with "almande milke, & with flour de rys," and seasoned with saffron.
And in *A Noble Boke Off Cookry*, about 1470, a dish for *Yonge pessene*
is bound with pounded peas and bread; the following recipe for
yonge pessen ryalle, an appropriately elaborate dish based on rabbit
and calling for almond milk, saffron, and mint, instructs that
12 egg yolks are to be added to 4 gallons of liquid, in addition to
an unspecified amount of brayed peas and bread, as in the more
plebian recipe. Even so, we are cautioned to "let the pessen be
rynyng."

 The English have long been inordinately fond of mint
(spearmint, *Mentha viridis*) in cooking and medieval medical opinion backed them up. Gerard says: "It will not suffer milke to cruddle in the stomacke," and cites Pliny as saying that the very smell
of mint "doth stir up the minde and the taste to a greedy desire
of meat [food]." Also see S 140.

 According to Gerard, the marigold flower "is thought to
strengthen and comfort the heart very much, also to withstand
poyson." The leaves were thought to "mollifie the belly . . . if it be
used as a pot-hearbe." *OED* claims that the flowers are still used
to flavor soups, so perhaps it is the flowers wanted here. There
may be some continuity with the yellow coloring of the saffron in
the early recipes cited above. (Also, see S 83.)

33   TO MAKE TOSTES OF VEALE

Shread veale & suet small together, & boyle them well
in a little faire water. & boyle some currans by
themselves, then mingle together with grated bread,
then season them with a little nutmegg & sugar, & lay
them upon toasts of manchet, & fry them with fresh
butter.

I believe this to be an old recipe; similar ones are common in
Elizabethan cookbooks. Finally, it is a sort of mincemeat on toast.
The toast must be crisp fried at absolutely the last moment or there
is no point to this dish at all. *Manchet* is finest white bread
(see C 95).

34   HOW TO ROULE A COLLER OF BEEFE

Take a 9 hide piece of beefe, which is ye thin end of y^e
breast, & cut away ye but end where the shoulder is.
bone it, & lay it in spring well water & salt 3 days & 3
nights. then take it out & strow good store of sal[t] on
ye insyde of ye beefe, & put in gross pepper, whole
mace, & some cloves, & bay leaves cut in small long
pi[e]ces, & leamon scinn cut with slyces of leamon cut
in bit[s] & layd all over it. season it good & high. you
may allso[e], If you please, put in some sweet hearbs
shread small. then roule it up like a coller of brawne &
tie it with corse mele. it will require 5 hours boyling.

The cut wanted here is flank. The *9 hide* designation is in error for
9 hole (unless it be a local corruption). *OED* gives *nine-holes*, describing it as Scottish; one of the meanings is: "That piece of beef
that is cut out immediately below the brisket, or breast, denomi-
nated from the vacancies left by the ribs." Elizabeth David tells me
that "Meg Dods* says it's the Scotch name for flank or runner,"
and that it may still be in use in some parts of the country. (This
is one of the traces that caused me to suspect a Northumbrian
origin of certain recipes.)

* Mistress Margaret Dods in *The Cook and Housewife's Manual*, Edinburgh,
1826 on.

Hannah Woolley, in *The Gentlewomans Companion*, 1682, says: "In the right making of a *Collar of Beef* you must take the flank and lay it in *Pump-water* two or three days." (Note how much more modern her instructions are than those in our manuscript.) In 1755, Hannah Glasse also specifies a "thin Piece of Flank Beef," to be laid in *Pump-water*. A scribal error gives *spring well water* in our manuscript. Most writers specify well water; because it is usually hard, the meat will keep its shape better. (For broth, on the other hand, spring water is favored.) The thick butt end is cut away in our recipe so that the meat can be salted and rolled up evenly; Mrs. Glasse beats it even. After the poaching, it is hung in a cool place and served cold, very thinly sliced.

For *corse mele*, use kitchen twine. (Under scores of entries in *OED*, I found only one with any relationship, however far fetched; *mell*, an obsolete and rare word for horse's tail. Horse hair was in common use for many household chores as late as my childhood, so that this is not impossible.) *Brawne* is the fleshy part, the muscle, of the leg.

---

35 TO SOUCE A PIGG OF 3 OR 4 SHILLINGS PRICE

First scalld y^r pigg very clean, y^n cut it thorough ye back & take out ye bones, & let it lie a night in water at least, to soak out ye blood. y^n cut it in 3 or 4 pieces, as you please, & roule them up like coller[s] of brawne, & sow them up in cloaths. y^n set on faire water & a little salt & let it boyle. y^n put ye collers in, & let y^m boyle till they are tender as a rush will goe thorough y^m. y^n put them in a clean pot, & cover them with souce drink thus made. take some of ye liquor they were boyled in, & put to it one quart of white wine, & a pint of white wine vinegar, a race of ging[er] slyced, & a nutmegg, some 20 graynes of whole pepper, & halfe a dosin bay leaves. boyle this halfe an houre, y^n put it in an earthen pot, both pigg & it together, eyther both hot or both cold. If you pleas, you may stre[w] a little cloves & mace beaten, on ye inside of y^r collers afte[r] you roule them up.

This is an excellent recipe for souse; the counsel to have both meat and souse the same temperature is most perceptive. If kept cold, pork may be kept a week or ten days in this light souse, but it is at its best after two or three days. No indication is given as to the amount of cooking broth to be added to the *drink* (not a common usage); the keeping qualities depend on the acidity, of course, but with refrigeration, you may have as light a souse as pleases you. The meat must be kept covered with the souse. (The rest of the broth makes a fine basis for lentil soup, or any bean dish, particularly if you use the feet, ears, and other lowly parts.)

From the context, a *Pigg of 3 or 4 shillings Price* appears to correspond to what came to be known in Virginia as *shote*, described by Mrs. M. C. Tyree in *Housekeeping in Old Virginia*, 1879, as a pig killed between two and three months of age; it is cut in four quarters, she says, and "is more delicate and wholesome eaten cold," so that historical continuity seems to support this. Mary Randolph, in 1824, specified that each quarter weigh 6 pounds. Such figures as I have are not conclusive, but prices paid for various butcher meats at Ingatestone Hall in 1561, for example, do not seem to be out of line: an entire veal cost 10 shillings and a whole mutton was had for 7 shillings. In any event, until the eighteenth century, *pig* specified a very young animal.

A *race* refers to a hand of ginger (S 92). *Souse* is related to sauce; see C 4.

---

[36]   TO ROSTE A HARE

When y^r hare is dres'd, take time, parsley, &
margerum, shread them small & mingle them with 3 or
4 youlks of eggs & therewith fill ye belly of ye hare &
roste it. y^n cut all ye meat from ye bones, & mince it
small, & mingle with it y^t which was in ye bellie, & put
in a good deale of butter & a little verges or vinegar, &
soe let y^m heat together. serve it up in a faire dish, y^e
bones lying about it & ye back bone in ye midst. you
may boyle some currans & put in If you like them.

The practice of roasting a hare, only to mince it marks this as an ancient recipe. There may have been certain modifications of the seasoning in the direction of suavity—herbs rather than spices, for example—but the structure and the presentation are old. It is difficult to know just how *small* the meat is to be minced, but I think that what is wanted is bite-sized pieces, not a hash. The hare is properly roasted on the spit but oven roasting will do; it should be barded or basted frequently with butter, and must not be overdone.

---

37   TO ROSTE A CAPON WITH OYSTERS

Take a fat Capon & pull & draw it, y^n stuff ye body wth raw oysters, y^n truss & lay it to ye fire, & set a clean dish under it to save ye gravie. y^n make ye sauce for it, with water y^t cometh from ye oysters, & a little clarret, a little pepper & vinegar & ye gravie, & rub an ounion up & downe ye sauce, y^t it may taste well of it. when it hath boyled a little, put in some butter & mince in some leamon and leamon pill, then serve it up with slyced leamon on ye capon & round about ye dish.

This is an excellent recipe. American oysters are quite different in flavor from those of European waters, being fatter and blander. However, they cook up well and are perfectly suitable. Our chickens, however, have little taste or texture, even fancy capons, but if you have the good fortune to lay your hands on a fine roasting chicken, this is a great and festive dish. Roasting means spitting the bird, but with care, you can do an acceptable job in the oven. Above all, be sure that the roasting pan is an oval one of just the right size; this helps to assure that the pan juices do not burn. The sauce is excellent; I would omit the shreds of lemon peel but I find the diced lemon delightful. I believe that the amount of vinegar is minuscule, just enough to sharpen the taste a bit. The specification of raw oysters strengthens my surmise that in most recipes, they are pickled.

To *pull* a fowl is to pluck it, but see S 268.

---

38   A CAPON AFTER Y^e FLANDERS FASHION

Boyle y^r Capon in a quart of white wine, another of water, & ye rest of muton broth; cut in some carrets & put in 2 marrow bones, whole mace & some sugar. serve it up in some of ye broth with sops, but leave out ye marrow bones.

Poaching a capon in mutton broth did not offend the taste of the period. Mutton broth is something few Americans have tasted; it is a bit strong (here, it would make up about one third of the liquid) but if well made, it has character. Modern French technique would call for veal broth but in the spirit of the recipe, you could substitute a good beef broth, homemade, of course; it would lend a bit of savor to the bird. Poaching must be carried on at an imperceptible simmer, but the liquid must be boiling when the bird is first put in. I would personally omit the sugar, but if you wish to be authentic, wait until the bird is tender and sweeten only the amount of broth you intend to serve as accompaniment so that the remaining rich broth can be used for some other purpose. An oval pan of appropriate size is very nearly essential for such cooking.

I have no reason to believe that the recipe is particularly Flemish, but it is possible that some element of construction or garnish in this recipe corresponds to such usage, or to some English cook's concept of such usage.

---

39 TO SOUCE VEALE

Halfe boyle a joynt of Veale in water & salt, y^n put to it a pinte of white wine, & halfe a pint of vinegar, 3 or 4 large mace & a bundle of sweet hearbs. when it is boyled enough, take it up & let it ly in ye broth 3 or 4 dayes, before you eat it.

A delightful dish that shows the imagination with which women dealt with the lack of refrigeration, often ending up with a dish of more interest and charm than handling it straight would have given. This is a light souse, and while it improves on maturing for a few days, as our scribe notes, it is not intended for long keeping, although refrigeration will lengthen that time. In cooling it, make sure that the meat is well covered with liquid, choosing a dish in which the joint just fits nicely; do not cover it until perfectly cool.

---

40 [TO R]OSTE A SHOULDER OF MUTTON WITH BLOOD

When [you] kill a sheep, save ye blood & strayn about a pint of it; & to y^t blood put a good quantety of time, pick'd & shread small. when you take ye caull out of ye sheeps bellie, spread it on a great trey wet wth water, & cut of y^r shoulder as large as you can, & stuff* both y^e

* Written *suff.*

75

inside & out side with ye time steeped in blood, & in every hole poure in with a spoone some of ye blood. then, lay ye shoulder into ye caule, & fasten it with scewers. y^n lay it in a trey & poure ye rest of ye blood upon it. in the winter you may let it ly thus in ye blood 24 hours before it be roasted, but in ye summer it must ly halfe soe longe.

Most of us are not likely ever to have the opportunity of trying this ancient dish. The meat gains in flavor and tenderness in this marinade, and wrapping it in caul is the most effective possible way to roast it; the fatty membrane provides automatic basting and the lacy open texture allows the proper crusting of the meat, unlike barding. Certain foreign butcher shops, especially those catering to Italians, do sell pork caul; it is worth seeking out for roasting.

---

41   TO ROSTE A SHOULDER OF MUTON WITH GARLICK

First boyle ye garlick in 2 or 3 waters, & let ye shoulder of muton be green roasted. y^n scorch it to let out ye gravie into a dish, & to it put ye garlick & a little clarret wine & some nutmegg. Let them stew a little together, & when y^r shoulder of muton is layd in ye dish, you may eyther take out ye garlick or leave it in as you like it.

This dish has a French air; it is not so much the discreet presence of garlic as the technique of green roasting and finishing up the meat rather as a *salmis*. (Green roasted meat is virtually raw in the center.) The roasting was done on the spit (see page 21); the stewing would have been done on the *chafing dish* (C 15). There is no clue to how much garlic would have been used, but the flavor is remarkably mild with this treatment.

    Garlic (*Allium sativum*) derives from Old English *gar*, meaning spear, and *leac*, meaning leek (*OED*). Gerard reports that: "Garlicke is very sharpe, hot and dry (as *Galen* saith) in the fourth degree . . . it cutteth such grosse humours as are tough and clammy . . . it engendreth sharpe and naughty blood." (Parboiling attenuates these qualities.) It is also considered good for an old cough, "it breaketh and consumeth wind," it kills worms, and is effective against the pestilence. A number of sixteenth-century writers on health allowed that garlic would be beneficial to the English because of the climate and their predisposition to "cold and clammy phlegm," but thought that they were too discerning a people to resort to such a medicine except *in extremis*. And garlic was, and remains, rare in English cookery. Our manuscript is rather unusual in this respect as it enters three recipes, C 31 and 199 in addition to this one.

Scorch means to slash. Obsolete in this sense, it is an alteration of *score* and related to *scotch* (C 4). *OED* suggests that the form was influenced by *scratch*; certainly the meanings are close. But the influence of Old French *escorcier* (*escorcher* in Cotgrave, 1611), to flay, is difficult to dismiss, I think; the forms are virtually identical and flaying does involve slashing.

---

42   TO ROSTE A PIGG

When ye pigg is halfe rosted, pull of ye scinn & stick it full of sprigs of time, & baste it with butter & crumbs of bread till it be enough. for ye sauce, take grated bread & water, a little vinegar, nutmegg, & sugar, & boyle all these together, then put in some butter & serve them up.

From other sources of the period, we learn that the young pig (C 35) was put on the spit with hide and hair; apparently the rind peels off easily, leaving a layer of fat to protect the meat. It obviates the tedious operation of getting the hair off but the delectable crackly crisp rind, considered by many as the most delectable part of the roast, is lost. The sprigs of thyme are a nice touch. The sauce is of less interest, but not untypical.

---

43   TO STEW CALUES FEET

Boyle & pill them, then put them between 2 dishes over a chafing dish of coles, with some water, & put therein a little vinegar, some currans, suger, cinnamon, & mace. & when they are enough you may, If you pleas, put in a piece of fresh butter, & so serve them up.

Sweet and sour preparations were evidently in favor in this household (see C 11). Cooking *between 2 dishes* is discussed in C 1.

44   TO BUTTER EGGS

Take ye gravie of A loyne of muton, wherein an
anchovie hath been melted, & mingle it with y^r beaten
eggs, & put in A little [salt ?] & some butter, & set
them on ye fire, & when they are enough, grate in
some nutmegg.

It is by no means clear whether this is an omelet or scrambled eggs;
there are no directions for stirring as the mixture cooks, but scrambling better fits the nature of the dish and its history. The gravy,
as always, is the running juices of rare roast mutton. Mash an
anchovy fillet (soaked and rinsed if heavily salted) with a wooden
spatula in the gravy; the amount depends on taste, but 1 fillet to
½ cup of pure meat juice should suffice for 8 eggs, or so. Easy on
the salt. The amount of butter should be generous—about a tablespoon per egg—particularly if you scramble the eggs, where it
helps to assure the characteristic velvety texture. An exceedingly
gentle heat and and good store of patience are also necessary.

The name *buttered eggs* was indifferently applied to many
egg dishes, including sweet custardy ones. This one is actually a
recipe for *oeufs à la Huguenote*, the characterizing note of which is
mutton gravy. (Anchovy is not classic, it should be noted.) Nowadays, the eggs are cooked unbroken, *au plat*, but in *Les Délices de
la Campagne*, 1662, by Bonnefons, we learn that whether you cook
the eggs unbroken in the *jus de Gigot* or scramble it all together,
the dish is called *à la Huguenotte*. The dish was popular in England.
Robert May gives a recipe *To dress Eggs called in French, a la Hu-
genotte, or the Protestant Way*, in *The Accomplisht Cook*, 1671, which
calls for scrambling the eggs. However, in *L'Art de Bien Traiter*,
1674, *huguenottes* were listed with *terrines* among necessary kitchen
utensils, and they are described in French sources as being earthenware casseroles, unfooted, for use with a chafing dish, an
ideal arrangement for cooking eggs. What is not agreed upon is
the origin of the word, but the French habit of naming a dish after
its cooking vessel calls for a bit of reflection on the pat Protestant
connection.

45   TO STEW BEEFE STEAKS

Take some pieces of fresh beef y^t is interlarded with fat,
& cut them in thin slyces. Then lay them in a dish &

put to them some water, a little vinegar, a little time, mint, savory, & moste parsley, & a few ounions, all chopt small together, & put them to ye steaks with a little pepper & salt & an anchovy or 2, if you have them. set them on ye fire to stew between 2 dishes or in a pipkin. turne y^m very often, & when they are enough, lay them & theyr sauce upon sippets & serve them up.

The seasoning of this little stew is interesting. The inherent problem of stewing slices of meat is that the braising liquid should nourish the meat, not the contrary. To be sure, fat beef is specified, but I suggest good veal broth instead of water. (See C 1 for cooking *between two dishes*.)

---

46   TO BOYLE A RUMPE OF BEEFE

Take a rumpe of beefe, beeing clean washed, & put it into a good deale of water in a stone pot, then take a quarter of a peck of pot hearbs shread small, & put them into ye beefe. when it is seasoned with salt to your likeing, allsoe put in 2 or 3 shread ounions. & when it hath boyled an houre & halfe leasurely, cut 6 carrets in quarters & put into it, & a spoonfull of whole pepper. soe let it stew 5 or 6 houres, then serve it up with sippets & as much liquor poured on it as ye dish will hould. but before you take it up, season it to y^r taste [with white]* wine vinegar & let it have but one boyle after.

This is actually a *pottage* (C 28) and is a splendid example of those fine green soups that were so popular at one time. Pot herbs include all manner of green leafy vegetables, such as spinach, sorrel, chard, and lettuce. The caution about allowing the soup to "have but one boyle" after adding the vinegar is perceptive.

* Supplied for *wite*.

47 TO BAKE A RUMPE OF BEEFE

After y^r rump of beefe is salted over night, take time,
parsley, winter savory, pot margerum, & a little
penneroyall; chop ye hearbs wth youlks of hard eggs, &
put in a little grated bread, salt, & a good piece of
butter; stuff y^r beefe well wth these, y^n put it in a[n]
earthen pot with a little water, some pepper, & an
ounion [or] 2 slyced, & some pickt time, parsley, &
winter savory. then make up ye pot very close wth
paste & set it in ye oven wth hou[s]hould bread, &
when it is baked, put y^r beef in a dish wth white* bread
sops, & poure ye liquor on it.

This is a pot roasted, lightly corned piece of beef. I assume that you
make a pocket into which you place the stuffing. Sealing earthenware vessels with a strip of dough was an efficient way of com-
pensating for ill-fitting lids; it is still good practice. An oven hot
enough for bread seems to me to be too hot for a pot roast, but it
is true that after the initial blast of heat the oven abates considerably, so perhaps it would work out. I suggest a moderate oven
of 350° F.

Winter savory (*Satureia montana*) has a rather different
taste from the more common summer savory. It was regarded as
having the same virtues as thyme (C 10 and S 246); being hot and
dry, it combatted melancholy and phlegmatic humors. For pennyroyal, see S 246.

48 TO MAKE RED DEAR OF BEEFE

First take a piece of young buttock beefe & lard it. y^n
season it wth nutmegg, ginger, pepper & salt. y^n lay it
in clarret wine, & a little wine vinegar for a day or two,
then put it in corse paste with a good deale of butter, &
when you set it into ye oven, put in the vinegar & let it
be well soaked. A neats tongue soe seasoned is
excellent good meat, & allsoe veale.

* Written *whie.*

Recipes for making red deer of beef abound in early seventeenth-century English cookbooks. Markham claims for his version in *The English Hus-wife*, 1615, that "a very good judgement shall not be able to say otherwise, then that it is of itself perfect Venison . . ." It is true that venison was a more princely dish than beef—it was, in fact, a royal prerogative—and that among the nobility, deer were becoming scarcer in the family parks, but I doubt that many were deceived by such dissembling. Certainly, Pepys was not; among the earlier entries in his diary, he complains that the venison pasty was "palpable beef, which was not handsome." It has been suggested that since venison was frequently marinated, the masquerade may have been more successful than one might think. However, the venison in C 51 and 52 is not, nor is it unusual. Similar practices may be found in old French recipes; marinating pork to suggest *marcassin*, wild piglet, was especially popular and persists to this day. The wine and vinegar announce their presence by their flavor, of course, but they also act to tenderize less tender cuts of meat and to assist in their preservation against time of use.

This recipe also marks the beginning of an extended section (through C 70) of dishes baked in crust, of which the English were inordinately fond. Many of these dishes may be enjoyed using perfectly ordinary pastry but for those of you who enjoy baking, there is much to be said for going back to older recipes. Markham goes into some detail on the use of coarse pastry, explaining that very large pieces should be baked in "a moist, thicke, course and long lasting crust." It is to be made of rye flour, a little butter or lard, and hot water (boiling mutton broth is suggested by some writers) and must be very stiff, "that it may stand well in the raising, for the coffin thereof must ever be verie deepe." It must be well kneaded, and rolled out to a thickness of at least ½ inch, according to others. A somewhat finer crust of whole wheat flour is suggested by Markham for middling-sized pieces such as lamb or turkey.

Dorothy Hartley gives a recipe for raised crust in *Food In England*: 14 pounds of flour, and 4 pounds of lard melted in 80 ounces of salted boiling water, or about 3 tablespoons of lard and ¼ cup of water to each cup of unbleached flour. (Hannah Glasse, in 1755, calls for 6 pounds of butter for the same amount of flour.) The hot paste is pummelled for half an hour (1 ½ minutes in the food processor), and allowed to rest for an hour, keeping it warm so that it remains pliant. "The art is to get the crust crisp and firm, but not hard," Mrs. Hartley says. Indeed it is. Most American flours absorb more water than English ones but the paste is stiff, although surprisingly plastic and easy to work. Using these proportions, my rye paste was successful.

Mrs. Hartley describes the raising of the crust. It is a daunting procedure unless you have the equipment and love this sort of work. In most cases, you may simply line a suitable mold as evenly and as seamlessly as possible. All of these pies are baked closed. Mrs. Glasse makes these *Observations on Pies*: "Raised pies should have a quick oven, and well closed up, or your pie will fall in the sides; it should have no water put in till the minute it goes to the oven, it makes the crust sad, and is a great hazard of the pie running."

It is my understanding that these coffins and crusts were not necessarily eaten by the privileged, any more than trenchers were. The main function of coarse pastry was to protect the meat during the baking, but it also provided an impressive presentation at baronial banquests for cuts of meat that required long moist cooking. For *coffin*, see C 49.

This recipe is for a *pasty* (from Old French *pasté*), defined as a meat pie not baked in a mold. All of the large pieces (recipes C 48 through 52 and 58) qualify as pasties. These pieces are simply wrapped free-form in the pastry as handsomely as possible, corresponding to fish or meat *en croûte*. For very large pieces, Markham is right; coarse pastry is best. For smaller pieces, fine pastry is more elegant. Such recipes are found in C 145 through 148, especially the two last ones.

A *neat* is an animal of the ox-kind, as *OED* puts it. The word is unchanged from Old English and survives only in such expressions as "neat's foot oil."

In addition to the pastry dishes in this section, there are twelve others scattered throughout the manuscript (C 102, 106, 107, 108, 145 through 149, 193, 199, and 201).

---

49   ANOTHER WAY TO MAKE BEEF LIKE
       RED DEARE

Take a piece of ye clod of beefe next ye legg & cut ye sinews from it; then put it in a clean cloth & beat it extremely; y^n lard it very well, & season it with nutmegg, pepper, & salt; then lay it on a clean dish & poure upon it halfe a pinte of white wine & as much wine vinegar. let it ly in steepe all night, & ye next day poure away ye vinegar & wine. put ye meat in a round coffin of paste crust & lay 2 or 3 bay leaves under & as many above it. put in store of butter, & let it stand 6

hour in ye oven. make a hole in ye lid & fill it up with
buter when it comes out of ye oven.

This is essentially the same recipe as that presented in C 48, which see. Discarding the marinade seems an improvement in procedure, particularly with regard to the effect on the crust. The *clod of beefe* is the coarse part of the neck of a steer, nearest the shoulder. (The cut exists in American butchery but if not easily available, I suppose that better end of chuck will do.) If the meat be well larded, it should not be necessary to pour in all that butter. I find it excessive; use your judgment.

A *coffin* is a mold made of pastry. The word comes from Old French *cofin* and finally from Greek *cophinos*, meaning basket (*OED*). While they could be of any shape, they seem to have been rectangular as often as not, judging by the occasional specification for a round coffin, as in this recipe. They were closed unless directed otherwise.

This cut could just as well be baked as a pasty (C 48); it would be far simpler.

---

50 TO BAKE MUTON IN BLOOD

Bone a breast or neck of muton, stuff it wth time chopt
small & lay it all night in sheepes blood. when you
have made & rouled out ye pasty, lay in ye bottome
some beefe suet or butter, y^n season ye meat with
pepper & salt, & lay it on ye suet with some shread
time [&] butter or suet layd on ye top, & over y^t lay a
piece of ye caule y^t hath been steeped in ye blood. y^n
close up ye pasty, & when it is baked put in some claret
& melted butte[r].

This recipe is related to the one presented in C 40, where the mutton was roasted; some of the details are discussed in more detail there. This is a pasty; see C 48 for information on the crust.

---

51 TO SEASON A VENISON [PASTY]

Take out ye bones & turne ye fat syde downe upon a
board. y^n take ye pill of 2 leamons & break them in
pieces as long as y^r finger & thrust them into every
hole of y^r venison. then take 2 ounces of beaten pepper

& thrice as much salt, mingle it, then wring out ye juice
of leamon into ye pepper & salt & season it, first
takeing out ye leamon pills haveing layn soe a night.
then paste it with gross pepper layd on ye top & good
store of butter or muton suet.

The piece of venison in question must have been an entire haunch
to require 2 ounces of pepper (a scant ½ cup) and 6 ounces of salt
(½ to 1 cup, depending on coarseness of grind), in addition to the
gross pepper, or cracked pepper, to be laid on top. It is true that
venison seems to call for a lot of pepper. The insertion of strips
of lemon rind, to be left overnight, is a subtle touch. *Paste it* means
to enclose it in pastry; see C 48.

---

52   TO BAKE VENISON RED DEERE OR ANY
       GREAT MEATS

You must first perboyle y^r meat or however; press it all
night in a press very dry, & season it according to y^e
meate baked, & you must clarefy ye butter you put into
it.

The recipe neglects to say so, but the boiled meat is then to be
baked in a crust, as in the previous recipe. Indeed, *baked meats*
were in a crust by definition, virtually. I do not understand the
specification for clarified butter, as opposed to fresh. There were
certain conventions in the seasoning of various meats, but there
was also a good deal of latitude; I can only refer you to other
recipes in our manuscript and early seventeenth-century cookbooks. The recipe is not very useful. This is a pasty; see C 48.
    Perboyle, a sixteenth-century form, means to boil thor-
oughly. It comes from Old French *parboiller*, of the same meaning;
somewhere along the way, *parboyle* erroniously became associated
with its modern meaning of *part boil* (*OED*), and is so used elsewhere in our manuscript.
    The *red Deere* is a member of Cervidae, as are reindeer,
fallow deer, etc. Both *deere* and *deare* were current forms only
through the sixteenth century (*OED*).

---

53   TO MAKE A PIE OF SEUERALL THINGS

First make y^r coffin in what fashion you pleas; then
boyle roofes of beefe, calves or sheep, & cocks combes;

84

pill ye roofes, & cut them in little pieces; allsoe take
sweete breads & kidneys of veale, with theyr tongues,
& sheepes tongues & kidneys, all which must be pilled
& perboyled. put these things into ye pie, & add to fill
it up chicken, rabbit, or any foule in season, hartychoak
bottoms, scirits, potatoes, orringes, cytron, dates,
suckets, long bisket. If you have none of them, use
goosberies or grapes, barbaries, either green or
pickled. season ye meat with a very little salt & pepper,
blades of mace & nutmeggs. when ye pie is filled to y^e
lid, put in bits of butter, & when it is goeing into y^e
oven, put in hash broth y^t may be stewing by, made
with wine or such like, eyther syder or a little vinegar,
and suger. then bake it. this is called an olio pie.

The interest of this recipe is largely historical. It is not that it could
not be more or less duplicated, but the difficulty of assembling and
preparing well over a score of ingredients, as well as raising the
crust, hardly seems to justify the results. Also, see C 199.

Roofes are palates. *Roof* is a rare usage in cookery; I know
of only one other instance, and that occurs in Harleian MS. 4016,
about 1450: "Kutt a Swañ in the rove of the mouth," and that does
not refer to the roof as a piece of meat. *Sweete breads* are the thymus
and pancreas glands of the unweaned calf.

Scirets, skirrets (*Sium sisarum*), are a species of water parsnip (*OED*). Gerard, in 1597, claims that the roots, "most commonly not a finger thicke, . . . are sweet, white, good to be eaten,
and most pleasant in taste . . . The women of Sueuia, saith *Hi-
eronymus Heroldus*, prepare the roots thereof for their husbands,
and know full well wherefore and why, &c.," referring to the
putative aphrodisiac qualities of skirrets. They began to fall into
neglect at the turn of the century and were rapidly displaced by
carrots (C 29).

The sweet potato, *Ipomoea batatas*, and the white potato,
Solanum tuberosum, both plants from the New World, are not re-
motely related, yet their identities were hopelessly entangled in
the sixteenth and seventeenth centuries. Sources, even highly regarded ones, are contradictory, not to say self-contradictory.
Turner, in 1548, makes no mention of either potato, but in 1577,
Harrison speaks of "the potato and such venerous roots as are
brought out of Spaine, Portingale and the Indies to furnish up our

85

A Booke of Cookery

bankets [banquets]."* By 1586, there appears in Thomas Dawson's *The Good Huswifes Jewell, Part I,* a recipe entitled: *To make a tart that is a courage to man or woman,* that calls for *Potaton.* (The title refers to the aphrodisiac virtues of this *olio pie.*) In 1597, Gerard correctly identified the two plants. (He was by no means the first to have done so, but his work was popular and had clear drawings.) He called sweets simply *Potatoes,* saying that they grew in Spain; what he called *Potatoes of Virginia* are whites. (Thomas Hariot, a member of the Raleigh expedition, in *A Briefe and True Report of the New Found Land of Virginia,* 1588, described what would seem to be white potatoes, cultivated by the Indians.) This nomenclature persisted till nearly mid-century. Both kinds grew in his garden, Gerard says, but the sweet potatoes "perished" of damp and cold. Sweet potatoes "comfort, nourish, and strengthen the body, vehemently procuring bodily lust," he claims. And in 1598, Shakespeare wrote the famous line in *The Merry Wives of Windsor*: "Let the skye raine Potatoes . . . hail kissing-Comfits, and snow Eringoes." Shakespeare knew his audiences; rest assured that this boisterous joke about the most popular aphrodisiacs of the day was boisterously received; it seems arcane to us only because it is no longer topical. The potatoes of Shakespeare were sweet potatoes, and they were frequently sliced and conserved with sugar exactly as eryngo roots (see S 34).

Markham, in 1615, mentions potatoes at least twice: in a recipe for *Olepotrige,* a dish from *Spaine,* and again in discussing a potato pie; they could only have been sweet potatoes. It seems to have taken several decades for the Virginia potato to move from horticultural displays to general cultivation. Of a fair number of early seventeenth-century gardening manuals to which I have had access, not one so much as mentions potatoes. This includes Lawson's *The Country Housewives Garden,* 1637, the 1660 edition of the ever popular Markham work (although numerous other modernizations had been made in his name), and two manuscript books, about 1650, among other works.

The sweet potato was never cultivated in Britain, but trade with Spain was lively and continued to flourish; the price was high, but such white potatoes as reached the market, around midcentury, were nearly as dear. As for the potatoes in our manuscript (this is the only mention), we can only speculate as to what was in the mind of the copyist, possibly as late as the second half of the seventeenth century. The ancient recipe, however, with its medieval traces and "restorative" overtones, is pure Elizabethan;

* William Harrison, *Description of England,* 1577, Bk. II, New Shakespeare Society, 1877, and cited in Radcliffe Salaman's *History and Social Influence of the Potato.*

86

historically and gastronomically, only sweet potatoes are congenial with dates, suckets, *biskets*, oranges, citron, skirrets, barberries, and grapes. Usually two or three would be added, I believe, and they must have been sliced. (For more on potatoes in seventeenth-century England, see John Forster entry, page 475.)

Hash broth is a liquor of slices of meat in wine (C 7); *per-boyled* means thoroughly cooked (C 52); and a discussion of *coffin* and pastry will be found in C 48 and 49. For *hartychoaks*, see C 65; for *suckets*, S 93; for *bisket*, S 176.

---

54   TO MAKE A CHICKEN PIE

Season y^r chicken with a little pepper, some salt, nutmegg, & suger, & lay them in a round coffin with good store of marrow cut in square bits biger then dice; roule them up in egge youlks, & a little white wine & grated nutmegg, & put in some hartichoak bottoms, boyled; & lay amongst ye chicken some egg youlks boyled hard. & If you would have [it] a sweet rellish, put in dates shread, suckets & citron, suger & some candied lettis stalks, raysons of ye sun stoned & currans, & a little whole mace, & lay on good store of butter. make a sweet caudle of white wine & sack or muskadine, & put it in when ye pie comes out of ye oven. but If you would have it a sharp rellish, put a little vergiece* to ye white wine & juice of lemons.

This is another very old recipe. I believe that the pieces of chicken and marrow are to be dipped in the egg yolk and wine mixture before being laid in the *coffin* (C 48). The sweet version threatens to be cloying; English cooks did not seem to understand the rectifying breath of hot spices in these sweet dishes, as so brilliantly employed by Chinese and Moroccan cooks, for example. The alternate "sharp rellish" version, obtained by omitting the sweet fruits and adding verjuice and lemon juice to the white wine, mentioned earlier, seems a modernization. I believe that the *caudle* (C̄ 105) is to be added to both versions, but it is uncertain.

For candied lettuce stalks, see S 97 and C 163. *Muskadine* is an obsolete word for muscatel, a strong sweet wine made from

* This was ineptly reworked from what seems to have been *ueriuice*, which would have been correct but was beginning to look archaic to the copyist. The ȝ comes from the more popular form of *uerges*, or *verges*.

the muscat grape. In practice, the name was often applied to any strong sweet, or sweetened, wine.

---

55   TO MAKE A PIGEON PIE

When you put y^r pigeons into ye coffin, lay butter under them, & put in some bacon, cut dice wayes, and halfe a dosin sassages, cut in little pieces. season your pigeons with pepper & salt & lay on more butter. then close up y^r pie & bake it 2 hours. when it comes out of ye oven, put in a little thick butter beat up with a little white wine & a drop of vinegar. shake it & soe serve it up. you may bake eyther veale or rabbit on this manner.

This is a fine recipe; the sauce that is poured in the pie is particularly attractive. Use a sparing hand when laying in the butter beforehand. The bacon should be blanched and the sausages partially cooked before laying the pieces among the pigeons in the *coffin* (C 48). They are meant to be baked whole, I believe, but I suppose that you might split them lengthwise if it seems more convenient. This is a feasible recipe for today, as modern pigeons, while surely not as tasty as those of yore, still have a memory of taste and texture. Do not substitute those horrid Cornish game hens.

---

56   TO MAKE A VEALE PIE

First make y^r Coffin on what fashion you please. then lay some butter all over ye bottom with capers & pickld oysters. y^n cut y^r veale in pieces & lay it in, & on it lay more butte[r], oysters, capers, & ye youlks of hard eggs with balls of mincd veale, suet, & hearbs, all chopt small, & mixed together wth som salt & nutmegg, & make up ye balls with whites of eggs. season y^r veale allsoe with salt, nutmegg & pepper & cut in some slyces of leamon.

This is an interesting recipe and, while rather elaborate, is perfectly feasible; for one thing, this *olio* could be made in more reasonable proportions than some of the great pies. You will want to pickle a few oysters ahead of time; instructions are given in C 173 and while they improve on maturing for a time, even a couple of days will give some of the requisite effect. For *coffins*, see C 48. For the veal, I suggest thickish scallopine cut into manageable squares; season them as you lay them in the coffin, not forgetting a few slices of lemon, a brilliant touch. Using the ingredients listed here, I suggest following the general instructions given in the sausage recipe, C 25, for the veal balls, substituting egg white for the binding agent, as suggested. (Perhaps it holds up better in the long baking.) They are to be shaped to match the hard-cooked egg yolks. With large households, other uses were surely found for the discarded hard-cooked egg whites. I suppose that you might use the entire hard-cooked egg, shaping the little veal sausages accordingly, but some of the charm of the dish would be lost.

---

[57]   TO MAKE A VEALE & B[ACON PIE]

Take time, margerum, parsley, winter savory, of each a little; chop them small with ye youlks of 4 hard eggs. then cut a neck of veale in single bones, & stuff in the hearbs, beeing mingled with a little pepper, salt, and butter; & rub a little pepper & salt on ye outside of ye veale, & lay it in y^r crust, peece by peece, with a good deal of butter. when it is allmoste baked, take bacon, beeing well boyled before, & cut it into slyces; put y^m into ye pie, then set it into ye oven againe for a little time.

The cut wanted here is rib chops, which you are to slit so that you will have a pocket into which you force the little stuffing. I approve the boiling of the bacon but I do not understand why it is added toward the end. For the crust, see C 48.

---

58   TO MAKE A PORKE PIE

Take a legg of porke & season it well with salt, y^n lard it with bacon & season it with cloves, mace, and pepper, & lay it to soak in claret white wine or verges, & culler it with sanders or blood, If you please. then make up your coffin, & with butter fill it up after ye meat is layd in; & when you set ye pie in ye oven put in with a funnell some of ye liquor.

89

Elizabeth David believes that in this instance the larding calls for
the insertion of strips of bacon into the flesh; it was a way of
introducing salt into the interior (see C 6). In this case, perhaps
the bacon is meant to be seasoned with the spices. I strongly counsel not adding butter at the end; the bloated pork of today is very
fat.

The color of the wine is an interesting exercise. It is possible that the scribe meant to write "claret *or* white wine," but I
think it correct and that other designations of *claret* in our manuscript may be elliptical (C 22, 161, and 198). Red wine would
impart an unappetizing color and would muddy the strikingly
beautiful red of the *sanders*. (Red wine would be better with blood,
however.) If you marinate the pork in the refrigerator, it will take
at least 48 hours, turning it twice daily. The baking will take about
four hours; the liquor refers to the marinade. For *coffin*, see C 48,
but this is more properly a pasty, or fresh ham in crust, I believe.
In any event, it is simpler.

Sanders, red sandalwood, is used here only for its color.
Its highly astringent qualities (S 186) would surely have had an
adverse effect on the meat; perhaps the tenderizing effect of the
verjuice or wine counterbalanced it.

---

59   TO MAKE A SHEEPES TONGUE PIE

Boyle ye tongues tender, then pill them & slit y^m in y^e
middle, and lay them in ye pie, like an oyster pie, with
sum butter, grated bread, & nutmegg, & some salt; and
when it is baked, melt & beat some butter and white
wine together, and some capers which have been
scallded in water, & as much sugar as you please. then
cut ye lid open, and poure it all in, & then serve it up,
without setting it into the oven againe.

Sheep tongues are said to be a delicacy; I doubt that they are to
be had. I suppose that you could use the basic principle of the
recipe with some other variety meat. Since the meat is already well
cooked, it will be primarily a question of baking the crust. *Coffins*
are discussed in C 48.

---

60   [TO] MAKE A CALUES HEAD PIE

First perboyle ye head, then take out ye bones & season
it with nutmegg, & salt, & a very little pepper, & a little

90

white wine or white wine vinegar, some raysons of y^e
sun, some minced leamon pills; soe close it up after you
have put in a pritty quantety of butter. & If you have
noe wine, put in a little verges & suger when ye pie
comes out of ye oven. you may put ye brains into y^{r*}
pie before you close it up.

It is not clear how the head is to be presented; assuming that you
can lay hand on one, I suggest cutting the meat into manageable
chunks after taking out the bones. *Perboyle* means to cook thoroughly (C 52); pastry *coffins* are treated in C 48.

---

61   TO [M]AKE AN EGGE PIE

Roste 12 eggs very hard, then mince them very small,
& soe doe a pound of beefe suet, & grate in a nutmegg,
& put in a pound of currans. mingle all these together
with a little rose water & sack, & a little salt & some
sugar. soe make it up in a pie. an houre will bake it.
when it is drawne, pu[t] in 2 or 3 youlks of eggs beaten
with sack, & sweetened wth sugar. & mince† in some
orring or leamon pill y^t is candied in ye first ingrediens
before ye pie is set in ye oven.

Not an inspired pie, I'm afraid, but one that is not untypical of
certain aspects of sixteenth- and seventeenth-century English cookery. The minced candied orange peel goes in at the beginning; the
uncooked *caudle* of sherry (see C 105) and egg yolk goes in at the
end where the heat of the pie will turn it into a soft custard. The
proper crusts are discussed in C 48.

---

62   TO MAKE A CALUES FOOT PIE

After ye feet are boyled & pickt cleane, cut them in
smal slyces, & season them with spice to y^r oune
likeing. then put in some carraway seeds, currans, &
rose water, a little sack, noe butter, but suet shread
small. & a little salt.

* Or *y^e*
† Written *mine.*

91

There is no sugar mentioned and I have the feeling that the omission is inadvertent; rose water and spices are seldom used without it and the spirit of these ancient pies call for it, as evidenced by all the other pies in this section (see C 48).

---

63   TO MAKE MINCD PIES

Take to 4 pound of ye flesh of a legg of veale, or neats tongues, 4 pound of beefe suet, 2 pound of raysons stoned & shread, 3 pound of currans, halfe a pound or more of sugar, 3 quarters of an ounce of cloves, mace, nutmegg, & cinnamon, beaten, halfe a dosin apples shread, some rosewater, a quarter of a pinte o[f] muskadine or sack, some candied orringe, leamon & citron pill minced. shread y^r meat & suet very fine, & mingle all togethe[r]. for plaine mincd pies, leave out ye fruit & put in blanchd almond[s] minced small.

Mince pie is one ancient dish that has come down to us in a recognizable form, albeit an emasculated one; this is changing rapidly, however. It has also moved from being one of the principal dishes to the dessert course. This is a most excellent recipe and deserves to be treasured and used. Since the minced meat is cooked in the filled pie, it will be more like a sweet, fruited *pâté* in texture than the loose-textured fruit pie of today. Most modern mince pies are overly sweet and drenched in mediocre brandy or rum, from which this is mercifully free, and we have instead the ancient Middle Eastern fragrance of rose water.

One ounce of spice is equivalent to about 4 level tablespoons when ground, so that 3 tablespoons in all, in roughly equal proportions, but light on the cloves. (I find a good proportion of dried ginger root a great improvement in these spice mixtures.) The strength and fragrance of spices dissipate dramatically on grinding. *Muskadine* is muscatel (C 54); *sack* is sherry (C 21); ½ pound of sugar is 1 cup. Pastry is discussed in C 48. I do not think much of the *plaine* version without fruit; I suspect that it was tacked on by an interim hand.

If you would like to serve this as a dessert, I see no reason why you could not reduce somewhat the proportion of veal and suet; the texture will change, of course.

64   TO MAKE AN HUMBLE PIE

Take ye humbles of a deere, or a calves heart, or pluck,
or a sheeps heart; perboyle it, & when it is colde,
shread it small with beefe suet, & season it with cloves,
mace, nutmegg, & ginger beaten small; & mingle with
it currans, verges & salt; put all into ye pie & set it in
the oven an houre; then take it out, cut it up & put in
some clarret wine, melted butter & sugar beat together.
then cover it a little & serve it.

Finally, this recipe is for a sort of mince pie (C 63). The instruction
to "cut it up" means to carefully cut out the top in such a way as
to form a lid that will lift out neatly, so that you can distribute the
wine mixture evenly about. Then let the pie rest to allow the flavoring to permeate the filling, as the recipe counsels.

The *humbles* are the heart, kidneys, liver, and other organs
of the deer. The word comes from Old French *nombles*, cited by Du
Cange as early as 1239; the Late Latin is *numbli*. (The occasional
medieval meaning of *loin* arises from an apparent confusion with
lombles, Old French for loin.) *OED* is firm; *humbles* is an occasional
spelling of *umbles*, itself a later form of *numbles*. It is interesting to
note that Norman French still retains the Old French *nombles*, with
the customary meanings, while all the forms in English are long
since obsolete. The *n* of *numbles* appears to have been absorbed by
the article, much as happened with Arabic *nāranj* to *orange* (see S
28); it is difficult to see how it could have been the other way
around, as proposed by some writers, since *umbles* seems not to
have appeared until the fifteenth century, according to *OED*, at
which time *numbles* had long been established. (Actually, either
construction poses certain problems, since the word seems always
to have been plural in both French and English.) In due time, *umbles*
became confused with *humble*, meaning meek or lowly. There is
no basis for this in early culinary history. Indeed, *noumbles* was a
royal dish, and recipes appear in *The Forme of Cury*, about 1390,
which was compiled by master cooks to Richard II. The earliest
citing of *humble pie* in the figurative sense of suffering humiliation
is given in *OED* for 1830. Perhaps the substitution of pluck from
other beasts, as evidenced in our manuscript, gradually lowered
the status of the dish and so contributed to the figurative meaning,
already prepared for by the homonyms *umbles* and *humbles*.

Pluck is the innards of any animal used as food. The word
is still current in Britain. *Perboyle* means to boil thoroughly (C 52).

65   TO MAKE AN HARTICHOAK PIE

Take 12 hartychoak bottoms y^t are good & large; after you have boyled them, take them cleere from ye leaves & cores, season them with a little pepper & salt, & lay them in a coffin of paste, with a pound of butter & ye marrow of 2 bones in bigg pieces. then close it up & set it in ye oven, then put halfe a pound of suger to halfe a pinte of verges, & some powder of cinnamon & ginger; boyle these together & when ye pie is halfe baked, put this liquor in & set it in ye oven againe, till it be quite bak'd.

I have no reason to believe that artichokes were appreciably larger in those days than now, so that with 2 cups of butter, the marrow, 1 cup of verjuice, 1 cup of sugar, and the spices, the concoction must have given the impression of greasy sweet and sour pickles in a pie. All that liquid sloshing about in the pastry coffin worries me as well. I believe this recipe to date from the sixteenth century. It is monstrously rich and while the proportions could be reworked, I suppose, it is not a beguiling project.

The word *artichoke* (*Cynara scolymus*) comes to us from Arabic *al-kharshūf* by way of Spanish Arabic *al-kharshōfa*, North Italian *articiocco*, and French *artichaut* (*OED*); in short, the usual path. The *carduus* of antiquity could have been either cardoon or artichoke, but in Spanish, the unarguable *carchofa* had appeared by 1423, according to Corominas. None of this is arcane, yet I have read in our most serious journal, *The New York Times*, that the artichoke was "discovered" by Lewis and Clark on their expedition (1803-07), whence it made its way to Italy.

If we can believe a reading in *OED*, the artichoke came to England only during the reign of Henry VIII (1509-47), but Turner, in 1548, correctly identifies the *gardin Archichoke* as *Cinara*, mentioning *Scolimus* as well. He also noted that the *wylde Archichoke* was *Carduus*, or thistle. Gerard, in 1597, describes it as "cholerick," and goes on to say: "I find, moreover, That the root is good against the ranke smell of the arme-holes, if when the pith is taken away the same root bee boyled in wine and drunke: for it sendeth forth plenty of stinking urine, whereby the ranke and rammish savour of the whole body is much amended." It quickly became a staple in English gardens and cookery, judging by the manuals and cookbooks. It seems to have been most popular in pies but, surprisingly perhaps, it was also in great favor eaten raw with oil and vinegar, according to Gerard.

---

66   TO MAKE A QUINCE PIE

Lay y^r quinces, beeing coared, an houre in faire water after they are well washed out of ye pickle; then scald them till they will pill apace; y^n let y^m ly 2 inches under water in a preserving pan, y^n put in 3 parts of their waight in suger & let y^m stew all day softly, close coverd. turne y^m often till they are red enough, y^n put them in a deepe coffin of paste, & put more sugar to y^m. If ye quinces wth theyr sirrup will not fill ye pie to ye top, y^n fill it up with faire water just as it is goeing into ye oven, stop ye vent close you put ye water in at. 2 hours will bake it at the moste.

There is a recipe *To keepe quinces all ye yeare*, C 152, but it is not a pickle. In any event, the soaking is to rid the fruit of the preserving element, most likely vinegar. "3 parts of their waight in suger" must mean three-fourths of their weight; either quarters was understood or our scribe absent-mindedly wrote parts. This is quite a lot of sugar for a pie, but quinces are an acid astringent fruit (see S 7), so that compared to the following recipe, it does not seem out of line. I would tailor the size of the *coffin* (see C 48) to the amount of fruit rather than adding water.

---

67   [TO MAKE] A CODLING TARTE EYTHER TO LOOKE CLEAR OR GREENE

First coddle ye apples in faire water; y^n take halfe the weight in sugar & make as much syrrop as will cover ye bottom of y^r preserving pan, & ye rest of ye suger keepe to throw on them as they boyle, which must be very softly; & you must turne them often least they burne too. then put them in a thin tart crust, & give them with theyr syrrup halfe an hours bakeing; or If you pleas, you may serve them up in a handsome dish, onely garnished with suger & cinnamon. If you would

have y^r apples looke green, coddle them in faire water,
then pill them, & put them into ye water againe, &
cover them very close. then lay them in y^r coffins of
paste with lofe suger, & bake them not too hard. when
you serve them up, put in with a tunnell to as many of
them as you pleas, a little thick sweet cream.

We like to say "as American as apple pie," but in the Pegge manuscript of 1380 (appended to *The Forme of Cury*), we find a recipe,
For to make Tartys in Applys, that starts out: "Take gode Applys and
gode Spycis . . ." The proportion of sugar in our recipe above is
high, but perhaps the apples were very sour.

Tarte comes unchanged from Old French. A tart differed
from a pie in that it was baked open, a distinction that did not
always hold true, however. A more important difference lay in the
choice of paste; in principle, a tart was made of thinly rolled fine
rich paste that could not be *raised*, as coffins were. There is a group
of recipes for these more fragile pastes, C 145 through 148 and also
C 108.

There are actually three recipes here: one for a tart, one
for compote, and one for a pie. The baking time for the tart is so
brief that I wonder whether the shell might not be prebaked, a not
uncommon practice.

Some writers describe *codlings* as immature or windfall
apples, and this may have been true at times, but the term also
designated a specific apple, rather elongated and tapering toward
the flower end. (There is a modern codling apple.) All sources
agree that the codling was good only for cooking. Palsgrave, for
instance, translates it into French as *pomme cuite*, cooked apple. It
has been suggested that its name comes from its shape, but to me,
this smacks of folk etymology; as early as 1314, the form of *codling*
applied to the fish and remained unchanged. The first appearance
of the name of the apple was as *querdelynge*, in 1440 (*OED*), so that
it seems more reasonable that the word derives from Middle English *quert*, meaning sound or hard, and its history as a hard apple,
fit only to be cooked, supports this derivation.

Coddle, to poach, and *codling*, the apple, came to be related
in the popular mind, but *OED* is properly dubious. It is inexplicably
cautious on another possible derivation, but once said, there seems
little question that *coddle* is from Norman French *caudeler*, to gently
heat. This would make it related to *caudle* (C 105), which is entirely
logical.

Tunnell is an obsolete word for funnel.

68 TO MAKE A TART OF HIPPS

Slyce them & cut out ye kernells, & seeth them in white
wine, & when they be soft, streyne them as thick as
you can; then season them with sugar, cinnamon,
ginger, & rose water, then put this in crust made of a
tart fashion.

There is little question that the cooked pureed filling is put into
a prebaked tart shell without further baking, although there are
no specific instructions to this effect. *Tarts* are discussed in C 67.

Hipps are the fruit of the wild rose, or eglantine (see S
127). *OED* gives the first appearance of the word as *heopan* in a
manuscript of about 725. It also quotes Chaucer singing: "Sweete
as is the Brembul flour That bereth the rede hepe." *Hipp* was
current only in the sixteenth century; *hypes*, from the scribe's index,
appeared before 1100 and was in use through the fifteenth century.
(*Hype*, it should be noted, referred to the anatomical *hip*; since the
two words are homonyms, this should pose no problem.) Turner,
in his *Herbal*, 1562, talks of "tartes of Heppes." Gerard informs us
that the Eglantine, or sweet briar, is also called the *Hep tree*, and
gives us a number of uses in medicine, quoting Galen, that could
be construed as understanding the healing and detoxifying effects
accepted today for vitamin C, in which the rose hip is very rich.
He also discusses tarts, "the making whereof I commit to the cunning cooke, and teeth to eate them in the rich mans mouth."

69 TO MAKE A TART OF PARSNEPS & SCYRRETS

Seeth y^r roots in water & wine, then pill them & beat
them in a morter, with raw eggs & grated bread. bedew
them often with rose water & wine, then streyne them
& put suger to them & some juice of leamons, & put it
into ye crust; & when y^r tart is baked, cut it up & butter
it hot, or you may put some butter into it, when you
set it into ye oven, & eat it cold. ye Juice of leamon you
may eyther put in or leave out at y^r pleasure.

At first glance, this pie seems odd, but you will note that it is
constructed on essentially the same principle as our pumpkin pie.
Aside from wine replacing milk, there is little structural difference,

although the bread crumbs will produce a denser texture than that to which we are accustomed. Carrots are occasionally suggested as a substitute for skirrets in Elizabethan recipes; the color is wrong, however, and I would prefer using only parsnips. Figure 4 eggs for about 4 cups of strained pulp, a scant cup of white wine, barely enough bread crumbs to be true to the recipe (perhaps ¼ cup), and sugar and rose water to taste. (You might refer to a standard pumpkin pie recipe, remembering that parsnips and carrots are sweeter than pumpkin.) The tang of lemon juice is interesting, and a tablespoon or two of butter in the basic mixture, as suggested, will enrich and smooth out both taste and texture. I believe this to be a very old recipe, and the charming language bears me out; how often have you been instructed to "bedew" a mixture with rose water?

As noted elsewhere, "cut it up" means to lift up the carefully cut out lid, not to divide the pie. This tart is clearly intended to be a closed pie (C 67), but I would counsel briefly pre-baking a blind shell, pouring in the filling, and finish baking at a moderate temperature, exactly as for any custard type pie; your crust will be much more successful.

Parsnip (*Pastinaca sativa*) seems to have come from Old French *pasnaie*. It is suggested that the final syllable became *nep* because it was considered a kind of turnip, giving us *pasnep* in Middle English (*OED*), although *pasternak*, from the Latin, was also a common name. Gerard in 1597 says that they are "moderately hot and more dry than moist," and that "they provoke urine, and lust . . . [and] be good for the stomacke, kidnies, bladder, and lungs." For skirrets, see C 53.

---

70   TO MAKE A LETTIS TA[RT]

When you have raised ye crust, lay in all over the
bottom some butter, & strow in some sugar, cinnamon,
& a little ginger; then boyle y^r cabbage lettis in a little
water & salt, & when ye water is drayned from it, lay it
in y^r coffin with some dammask pruens stoned; then
lay on ye top some marrow & such seasoning as you
layd on ye bottom. y^n close it up and bake it.

I assume that the lettuce should be roughly chopped after boiling and draining, and that the prunes be well soaked. Historically, this is a very interesting recipe. It is not so different from various sweetened spinach and chard tarts, usually made with currants and pine nuts, that we have encountered in the Mediterranean; one of these was in Nice, which might be surprising to those who do not know the history of Nice cooking. *Tarte* is a misnomer in this recipe; it is a closed *coffin* (see C 48 and C 67). I see no reason why you could not use any fine paste recipe, however, since there is no structural need for a coffin paste.

Lettuce (*Lactuca*) appeared in Middle English as *letuse*, derived from Old French *laituë*, milky, and finally from the Latin. *Lettis* appeared only in the sixteenth century (*OED*.) Lettuce was a popular vegetable in England, and there was an astonishing number of varieties cultivated in Tudor times, including Lombard lettuce, red lettuce, curly lettuce, and cabbage (head) lettuce, for instance; several of these varieties are listed much earlier. Gerard in 1597 says: "Lettuce cooleth the heat of the stomacke, called the heart-burning . . . it quencheth thirst, causeth sleepe [and] maketh plenty of milk in nurses." He also noted that it "maketh a pleasant sallad, being eaten raw with vinegar, oil, and a little salt," saying that, "it is served in these daies, and in these countries in the beginning of supper, and eaten first before any other meat." He cites Galen, Pliny, and the poet Martial, writers of antiquity, showing their acquaintance with lettuce and salads. (It is amusing to note that, by and large, salads are eaten at the beginning of the meal in non-wine-drinking countries and at the end in wine-drinking countries.)

It is not clear whether *dammask pruens* be prunes imported from Damascus or prunes made from Damson plums, a variety which originated near Damascus. *OED* cites a reading from around 1400: "Drie prunis of damascenes," and Gerard cites Galen, second century, as saying the "the best doe grow in Damascus, a city of Syria."

---

71 TO STEW WARDENS

> Boyle them first in faire water, then pare & stew them
> between 2 dishes with cinnamon, suger, and rosewater;
> or wth ye same seasoning you may put them in a pie &
> bake them.

This recipe is very like one in Harleian MS. 279, about 1430: "Take wardonys, an caste on a potte, and boyle hem till they ben tender; than take hem up and pare hem, an kytte hem into pecys; take y-now of powder of canel [cinnamon], a good quantyte . . . ," with this important difference: the second simmering was in red wine. As the recipe notes, you may bake these stewed pears; I refer you to recipe C 48 and 67.

Wardens are an old variety of cooking pear (see S 104). It is interesting to note that in *Pears of New York*, U. P. Hedrick writes that on the date of the Battle of Lexington, April 19, 1775, graftings were made with the "Pickering or English Warden," so that the warden came to America. Any firm pear of good flavor may be used in these recipes.

---

72   A MADE DISH

Take stale white bread & slyce it, & lay it in steep in white wine all night. ye next day take youlks of eggs & creame & sugar & beat them well together; then take the bread out of ye wine, & put it in ye cream, & when it hath been in a quarter of an houre, take it out & lay it in a frying pan, & poure ye cream y^t is left upon it; & when it is fryed enough, lay it in a dish, & strew on it sugar & grated nutmegg, & soe serve it up.

You may not recognize it at first glance, but this recipe is a rich and elegant version of *pain perdu*, or French toast. There is a recipe for *payn pur-dew* in Harleian MS. 279, about 1430, with neither wine nor cream, very like any modern recipe. (For that matter, Apicius gives a perfectly recognizable recipe, sweetened with honey, under *Dulcia Domestica*.) The English early took to *pain perdu* and made it their own; it was rarely omitted from a cookbook, usually listed under *made dishes*, and there have been some charming corruptions of the name, such as Markham's *panperdy*, which he listed under *Fricase* (see C 2).

A *made dish* was any dish, apparently, that amused the cook or showed off her skill. They are never major dishes and they frequently involve eggs in some way. Although *kickshaws* (from French *quelque chose*) and made dishes seem to have overlapped to some extent, the kickshaw appears to have been a sort of scrambled egg dish, usually overloaded with odds and ends of meats and herbs. The lines between many of these dishes became increasingly blurred and twisted with time.

---

73   A MADE DISH OF GOOSBERIES

Put as much water to a pinte of goosberries as will wet them & let them boyle all to pieces; then put in as

100

much suger as will sweeten them well; then take youlks
of 6 eggs & beat them with 3 spoonfulls of dammask
rose water; y^n mingle it with ye goosberries, & let it
boyle 2 or 3 walm[es], & after, dish it up. it is good
eyther hot or cold but it is best cold.

This is, of course, really a recipe for gooseberry fool, save for the
lack of straining that is the peculiar characteristic of that dish. For
fool, see C 109 and 124; for gooseberries, see S 56; for *made dish*,
see C 72.

---

74 TO MAKE A MARROW PUDDING

Take a pinte or more of sweet creame, & boyle it wth
whole blades of mace & quarterd nutmegg, & 2 or 3
youlks of eggs, & swetten* it wth sugar. then butter a
dish & slyce thin manchet & lay in ye bottom of it. &
lay on that 20 or more raysons of ye sunn, & some
hartychoak bottoms or apples slyced thin, & raw
marrow in bits, but if you have it not, mince & strow in
some beefe or muton suet. then to y^t, put in some
boyled creame, & begin with manchet as you did
before, till ye dish be full. then put ye creame y^t is left
upon it, & bake it, eyther by ye fire or in an oven.

This recipe might better be called bread pudding with artichoke
bottoms. I am concerned about the custard; it will have wheyed
by the time the pudding is baked, particularly if you boil the egg
yolks with the cream, a worse than needless operation. I counsel
baking the pudding in a shallow pan of hot water; as with any
custard, the water must not be permitted to boil. The artichoke
bottoms are boiled before slicing. The dish is interesting historically, but not very enticing.

This marks the opening of a section of pudding recipes
(through C 91) and so is a good place to explore the meanings of
pudding. OED is disappointing: origin obscure. It may well be, but
I would have expected a discussion of French *boudin*, fresh sausage.
Palsgrave in 1530, translates *Puddying* as *boudayn* and Cotgrave, in
1611, translates *boudin* as pudding, with no further ado. Once said,

---

* Written *sweeten*, but corrected by the scribe to *swetten* with a heavy
stroke. See C 137 and S 271.

it could hardly be otherwise. There are no problems phonetically and the old meanings of the word in both languages are parallel and this holds true for popular usage as well, particularly in the scatological sense. According to Godefroy, *boudine, bêdaine*, and *bodyn*, in Old French, meant navel, belly, and bowels, respectively. *OED* duly notes, to be sure, that *pudding* means bowels or guts, chiefly in dialect. And Halliwell gives a wonderfully descriptive Northern dialect expression: "An untidy slovenly person is said to have his puddings about his heels."

In any event, the word showed up as *poding* in Middle English by the thirteenth century. While black puddings (made of blood) and white puddings (made of veal or chicken) encased in intestines, comparable to the French *boudins noirs et blancs*, continued to be made, the fact is that English puddings early on became ever more farinaceous, more porridgy, than their French counterparts, where such practice is regarded as adulteration. Most fifteenth-century pudding recipes already call for bread crumbs or *ote-mele*, and eventually, the *pudding-bag* (C 76) became a surrogate maw or intestine for boiling the gutless—and meatless—sweet pudding. Perhaps the early evolution of *pudding* into the now more familiar sweet porridge has obscured the older meanings of the word in English. Amusingly, *le pudding* returned to France thoroughly anglicized, with its new meaning pertaining to these all too often stodgy desserts.

The word came to have homey connotations involving well-being and hospitality. To come in pudding-time meant "in the nick of time, at the commencement of dinner," according to Halliwell, who also reports a charming welcoming ritual called *puddining*.

---

75   TO MAKE A BAK'D ALMOND PUDDING

Take halfe a pound of blanch'd & beaten almonds, a pint[e] of creame, 5 youlks of eggs, & one or 2 whites, well beaten; you must beat ye almonds with 2 or 3 spoonfulls of rose water; & put in salt & suger to your likeing, then streyne it thorough a cloth & mingle all together; y^n roule a piece of ordinary paste out & lay in ye bottom of a dish, put in bigg bits of marrow, & then cover it with puff paste.

This is more of an almond custard pie than a proper pudding. The combination of almonds and rose water is particularly beguiling and the recipe is worth attention. I personally find the marrow a bit much, traditional as it was. Also, I would be inclined to proceed as I would for any custard pie: partially prebake the tart shell, fill it, and bake it at a moderate temperature, omitting the puff paste topping. The result would be less authentic, but more delicious and certainly less fussy. See *tarte*, C 67, for discussion of suitable pastes and C 76 for further suggestions on the filling.

For *puff paste*, see C 145 and 146.

---

76   TO MAKE AN ALMOND PUDDING
        TO BOYLE

Take a quart of creame, 6 whole mace, a nutmegg
quarterd, 2 spoonfulls of flowre, a quarter of a pound
of almonds beaten with 2 or 3 spoonfulls of rose water,
9 eggs beaten & streyned with ye almond[s], & put in a
little ambergreece & soe boyle it up.

This is an excellent recipe; actually, it is for a *quaking pudding* (C 84), a far lighter affair than most of the puddings in this section. I find the combination of almonds and rose water a hauntingly successful one. I must assume that the cream is heated with the spices and allowed to steep so that it may be infused with their aroma. It is then to be mixed with the beaten almonds (a food processor or blender is useful for this tedious chore) and allowed to stand to extract the goodness from the almonds before straining. This fragrant liquid is then mixed with the lightly beaten eggs and other ingredients. No sugar is mentioned; this is surely inadvertent, so sweeten to taste. For nutmeg, see C 6.

This is the first of the boiled puddings, so it is not amiss to give Hannah Glasse's instructions on the subject, taken from *The Art of Cookery*, 1755.

In boiled Puddings, take great Care the Bag or Cloth be very clean, not soapy, but dipped in hot Water, and well floured. If a Bread-pudding, tie it loose; if a Batter-pudding, tie it close; and be sure the Water boils when you put the Pudding in, and you should move the Puddings in the Pot now and then, for fear they stick. When you make a Batter-pudding, first mix the Flour well with a little Milk, then put in the Ingredients by Degrees, and it will be smooth and not have Lumps; but for a plain Batter-pudding, the best way is to strain it through a coarse Hair Sieve, that it may neither have Lumps nor the Treadles of the Eggs: and for all other Puddings, strain the Eggs when they are beat. If you boil them in wooden Bowls, or China Dishes, butter the Inside before you put in your Batter; and for all baked Puddings, butter the Pan or Dish before the Pudding is put in.

There is some doubt as to whether ambergris (S 20) was actually much used in seventeenth-century cooking. Cotgrave, in 1611, defines it thus: "Ambergreece or gray Amber: used in perfume." In view of the date, this is a telling entry because he says nothing about its use in either cooking or medicine. Nor was I able to find any mention of it in the cookery section of Markham's *The English Hus-wife*, 1615. I hesitate to say that it was not used, but I cannot help but feel that its use had become archaic by 1600 and that recipes in manuscripts and cookbooks continued to call for it through conservatism or ostentatiousness. At the least, it was more often omitted than not; not only had taste changed, but it had become prohibitively costly.

---

77   TO MAKE A RISE [PUDDING]

Take a quarter of a pound of rise & as much new milk as will boyle it soft; y^n put to it A quarter of a pound of muton suet minced small, 6 youlks of eggs & 2 whites, a little rosewater, & some cinamon, a pritty deal of salt, sugar, & currans. when all these ingredients are mix'd together, bake it.

Most of us would be unhappy with mutton suet in a dessert, even were it available. Beef suet or marrow may be substituted, or even butter, with different but finer results. Cooks of the time understood certain principles very well, and one of them was the proportion of egg yolk to white. Yolks provide richness and, carefully handled, a delicate texture; whites strengthen, but also toughen. (Whites may be beaten to a froth and thus provide airiness, but it is precisely the quality of toughness that permits this; the air is trapped.) Anyone who makes custard with whole eggs only, does not altogether understand the structure of the dish, or does not appreciate the delicacy of texture. The directions for boiling the rice are elliptical. First parboil the rice for 5 or 10 minutes in a lot of water, and drain well. Then cook the rice in the milk until perfectly tender; this is most easily done in a double boiler. Then add a little to the lightly beaten eggs, stirring, and mix all the ingredients together. Bake as a custard, in a pan of not ever boiling water in an oven about 300°F, for most of an hour.

Four ounces of rice is a generous ½ cup. The proportion of fat is high; I suggest halving it, using 4 tablespoons of butter, for example. You will need 3 cups of milk, or more. About ⅓ cup of sugar and a pinch of salt should please most palates. If you have no rose water, you may put in some zest of lemon when you cook the rice; it is very good. For that matter, a stick of cinnamon used in the same way, is much nicer than ground cinnamon. Use a good ½ cup of currants, picked over and rinsed. This is a fine recipe for this old English sweet dish.

---

78   TO MAKE A HAGGIS PUDDING

Seethe a calves haggis, & when it is cold, chopp it with beefe suet, & put into it parsley, time, penneroyall, violet leaves, & margerum, of each an handfull chopt together small. then put in creame, grated bread, cloves, mace, pepper, salt & suger; mingle all these well together & make up ye puddings & boyle them.

This recipe differs little from one of the early recipes, *Hagws of a schepe*, given in Harleian MS. 279, about 1430. They both contain bread crumbs and cream, for instance. The older version is seasoned with saffron and pepper and is boiled in the maw of the sheep, while ours seems to be boiled in pudding-bags. The use of violet leaves in our haggis is interesting; it is rare in our manuscript but was very popular in Elizabethan cookery. According to Gerard, 1597, violet leaves, "inwardly taken, do coole, moisten, and make the belly soluble." (For violets, see S 86.)

The *English Dialect Dictionary* defines *haggis* as the smaller entrails, or chitterlings of a calf. From Halliwell, we learn that *hag* is Northern dialect for belly, and that "to cool one's haggis means 'to beat him soundly.' " Palsgrave, 1530, gives: "*Haggas, podyng, Cailette de Mouton.*" (*Cailette* is the fourth stomach.) *OED* rejects one common theory that the word comes from French *hachis* (see C 7); certainly the case for the meaning of guts is compelling. It should be noted that although haggis is today considered Scottish, it was common in English cookery until about the seventeenth century. Indeed, the use of bread crumbs tends to mark this recipe as English; Scottish recipes call for oat grits, and quite likely always did.

---

79   TO MAKE LIUER PUDDING

Take a piece of hoggs liver, boyle, grate, & sift it thorough a cullender; y^n take 3 times as much grated bread, suger & currans as you please, beef suet shread small, marrow If you have it, If not take ye more beefe suet; allsoe put in cinnamon & cloves small beaten, & some rosewater with a little ambergreece steept in it; all this must be wet moderately with a little boyling creame & youlks of eggs. ye quantety of a quart of liver will require a pound of suger, & bread answerable; it must be pritty stiff. then fill them up in scinns & boyle them.

The combination of pork liver and currants is interesting and very old, but these are exceedingly odd black puddings. (See C 83.) However, a reading of pudding recipes in English cookbooks down through the centuries shows that they are not out of line. Stuffing sausage skins with such a bready mixture seems risky to me; do leave room to expand. A pound of sugar is 2 cups.

---

[80]   [TO] MAKE WHITE PUDDINGS

Take 3 pintes of milke & when it is boyled, put in tw[o] quarts of great oatmeale bruised a little, & stirr it over ye fire till it be ready to boyle. then take it of & cover it close all night. 3 pound of suet minced small, put in wth 3 grated nutmeggs, ye youlks of 8 eggs, 2 whites, & a little rosewater, a pound of sugar, & a little grated bread, currans, & creame as you think fit. this quantety will make 3 or 4 dosin.

Like the curious liver pudding in C 79, this mixture is to be stuffed into sausage skins, I believe. Three pints of liquid will not suffice for 2 quarts of cracked oats, even for this use; perhaps the scribe made an error. I suggest equal amounts by volume. (Rolled oats will not do.)

Great is not used here in the common sense of large, but as a homonyn for *grete*, a variant of *groat*, which *OED* defines as hulled, or hulled and crushed, grain, chiefly oats. (*Great* and *groat* may be cognate, but not all authorities agree.) *OED* notes that *grete* was commonly pronounced *grit* in certain areas, so that it is easy to see where *grits*, the word for parched cracked corn in our own South, came from; the word was naturally applied to whatever grain was in use.

Oats (*Avena sativa*) seem to have become established in Britain by the Iron Age, according to the *Oxford Book of Food Plants*, and they are mentioned in early Saxon manuscripts (*OED*). While the English have historically tended to look down their noses at the Scots as eaters of oats, the fact is that in times past, the English ate quite a lot of oats themselves (especially in certain regions), as is confirmed by this manuscript. As late as the 1896 edition of *The Art of Cookery* by Hannah Glasse, we find a fair number of recipes calling for oats.

---

81   TO MAKE PUDDINGS TO STEW

Take a little veale minced small, a little grated bread, & 3 eggs beaten, a good quantety of sugar, & allsoe currans, then take twice as much suet as all these shread small, grate a nutmegg in, & mingle all these well together. y^n make them into balls & stew y^m in a little strong mutton broth, & beat a littl verge[s], butter, & suger together for sauce.

These are not what we would consider puddings at all, but meat dumplings; the distinguishing difference is that these puddings are poached. As usual, the proportion of suet seems excessive and I would cut it by half.

---

82   TO MAKE A CURD PUDDING

Take of ye best wilde curds, beeing dreyned from ye whey; put to them a little suet shread small, & a little nutmegg, rose water, a little salt, 3 or 4 eggs beaten, & a little fine flower; mingle it not to stiff. put in allsoe some currans, & a little marrow, If you pleas[e]. bake it in a pann.

This is, effectively, a cheesecake without a crust. It is not a bad recipe, although the sempiternal suet and marrow begin to pall. The rose water would be a delightful touch to any cheesecake.

Wilde curds are naturally formed, or induced, by slipping in spoonfuls of clabbered milk under the surface of a pan of milk; that is, *not* made with rennet. I could find no discussion of this in any source available to me, although the technique of slipping in curd is alluded to fairly frequently, including our own manuscript (C 118). Those accustomed to making their own yogurt will recognize the process, and because pasteurized milk refuses to clabber properly, yogurt cultures may be the answer here, perhaps fortified with a truly minuscule amount of rennet to give a curd. Wild curds have a delightful tang that rennet-induced curds lack, and an infinitely finer texture; there is the same difference in quality as between wild yeasts and store-bought and, in the same way, they are a bit trickier to handle. (For *curd*, see S 303.)

---

83   TO MAKE A GOOSE PUDDING

Take ye blood of a goose, great oatmeale steeped in milke, ye fat of ye guts, or beefe or muton suet, pepper, sal[t], & a little wine, 3 youlks of eggs; & If you like a sweet seasoning, put in sugar, cloves, & mace, allsoe currans, If you like them. make it up in ye scin of ye neck & boy[le] it, or bake it in a dish with crust over it.

This is a fascinating recipe, and a very old one, I believe. It is, of course, a variation on the ancient black pudding. In her recipe for *Black Puddings* in *The Art of Cookery*, 1755, Hannah Glasse says: "In Scotland they make a Pudding with the Blood of a Goose. Chop off the Head and save the Blood, stir it till it is cold, then mix it with Gruts [*Grits*, in later editions] . . ." Spice, salt, sweet herbs, and some beef suet are the other ingredients. For *great oatmeale*, see C 80.

(Curiously, I have not encountered a similar use of goose blood in France; all over the Southwest, women make *sanguette*, which can only be described as a sort of blood omelet. The neck of the goose is indeed stuffed, but usually with a marvelously aromatic and rich mixture of sausage, scraps of *foie gras* perhaps, and peelings of truffles.)

Clearly, the main interest here is historical; few of us raise our own geese. For those of us who do, no fat but the fat of the goose should be used.

---

84   TO MAKE A QUAKEING PUDDING

Take a quart of creame & put 2 or 3 spoonfulls of it in a dish, with a spoonfull of wheat flowre; beat it a good while, y^n put in halfe a nutmegg, a little salt, a quarter of a pound of suger, & 10 eggs, youlks & whites; beat all these together a quarter of an houre. y^n put in all ye rest of ye creame & keep it* stird, then wet a cloth in

* Written *is*.

faire water & butter it as far as you think ye batter will goe; y^n tie it up & put it into a pot y^t boyles as fast as may be for halfe an houre.

Quaking pudding was one of the conceits of seventeenth-century English cookery. It is no small feat to put in enough flour to obtain the cohesiveness necessary to withstand boiling and yet have some of the characteristics of a fluffy custard. A mixer will make a breeze of the work involved here. The spoonful of flour was likely a rounded one of a fair size; say, about 4 tablespoons. (The first time, it is prudent to add a bit too much, perhaps, rather than not enough.) The cream must be fresh heavy cream (*not* sterilized), and on no account should you ignore the instruction to leave the bulk of the cream aside until the beating is finished. A quarter of a pound of sugar amounts to ½ cup. That the water be at a full boil is especially critical here (see C 76); the outer surface of the pudding must form a skin instantly.

---

85   TO MAKE A LIGHT PUDDING

Take a penny loafe & slyce it thin into a pinte of milke, & set it to boyle; & when it is boyled thick, take it of ye fire & break it small. then put in 6 eggs, sugar as you please, & rosewater & grated nutmeg & a little salt; then let it boyle an houre & noe more, least it burne too. y^{n*} take it up & stick it full of blanch'd almonds. ye sauce must be rose water, butter, sugar, & a numegg grated or slyced on ye top of it.

For this pudding we start off with a panade; considering the proportions, I think that it must be a manchet loaf of about 6 ounces that is wanted here. Despite the confusing directions, the pudding is to be boiled in a pudding bag (C 76). The presentation is the ancient porcupine conceit, popular for all manner of dishes since medieval times. The sauce is actually a hard sauce (equal parts of fine sugar and sweet butter) beaten with rose water until fluffy. Do grate a bit of nutmeg; the shreds are disagreeable (C 6).

The size of the *penny loafe* in recipes is a vexing question. It is not just that the size changed with the price of wheat and extent of bolting, already quite complicated enough, but that in late Elizabethan times, it came to be an *understood* size, whatever

* Written y^t.

109

the actual cost might be. Understood, that is, to readers of the day. Still, there are clues. The Countess of Kent in *A True Gentlewomans Delight*, 1653, in a recipe for baked pudding, calls for a penny loaf to a quart of cream and 8 eggs; in a recipe for boiled pudding, she takes a penny *roul* to a pint of cream and 6 eggs, the very proportions of our recipe above. This apparent inconsistency can be explained by the fact that a roll is deemed to have been half the weight of a penny white; rolls and manchets were made of the very finest flour. In *English Bread and Yeast Cookery*, Elizabeth David* suggests that in most recipes, a penny roll or manchet may be considered to have been from 6 to 8 ounces and a penny white loaf about twice as big.

---

86   TO MAKE A GOOD PUDDING

Take a penny loafe & grate it, & put it into a pinte of seething creame, 4 eggs, a quarter of a pound of beefe suet minced small, nutmegg slyced thin, a little rosewater, & sugar, & a little salt. when it is served up, make the sauce of butter, sugar, & vinegar beat together & put in, or leave out, currans at your pleasure.

This recipe employs the same technique as the preceding one, and pretty much the same comments may be made. It is a good deal richer, and the addition of vinegar to the hard sauce, to counteract the richness, is an interesting touch. The currants are to be added to the pudding, not the sauce. (For *nutmegg slyced*, see C 6. Or grate it.)

---

[87]   TO MAKE A BAGG PUDDING

Take 2 pennyworth of grated bread, as much flower, 5 eggs beaten, & fruit as much as you pleas, a little salt; mingle all these with cold water & put them to boyle in y^r bagg or cloth.

Whatever the penny loaf weighed (C 85), this is a stodgy pudding. Assuming that rolls of 6 ounces are indicated, this means about 2¼ cups of flour; if regular penny loaves, it would be more like

* I am indebted to her for illuminating this question; she not only suggested sources but wrote out examples from cookbook literature for me.

110

4 cups of flour. The amount of water is not specified; the dough must be fairly consistent. See C 76 for boiling directions.

---

88   TO MAKE AN HEARBE PUDDING

First take oatmeale & bruise it a little, & lay it to steep all night in good hot milke. then in ye morning get good store of sweete hearbs & chopp them very small, & mingle them with ye oatmeale, with 3 or 4 eggs beaten, & some salt & pepper. but If you would have it a sweet pudding, leave out ye pepper, & put in lew thereof some nutmegg grated, sugar, & currans, & a little rose water. when these are well mixed, put them into y^r bagg or cloth to boyle, & when it is enough, lay it in a dish & poure good store of melted butter on it, & strow some sugar on it & about ye dish.

I find this an interesting recipe. The cracked oats (C 80) give textural interest and the "good store of sweete hearbs" might include not only the expected parsley but thyme, spinach, violet and strawberry leaves, and so on. The idea of mixing herbs and sweets is very ancient; raisins from Corinth and rose water from Persia must have found oatmeal a strange companion, but why not? (Rolled oats will not do.) For boiling puddings, see C 76.

---

89   TO MAKE A FRYDE PUDDING

Take 8 eggs & leave out 4 of ye whites, a good porrenger of creame, grated bread sifted thorough a cullender; put in sugar, cinnamon, & nutmegg. when it is well sweetned, beat all well together; it must [not]* be soe thick as for a pudding nor soe thin as for pancakes. you must put in a good many currans & a handfull of wheat flowre; put this into a frying pan, & keep it continually stird over a quick fire. fry it in good butter, & turne it with a pieplat like a tansey, & fry ye other side, then serve it up with sugar strowd upon it.

* The word *not* was inadvertently omitted.

111

This is a sort of *galette*, or thick pancake. By stirring, the scribe means lifting up the edges of the galette and letting the batter flow underneath as some do in making an omelet. For *tansey*, see C 101.

A *porringer* is an individual bowl (the word is related to porridge); those I have seen would contain about 8 ounces, or 1 cup, but they could well have varied.

---

90   TO MAKE UERY GOOD PUD[DING]

Take a pinte of creame or good milke, & beat 2 or 3 eggs with a little rosewater & grated nutmegg & put it into ye creame, & thicken it with a little grated bread & flower, & shread into it a little marrow or suet. alsoe put in sum currans & a little suger, then make them up in little cakes & fry them in fresh butter; then lay them in a dish & strow some sugar & cinnamon on them.

This recipe differs little from some of the previous ones except that the mixture is formed into cakes and fried. The dough should be stiff enough to hold its shape.

---

91   TO MAKE A PUDDING IN A LOAFE

Take out all ye crume & lay it to soake in new milke boyled, then put in 4 youlks of eggs, A few currans, wth a little nutmegg & salt, a quarter of a pound of beef suet; then put on ye top againe, & put y^t lower moste in ye bagg. tie it up & boyle it halfe an houre. ye rest y^t you leave, put to ye whites of eggs & a little sugar. this pudding may be baked or fry'd, onely adding raysons of ye sun to it.

The loaf in question must have been a round white loaf of about 2 pounds; it could not have been much bigger, considering that only 4 egg yolks are required, perhaps smaller. For boiling puddings, see C 76. The instructions for making use of the rest of the mixture are interesting; the egg whites will cause the pudding to puff.

92   TO MAKE FRENCH BREAD

Take a gallon of flowre & put to it a little salt, a pinte of ale yeast, a quart of new milke heated, but not too hot. poure these into ye flowre, & mix them with one hand, you must not knead it at all. y^n heat a woollen cloth & poure your paste on it, flower ye cloth, & lap it up. y^n make it into a dosin of loves & set y^m on a peele, flowred, & lay a warm wollen cloth on y^m. y^r oven must be allmoste hot w^{hn} you mix y^r bread. heat y^r oven pritty hot, & chip y^r bread when it comes out.

Historically, *French bread* in England denoted a very different loaf from the bread to be bought in a French *boulangerie*; it was also different from ordinary traditional bread in England where, as in France, bread was normally made with flour, water, salt, and leaven or yeast. One telling difference between French and English baking methods lay in the widespread use of ale yeast in England, accounted for by the prevalance of home brewing; the French were vintners, and the use of *levain* (sour dough) was nearly invariable. (The long maturing process and more vigorous kneading techniques are related to the sour dough method, as well as to differences in flour.) But not quite. In *Délices de la Campagne, Dedié aux Dames Mesnageres*, 1654, Bonnefons gives a recipe for *pain à la Montoron* which differs markedly from most traditional French recipes for bread, but resembles our recipe above, in that it calls for milk, *Leveure nouvelle* (new ale yeast), and is to be worked *en molle* (soft dough lightly kneaded); it retains, however, the typically French long multistage sponge system and is proved upside down in wooden bowls. Several other fancy breads call for ale yeast, among them a *cousin* (cushion or *puffe*, if you will), calling for butter, eggs, and soft cream curds, a version of *pain benist*, blessed bread. (The *brioche*, of Norman origin [from *brier*, to beat], is yet another version.)

Most authorities state that the use of yeast came to France only in the seventeenth century. It is true that the use of ale yeast was not made legal there until 1670 by parliamentary decree,[*] and only for *pains de luxe*. But yeast had been proscribed only in *commercial* baking. I believe that the nobility had always eaten the more delicate yeast-leavened bread and that the bourgeois simply

[*] *Histoire Illustrée de la Boulangerie en France* by Ambroise Morel, cited by Elizabeth David.

wanted to be able to buy the same aristocratic sort of bread. Bonnefons was *valet de chambre* to Louis XIV, and his recipes show
easy and long familiarity with the use of ale yeast. Cotgrave in
1611 says that *pain de cour* (bread of the court) is *pain mollet*, which
he describes as "A verie light, verie crustie, and savorie white
bread, full of eyes, leaven, and salt," surely leavened with yeast.

Also, Elizabeth David, citing *Liber albus*, reports in *English
Bread and Yeast Cookery* that, "Already in the reign of Edward I
(1272-1307) the London bakers of white bread were making 'Light
Bread known as French bread,' also called puffe and pouf." No
bread leavened with sour dough would have been called a *puffe*,
at least not in England where *yeast* and *barm* appear in Saxon
manuscripts around 1000 (*OED*) and there is reason to believe that
the ancient Celts—and for that matter, the related Gauls—were
using it in antiquity. Altogether, it seems reasonable to suppose
that these *puffes*, so associated with the French that they were called
French bread by the English, were brought to England by French
bakers to the royal court, which was still French-speaking at that
time. Anne Wilson, in *Food and Drink in Britain*, thinks that these
puffs were "a kind of milk bread, confected with butter and eggs."
I am less convinced, but whatever the precise early history, *French
bread* in England came to designate these light enriched breads as
distinguished from ordinary bread.

To *chip bread* is to pare bread of its crust. The custom may
have originated in removing clinging ash or burnt crust but it became a mark of social distinction and finally, of snobbery. *The Boke
of Kervynge*, printed by Wynken de Worde in 1508, instructs the *panter*
(in charge of *pain*, bread, in the *pantry*) to "chyppe your soveraynes
brede hote" with a *chyppere*. Others had to do with day-old bread;
servants' bread was not chipped. This chipping persisted well into
the eighteenth century, and I suspect that the reason the English
took to baking pan bread (unlike most Europeans, who prefer cast
bread) was the ease with which a soft crust might be obtained. It
also accounts for the generally lower baking temperatures of English bread, particularly of manchet, whose chief charm was a soft
crust; the "verie light, verie crustie . . . white bread" noted by
Cotgrave requires intense heat. This curious antipathy of the English toward crust was brought to the colonies; American bread recipes often advise how best to produce a "nice soft crust." Our
manufactured bread today has neither crust nor crumb, and a *New
York Times* food writer pronounces that "an untrimmed sandwich
is to my mind vulgar, crude and uncouth." In France, all the baker's
cunning is bent on producing good crust, and lots of it.

A gallon of flour, old measure, is said to have weighed
7 pounds (equivalent to about 21 cups of unsifted American flour),

which would make an unworkably stiff dough with 3 pints (6 U.S. cups) of liquid. In S 142, "3 ale quarts of fine flowre" are specified, and "To make a Cake," Digby calls for "eight wine quarts of flower" (1669). I am convinced that in the home kitchen, use of the *ale pinte* (S 1) was understood in all volume measuring and was only rarely expressed. Because American flour is rather more absorbent, start with about 15 cups.

For *ale yeast*, I find that from 1 to 1½ ounces of fresh compressed yeast (depending on proportions and time), liquified in a pint (2 U.S. cups) of water at blood temperature, gives excellent results used pint for pint in period recipes. (Use 2 or 3 *scant teaspoons* of preservative-free dry yeast, if you must, adding a cup or so of flour to the mixture when the yeast is soft, and allowing to ferment for 15 minutes, at least. Nearly everyone uses far too much dry yeast.) The lesser amount of yeast always works; it may take a bit longer than indicated. I like to replace about half the water with best imported ale (not beer); it gives a fine sixteenth-century air to baked goods, or so I fancy. The same system works for *barm*.

In bread making, I figure a teaspoon or so of sea salt to each cup of liquid, *in toto*. This proportion of salt may be lowered, but cannot be eliminated without drastic change in crust and crumb, to say nothing of savor.

A *peele* (from Old French *pele*) is a baker's wooden paddle, rather like a spatulate oar. *Lap it up* is to lap it over. A woolen cloth is lovely; it keeps the dough warm, allows breathing, and does not stick to the dough. It takes from 1½ to 2 hours, depending on size and fuel, to heat home brick ovens. As noted above, these small round loaves are baked in a quick oven (450° F, or so) giving a more characteristic "French" crust. For further notes on choice of flour and baking procedures, see C 95 and *bread*, page 17.

---

93   [TO] MAKE A BUTTERD LOAFE

Take 4 quarts of milke, put runnit to it, & whey it, & hang ye curd up in a cloth to dreyne for an houre or 2. then take 10 eggs & leave out 3 of the ye whites, y^n take a little ginger, a pinte of ale yeast, as much fine flowre as will make it up to a loafe. when it is well baked, cut it up, & butter it with sweete butter & sugar. your butter must be melted & beat up with ye sugar before you put it into y^r loafe.

The *butterd Loafe* of the sixteenth century harks back to the earlier *raston,* an Old French word that Cotgrave, 1611, translates as "A fashion of round, and high Tart, made of butter, egges, and cheese." The English raston did not contain cheese. The relationship has to do with slicing off the top of a raston "in the manner of a crown" (Harleian MS. 279, about 1430), scoring the crumb with a knife but leaving the crust whole, drizzling melted butter about, and re-covering it with the reserved top before reheating it for a moment. Elizabeth David thinks that the word may be related to Old French *rostis de pain* (slices of bread put under roasting meat to catch the drippings); in light of the history of the dish, it is a beguiling construction. The texture of the raston must have resembled that of a brioche; the *rostand* in the *Noble Boke off Cookry* (mid-fifteenth century) is supposed to "ryse as frenche bred."

The recipe for *A buttered Loafe* given by A. W. in *A Booke of Cookrye,* 1591, has no cheese either, and this is usual. Perhaps our own *butterd Loafe* is more closely linked to the Old French *raston,* for which I know no recipe. It can be noted that the texture of the *cousin* mentioned in C 92 cannot have been so different from that of our loaf above; the basic ingredients are the same (proportions are difficult to determine).

I have not tried this recipe. The amount of flour will vary a great deal with the dryness of the curds and the size of the eggs, as well as the type of flour. Lacking directions, this may have been a cast loaf, but there is no reason why you cannot bake it in a mold suitable to these enriched breads. You may follow the general rules for a brioche or a kugelhopf. Oven temperature is 375° F. For ale *yeast,* see C 92; for choice of flour and suggestions on baking proprocedures, see C 95 and *bread,* page 17.

I believe that *cut it up* means to scalp it, much as was done with the ancient *rastons* above. A very late recipe for *Resbones,* given by Thomas Dawson in *The Good Huswifes Jewell, Part I,* 1586, directs that they be baked in tiny loaves the "bignesse of Ducks egges," cut crosswise into four pieces, and soak them with melted butter and sprinkled with sugar and spices before being reconstituted.

Runnit, rennet, is the mass of curdled milk found in the stomach of the unweaned calf, which is then prepared for keeping. It is to be bought commercially, in liquid or tablet form. The word also applied to anything that would coagulate milk, such as nettles or rennet wort (C 130). The word appeared in Old English as *rynet* and has charming variants, such as *rendlys* and *rendles* (*OED*). Also, see *earning,* C 107. The curd for this cake should be very soft, so use less than recommended by the manufacturer. Or better, use the procedures suggested in C 106 and C 82.

To *whey* is to separate the whey from the curd. It is an old word in English; *OED* cites an appearance in a Latin glossary of 725 as "*Serum*: hwaey." An old-fashioned flour sack dish towel, impeccably rinsed, is the best possible device for accomplishing this; hang it over the sink.

---

94   TO MAKE CHEESE LOAUES

Take as much creame & new milke as you please & put to it as much runnit as will make it come; then break y^r curd very small & put to it 6 eggs and season it with sugar, mace, cloves, & a little salt; & put in as much grated bread as will make it up into little loaves about ye bigness of halfe penny loaves. then wash them over with melted butter & put them on butterd papers. when they are well baked in ye oven, cut them up on ye top, & put into them melted butter, rosewater, & sugar beaten together, & soe serve them up.

This is a variant of the *butterd Loafe* in C 93. They will not be light, of course, but made with care, they should have an interesting texture and be quite good. Use only homemade bread for such work. For making curds, see C 106 or C 93; I suggest 4 quarts of milk. Let us suppose that the half-penny loaf was the size of a big roll. *Cut them up* involves slicing off the tops, then scoring the crumb as for the *rastons*, page 116.

---

95   TO MAKE WHITE BREAD

Take 3 quarters of a peck of fine flower, & strow salt in as much as will season it. y^n heat as much milke as will season it luke warme, & hould it high when you poure it on to make it light. & mingle wth y^r milke 4 or 5 spoonfulls of good yeast. worke y^r paste well, & y^n let it ly a rising by the fire. y^r oven will be hoted* in an houre & halfe; y^n shut [it] up a quarter of an houre, in wch space make up y^r loaves & y^n set them in ye oven. an houre & halfe will bake them.

* There is an indecipherable mark between *o* and *t*.

Given the period, a curious aspect of this recipe is the inclusion of milk in *white bread;* the only differences between this recipe and that for *French bread* (C 92) concern kneading instructions and the form of yeast. Recipes for white bread are rare in cookbooks until we come to the eighteenth century. This is understandable if we remember that the quality and price of standard breads were severely controlled by law in England (page 17 and C 85), so that the composition of say the *penny white* loaf was unchanging: fine white flour, yeast, salt, and water. Milk and other complications were reserved for French bread and other fancy breads (*rouls,* for example, in C 107), which were correspondingly more costly. Certainly this is what Hannah Glasse was saying in her recipe for *White Bread* in *The Art of Cookery,* 1755, which calls for finest flour, "Water (which we call Liquor)," yeast, and salt. Her recipe for *French Bread* calls for butter, eggs, and equal parts of milk and water, in addition.

Let us assume that a peck of flour was based on the household ale measure (see C 92), so that 24 cups of flour is wanted, which will require 9 cups or so of liquid at blood temperature for a medium dough—8 cups or so for a stiff dough. (Equal parts of milk and water make better bread.) To approximate a little the flour of the day, use only natural unbleached flour, of which part of each cup may be a tablespoon of wheat germ and 2 tablespoons of whole wheat flour, sifted if you like. (See *flours,* page 18.)

In my experience, ½ ounce of fresh compressed yeast does the work of each *spoonfull* of yeast in period recipes; 2½ ounces will aerate 8 pounds of flour easily, but it may take a little longer than indicated here, so you may increase the amount to 3 ounces. (The equivalent in dry preservative-free yeast is 1 scant teaspoon to each ½ ounce of fresh, or no more than 2 scant tablespoons in all. Nearly everyone uses far too much.) I figure a good teaspoon of sea salt for each cup of liquid.

These are cast loaves, and quite hefty ones, judging by the baking time. For suggestions on baking, see *ovens,* page 19.

Manchets are referred to throughout the manuscript although no recipe is given for them. An early appearance of the word is *manchete* in *Liber Cure Cocorum,* about 1420. The origin of the name is obscure; *OED* notes several theories, the most likely being a relationship with *pain de Maine, panem domenicum,* the Lord's bread. An attractive construction is that it represents a diminutive of old forms of *dimanche,* making it mean small Sunday bread. Early usage, as *mengyd Flowre* (Harleian MS. 279, about 1430) and *Floure of payndemayn* (*Liber Cure Cocorum*), tends to emphasize the superior quality of the flour used in the breads. Phrases like "manged brede or paynman" (Harleian MS. 4016, about 1450) and "of paynemayns or elles of tendre brede" (Douce MS. 55, about

1440) only indicate that one bread might be substituted for the other. Thomas Cogan, in *The Haven of Health*, 1584, discusses *pain de Maine* and manchet as quite different breads, but maddeningly gives no hint of the difference except to say that the former was best made in Yorkshire.

It is agreed that the manchet was a small tender loaf made of the finest whitest flour of the day and, like all fine white bread, was leavened with yeast or barm, not sour dough. The shape, so definitively described by Markham as being round, seems nevertheless to have frequently been that of an elongated or oval roll with characteristically bobbed ends. The official size varied with the price of wheat, as did all bread (page 17). But William Harrison, in *Description of England*, 1577, says that it was "eight ounces into the oven and six ounces out," and this is regarded as typical. Home bakers quite likely followed this pattern.

While *rouls* and manchets seem to have been comparable in size, my understanding is that rolls were made of enriched dough, as in C 107, while manchets were not. (*Rouls* appeared in late Elizabethan times, and would almost appear to have replaced *pain de Maine*, which hardly survived the century.) As with white bread, this would explain why recipes for manchet were so rare; their only peculiarity, aside from the choice of flour, seems to have been the fact that they were baked "with a gentle heat," making a recipe hardly necessary. This distinction began to blur in the seventeenth century, and in *A True Gentlewomans Delight*, 1653, the Countess of Kent gives a recipe for *Lady of Arundels Manchet* that contains eggs, butter, and milk.

I know only three early recipes for manchet. Markham's is the most illuminating and, I believe, the most typical.

Of baking Manchets

Now for the baking of bread of your simple meales, your best and principall bread is manchet, which you shall bake in this manner; first your meale being ground upon the black stones if it be possible, which makes the whitest flour, and boulted through the finest boulting cloth, you shall put it into a clean Kimnel [kneading tub], and opening the flower hollow in the midst, put into it of the best Ale-barme the quantity of three pints to a bushel of meale, with som salt to season it with: then put in your liquor reasonable warme, and kneade it very well together, both with your hands, and through the brake [kneading device], or for want thereof, fould it in a cloth, and with your feete tread it a good space together, then letting it lie an howre or thereabouts to swel, take it foorth and mould it into manchets, round, and flat, scorcht [slashed] about the wast [waist] to give it leave to rise, and prick it with your knife in the top, and so put into the Oven, and bake it with a gentle heate.

Gervase Markham, *The English Hus-wife*, 1615

An earlier recipe, in *The Good Huswifes Handmaide for the Kitchen*, 1594, specifies water (also, see Hannah Glasse on *Liquor* above) and says that the dough must be "as hard as ye can handle it." A stiff dough usually requires a pound of flour to each 8 ounces of liquid. For a manageable batch, take 3 cups of unbleached flour, of which 3 tablespoons should be wheat germ and 3 tablespoons sifted whole wheat flour (see *flours*, page 18), 1 cup water at blood temperature, and just ½ ounce of fresh compressed yeast (see *ale yeast*, C 92), and a good teaspoon of sea salt. This will make three beautiful manchets. They are to be baked at a temperature of 350° F. There a number of references to oven temperature for manchets in our manuscript; see *mackroons*, S 184. For further suggestions on baking methods, see *ovens*, page 19.

In *English Bread and Yeast Cookery*, Elizabeth David explains that it was "the precision of the grooving and the extreme hardness" of the black Andernach lava stones from near Coblenz on the Rhine that permitted exceeding fine grinding of flour.

---

96   TO MAKE PANCAKE[S]

Take warme creame & mingle y^r flowre with it & eggs well beaten; leave out halfe ye whites; put in what spice you will, & a little grated bread, but noe sack, sugar, nor ale; put in a little rosewater & stirr all well together; let it be noe thicker then batter uses to be, then fry it with butter first melted.

We have here a group of pancake and fritter recipes, the batters for which were frequently interchangeable, as noted in C 99 (also, see C 202). The word *pancake* appears in Harleian MS. 279, about 1430, sufficiently familiar to be used in explaining another term. The English remained faithful to the paper-thin pancake, and it came to the colonies. Mary Randolph, in *The Virginia Housewife*, 1824, gives a recipe for a *Quire of Paper Pancakes*, essentially a classic *crêpe* recipe, that was to remain popular for decades. Thick pancakes leavened with baking powder do not seem to have appeared until mid-century; by the end of the century, they had edged out the finer thin ones.

It is quite likely that the early English pancakes were fried to be crisp, at least on the edges, in accordance with the origin and early association of the words *crisp* and *crêpe* (as is still frequently the case in Brittany), and the emphasis on butter in the frying raises the possibility that it is true for the recipes in our manuscript.

In any event, these pancakes are far more delicate than the *crêpes* usually encountered in fancy restaurants or cookbooks, which are purposely made pliable for wrapping or folding.

This is an interesting recipe in spite of the maddening lack of precision. I offer a version, based on the general lines of the other recipes, which I found delightful: for each cup of hardly tepid cream take 1 whole egg and 1 extra yolk, 1 tablespoon fine bread crumbs, 3 tablespoons of flour, 2 tablespoons of rose water, and what spice you will. (I prefer the contrast between the fragile unspiced cake and the ancient strewing of sugar and cinnamon.) You must be prepared to adjust the amounts of flour and liquid to obtain a batter that is no heavier than cool heavy cream. It improves on standing a couple of hours. Butter *first melted* most likely refers to clarified butter. Fry your cakes as thin as possible, turning to nicely bake the other side. Do try crisping the edges, done by slipping a little extra butter under the baked cake and allowing to sizzle for a moment. Serve immediately or most of the charm is lost.

Uses to be is a use which used to be and now uses to be only in the past imperfect. (Note the Markham citation in C 101.)

---

97   TO MAKE PANCAKES ANOTHER WAY

Take a quart of ale & warme [it],* then mingle with it 4 or 5 eggs well beaten, a little flower, a nutmegg grated, a little rosewater, a quarter of a pinte of sacke, & a little salt; mingle all these together, then fry ye pancakes very thin with fresh butter, & serve them up with cinnamon & sugar strowed on them.

---

98   TO MAKE FRITTERS

Take a pinte of very stronge ale, put it to a little sack & warme it in a little scillet; then take 8 youlks of eggs & but 2 whites, beat them very well; y^n put to them a little flowre & beat them together, y^n put in y^r warme ale; you must put noe more flowre to ye eggs after ye ale is in. y^r batter must be noe thicker then will just hang on ye apples. season ye batter with ye powder of

* Supplied.

121

nutmegg, cloves, and mace; then cut your apple into little bits & put them into ye batter; y^n set on ye fire a good quantety of tryed suet or hoggs lard, & when it is very hot drop in y^r apples one by one with y^r fingers as fast as you can. when they are fryde, lay y^m on a cleane cloth put over a cullender, y^n lay y^m on trencher plates, & strow on y^m sugar & cinnamon.

This is an excellent recipe and well presented. I like the description of the desired consistency of the batter: "noe thicker then will iust hang on ye apples," which is ever so much more helpful than the pseudoscientific level-measurement fetish. The proportion of 8 egg yolks to 2 whites and the careful instructions on draining the fritters are other signs of a perceptive cook.

Fritter comes from French *friture*, meaning both frying fat and that which is fried. (*Fritelles* appears in the Mazarine MS. of *Le Viandier*, early fifteenth century, but soon gave way to forms of *beignet*.) There are recipes for *frytours* and *fretourys* in the Pegge MS. of 1381; their popularity continued down through the centuries. The recipes varied little from those at hand; a few of them used yeast instead of eggs, but sugar and cinnamon were almost invariably strewn over the fritters before serving.

Originally, a *trencher* was a thick slice of heavy household bread (hence the name, which comes from Old Norman French *trencheor*, to cut) which was used as a sort of service plate on the medieval table. By the time of our manuscript, the word was applied principally to large flat serving plates of wood, metal, or earthenware. Because the bread trenchers had been squared off, as a rule, the serving plates seem to have occasionally been of a square shape. (See *voyder*, S 161, and *charger*, S 162.)

99   [TO MA]KE FRITTERS ANOTHER WAY

Take nutmeggs, mace, cloves, ginger, & cinnamond, beat & sift them, y^n bruise some safron, 5 eggs, whites & all, [&] beat well with 6 spoonfulls of rosewater; y^n mingle 3 pintes of new milke colde with fine flowre of a fit thickness for fritters; then poure in ye eggs & spice, & beat it alltogether. If you are not in haste, let it stand 3 or 4 houres, covered; when you fry them put liquor enough into ye pan, & make it very hot before you

drop them in. y^n put ye apples in cut thin & shorte.
drop them in with your fingers. this batter will make
good pancakes. strow sugar & cinamon on y^r fritters
when they are fryde.

It is interesting that a point is made of using whites and all when
speaking of the eggs; compare with C 98. Six spices, plus rose
water, seem a little difficult to harmonize, but it is typical of the
earliest recipes. Allowing the batter to stand is still standard French
practice; it allows the gluten to "relax" and there occurs a maturing
and fermentation which improve not only the flavor but the light-
ness and crispness of the fritter. I believe this recipe to be older
than the preceding one, although the language does not reflect
this. The advice that it makes good pancakes does, however; the
earliest recipes seem to have served indifferently for both *frytours*
and *cryspels* (a Middle English form of *crêpe*), and Pegge cites *Fritter
Crispayne* from another manuscript.

Liquor here is fat or oil, an obsolete and rare usage (*OED*).

---

100   TO MAKE FIRMETY

Take 3 pintes of new milke & one pinte of creame, and
boyle it with a flake or 2 of mace & some nutmegg; &
y^n put in y^r wheat, & keepe it boyling & stirring; & y^n
thicken it with eggs well beaten, or wheat flower, & put
in some raysons of ye sun, beeing before plumpt; &
streyne in some saffron If you please, & sweeten it well
with sugar, & soe serve it up.

Firmety, frumenty, is a dish made of hulled wheat boiled in milk
or other liquid. The word came into English from Old French
fromentée and *fourmentée*, showing that metathesis, or transposition,
had already taken place; to this day, *furmety* is a recognized form
in the *OED*. (The word meant of grain, now specifically wheat.)
There is a recipe for *formentée* in the Sion MS. of *Le Viandier*, before
1300, which is quite detailed: the wheat is parboiled, simmered in
milk, and egg yolks, saffron and other spices are added. Several
recipes in *The Forme of Cury*, about 1390, and the Pegge MS., 1381,
specify almond milk. Boiled grain is universal, but the presence,
and persistence, of Middle Eastern fragrances give pause. (One
recipe for *Formete* in *The Forme of Cury* is finally a sort of *couscous*,
made with *etemele*, hulled oats.) In general, one was to "mess yt
forth wyth fat venyson and fresh moton," or other meat.

Frumenty seems to have gone out of fashion towards the end of the sixteenth century; recipes for it all but disappeared from published cookbooks; Markham gives none in 1615, for example. Apparently the dish continued in rural areas, however, because one does find references to it in literature. And in recent times, frumenty has enjoyed a certain revival, part of a general resurgence of interest in folklore. (*Flummery*, a jellied dish made of the liquid of successive soakings of cereal, usually oatmeal, seems to have started appearing in seventeenth-century cookbooks; the name comes from Welsh, however, and appears to have no relationship with frumenty. Aside from both being based on cereal, they are very different dishes—one is slithery and the other is whole grain.) The recipe fails to specify *creed* wheat, a serious omission if one is unfamiliar with frumenty (see C 102). Take hulled wheat, either whole grain or cracked, and bring it to a boil in four times the amount of water by volume; allow it to stand overnight, and it may then be used in this recipe.

The phrase, "or wheat flower" was inserted; it may well be the scribe's own idea. In any event, it demonstrates how small modernizing touches were introduced and incorporated into recipes, with a decline in quality. The original recipe is for rich and elegant frumenty, not so different from a rice pudding but with a taste and texture that many will find more attractive.

---

101   TO MAKE A TANSEY

Take spinnage, sorrell, & tansey, but moste of spinnage; beat them & take theyr juice to mingle with 14 beaten eggs, both yolks & whites, & allmoste halfe A pound of beaten loaf sugar, & halfe a pinte of creame, & one nutmegg, & halfe a penny loafe grated. fry it with fresh butter, & when it is dished up, sprinkle a little verges or juice of orringes, & some sugar upon it.

The *tansey* harks back to the earlier *Erbolat* of *The Forme of Cury*, about 1390, which contains eggs and a good many herbs, among them tansy. There is a very similar recipe called *Arboulastre* in *Le Ménagier*, about 1393, which calls for frying the mixture in two *alumelles* (later to become *aumelette*) or thin cakes. The *tansye* appears in Harleian MS. 279, about 1430, and it contains only tansy and eggs; elaborate directions are given for turning the large flat omelet over. (It took centuries, apparently, for the term *omelet* to cross the channel; the first appearance seems to be in 1611 when

Cotgrave described it as "a pancake made of egs.") Gradually, spinach and other herbs were added, as in our recipe, and by 1615, the dish was undergoing an interesting change noted by Markham in *The English Hus-wife*: "Some use to put of the hearbe Tansey into it. . . ." I believe our recipe to be appreciably older than Markham's. Tansies persisted into eighteenth-century cookbooks—some even contained a little tansy—so that recipes came to the colonies, but the dish never became naturalized.

The amount of bread in the recipe would have been about 6 ounces.

The herb tansy (*Tanacetum vulgare*) has a strong aromatic scent and a bitter taste, according to *OED*. The Latin and all derived names are aphetic forms of Greek *athansia*, meaning immortality. Gerard tells us about the "cakes or tansies, which be pleasant in taste, and good for the stomacke. For if any humours cleave thereunto, it doth . . . scowre them downewards." *OED* says that tansy is associated with the bitter herbs of Passover. In French and English cookery, it was invariably associated with eggs. (I should note that the French forsook it very early, relegating it to medicine where it was specific as a treatment for parasitic worms.)

---

102   TO MAKE A RISE FLOR[ENTINE]

Take a pound of rise & cree it in milke with a little whole mace, then season it with cinnamon, cloves, sugar, & a little sack, & a little rose water, & halfe a pownd of raysons, & halfe a pound of currans, 3 or 4 eggs, & a little butter. y^n lay it in puff paste in a dish, & when it is baked, scrape on some sugar.

A *florentine* in English cookery was a pie, most often a meat pie, according to *OED*, and the cookbooks support this, with veal kidney having been a frequent choice. Early examples from the mid-sixteenth century, however, were often classed among custards and similar sweets and many of the meat florentines do have a custard filling. The one constant that I find is the use of fine paste rolled exceeding thin, or puff paste (often identified with Florence), which came into general use in the last years of the Elizabethan era. (See C 145.) When baked, the top crust was strewn with scraped sugar, which was often dampened with rose water and set back in the oven to glaze.

To *cree* is to soften grain by boiling or soaking, causing it to swell. The word comes from French *crever*, to burst, a word still so used in speaking of rice; in English, it was more commonly applied to wheat and oats. Rice benefits from a quick parboiling before being cooked in milk (C 77). The mixture could be baked as a rice pudding with much less fuss; I would increase the number of eggs. It would no longer be a florentine, of course.

---

103   HOW TO MAKE SET CUSTERD MEAT

Take 2 quarts of cream & put to it whole mace, nutmeg, & cinnamon slyced; y^n boyle it with a bay leafe, y^n break 16 eggs, except 8 whites, & beat them well together with a little sack. when y^r creame is taken of the fire sweeten it well with sugar, & keepe it stirring, & when it is halfe cold put in y^r eggs; beat some blanched almonds with ye end of y^r rouling pinn with a little rose water; strow it in & y^n fill into ye coffins.

The word custard is a metathetic form of French *crustarde*, which was a custardy meat pie, one of those into which court fools leapt to amuse the guests at royal banquets in medieval Merrie England. Eventually, the dish took on the name and general composition familiar to us today. Using the word in conjunction with *meat* is an interesting and archaic usage, and was when the recipe was last copied; it dates back to a time when meat meant food, as distinct from drink. *OED* notes bake-meat, etc., and we have sweet-meats in our manuscript, all slightly archaic. *OED* says nothing about a relationship of Saxon *meat* with French *mets*, prepared food, but the similarity of the words and overlapping of meanings gave rise to a certain amount of confusion. (The spelling of *meats* as *metes* in Wynken de Worde's *The Boke of Kervynge*, 1508, shows how the confusion arose.) According to Robert, *mets* comes from popular Latin *missum*, which meant anything set on the table, and is still so used in French. Under *mess*, in *OED*, there are found all the meanings one would expect to find in the Anglicized *mets*. While many are obsolete, as "mess it up," or *mess*, meaning a service or cover for two persons, a few survived and in the United States Navy, there is mess hall and officers' mess, for example.

As for the custard pie, it is a most excellent recipe. The proportion of egg yolks to whites is good and the strewing of crushed almonds, scented with rose water, is delightful. You will find it prudent to prebake the pastry crust; this amount will fill two pie crusts. Fine paste recipes are given in C 108 and C 145 through 148.

104   TO MAKE A CUSTARD

Take a quart of sweet creame & strayne therein 2
whites of eggs & 8 youlks well beaten; put them in a
dish with a grated nutmegg, a little salt, & halfe a
pound of sugar, stir them well together & soe bake it.
you may allsoe put in some rose water, If you please.

Another custard, this time without a crust. The dish is oversweet-
ened for many tastes; ½ pound of sugar is a cupful. The custard
should be baked in the customary *bain marie* arrangement, the oven
at 350°F, or lower. The water must never be allowed to quite boil;
if you place an old folded towel in the water under your custard,
it will have additional protection. Do not overcook; it continues
cooking with retained heat.

105   TO MAKE AN ALMOND CAUDLE

Blanche y^r almonds & grinde them with a little ale or
posset ale very fine, then streyne it as thick as creame
& boyle it with whole mace, cinnamon, & sugar.

By the seventeenth century, a caudle is considered to have been
a warm drink of thin gruel made with ale or wine, sweetened and
spiced. In was typically given to sick people, especially women in
childbed, according to *OED*; this agrees with all sources and may
be associated with the figurative meaning of *coddle*, to treat with
tender loving care. The word derives from Old French *caudel*,
warm. (See *coddle*, C 67.)

This rich and elegant mixture, however, harks back to a
much earlier tradition; it differs from the *Cawdelle de Almaunde*
given in Harleian MS. 279, about 1430, where one is to *grynde* the
almonds and temper them up with *gode ale*, only in seasoning,
which is saffron and sugar in the older one. The most enlightening
aspect about the recipe is the instruction to "serve it forth al hotte
in maner of potage." Another *Caudell*, from Harleian MS. 4016,
about 1450, calls for cooking "good ale, or elles good wyne" with
egg yolks in custard fashion. Earlier recipes for *Cawdel* in *The Forme
of Cury*, about 1390, and the Arundel MS. 344, around 1400, for
example, are more often for meat-based soups, with mussels being
a Lenten version. Our almond caudle was quite likely originally
a fast-day version, as well. How it was used at the time it was last
copied into our manuscript I cannot say, but it is more likely to

have been served as a fortifying potion rather than part of the meal proper. It must be perfectly delicious and would make a lovely dessert drink of a winter's evening.

---

106   TO MAKE CHEESCAKES

Take 6 quarts of stroakings or new milke & whey it with runnet as for an ordinary cheese, y^n put it in a streyner & hang it on a pin or else press it with 2 pound weight. y^n break it very small with y^r hands or run it thorough a sive, then put to it 7 or 8 eggs well beaten, 3 quarters of a pound of currans, halfe a pound of sugar, a nutmegg grated or some cloves & mace beaten, 2 or 3 spoonfuls of rosewater, a little salt. y^n take a quart of cream, & when it boyl[es] thicken it with grated bread & boyle it very well as thick as for an hasty pudding. then take it from ye fire & stir therein halfe a pound of fresh butter, then let it stand till it be allmoste cold, & y^n mingle it with your curd very well; y^n fill y^r coffins of paste & when they are ready to set into ye oven scrape on them some sugar & sprinkle on some rosewater with a feather. If you love good store of currans in them, you may put in a whole pound, & a little sack If you please. & soe bake y^m.

This cheesecake has a flavor and texture quite unlike that of the bland slick type familiar to most Americans, but not that different from those still being made in many parts of Europe. It is the use of homemade fresh cheese rather than gummy factory cheese, of course, that gives these particular cakes their character and cachet. The basic principles of cheesecake—more accurately, cheese tart—are very old, and we have remarkably similar recipes in Harleian MS. 4016, for example. One recipe, *Auter Tartus*, although differing in certain respects, is especially informative: the *brinkes* of the pastry coffin are to be reared more than an *enche* high; it is to be let "harden in the oven" before being filled and is baked "with-oute lydde," showing considerable finesse and underlining the fact that most pies were covered. The name *Chesekake* shows up in the *Parvulorum*, 1440; in 1530, Palsgrave defined *Chese cake* as *gasteau* or *torteau* (cake or tart). All this may surprise those food experts who have written that cheesecake is an American invention.

Six quarts of milk give between 1½ and 2 pounds of curd (about 4 cups), depending on the milk and how well drained the curd is. (*Stroakings* refers to the milk expressed in the stripping process, sometimes called the *afterings*. It is richer than the main flow of milk, and has a different quality. Nowadays, of course, it is all mixed, not to say homogenized.) You will have the tastiest cottage cheese working with wild curds (C 82) but you may use commercial rennet, following instructions for soft curds (see C 130). The amount of sugar is 1 cup; the amount of bread crumbs depends on how dry they are, the wetness of the curd, the desired texture, etc. I tried using ½ cup of dry fine crumbs with well drained curds, with excellent results, but I suspect that normally the cake should have been denser, in line with the three large *rouls* called for in C 107. The crumbs must be in sufficient quantity to absorb the cup of butter in this recipe. The curds should be sieved or run through the food processor. The currants, as always, should be plumped in hot water and thoroughly dried.

Partial pre-baking of the crust, as suggested by the ancient recipe above, was still being counselled by William Penn's wife in mid-seventeenth century and is good practice today, allowing you to bake the custardy cheese filling at an even 325°F. There are pastry recipes given in C 108 and 145 through 148. This recipe will yield two good-sized cheesecakes. The rose-scented sugar glaze is delightful.

---

107   TO MAKE CHEESCAKES ANOTHER WAY

Take 2 pound of fine flower, & rub into it halfe a pound of fresh butter, y^n make some new milke blood warme, put ye[ast] to it, & make y^r bread into rouls, & bake it. let it be 2 or 3 days old, y^n put a little milde earning in a gallon of new milke b[lood] warme; when it is come, seperate ye curd from ye whey with a sciming dish, y^n toss it betwixt 2 in a thin streyner, till all ye whey be dreyned away. y^n slyce in 3 of y^r rouls into ye curd & put in some cream & rub it to & fro till all comes thorough y^r clo[th] y^t will come. season it with white sugar, cloves, & a nutmegg beaten, currans, a little sack, or rosewater. to this quantety of curd you must put 8 or 10 eggs beaten, & bake them in puff past.

We have two separate recipes here: one for *rouls* and one for cheesecakes. For the rolls, I refer the reader to C 92 and 95. Obviously, it is not necessary to actually bake these buttery rolls for the express purpose of making cheesecake; any stale homemade bread of good crumb may be used. It is, however, an excellent recipe. Two pounds of flour come to about 6 cups of unbleached flour, of which ⅓ cup should be wheat germ and ⅓ cup should be sifted whole wheat flour. With a cup of butter, 2 cups of milk (half water is good) or a little more, should suffice. About ½ ounce of fresh compressed yeast will give excellent results, but a scant teaspoon of preservative-free dry yeast may be used instead, if necessary (see C 92). This amount will make 8 rolls weighing a good 6 ounces when baked, the customary size. For oven management, see page 19.

As for the cheesecakes, the recipe differs only in details from the previous one, although the details do have their importance. *Earning* is curdled milk or rennet. The word comes from Old English *iernan*, to curdle, a metathetic form of *rinnan* (*OED*), related to *runnit* of C 93. We have a charming description of how to assure proper draining of the curd; allowing it to remain suspended in cheesecloth is more efficient. A *sciming dish* is a perforated saucer-shaped, short-handled utensil (often of brass) used for skimming. The bread crumbs and curd may be sieved, as directed, or run through a food processor. As noted in C 108, the beaten eggs are to be combined with the bread and cheese at this point. As for the other ingredients, I suggest following the general proportions given in C 106. I consider the lack of additional butter an improvement. Puff paste is suggested; there are period recipes given in C 145 and 146, but more ordinary fine paste will do. See C 108, 147, and 148.

108　　TO MAKE UERY GOOD CHEE[SCAKES WITHOUT] CHEESE CURD

Take a quart of cream, & when it boyles take 14 eggs; If they be very yallow take out 2 or 3 of the youlks; put them into ye cream when it boyles & keep it with continuall stirring till it be thick like curd. y^n put into it sugar & currans, of each halfe a pound; ye currans must first be plumpt in faire water; then take a pound of butter & put into the curd a quarter of y^t butter; y^n take a quart of fine flowre, & put ye rest of ye butter to it in

little bits, with 4 or 5 spoonfulls of faire water, make y^e
paste of it & when it is well mingled beat it on a table
& soe roule it out. then put ye curd into ye paste, first
putting therein 2 nutmeggs slyced, a little salt, & a little
rosewater; ye eggs must be well beaten before you put
them in; & for y^r paste you may make them up into
what fashion you please. ~~~~~~~~~~~~~~~

as for ye latter receipt of cheescakes on ye other side of
ye leafe, ye eggs must be put in with ye bread.

The filling for this cheesecake is one of those curded custards that occur in a number of recipes throughout the manuscript,
C 128, for example. The practice went back to medieval cookery;
in Harleian MS. 279, about 1430, there is a recipe for *Let lory* that
directs you to stir milk and strained eggs over the fire "tyll it crodd
[curd]." The curd was served with a spiced custard sauce. By the
seventeenth century, however, such recipes are exceedingly difficult to find; Markham does not give one in 1615, for example.

The use of heavy cream in these proportions gives a soft
curd, rather more attractive than I had anticipated, but lacking the
distinctive and delightful tang of genuine curds. I counsel use of
the double boiler; as belatedly noted, the eggs are to be well beaten.
I also suggest steeping the *slyced* nutmeg in the hot cream before
adding the eggs, straining it out before continuing, or simply grate
it in judiciously, tasting as you go (see C 6). I suggest no more than
¼ cup of fine bread crumbs, depending on how dry they are. For
further discussion of cheesecakes and their baking, see C 106.

Now for the pastry. If you use 4 cups of pastry flour (see
C 92 on old flour measures) the ¾ pound of sweet butter will be
just about right. (See *flours*, beginning page 18.) If you must use
all-purpose *unbleached* flour, add 4 tablespoons of lard to make it
less intractible; it does not interfere unduly with the buttery taste
and can be defended historically—English flours were soft flours
and better suited for pastry making. Also, I suggest ½ teaspoon
of sea salt. Chill for an hour or so before making up.

---

109   TO MAKE A FOOLE

Take a pinte of cream & boyle it with a little mace, y^n
take it from ye fire & put to it ye youlks of 3 or 4 eggs
well beaten; then take some sippets of white bread &
lay in ye bottom of y^r dish, but first they must be dipt

in cream; y^n poure on y^r boyled cream, but not to hot, on the sippets. let it stand all night. when you beat y^e [egg youlks]* put in as much sugar as will sweeten ye cream, & some rose water; when you serve it up, scrape on some sugar & stick in some long narrow bits of candied leamon or citron.

The oldest meaning of *fool* in English cookery, long since obsolete, is a custard dish. There is some dispute over the derivation of the word; a cook might opt for French *fouler* (to press or crush) given the present composition of the dish, but *OED* spurns this construction and agrees with those who link it with *trifle*, or a bit of foolishness. The earliest citation, from Florio, 1598, "a kinde of clouted cream called a foole or a trifle in English," is compelling. (See C 121 for the sort of *clouted cream* referred to.) For the word to have found its way into an Italian dictionary means that it must have been current during the last quarter of the sixteenth century, if not earlier.

In later English cookery, the sort of dish described in our recipe above came to be known as a trifle, nowadays typically made of stale sponge cake, custard sauce, and sherry. The word *fool* came to be applied to a puree of fruit, typically raspberries or stewed gooseberries, sweetened and mixed with custard (much as in *made dish of goosberries*, C 73) and finally, more often simply with heavy cream (exactly as in the *creame* given in C 124). I cannot place these changes exactly, but the 1755 edition of Hannah Glasse's *The Art of Cookery* gives three recipes for fool: Westminster fool, hardly differing from our own recipe above, and gooseberry and orange fools, each made with a custard base. Her fruit fools are virtually the same as her fruit creams. Elizabeth Raffald gives a recipe for a frothy *Raspberry-Cream* in *The Experienced English Housekeeper*, 1789, that has cream rather than custard. Apparently, the name *fool* was not applied to these custardless fruit dishes until the nineteenth century; Mrs. Beeton, in 1861, gave a recipe for a *gooseberry fool* that did not call for custard.

---

110   [THE] BEST WAY TO MAKE A
       SACK POSSIT

Take a quart of cream & boyle it with a quartered nutmegg, y^n set it by & keepe it blood warme; then take halfe a pinte of sack, & above halfe a pound of

* Supplied.

sugar, & A little muske or ambergreece grownd with a little of ye sugar. let ye sack stand on ye fire till ye sugar be all melted, then take ye youlks of 14 eggs & ye whites of 7. If it be not good cream, you must keep out ye fewer whites. strayne them thorough a cloth, & let ye sack coole a little, y^n stir in all ye eggs & set it on ye fire againe, & keepe it stiring till it be pritty thick; then put in ye cream & stir all well together, y^n take it of ye hot fire & set it where it may onely keepe warme for halfe an houre, & let ye bason be covered. then serve it up with cinnamon strowed on ye top.

Posset is described in all sources as being a bracing drink composed of hot milk that is sweetened, spiced, and curdled with ale or wine. This posset is a warm custard spiked with sherry, much too rich to be bracing. It more resembles a warm eggnog, or the "styf poshotte of Ale" that one is to make with eggs for *Vyaund leche* (Harleian MS. 279, about 1430) in spite of deliberate overcooking. (See the *tender possit* called for in *A Great Cake*, S 152.) It also rather resembles the *Caudell* (Harleian MS. 4016) mentioned in C 105. (See the *sweet caudle* of wine called for in a pie, C 54.) It can be seen that the line between the two drinks was a blurred one, and that our recipe for posset is an old one. Like the *almond caudle* in C 105, it would make a delicious dessert drink.

The derivation of the word is obscure. Palsgrave, in his English-French dictionary, 1530, gives *posette* in French, but *OED* notes that French scholars drily comment that they do not otherwise know the word. It is true, however, that the word has a French ring to it and one may speculate that it was an Anglo-Norman witticism involving *pousser* (push) in the spirit of the modern French *pousse-café*, the post-prandial brandy.

---

111   TO MAKE A SACK POSSIT ANOTHER WAY

Take a pinte of sack, ye youlks of 16 eggs & ye whites of 4, halfe a pownd of sugar finely beaten; put these together & set them on a charcoale fire ready kind[led], & with a spoone beat it together as it standes on ye fire till it froth very well. then boyle th[ree] pintes of cream, & take ye sack of the fire & poure ye cream on [from]*

* Supplied.

A great height; then cover it with A hollow dish & set it
on A clear fire for A quarter of an houre, & y^t will
make it froth. then set your bason in A handsome dish
& strow some suger about it & serve it up.

This dish is perhaps even more like a cooked eggnog than
C 110 (which see), with a bit of *zabaglione* technique as well. It
seems unwise to allow the mixture to stand on the fire after the
initial cooking as instructed; I counsel whisking it for a few moments instead to produce the characteristic froth.

---

112   TO MAKE A SACK POSSIT [WITHOUT
        MILKE]

Take a pinte of sack & A pinte of ale, & let it boyle.
then take 10 eggs both whites & youlks, beat & strayne
them & put them into your sack with a quarterd
nutmegg; let them boyle together, then put in halfe a
pound of sugar. let it stand A while & soe serve it up.

See recipe C 110. For the quartered nutmeg, see C 6.

---

113   TO MAKE WHITE BROTH

Take some of ye broth ye veale or muton is boyled in &
put into it mace, cinnamon, & nutmegg. y^n you must
boyle pruans & currans by themselves in water & put
to ye aforesaide broth when it is served in. & when y^t
broth is ready to boyle, thicken it with youlks of eggs &
sack or muskadine, & serve it up with sippets. If you
please, you may make ye broth with a Capon & let y^e
Capon be served up in ye broth & eyther put in or
leave out ye fruit at your pleasure, & put A little sugar
into ye seasoning of ye broth If the sack or muskadine
makes it not sweet enough.

Most of the old recipes for *white broth* known to me previously had
been on the order of the recipe given in C 203, that is, made white
with almonds or cream, or both. The recipe given by Markham in
1615 is such a recipe, and Hugh Plat, in *Delightes for Ladies*, 1608,
suggests in a recipe *To boile a Capon in white broth*, that "if you have

no Almonds, thicken it with creame, or with yolks of eggs," reinforcing my impression that the recipe given above was atypical, indicating a sloughing off of older characteristics. On closer study, however, it appears to be quite in line with earlier sixteenth-century recipes, such as one, *To stewe Capons in Whyte Brothe* in *A Proper Newe Booke of Cokerye*, 1545 (?), or those in *A Booke of Cookrye* by A. W., 1591. There are certain differences, but the meat broth, the prunes, and the liaison of egg yolk are present in all. (The Scottish cock-a-leeky, which is characterized by prunes as well as leeks, was a parallel development.) It was always considered nice to boil the prunes and any other fruit separately.

---

114   TO MAKE PLUMB BROTH, OR STEWD
       BROTH

Take a piece of fresh beefe or 2 or 3 marrow bones* and
boyle it in 7 or 8 quarts of water. when it is cleane
scimed & halfe boyled, put in some blades of mace, &
currans, raysons, & pruands, 2 pownd; let them be
clean washt & pikt; allsoe put in allmoste 2 penny
loaves grated & 3 quarters of a pownd of sugar. you
may culler it with sanders If you please, & serve up y^e
marrow bones in ye broth or leave them out at y^r
pleasure.

The confusing practice of applying *plumb* to both raisins and prunes seems not to have started until 1725 (judging by a citation in *OED*), well past the date of our manuscript. Since both fruits are called for here, the question is of historical interest only; in any event, it should be noted that while prunes were occasionally omitted from eighteenth-century recipes for *plumb broth*, it was their presence that gave the dish its name in the first place.

This is a typical seventeenth-century recipe. Two *penny loaves* probably amounted to 1½ pounds or so of bread (C 85); the sugar is 1½ cups. The 2 pounds of fruit must refer to the sum total. This sweet porridgy dish survived into the eighteenth century and recipes appeared in the earliest cookbooks published in the colonies.

The suggested substitution of *bludy neck or leg* was inserted at a much later date, judging by the handwriting. Chuck and shank would be the equivalent cuts in American butchery.

* *marrow bones* is crossed out and *bludy neck or leg* written in by a different hand.

135

115   [TO] MAKE BARLEY BROTH

*Frances**

Take A neck of muton & boyle it in 5 quarts of water &
scim it clean; then take halfe a pound of barley which
must be boyled in 2 or 3 waters; y^n put it to ye neck of
muton, with a pound of raysons of ye sun, & 3 or 4
whole mace, french sorrell & spinnage, halfe a
handfull, & a little parsley. when this is boyled enough,
season it with sugar & salt & dish it up. ~~~~~~~~
it must not be fat.†

This is a more interesting recipe than the two previous ones, at
least from a gastronomic point of view. Raisins go better with
mutton than with beef; the barley provides textural interest as
compared to the sempiternal bread crumbs. The cautionary note,
"it must not be fat," is a wise one; nor too sweet, I might add. A
rack of mutton is the indicated cut of meat.

116   TO MAKE GRUELL OF FRENCH BARLEY

Take a little quantety of french barley & boyle it in
t[wo] or 3 waters till it be very tender, then boyle it in
good sweet cream, & season it with a little mace &
sugar, fitting y^r taste, 2 eggs well beaten, & a spoonfull
or 2 of rose water. soe serve it up.

Gruel is a very old word, finally related to *groat* (*OED*); see C 80.
Recipes for gruel were appearing in early fifteenth-century manuscripts; it had been made since time immemorial. In those early
recipes, gruel was usually based on meat broth and was, or came
to be, associated with invalid cookery, at least in wealthy homes.
(See barley cream in C 122.)

117   TO MAKE A COLD POSSIT OR SULLIBUB

Take a quart of sweete cream & boyle it with a nutmegg
cut in 4 quarters, y^n take it of & stir it till it be quite

* In a different hand. See page 460.
† In yet another hand.

make Barley Broth

115. Take a neck of muton & boyle it in 5 quarts of water, & scim it, clean, then take halfe a pound of barley which must be boyled in 2 or 3 waters, y'n put it be y'e neck of muton, with a pound of raysons of y'e sun & 3 or 4 whole mace, french sorrell & spinnage halfe a hand full, & a little persley, when this is boyled enough, season it with sugar & salt & dish it up.

it must not be fat

To make Gruell of french Barley

116. Take a little quantety of french barley & boyle it 2 or 3 waters till it be very tender, then boyle it in good sweet cream, & season it with a little mace, & sugar fitting y'r taste 2 eggs well beaten & a spoonfull or 2 of rose water, soe serue it up.

To make A cold Possit or Sullibub

117. Take a quart of sweete cream & boyle it with a nut megg cut in 4 quarters, y'n take it of & stir it till it be quite cold, y'n powre it into a bottle glass over night if you would haue a sullibub, then you must take halfe a pinte of water & as much white wine & 2 spoonfulls of rosewater, & lay in it halfe a lemon pill green or dry, & some rosemary, & sweeten it, then stand high on a table & poure y'e boyled cream into y'e white wine, let it stand 4 or 5 hours & it will come.

To make A Sullibub another way

118. Take what wine you like, & mingle it with ale or beere, sweeten it with sugar, y'n milke into y'e drink, & let one poure in w'th a spoone some cream, as if they were makeing wilde curd, y'n milke againe, & soe doe till it be full, If you like y'e you may strow currans on y'e top of y'r sullibub.

cold; y^n powre it into a bottle glass over night y^t you
would have A sullibub. then you must take halfe a
pinte of water & as much white wine, & 2 spoonfulls of
rosewater, & lay in it halfe a leamon pill, green or dry,
& some rosemary, & sweeten it. then stand high on a
table & poure ye boyled cream into ye white wine. let it
stand 4 or 5 hours & it will come.

The origin of *syllabub* is obscure, according to *OED*. The earliest
citation is 1537 and, as is so often the case, it is a literary allusion
rather than to a recipe. There are a number of amusing variants,
among them *sillybob*. The typical syllabub is made of milk, frequently drawn from the cow directly into the serving bowl already
partly filled with white wine, enriched with cream, sweetened and
flavored. The wine was a clabbering agent. This recipe is then
fairly classic.

The differences between *syllabub*, *posset*, and *caudle* became blurred and twisted as can be seen in the recipes of our
manuscript (C 105, 110, 111, 112, 118, and 204). A syllabub was,
however, always served cold. The drink was very popular in colonial America and recipes appeared in *American Cookery* by Amelia
Simmons in 1796 and succeeding editions.

---

118   TO MAKE A SULLIBUB ANOTHER WAY

Take what wine you like, & mingle it wth ale or beere;
sweeten it with sugar, y^n milke into ye drink, & let one
poure in wth a spoone some cream as If they were
makeing wilde curd[s]. y^n milke again, & soe doe till it
be full. If you like y^m, you may strow currans on ye top
of y^r sullibub.

The ale or beer is unusual in a syllabub, I believe. Few of us have
a freshened cow at our disposition; whisking the mixture will produce a fine froth, but it will disturb the layered effect of the cream
and milk. Raw milk produces ever so much more successful syllabubs than pasteurized milk, which has no character and does
not much like to clabber.

119   TO MAKE A FINE [CREAM]

Take a quart of cream y^t is sweet & thick & put to it 6
spoonfulls of sack & 4 spoonfuls of rose water, y^n
worke it in A glass churne till it be curdled. then
sweeten it with sugar & shake it a little; then put it in a
dish & let it stant halfe an houre before it be eaten.

This is a delightful recipe, and one I believe to be very old. (*Stant*
is the third person singular of *stand* and was current until nearly
1600, according to *OED*. The final *t* is pristine.) There is no point
in using any but the finest sherry you can find ; sweet thick cream
will pose greater problems. The glass churn is a nice note; in lieu
thereof I suggest agitation with a wooden whisk. The idea is to
produce a fine even curd, not butter, so take care. You may allow
it to set in the refrigerator but it should not be icy cold.

120   TO MAKE A CREAME WITH SNOW

Take 3 pintes of cream & ye whites of 7 or 8 eggs;
strayne them together with a little rose water & as
much sugar as will sweeten* it; then take a stick slit
cross, or a bundle of white twiggs, & beate it, & as y^e
snow riseth take it up in a spoone & put it in a
cullender y^t the whey may run from it; & when you
have enough of ye snow, take the cream y^t is left & put
it in a scillet & put therin whole cloves, sticks of
cinnamon, & ginger bruised. then seeth it till it be
thick, & then strayne it & when it is cold, put it in a
dish & lay your snow upon it.

The making of snow creams was an elegant conceit of Tudor cookery. In the *Proper Newe Booke of Cokerye*, 1545 (?), there is a recipe
very like ours: "Take a pottell [2 quarts] of swete thycke creame
and the whytes of eyghte egges . . . a saucerfull of Rosewater, and
a dyshe full of Suger wyth all, then take a stycke and . . . cutte it
in the ende four square, and therwith beate all the aforesayede
thynges together, and ever as it ryseth take it of and put it into a
Collaunder . . ." There are turns of phrase in our own recipe that

* Written *sweetet*.

are tantalizingly evocative. Our recipe, however, records an important improvement in technique: a true whisk. Knowing the way print cookbooks lagged behind usage, it is possible that it had been in long use, but the whisk was inexplicably slow in showing up considering the simplicity and efficiency of a bundle of willow twigs. (See C 204.)

Snow cream is the English version of *crêmets d'Anjou*, those delightful heart-shaped desserts that one finds down river from Tours. Instead of being sweetened, they are served with sugar and fresh cream on serving. It seems likely that the Plantagenets brought the sweet to England.

---

121   TO MAKE CLOUTED CREAM

Set on 2 gallons of new milke, & make a quick fire under it, & stir it all ye while. y^n take 3 pintes of sweet cream, & when it is ready to boyle, poure in ye cream by little & little, very softly, & when it is ready to boyle againe, take a pinte of cream more, well beaten with 3 new layd eggs (onely ye youlks)* and poure in, but be sure it boyle not after. y^n strayn it as hot as you can into as little a pan as you can get.

This is more properly a rich custard and has little in common with the clotted cream as traditionally made in Devon, Dorset, and Cornwall. Elizabeth David tells me that such clotted cream is cream from the top of a wide earthen pan of milk which has been set over a very low fire (they had special stoves) and scalded until a ring (the size of the hot plate underneath) appeared in the middle. The pan was then set on the shelf for two days or so, and the thick cream lifted off, as in *Cabbage Cream,* C 126. (I paraphrase.) I have not found any other authority for the use of egg yolk in *clouted cream.* It should not be necessary to note that the cream must be heavy cream and not super-pasteurized.

---

122   [TO M]AKE CREAM OF FRENCH BARLEY

Take ye third part of a pound of french barley, wash it well in faire water; in ye morning set 2 scillets with faire water on ye fire, & in one of them put y^r barley; let it boyle till ye water look red, then dreyne it from y^e

* Scribe's parentheses.

water & put it into ye other warme water. thus you
must do severall times, till it looks white. y^n strayne y^e
water clean from it & take a quart of cream & put into it
a nutmegg or 2 quartered, a little large mace, & some
sugar. set it on ye fire & when it is ready to boyle, put
in y^r barley into it & let it boyle a quarter of an houre.
y^n put in it ye youlks of 2 or 3 eggs well beaten with a
little rose water, then dish it up & eat it cold.

This is a recipe for an elegant barley custard cream, done with the
utmost nicety. I believe that overnight soaking of the barley is
elliptically indicated. It is then to be brought to a boil in several
waters. The use of whole spices, to be removed before serving, is
a subtle touch. The rules of custard making are to be observed.

---

123   TO MAKE CREAM TO BE EATEN WITH APPLES OR FRESH CHEESE

Take ye pap of scalded or rosted apples & put it into a
dish. If they be sower, sweeten them with sugar & rose
water, & bruise y^m with a spoon & spread them a[ll]
over ye dish. y^n take thick sweet cream & set it on y^e
fire, & put to it rosewater & sugar. let it boyle apace &
when you see it soe thick y^t it froths, with a spoon or
silver ladle take of ye froth as fast as you can, & put it
in ye dish with apples till ye dish be full. when y^r cream
is cold, you may put it into fresh chees, y^t you must
have ready prepard before; or If you pleas you may
poure it into the dish where the apples are, & soe serve
it up with sugar scrapd about ye dish.

I suggest using the pulp of baked apples for this dish; it gives a
far more intense flavor and appropriate texture. The final assembly
of the dish is not altogether clear; I believe that the cream allowed
to get cold is that which did not froth and is to be mixed with fresh
cheese (see C 137 and 138) or poured over the apple mixture. The
final strewing of coarse grained sugar over the dish is an important
element of contrast.

124 TO MAKE GOOSBERY OR [APPLE] CREAME

Take goosberries or apples & scalld them very tender, then put them in a little hearb sive, or cullender & bruise them with ye back of a spoone; & the pulp y^t comes thorough A sive or Cullender, you must take & season with rosewater & sugar. y^n mix some good cream with it and make it of what thicknes you please, & soe serve it up.

Except for the rose water, this cream is actually what we know today as gooseberry fool (see *fool*, C 109). It makes a delightful and refreshing summer dessert, one that should be more popular.

125 TO MAKE RASBERRY CREAM

Take a pinte of cream & boyle it with 3 whites of eggs beaten well with warme cream, put in a blade or 2 of mace & some leamon pill, & when it is pritty well boyled take it of & season it with sugar & put in some Juice of rasberries. stir it well together & when it is cold serve it up. thus you may make curranberrie, sorrell, or leamon cream.

This cream is also a kind of fool, the kind that combined custard and fruit (see *fool*, C 109). Omitting the egg yolks is perceptive in this case as they veil the intensity of these fruit flavors; it also makes the cooking of the custard a bit tricky, although the use of heavy cream makes it possible. Observe all rules of cooking custard and be especially careful about not overcooking. The use of sorrel in these creams was fairly common and not at all outré.

126 TO MAKE CABBAGE CREAM

Set some new milke on ye fire with a little salt in it. let it boyle a walme or 2, y^n set it to cool in severall panns, & when it is cold, scum of ye cream gently & lay it in wrinkles on a dish with a plate under it like a little

cabbage roled up. & upon every leafe str[ow] some
sugar; & tie some rosewater in a glass with A leather
full of holes over it, out of which you must sprinkle
some of ye water betwixt every leafe. & soe you must
keepe it two dayes before you eat it.

Cabbage cream was another elegant conceit of the sixteenth- and
seventeenth-century English kitchen. Finally, it is an elegant way
of serving clotted cream (see C 121). Heated milk is allowed to
stand in a broad pan until a heavy, wrinkled sheet of cream forms,
which is carefully lifted and artfully arranged on a serving plate
in a pattern vaguely suggesting cabbage leaves. (I suppose that a
small bowl is to be used as an armature.) Allowing the dish to
mature is an important aspect of its special character, as is the
layering of scraped sugar and bedewing with rose water. (There
are, to be sure, more efficient ways than resorting to leather-bound
bottles.) It is now next to impossible to find the beautiful quality
of milk necessary for this dish, but if it amuses you, you can turn
to C 130 for general directions. The clabbering of the milk with
yogurt is not in the recipe, but in proper clotted cream there is a
natural bacterial action—similar to that in *crème fraîche*—that gives
its characteristic taste, and our pasteurized milk simply does not
permit this. At the least, it will be necessary to add a quantity of
fresh heavy cream to the milk; what pathetically little cream is
present in today's milk is homogenized so that it could not rise,
given the will. The milk must stand long enough for the sheet of
cream to assume the requisite density. What I really counsel is
striking up a friendship with someone who owns a Jersey cow.

---

127   [TO] MAKE WHITE LEACH OF CREAM

Take a pinte of cream, 6 spoonfuls of rose water, 2
greyns of musk, 2 dropps of oyle of mace or a piece of
large mace; let it boyle with 4 ounces of Ising glass, &
y^n let it run thorough a Jelly bagg & when it is cold,
slyce it. this is ye best way to make leach.

The earliest meaning of *leach* in English cookery was the same as
that of Old French *lesche*, a long thin slice. Very early, it came to
mean almost anything that could be sliced, so that *OED* is able to
define leach as a dish of meat, eggs, fruits, and spices in jelly, or
a gelatine of almonds. The medieval gingerbreads were dry
leaches, for instance.

By the seventeenth century, the word most commonly referred to a stiff gelatine of almonds and this continued as late as E. Smith's *The Compleat Housewife*, first American edition, 1742. The dish had been declining in favor of the dessert *blanc manger*, a lighter gelatine of almonds. The disappearance of leach was no gastronomic loss; as can be seen from our recipe, it had to be unpalatably stiff in order to slice properly. I had thought that the omission of almonds here was inadvertent—and it may well have been—but Thomas Dawson gives a recipe for white *leach* in *The Good Hus-wives Jewell, Part II*, 1587, that calls for a quart of milk and 3 ounces of *Isinglass* that is also innocent of almonds. Markham, in 1615, uses milk, almonds, and isinglass, and this was more typical.

Isinglass is a form of leaf gelatine made from the bladder of the sturgeon; it may have been less concentrated than modern gelatine. I suggest one package (¼ ounce) of ordinary granulated gelatine, flouting authenticity. The prettiest way to serve this rich dessert is in decorative individual molds; paint the interior with almond oil. Sugar is omitted: 4 or 5 tablespoons should suffice.

It is worthwhile to turn to Eliza Leslie's recipe for *Blanc-Mange* in *Directions for Cookery*, 1837. She calls for 1 ounce of isinglass dissolved in rose water to cover, 4 ounces of almonds (half of them bitter) beaten to a paste, 1 quart of cream, 1 cup of sugar, and 1 spoonful of mace, all boiled together for 15 minutes, then strained and molded. (Note: 2 packages of granulated gelatine dissolved in ½ cup rose water may be substituted for the isinglass.) This dish is clearly related to the leach, but is infinitely more beguiling.

---

128   TO MAKE CREAM WITH EGGS, OR RATHER CURDS

Take a quart of cream & 8 eggs, & take out 4 of ye whites. set y^r cream on ye fire & put into it a nutmegg quartered with 2 whole mace. boyle it a quarter of an houre before ye eggs goe in; ye eggs must be well beaten with sugar before you put them in. y^n let them boyle together before you take them up, & when you see ye curds come from ye side of ye scillet, strayn them thorough a piece of tiffeny or thin strayner, & let it stand a quarter of an houre till all ye whey be dreyned from it. y^n season ye whey with sugar whilst it is

warme, & breake ye curds with ye back of a spoone
very small, & season it with sugar, & put it into a dish
& pour ye whey upon it when you serve it up. or you
may eat it with cream, white wine, or ale sweetned
instead of ye whey. stirr ye eggs & cream one way in y^e
boyling.

Or curds and whey. This is yet another of those curiously unappealing custard curd dishes discussed in C 108; indeed, it is not
unlike the medieval recipe referred to there. If you are curious, I
can say that it is better than you might think. The proportions are
excellent and there is nothing to keep you from using the recipe
for individual baked custards.

---

129 TO MAKE ALMOND BUTTER

Beat halfe a pound of almonds wth faire water till all
their whi[te]ness be out in ye water, y^n warme it a little
& set it in pans till there be a cream on it; y^n scum it &
season it wth sugar & what els you like, & churne it in
a glass churne to butter.

I do not altogether understand the charm of this dish. That it entered the English repertory in medieval times in lieu of butter on
fast days when "white meats" (dairy products) were proscribed
along with other meat, is understandable; the wonder is that it
survived as long as it did. Recipes for almond butter are not all
that common and those with which I am familiar are not, properly
speaking, for butter but for curds, as in C 134. The *Almond Butter*
presented by A. W. in *A Booke of Cookrye*, 1591, is such a dish: the
reader is to curd almond milk, whey it, mold it, and "plant it with
kernels of Pomgranets, and so serve it up." Dawson gives a similar
one 1586, which he claims to be "after the best and newest fashion."
Almond butter was also applied to cow's milk curds mixed with
almonds, as in C 206.

But our recipe above is for genuine butter in that it is
churned from almond milk. Either the blender or the food processor pulverizes the almonds nicely and should churn the butter
as well; I use it to churn butter from regular cream.

130 TO MAKE SEUERALL KINDE [OF CURDS]

Take a pan of milk as it comes from ye cow and set it over ye fire, & as it riseth, put in cream. doe soe 6 times, then take it of & let it stand upon nettles till next morning, y^n take of ye top & scrape some sugar on it & serve it up.

The English predilection for curds is lengendary. Lacking refrigeration, to be sure, most peoples who kept any animal for milk have always consumed the greater part of it in the form of curds, perforce. (Jane Grigson reports in *Good Things* that the first icehouse in Britain was built by Charles II in 1660, thus making frozen desserts possible.) The type and precise form of curd—liquid or solid, fresh or cured—depends on the quality of grazing lands, climate, and cultural preferences. In any event, the English, as most peoples, regarded curds as being more salutary than "milk as it comes from the cow," and curds included the various curdled milk drinks such as syllabub, and the custard curds, with which we are so frequently confronted in our manuscript (C 128). The reasoning was that new milk would curdle in the stomach, causing discomfort at the least. (This was long regarded as an old wives' tale; recent medical opinion indicates some basis for this preference.) Hard, long-keeping cheeses were also looked upon with suspicion by the English and were generally left to laborers and peasants to cope with.

Recipes for curds occur throughout the manuscript, particularly in the cheese-cake and syllabub sections, but here we have an entire series. The most interesting from a historical point of view are the almond curd recipes (C 134, 136, and 206). Originally, they permitted the eater to conform to the letter of the law concerning fasting, a luxury available only to the very wealthy. These recipes gradually disappeared with the lessening stringency of fasting regulations and became increasingly old-fashioned during the seventeenth century. There is also an interesting early recipe for slip-coat cheese (C 138).

Depending on the final use, clabbering may be induced by plain junket, rennet, wild curds (C 82) such as those found in yogurt or buttermilk, lemon juice, rose water, or white wine. For the first two, you will be guided by package directions, but err on the side of too little; what is wanted is a light clabber, not keeping cheese. I add a little yogurt even when working with commercial rennet; its use can be defended in that it restores to our antiseptic and denatured milk and cream a breath of life that will brighten dishes that can be unctuous and just a bit dull. Health food stores offer a rennet made of herbs; it works but imparts a slightly grassy taste. Markham, in 1615, tells us how to make curds using buttermilk: for three parts of buttermilk, one part of new milk is set on the fire. When it is ready to rise, take it off and allow it to cool a little; "then poure it into the buttermilke in the same manner as you would make a posset, and having stirred it about let it stand . . ." It takes several hours to clabber properly, during which time it must not be disturbed. It works even with cultured buttermilk; raw milk gives infinitely nicer curds. Other curdling agents are discussed in various recipes throughout the manuscript, as is the wheying in a muslin bag.

The recipe before us has much in common with *Cabbage Cream* (C 126). Here, a curdling agent is introduced rather than allowing natural fermentation to take place. I suggest using a minuscule amount of plain junket, along with a little added yogurt (a tablespoon to each cup or so of milk) to induce the characteristic tang that comes with light fermentation. The best yogurt is that you make yourself; health food stores carry excellent starter with directions. The proportion of cream to milk is not crucial; I suggest a pint or so of the freshest and heaviest cream you can find (*not* super-pasteurized) to a quart of milk, raw milk if you can lay your hands on the real thing from a pampered Jersey cow.

---

131   ANOTHER WAY

Take 3 pintes of cream & 14 eggs beaten; boyle y^m together till they are thick like a cheese and y^n season them as you please.

A custard curd recipe (see C 128).

---

132   ANOTHER WAY

Take a quarte* of thick cream & ye whites of 22 eggs beaten with some of ye cream, y^n set on ye other cream to boyle. & poure ye eggs into ye boyling cream, stirring it till it boyle againe. y^n take a quarter of a pinte of rose water, & poure it about ye pan till it curdle, then poure it into a strayner & whey it till it be as thick as almond

* *pinte* was ineptly changed to *quarte* by the scribe.

147

butter, y^n season it with sugar, strayn it out & eat it cold.

Yet another custard curd recipe (see C 130). It is more prudent to add a little of the hot cream to the egg white mixture, stirring, and pour that into the pot, stirring.

---

133   ANOTHER WAY

Set on milk as it comes from ye cow, cover it, and often wipe ye dish y^t noe dew may fall upon ye milke. when ye cream rises, take it of & lay it on a dish like cabbage; soe doe severall times, & between every leafe strow sugar. y^n put in ye dish you serve it up in a little runnet & cream warmed; soe put in ye cream you scimed of, & in a short time it will be like slip curds but much better.

We have here another recipe for cabbage cream (see C 126). If I read correctly, several milkings are involved put perhaps only several pans of milk. *Slip curds* are fresh unpressed curds. It is just possible that the cream cheese later called slip-coat (C 138) is being referred to here; there would have been little point in likening this rich matured cream to ordinary slip curds.

The *dew* refers to the pesky condensation that occurs on the inside of the cover; it would dampen the sheet of cream.

---

134   [TO] MAKE FRESH CHEESE OF ALMONDS

Take almonds & grind y^m very small, & strayne them with faire water to make milke. set it on ye fire & season it with salt; when it seetheth take a dish full [of]* it & put some sugar in it. y^n put to ye other y^t seetheth ye Juice of orringes & leamons, y^n take it of ye fire & let it stand a quarter of an houre. y^n poure it on a linnen cloth, lap it up, & hange it on a pinn for 4 or 5 houres. y^n with rose water & sugar & rosewater,† make it round like a chees & poure y^r cream upon it.

* Written *on*.
† There was punctuation neither before nor after this phrase. Several words were omitted by the scribe.

This is a delightful recipe and an interesting one from a historical point of view (see C 130). The use of citrus fruit with almonds is exceedingly rare in English cookery; the French preferred it to rose water—even their marchpane was flavored with orange or lemon. The fruit acid serves as the curdling agent and we have the rose water as well. I think I might prefer one or the other.

The omitted words probably directed the cook to season the curds; it is possible that the ball of cheese was to be coated with sugar and rose water as well, but the sequence makes it uncertain.

---

135   TO MAKE FRESH CHEES WITH ALMONDS

Take new milke & coole it, & put runnet to it, & when tis come, crush ye whey out & break ye curd small. then beat some blanchd almonds very small & put to y^m some rosewater y^t they may not oyle, & soake some musk comfits in ye rose water,* put in sugar & [stir]† it al together. y^n put it in porrengers & let it settle. when you use it, put a pritty deale of cream wth sugar & rose water in a dish, & put in y^r allmond cheese in layes.

Finally, this is fresh cottage cheese mixed with pounded almonds, seasoned with rose water and *musk comfits* (S 196 and 197), and served with sugar and fresh heavy cream. But the quality of the milk and cream made all the difference.

Layes is an old word for layers; *porrengers* are individual bowls.

---

136   TO MAKE ALMOND CURDS

Take A pinte of cream, 6 youlks of eggs beaten, a handfull of blancht almonds beaten wth rosewater, a quarter of a pinte of new milke; mix all together, & set it on ye fire & stir it till it is turned, y^n take it of & when it hath stood a pritty while, hang it in a thin strayner. & season it wth what spice‡ and sugar you please.

* Written *wate*.
† Supplied.
‡ Written *spie*.

This is not so much almond curds as custard curds with pounded almonds, an important distinction. (For proper almond curds, see C 134; for curds, see C 130.)

---

137   TO MAKE A FRESH [CHEESE]

Take a quart of cream or new milke & put to it a nutmeg quartered, a little cinnamon, & mace, y^n set it to boyle a good space, till it taste well of ye spice. y^n take ye whites of 5 eggs & ye youlks of 2, beat them very well, & put to them a pinte of creame & a little salt to make it taste brackish a little. y^n take away ye spice from ye milke, & put ye egg in & stir it together, & let it boyle till it comes to curds. y^n take it of ye fire & swetten* it with sugar; y^n put ye curds into y^r cheespan & as ye whey runs out, fill it up with curds. & If you pleas, before it be cold, put in some rose water & let it stand till ye next day, y^n put it out of y^r pan & serve it up wth cream.

This is yet another of those rather tiresome custard curd dishes (see C 130). An interesting note is the recognition that a pinch of salt improves the taste of any dish involving egg, even sweet dishes.

A *cheespan* was a special pan with a perforated bottom.

---

138   TO MAKE A CREAM CHEESE

Take a quart of stroakings from ye Cow, & put to it a pinte of sweet cream, & as much new milke as will make it up a gallon; put to it a spoonful of rennit wth salt & let it stand till it comes; y^n whey ye curd with a scuming dish & tie it up close in a fine clean cloth, & hang it up y^t ye whey may run clean from it for 4 or 5 hours. y^n put it in a fate & lay a small weight on it. at ye first, chang ye cloth 3 or 4 times a day. when it is fit to be taken out, put it in a cloth & chang it twice a day. ye coat will pill w^{hn} it is ready to eat.

* First written *sweeten*, but corrected by the scribed to *swetten* with a heavy stroke. See C 74 and S 271.

This is an interesting and early recipe for what later came to be called "slip-coat cheese," a well-known type of English cheese that might be described as a matured cream cheese. *OED* gives no reading for the name *slip-coat* before the appearance in 1669 of *The Closet of the Eminently Learned Sir Kenelme Digbie Kt. Opened* (written about 1648), and the cheese was long associated with Digbie. The cheese and its name also appear in *A True Gentlewomans Delight*, 1653, attributed to the Countess of Kent. It is evident that the cheese was being made before acquiring its name, derived from its prime characteristic so aptly described in our recipe: "ye coat will pill w^{hn} it is ready to eat."

Stroakings are discussed in C 106; a *fate* is a vat; see *sciming dish* in C 107. The reader should be reminded that our highly processed milk poses problems in cheese making, and inexperienced persons who would like to follow the recipes for matured cheeses, in particular, should consult specialized sources on the subject.

---

139   TO MAKE AN EXCELLENT WINTER CHEESE

To a cheese of 2 gallons of new milke, take 10 quarts of stroakings & 2 quarts of cream. put to it 4 spoonfuls of rennit, set it together as hot as you cam from ye Cow; you must not stir it at all when it is come. when you have dreyned ye whey from it, put it in a press, but press it lightly, espetially at the first.

The instruction, "set it together as hot as you [came] from the cow," brought me back to the Cantal where, some years ago, we were brought to visit an old Auvergnat couple just as they were bringing down the milk. The milk was poured into the wooden *fate*, the temperature checked, and the rennet added, drop by measured drop. All this time scarcely a word; it was like being witness to a silent ritual. Only when the fateful moment was past did they pause for a moment to welcome their guests with the equally ritual and solemn shaking of hands all around; our friend was a local boy who had made good in Paris. Then our host went back to the cheese room to check the presses, tightening here, loosening there, until he was satisfied that all was well. Later we visited the cave, carved out of the hillside, where the cheeses were in various stages of maturation. He was one of the last artisanal cheese makers in that corner of Auvergne; he had nothing but disdain for the cheese made at the cooperatives, and he was right.

For *stroakings*, see C 106. Also see C 130 and 138.

140   [TO] MAKE CHEESE BALLS

Take a quart of ye best creame & set it to come wth a
little milde earning, y^n dreyne it well in a cloth from y^e
whey; after rub it well in a trey or boule with y^r hand
till it be very small. y^n take a little grated bread, & a
little flower, 2 eggs, & a spoonfull or 2 of ale yeast.
season it with a little salt, cinnamon, nutmegg, sugar,
& a little sack & creame to make it thin as for fritters.
y^n take a pound of butter & put halfe of it into a frying
pan to melt, & when y^r stuff is pritty well risen, drop it
into y^r butter, like fritter[s], with a spoone. when they
are enough, take them up & beat a little butter & sack
with a little sugar, & soe serve them up with a little
sugar scrap'd upon them. when y^r butter grows black,
poure it out & put ye other halfe in.

This is a delightful recipe for what I would call cream cheese fritters;
there should be no problem for anyone who is familiar with that
sort of cookery. There is a recipe for *excellent Fritters the French way,*
C 202, that may be of some help in proportions, in spite of certain
important differences. Finally, the critical point is the consistency
of the batter. *Earning* is discussed in C 107. I suggest ½ ounce of
fresh compressed yeast, or a bit more (C 95).

The use of butter for deep frying, while very fine, is prodigal and quite unnecessary. It is also difficult to handle and I am
surprised that the recipe did not specify clarified butter; perhaps
it was understood. Any fried food must be eaten immediately or
it loses its particular charm (see C 202).

141   TO MAKE FRENCH CURDS

Take 5 whites of eggs & 2 youlks & beat them
togeth[er] & mix a pinte of sweet cream with ye eggs;
streyn[e] them together & put them in a scillet, & put
in a little rosemary, a little nutmegg, & a graine of
muske put in a linnen cloth. & soe set it on ye fire, &
stir it for fear of burning. & when it begins to come,
put in juice of orringes or leamons, A spoonful or 2, &

a little rosewater. when it is come, take it of ye fire, &
put it in a clean cloth that ye whey may run from it.
then beat suga[r] well with a spoone in a dish, & then
serve it up wth youlks of eggs, rose water, & sugar. & If
you please, you may put in some white wine.

Yet another of those curiously unappealing custard curds (C 130).
The flavoring is interesting, however, and you might wish to adapt
it to a more usual custard recipe, one with better proportions of
yolk and white. Directions for cooking the little sauce may have
been inadvertently omitted. I am not certain what would have
been considered particularly French about this recipe.

---

142   TO MAKE CURDES

Take 3 pintes of milke & set it on ye fire, y^n* beat 3
eggs very well with cold milke, & when y^r milke
boyles, put some inty y^r eggs y^t it curdle not. then put
ye eggs into ye milke & set it on ye fire, & when it
riseth, put in about halfe a pinte of butter milke & stir it
all ye while, & when it riseth againe, take it of ye fire,
& put it in a clean cloth y^t ye whey may run from it. y^n
eat ye curds with sack, french wine, ale, or creame,
according to y^r likeing, & strow on A pritty quantety of
sugar.

Thanks to the tang of the buttermilk, these curds will have a little
more interest than some of the other custard curds (see C 130).
The directions concerning custard technique are perceptive. *French
wine* is a frustrating designation, but I have the impression that it
often referred to French white wines, as distinguished from Rhine
wines.

    Inty may well be a slip of the pen for *into*, but *OED* does
note that certain dialect forms of *to* were pronounced and written
ti, making *inty* entirely reasonable.

    * Written y^e.

143   TO MAKE EXCELLENT WAFERS THE
FRENCH WAY

Take a pinte of cream & heat it luke warme, & mix it in
a basin with 2 pound of flowre, to wch you must add
halfe a quarter of a pinte of youlks of eggs beaten. but
before you mix in ye eggs, you must put in A spoonful
of thick yeast, & too this, halfe a pound of fresh butter
melted, & a little salt. allsoe put in some nutmegg;
cinnamon, & mace beaten, & some naple bisket grated;
dissolve a little ambergreece in rosewater & put in. y^n
lay a spoonful on y^r tongues & bake y^m, but before,
you must let y^m stand 2 houres in ye chimney corner to
rise.

Wafer comes from Old Norman French *waufre* and French *gaufre*.
(The Normans had a way of substituting *w* for the French *g*; see
wallnuts, S 72.) Both words had the sense of honeycomb, and
confections bearing that name, including wafers and waffles, are
duly so patterned to this day. Wafers seem to have had sacerdotal
beginnings but by medieval times, waferers made and called them
in markets and squares. *Le Ménagier*, about 1393, gives several
recipes: one calls for adding flour, wine, and salt to beaten eggs
and placing dough in the amount of "a slice of cheese" between
the heated irons. One recipe calls for a filling of cheese. Harleian
MS. 279, about 1430, gives a recipe for *Waffres* that calls for flour
and egg whites beaten together, seasoned with sugar and ginger,
and laid on hot irons in a thin layer; a cheese filling is detailed.
Markham, in 1615, gives a recipe for *best Wafers:* "Take the finest
Wheate flower you can get and mixe it with Creame, the yelkes
of egges, Rose water, Sugar and Cinamon till it be a little thicker,
then Pan-cake batter; and then warming your wafer Irons on a
Char-cole fire annoint them first with sweet butter, and then lay
on your butter [batter] and presse it, and bake it white or browne
at your pleasure."

    In spite of the untypical presence of yeast, I believe this
to be a recipe for the paper thin, crisp wafers known since medieval
times. Finally, they are pancakes baked under pressure. For those
who would like to try the recipe, a pound of flour amounts to 3
cups, the amount of egg yolk is ¼ cup, and a spoonful of yeast is
½ ounce of fresh compressed yeast (C 95). *Tongues* are tongs, or

wafer irons. Italian and Scandinavian irons are available in fancy kitchenware shops.

Naples biscuits are frequently called for in Tudor and Stuart cookbooks but recipes for them are so rare that I wonder if they might not have been imported, much as we import *amaretti* today. (Pegge gives a list of provisions for the wedding of Mary Nevill in 1530: in among the ginger, saffron, dates, etc., we find a pound of *Bisketts*.) There is a recipe *Too Make Naple Bisketts* in the seventeenth-century cookery manuscript of the William Penn family, and one by Mary Randolph that is virtually identical but more clearly detailed for what we now call *lady fingers*. (Mrs. Randolph's 1824 recipe: 12 eggs beaten light, 1 pound [3 cups] flour, 1 pound [2 cups] sugar, and beat all together "till perfectly light," and baked in pans "with divisions; so that each cake, when done, will be four inches long, and one and a half wide.") However, in *A Queens Delighte*, 1655, there is a recipe *To make Naples Bisket*: "Take of the same stuff the Mackaroons are made of, and put to it an ounce of Pin apple [pine nuts] in a quarter of a pound of stuff, for that is all the difference between the Mackaroons and the Naples Biskets." (For *mackroons*, see S 184.)

---

144   TO MAKE CRACKNELLS

> Take a pound of flowre, & a quarter of a pound of
> carraway comfits, & 2 spoonfulls of yeast, & halfe a
> pound of butter, suga[r]* put in, & 2 spoonfulls of rose
> water. make it up into little cak[es] or like mackroones,
> lay y^m on papers & bake y^m in a soft oven.

Because of a scribal error, the amount of sugar is unknown; also, eggs were customarily included in cracknel recipes. Cotgrave, in 1611, in defining *Craquelin* says: "A Cracknell; made of the yolks of eggs, water, and flower; and fashioned like a hollow trendle [a cupped disk or ring] . . ." OED says that it is a light crisp biscuit of a curved or hollow shape. Dawson in 1586 gives a recipe for *Cracknelles* that calls for them to be thrown into boiling water and when they rise, they are to be lifted out, wiped, and baked. This technique is one that survived from medieval—not to say classical—times and cracknels are thus related to *jumbals* (S 191), from which they differ primarily in shape, and *échaudés*. (Indeed, *Larousse Gastronomique* says that *craquelins* may be made by the *échaudé* procedure.)

* The scribe must have jumped a line in transcribing.

A recipe for "Cracknells: My Lady Howes Receipt" is found in the manuscript kept by Rebecca Price, started in 1681: it calls for a pound of flour (about 3 cups), a pound of sugar (2 cups), 4 egg yolks and 1 white, 2 ounces of butter, 2 spoonfuls of rose water, and about 2 spoonfuls of coriander seeds. "You must rowle your cakes as thine as paper; and prick them very much," before baking them in "an oven that is not too hott." Hannah Glasse, in 1796, gives a recipe that calls for half as much flour but only 3 egg yolks and no whites. Instead of yeast, Mrs. Glasse would have you beat the paste with a rolling pin "till it be light," roll it out thin, cut it in rounds with a glass, prick them, and bake on buttered plates in "a pretty quick oven."

For *comfits*, see S 146; for the characterizing shape, roll them over a broom handle while still warm.

---

145   [HOW] TO MAKE PUFF PASTE

Take a quartern of ye purest fine flowre & 3 pound of butter; work ye butter in little rouls & lay them in cold spring water all night. y^n mix ye flowr[e] up with egge whites & a little cold water; make it as stiff as you can. worke it well & roule it out in a square, pritty thin sheete; take a trencher & clame it & spread it pritty thin on ye paste, strow a little flowre on it, y^n clap it together, & roule it out again. y^n spread on some more butter as before, & soe continue till all ye butter be work'd up, & strow flowre every time you roule out y^r paste. If you have egg whites enough to wet y^r flower, you need not use any water at all.

Puff pastry was slow in coming to England—at least in cookbooks—and this is surprising because the English were inordinately fond of pastry, were fine practitioners, and were not diffident about borrowing good ideas. Puff paste is thought to have been perfected by the brilliant pastry chefs to the court of the dukes of Tuscany, perhaps in the fifteenth century. From there it made its way to the royal court of France, most likely brought by Marie de Medici. One of the difficulties in tracing the history of this pastry arises from its Italian name, *pasta sfoglia*, and its French name, *pâte feuilletée*, both of which simply signify leafed pastry. Now, thousand-leafed pastries have been made all around the Mediterranean since antiquity; the Greeks and Arabs, in particular, did splendid pastry work using thin *phyllo* or *warka* leaves and oil. What was different about this new pastry was the technique of interleafing tissue paper thin sheets of paste with cold butter in such a way as to cause the pastry to rise in a spectacular manner when baked.

Hugh Plat has been credited with naming the "new" pastry *puffe-paste* in *Delightes for Ladies*, 1605, but Florio, in 1598, had already translated *Fogliata* as *puft paste*, showing that the name had been in use for some years. Nor was Plat's recipe the first. Dawson gives a recipe for *butter paste* in *The Good Huswifes. Jewell, Part I*, 1586, that has been underestimated. It calls for a paste made with flour, eggs, and rose water or water, which is then beaten, rolled out, dotted with pieces of cold butter, layered, and rolled out again; this is to be repeated five or six times. In short, puff paste. In view of the lag of cookbooks behind usage at the time, it had been being made for some time.

This spectacular pastry must have been served at the court of Elizabeth early in her reign. I wonder if puff paste techniques were not the secret prerogative of royal pastry cooks everywhere. This would help to explain the slowness with which it was taken up among the nobility in France as well as England (who normally lost no opportunity for ostentatious display) and the otherwise inexplicable acceptance of the pop historians' tales of its "invention" by Feuillet, an eighteenth-century chef, and Claude Lorrain, the painter, who was born in 1600.

A *quartern* is a quarter of a *stone*, or of a *peck* (but see S 154). The stone varied in weight from 8 to 24 pounds, depending on the nature of what was being weighed; flour called for a stone of 14 pounds. (In principle, it was an eighth of a hundred-weight, which in 1474, was still counted as 100 pounds (*OED*), but the English now find 112 pounds, confounding language and logic.) In my experience with other recipes (C 92, for instance), I do not believe that millers' weights obtained in home kitchens. If the stone weighed 12½ pounds, we would have 3 pounds, 2 ounces of flour for 3 pounds of butter, constituting classic proportions for fine puff paste down through the centuries in both England and France. This amounts to 3 cups or so of American flour for each pound of butter, for which amount nearly a cup of liquid (egg whites and any additional water) is indicated. American all-purpose flour is unnecessarily recalcitrant in making pastry, although the practice of vigorous protracted working or beating of the paste, as directed by Dawson, does overcome this difficulty. Still, English flours were soft, and I propose unbleached pastry flour. Flours vary, so be prepared to adjust as necessary.

Egg whites were long the favored moisture in puff paste; they improve the ductile qualities. I add a little salt. Use best sweet butter; it should be washed, worked to force out all moisture, chilled, then beaten with a rolling pin to make it pliable, but still cool.

Clame, or cleam, is an old English word meaning to bedaub. A trencher is a large flat plate, apparently square in this instance (C 98). You are to butter the trencher and clap it down on the sheet of paste—the butter should stick to it. Dust it lightly, fold it over, roll it out, and start all over again, as in classic puff pastry technique. It if amuses you, try it; but simply dotting the paste with bits of butter works as well, I should think. This latter technique is what Eliza Acton uses for English Puff-Paste in Modern Cookery, 1855, in counterdistinction to the French method. (I assume knowledge of basic technique; novices should consult a standard cookbook.)

Fine bakers place the cut-out pastry on dampened baking sheets. Bake it in a thoroughly preheated oven at 425°F, lowering it to 400° at once. It is done when ethereal and thoroughly dry; allow it to stand in the turned-off oven a few minutes if there is any doubt.

---

146   TO MAKE PUFF PASTE A QUICKER WAY

Take A quartern of fine flowre & put in 10 eggs & keep out 4 of ye youlks, & put milke in to make up y^r paste. beat or roule it into a thin sheet, & lay pieces of butter all over; strow on a little flowre & fould it up & roule it out againe. do this 4 times. A pound of butter will serve.

The proportion of butter seems meager, even for what we might call mock puff paste; I suggest half the classic proportion, or ½ pound butter to 3 cups of flour. The technique is essentially the same as that presented in C 145.

---

147   TO MAKE PUFF KIDS

Take a quartern of flowre & beat in 10 eggs, & keepe out 4 of ye youlks. break in 2 pound of butter, & crush these together lightly. put in cold milk & work it up

158

very gently. use this paste for pasties, dishes, or patty
pans.

I could find no reference concerning the use of *kid* in pastry. However, both *OED* and Halliwell give pannier or basket as popular
meanings of the word. Since the original meaning of *coffin* was
also basket (C 49), there seems little doubt about the derivation.
A *puff* is any light small pastry, often triangular in shape. *Patty pan*
originally referred to minature pastries, a meaning long obsolete;
the term now refers only to the little pans. *Patty* comes from French
pâté (*OED*). But see *pasty pan* in C 199.

This is an excellent and useful recipe. For measures, see
C 146. The use of pastry flour is more critical here than for classic
puff pastry. The butter is to be "crumbed" in the flour with the
fingers, and requires a light hand, as the recipe says. Do not use
the machine.

---

148   TO MAKE PASTE [ROYALL]

Take halfe a pecke of fine flower, & put to it 6 eggs & 4
pound of butter. break it in small pieces & put in a gill
of rose water, a pinte of sack, & some sugar, & what
you need of spring water. knead all these together, but
take heed it be not made too stiff, nor worke it over
much, nor heat it with y^r hand. with this, you may
make a pastie or a made dish.

Let us say that half a peck of flour amounted to 16 cups (see C 92
and S 146). Flours vary, so be prepared to adjust. A *gill* is ¼ pint,
making it 4 ounces (½ U.S. cup) at the time. I believe that little
water is necessary.

This is another excellent recipe with a fine Tudor fragrance. The technique is identical to that of C 147 and the note on
flour applies here as well. Do heed the scribe's perceptive advice.

---

149   TO SEASON APPLES FOR PUFFS

Take apples, pare & cut them in quarters, & core them,
& put them into colde water; & set them on ye fire in a
pan; let them boyle softly, then put them into a dish, &
set them over a chafing dish of coles, & put to it some
slyced nutmegg, slyced ginger, & 2 or three cloves,

some slyced orring & leamon pill candied, or citron pill,
& a little red wine. & sweeten them with sugar, & then
put them into your puffs.

Most apples nowadays disintegrate when boiled, no matter how
softly. (Choose a hard flavorful apple, under no circumstances the
Delicious.) They keep their shape better if very gently simmered
in a syrup, so start them right off in the sweetened wine mixture.
It must be carried out in a large shallow pan as the apple quarters
must lie one deep. If you cover it, you may place the pan in a low
oven, cutting down on watching. A suitable pastry is that in C 147.

---

150   TO MAKE AN APPLE TANSIE

Take 12 eggs & leave out halfe of ye whites, & beat y^m
well. y^n put in 4 or 5 spoonfulls of rosewater, a
nutmegg, & halfe a pinte of cream. y^n take as many
apples, beeing pared & skread, as will thicken it; & fry
it in fresh butter. you must fry some apples in round
slyces & set y^m by till y^r tansie be turned once. y^n you
must lay those pieces on ye side you fryde last. serve it
up hot, & strow on some sugar & rose water, & shread
in a leamon with y^r apples & put in some sugar.

Tansies are discussed in C 101. The only characterizing note here
is that of being fried in a large flat omelet that was to be turned.
The apples are shredded and added to the egg mixture. At the risk
of compromising historical accuracy, I suggest using an omelet pan
of a size in which you can handle the turning without mishaps.
Cook the tansies gently in good butter, and serve them immediately with sauteed apple rounds and coarse sugar strewn over as
the recipe directs. The taste of apples cooked in butter is heavenly;
even rather ordinary apples can attain surprising heights done this
way.
    Skread may be a nod, but the *k* is clear. Old English *scrédian*
early turned to various forms of *shred*, but Halliwell says that *screed*
survived in Northumberland dialect very late.

151   [TO MAKE LI]TTLE FRYING CAKES
       WITH Y^e PULPE OF APPLES OR ANY
       OTHER FRUITE

Take about ye biggness of 2 or 3 eggs of ye pap of
rosted apples, or ye pap of any other fruite, & put it
into a dish with 2 or 3 spoonfulls of flowre, 6 eggs, & a
little salt. mix these well together, y^n melt some fresh
butter in a frying pan, & fry it in little cakes; & when
they are enough, dish them up with rosewater & sugar,
& stick them with candyed leamon pill.

This is a rather attractive little recipe for what amounts to pancakes
with baked apple pulp added. It is amusing to note that the writer
used the elegant word *pulpe* in the title but in the recipe itself, the
homier word *pap* prevailed. Do use baked apples; they have far
more intense flavor than applesauce. I hestitate to suggest the
amount of flour, but perhaps ¼ cup or so; the batter should not
much thicker than a *crêpe* batter, I believe.

152   TO KEEPE QUINCES ALL THE YEARE,
       FOR TARTS

First make a strong broth of y^r worser sort of quinces &
parings boyled together in water. y^n boyle ye quinces
you mean to keepe all ye year in y^t broth. you must
boyle them but a little, y^n take them up & put them in
a good bigg gally pot, & poure on them ye broth &
pareings they were boyled in.

Using a strong decoction made of the less presentable quinces and
the parings of the better ones, is an interesting way of preserving
quinces (S 7). They keep wondrously well; if any mold should
appear, it need only be skimmed off before bringing fruit and liquid
to a good boil and being stored in a clean container. (*OED* and
other sources describe *galley pots* as being small, but clearly they
were of larger sizes. See S 22.)

153 TO KEEPE CHERRIES Y^t YOU MAY HAUE
THEM FOR TARTS AT CHRISTMASS
WITHOUT PRESERUEING

Take ye fayrest cherries you can get, fresh from ye trees;
wth out bruising, wipe them one by one with a linnen
cloth, y^n put y^m into a barrell of hay & lay them in
ranks, first laying hay on the bottom, & then cherries,
& y^n hay & then cheryes, & then hay agayne. stop
them close up y^t noe Ayre get to y^m. then set them
under a fether bead where one lyeth continually, for y^e
warmer they are kept, ye better it is. see they be neere
noe fire. thus doeing, you may have cherries any time
of ye yeare. you allsoe may keep cherries or other fruits
in glasses, close stopt from ayre.

This recipe gives us a glimpse into a past where it was considered
reasonable to have in the household a feather bed "where one
lyeth continually." The charming language indicates that it is very
old. Fruits packed thus in hay do keep a remarkably long time (but
not all year) due to the exclusion of light and the cradling effect
of the hay. The French still use hay or straw in this way, although
more often in a cellar; and fancy fruits are packed in black tissue
paper and cotton wadding.

154 TO KEEPE PEASE [ALL Y^e] YEARE

Take Pease, shell & boyle them. then strow a good
deale of salt amongst them; dry them well, then melt as
much butter as will cover them in an earthen pot &
strow on good store of salt on them, & soe you may
keep them all ye yeare.

To keep produce during the long winter months was one of the
major concerns of a household. Many of the recipes in this section
will seem archaic, and perhaps they are, but some of our most
interesting foods are the result of such storage methods: ham,
stockfish, sausages, corned and smoked meats, *confit d'oie*, cheese,
dried and sugared fruits, dried legumes, pickled and fermented
foods, and even wine, for that matter. There is indeed a real change
in both taste and texture, often for the better. In any event, we

developed such a liking for many of those preserved foods that we continue to prepare them and buy them, although there is no longer the same compelling need to do so.

Every good housewife had her own tried and true method for preserving peas until Christmas, for instance, and it is surprising how varied these methods could be. In *American Cookery*, 1796, for instance, Amelia Simmons tells us simply to wipe the peas, salt them, and close them up in bottles with suet. The lady of our manuscript chooses a more elaborate way, using melted butter. Many of these traditions using salt and fat produce flavors and textures far more interesting than the pseudo-fresh quality of frozen food. To be sure, if fresh peas are well-frozen and well-stored, they can stage a convincing resurrection, so that we are not liable to try any of these old methods. For that matter, where would we get the fresh peas?

---

155   TO KEEPE TURNUPS ALL Y^e YEAR FROM SEEDING

First cut of ye tops of y^r turneps after michaellmass, & make A trench in ye ground y^t is light & sandy; though it be out of dores, it matters not; & lay in y^r turneps, about 3 quarters of a yerd deepe your trench must be; & ever as you have occasion to use them, digg them up, & cover up ye place againe; this way will keepe them from seeding.

Michaelmas is September 29. It is interesting to consider the phrase, "though it be out of dores, it matters not." Evidently they had pretty extensive root cellars to consider digging a 27-inch deep trench indoors. It is worth noting that we kept carrots in this fashion in my childhood.

Turnips (*Brassica rapa*) have been cultivated for food from ancient times. *Tur* quite likely comes from French *tour*, denoting its round shape, and *nip* comes from Latin *nāpus* by way of Old English *naep* (*OED*). I like the form *turnups*.

---

156   TO MAKE STRAWBERRIES COME EARLY OR GRAPES

Water y^r [strawberries]* once in three dayes with water wherein hath been steeped sheeps dunge or pigeons

* Written *staberries*. I find no trace of forms without initial *str*.

163

dunge, & they bear much earlier. plants waterd with
warme water will come up sooner & better then with
cold water or shours. as for grapes, If ye branches of A
vine be drawn into a roome wherein A fire is kept, [it]*
will make the fruit to ripen a moneth sooner then
without dores. allsoe, any other berries, fruits, or flowrs
wattered with ye afore sayd dung steeped in water, will
make y^m come early.

If it were not for this bit of gardening lore, it would have been all
too easy to conclude that strawberries were not cultivated by the
household from which our manuscript came. Indeed, it has been
written that the strawberry was not cultivated in Europe before
the seventeenth century. But the word appears in a glossary of
about 1000 as "*Fraga,* streaberige" (*OED*), and they are mentioned
in literature and cookbooks down through the centuries. Gerard,
in 1597, maintains that the wild strawberry is barren and concerns
himself only with cultivated varieties, of which there are several.
It is true that those strawberries (*fragolini*) were smaller and of a
more intense favor than modern varieties, which are of American
ancestry, but they were cultivated. Gerard says: "The ripe Strawberries quench thirst [and] coole heate of the stomack and inflammation of the liver."

As for the grapes, the archaic charm of the phrase, "will
make the fruit to ripen a moneth sooner then without dores,"
brings to mind damp and chilly English autumns; the grapes must
have been grateful for a fire. Many a year, the grapes must never
have ripened and Anne Wilson reports an entry: "No wine but
verjuice made, 9 Edw. IV [1470]." (See *uerges,* C 4.)

---

157   [TO] PLANT SPARRAGUS

To plant the rootes or seeds of sparragus, make ye bed
as bigg as you will have it, & digg ye earth out a yerd
deepe, & fill up ye place againe with old cows dung or
horse dung well rotted. & If you have any rams† horns,
or shaveings of horne, it will make it much ye better.
when you have filled up ye place with dung, tread it
downe well, y^n take earth y^t hath layn under a wood

* Supplied.
† May be a blotched *rems.*

pille, or any other fat earth, y^t hath neyther stones nor
sticks in it, & cover ye dongue a quarter of a yerd
deepe, ther rake it into long beds, & plant y^r seeds
halfe a quarter of a yerd asunder every way, & put
them full halfe a quarter of a yerd deepe into y^e
ground; and put three or foure seeds into a hole. If you
plant roots, set them a quarter of a yerd asunder, & a
quarter of A yerd deepe. it is good planting & sowing
towards ye latter end of march. you must not cut your
sparragrass that comes of seeds till the thirde* year, &
that which comes of rootes not till the second year.
towards winter, you must cut it all downe to the
ground & cover it with longe horse litter but in the
spring, you must take of the litter and rake ye beads
clean againe.

Sparragus, Asparagus officinalis, comes from Greek *asparagos.* It was
known in England at least by 1000; common names were *sperage*
and *sperach. OED* reports that in the sixteenth century, the influence of the herbalists brought the Latin name into general use but
in an aphetic form, *sparagus;* this was quickly corrupted and by
1650, by the same popular etymology that we have seen at work
so often, it had firmly become *sparrow-grass.* This took such a hold
that although botanists continued to write asparagus, the people
called it sparrow-grass through the eighteenth century. In the
American produce trade, it is still referred to as *grass.*

The practice of burying *rems horns,* or *rams' horns,* with
asparagus for better yield was solidly in popular tradition. John
Bossewell, in *Workes of Armorie,* 1572, writes: "Some reporte . . .
that of Rammes hornes buried, or hidde in the grounde, is broughte
forthe an Herbe, called Asparagus, in Englishe, Sperage" (*OED*).

---

158   TO HAUE EARLY COWCUMBERS

After y^r cowcumbers have done bearing, cut of the
stalks close by ye earth, & cast a pritty quantety of good
earth upon y^m, & they will bear very early ye next year.

* The word was ineptly reworked, having been corrected from *therde,*
or vice versa.

Cucumbers (*Cucumis sativus*) have been cultivated since ancient times. Wyclif mentions them in 1382, calling them *cucumeris*. *Cow-cumber* was current from 1500 to 1800 (*OED*) and would appear to be another example of popular insistence on giving some meaning to a word which was not understood, as happened with sparrow-grass and gooseberries, for example. Gerard claims that the "cucumber . . . taken in meats, is good for the stomacke and other parts troubled with heat . . . The seed . . . being stamped and outwardly applied in stead of a clenser, it maketh the skin smooth and faire." As part of a three-week diet, he promised that cucumbers would cure all manner of skin problems such as "shining fierie noses as red as red Roses," Cucumbers were considered to be cold and moist in the second degree.

---

159   TO PICKLE KIDNEY BE[ANS]

Take ye beans & string them very well, y^n lay lay them in ellegar with a good handfull of salt & let them ly covered over in ellegar or vinnegar 10 dayes. then take them out & set a kettle of water on ye fire & make it scallding hot. then put in ye beans, covering them close with a clean course cloth & when you disserne them to be greene & tender, take them up & when they be cold, pickle them in white wine vinnegar & salt, laying a clean course ragg upon ye pickle wch will keepe them from caneing. & wash ye cloth when it canes, with salt & water; & If you carefully take up ye cloth all ye canes will stick to it.

All of the many pickle recipes in our manuscript represent ancient ways of preserving vegetables against time of need as well as brightening winter menus, which could get monotonous after a few months. Some of the nutrients must have leached into the pickle, but I believe that the liquor was used in cooking as a seasoning.

Some of the recipes are perfectly straightforward pickle recipes; others present products and procedures that may be unfamiliar to us. I must emphasize that *modern table salt simply will not do for pickling*. Some use kosher salt, but I prefer sea salt, and it has been favored down through the ages (C 196). Straight pickling brine requires about 6 tablespoons of salt per quart of water; if vinegar is added, far less is required, perhaps 1 or 2 tablespoons will do. Pickles should be examined occasionally for mold; if there is as yet no sign of softening, all can be set right by draining off the liquor, boiling it for 10 or 15 minutes, rinsing off the pickles, and adding new cold vinegar to the cooled liquor in sufficient quantity to cover the pickles once again.

It would not be amiss to examine *Observations on Pickling*, given by Mary Randolph in *The Virginia Housewife*, 1824; "The vessels for keeping pickles should be made of stone ware, straight from the bottom to the top, with stone covers to them; when the mouth is very wide, the pickles may be taken out without breaking them. The motive for keeping all pickles in plain vinegar, previous to putting them in the prepared pot, is to draw off the water with which they are saturated, that they may not weaken the vinegar of the pot. *Pickles keep much better when the vinegar is not boiled.*" [Emphasis added.]

It should be noted that not all writers insisted on the final strong pickle. Markham, for instance, in 1615 thought that it was sufficient to boil the vegetables, drain them, spread them upon a table, strew them with "good store of salt," and when thoroughly cold, put them away in "close earthen pots [in a pickle of] water, salt and a little vinegar." He gives no proportions. Some pickled vegetables were put up raw, then boiled and cooled before serving as salads. Markham treated pickling of vegetables under *preserving of Sallets*, dealing with "Coucumbers, Samphire, Purslan, Broome, and such like." "Violets, Primrose, Cowslops, Gilly floweres of all kinds, Broome-flowers, and for the most part any wholsome flower whatsoever," were to be preserved in vinegar only. Preserved salads were most often served with olive oil and pepper. Lettuce was added as soon as it came up in the spring; it must have been a welcome change.

I should note that under no circumstances should copper, aluminum, or iron pots be used for pickling as they all give a disagreeable color.

These are green beans, *Phaseolus*. In 1548, William Turner calls *Phaseole* the name of *Kydney beane*, or "arber beanes, because they serve to cover an arber for the tyme of Summer." These beans were from the New World. But the *Faba vulgaris* had been known by the early Greeks and Chinese, as proved by their records and archeological evidence, and they appear to have been widespread in the Old World. *Bean* goes back to Old English *bean*, and so appears in Saxon manuscripts by A.D. 1000. There are recipes for *Benes* in *The Forme of Cury*, about 1390.

Ellegar is malt vinegar, for which a recipe is given in C 160. *Alegar* is the correct name, meaning sour ale, following *vinegar* from French *vin aigre,* sour wine, giving an interesting amalgam of Teutonic and French elements.

Cane is the "mothery" scum that forms during the fermentation process; the word is obsolete except in dialect, according to *OED.*

---

160   TO MAKE ELDER VINEGAR & ROSE VINEGAR

Take 5 or 6 gallons of strong wort & boyle it wth out hops, & worke it as you doe ale, onely tun it hot, & before it hath work'd too long in ye fate. when it hath done working, lay a tyle on ye top of ye runlet, & let it stand in ye sun in June or July; y^n put into it 3 or 4 handfulls of elder blossoms, first dividing halfe of it into another vessell, into which put 3 or 4 handfulls of dammask rose leaves. heat ye flowers & put in with y^m to each vessell a pottle of white wine vinegar.

This is actually *alegar* (C 159) to be flavored with flowers for two very popular vinegars. Most of us are unlikely to make our own malt vinegar, but we can make our own flavored vinegars simply by infusing elder blossoms or rose petals in excellent vinegar.

Wort is a strong infusion of malted grain to be fermented in the making of ale or beer (It is the same word as *wort,* the old word for leafy vegetables and herbs). To *tun* is to put fermented liquids into a tun, or large cask, and a *runlet* is a cask (S 254).

---

161   [TO P]ICKLE COWCUMBERS

Take white wine vinegar & clarret, of each a like quantety, & some salt. boyle them together & make good brine of it; scum it clean & when it is cold put in y^r cowcumbers. keepe it close & look to it once a weeke y^t they lack not brine.

If *clarret* refers to red wine from Bordeaux, it would give the pickles a bizarre color; if it refers to white wine, which seems reasonable in context (see C 180), the recipe may be quite old, since modern English practice in nomenclature dates from around 1600, or a little earlier (see C 22). I cannot believe that women who were so fastidious and so knowledgeable about the colors of their quince preserves would countenance the unappetizing color that even a light red wine would give (see C 58). For more on pickling, see C 159.

---

162   TO PICKLE COWCUMBERS GREENE

Take ye smallest cowcumbers & wipe them clean with a cours cloth, then make a pickle with salt & water as will bear an egge. boyle it & when it is cold, put in y^r cowcumbers & let them ly 24 hours. then make another pickle, but not soe salt as ye former; boyle it & when it is cold, put it into an earthen pot & put ye cowcumbers to it;* & in every one of them stick at ye end a clove, to every 2 quarts of y^t pickle & 3 pintes of white wine vinegar,* & add salt to y^r taste. put some dill both at ye top & bottom & lay a cloth on them, as is expresd in ye beans. keep y^r pot close covered y^t noe ayre come in. to a 100 of cowcumbers, put 2 penny worth of allom, which makes them crump & green.

This is a perfectly straightforward pickle recipe. Alum does indeed make pickles *crump* but too much also makes them bitter. Eliza Leslie, in *Directions for Cookery*, 1837, specifies a piece of alum "the size of a shelled almond" (¼ teaspoon) for every 100 gherkins (pickling cucumbers, most likely intended here). Fannie Farmer, in 1896, calls for a tablespoon and more to a gallon of water, which is far too much, in my opinion. It is now considered old-fashioned, but is still in use. The omitted line may have called for other spices.

   Crump is a Northumbrian dialect word that means brittle or crusty, according to Halliwell; crunchy, in other words. The bean recipe is C 159.

---

163   TO PICKLE LETTIS STALKS

Take lettis stalks about midsumer, stripping of ye leaves; then boyle them & when they are pritty tender, pill of all ye rinde, & when they are cold, make A pickle of salt and water, but not very salt, and A few cloves, and then boyle it. and when y^r pickle is cold,

---

* The punctuation between the two asterisks is original. Several words have been omitted.

169

put in the lettis stalks, and put in dill as before, both at ye top and bottom, & lay on A cloth as is mentioned in ye kidney beans.

I have never tried lettuce stalks, but they may well be delicious. Divested of their tough rind, broccoli stalks turn out to have an attractive crisp texture and more interest than the florets.

There is no vinegar in this pickle, and the directions indicate that the brine need not be up to strength, perhaps 3 or 4 tablespoons per quart of water. That seems a bit risky, particularly since the vegetable is boiled. I would suppose that the stalks are sliced before serving. For more on pickles, see C 159.

---

164   TO PICKLE PURSLAND

Gather ye pursland when it [is]* stalkie & will snap w^hn you break it. boyle it in a kettle of fayre water without any salt, & when it is tender, make a pickle of salt & water, as you doe for other pickles. & when it is cold, make it pritty sharp with vinegar & cover it as you did ye other prementioned pickles.

Purslane (*Portulaca oleracea*) is a refreshing and delicious green that has inexplicably fallen from favor. It has a fleshy succulent leaf of a taste and texture quite unlike any other green I know. It was eaten both raw and cooked. (Also, see S 239.) For more on pickling, see C 159.

The name comes from Old French *porcelaine* and Italian *porcellana*, which seem to have arisen from Pliny's use of *porcillaca* rather than the more customary *portulaca*, so that there is no real relationship with the identical forms for porcelain in both French and Italian (*OED*). (This is rank speculation, but if it was not a nod, could Pliny have been saying it was fodder for pigs, as *pigweed*?)

---

165   TO PICKLE BROOMEBUDS

Take your broome buds before they turne yellow at ye end, & fann all ye broome from them in a pewter dish. when they are pickt clean, make a pickle as before,

* Supplied.

with water & salt, & when it is cold make it sharpe
with vinegar, & then put in y^r buds.

Broom (*Sarothamnus* or *Cytisus scoparius*) is a shrub bearing large
handsome yellow flowers (*OED*). Gerard says that broom buds are
pickled and used much as capers, and that they "stirre up an
appetite to meate [food]."

---

166   TO PICKLE CLOUE GILLYFLOWRS
COWSLIPS BURRAGE & MARRIGOULDS

Clip your flowers clean from ye whites & cover them
over in white wine vinegar, sweetned with sugar, &
shake ye glasses you put them in often, & when you
discover your pickle to shrink, add more to it.

For *cloue gillyflowrs*, see S 67; cowslips, S 137; borage, S 88; and
marrigoulds, S 83 and C 32. All of these flowers were considered
to have medicinal qualities; in addition, they brought a sour-sweet
fillip to the winter table when pickled. As the recipe counsels,
pickled food must be kept covered with pickle. See C 167; for more
on pickling, see C 159.

---

167   ANOTHER WAY FOR KEEPING OF
FLOWERS WHICH IS ACCOUNTED
BETTER THEN ye FIRST

Take y^r flowers & shread them a little, then take about
halfe a pound of lofe sugar, & beat it small & put it in a
pewter dish with a little water. boyle it up to a candy
height, then put in y^r flowers, giveing of them a stir
together. when they are cold, put your flowers into
papers made into baggs, & hang them neer ye fire.
when you use them, put to y^m a little vinnegar, & soe
serve them up.

See recipe C 166. *Candy height* is discussed in S 5. Not all pewter
is able to withstand direct heat, so don't be tempted.

168   [TO P]ICKLE UP BARBARIES

Take bulles & boyle them in faire water with a little
salt, then put y^r barbaries into a glass. strayne out y^e
liquor, & then put some sugar in it, then poure y^e
liquor into ye barbaries boyling hot. you may take some
of ye same liquor, & more salt then aforesayd, & poure
it in cold to your barbaries without sugar. this will
keepe them A year y^t they shall have theyr perfect
culler.

Bulles is a variant of bullace (*Prunus insititia*), a wild plum; the
form was current only in the sixteenth century, according to *OED*.
(For barberries, see S 63.) The principle of using the plum juice as
the pickling vehicle is repeated in C 169 using the less presentable
barberries instead, and you could do the same here. Barberries are
called for as a garnish all through the manuscript; any of the three
recipes given here may be used. Barberries have been naturalized
in America but are not easily available. I don't know why cranberries could not be substituted, being hard, red, and acid as barberries are. I hestitate to suggest proportions as I have not tried
the recipes. However, if you are accustomed to pickling, you may
enjoy experimenting on your own; the sweet version presents
fewer problems.

169   TO PICKLE BARBARIES ANOTHER WAY

Take ye worst of y^r barbaries; stamp & streyne them,
then take halfe a pinte of vinegar & as much water & a
pritty quantety of salt, & boyle them altogether till it
will bear an egg. then put y^r barbarys into a glass or
earthen pot, & cover them with ye pickle, & it will last
to garnish with A year.

The reader is referred to C 159 for general pickling directions and
to C 168 for barberries. For a pint of vinegar and water and say a
pint of strained berries, I suggest starting with 2 tablespoons, or
less, of sea salt.

170   TO PICKLE GREEN SPARRAGUS

Let y^r water be boyling, then bundle up y^r sparragus as
it is when it is sould; hould ye roots in your hands &
dip in ye green ends whilst ye water boyls. soe doe by
every bundle you have, & when y^r sparragus is cold,
put it into A glass with verges & salt, & it will keep all
ye year.

The blanching procedure suggested here seems unnecessarily
risky; use a fry basket instead. If you have no verjuice, excellent
vinegar will do. For pickling directions, see C 159.

171   TO MAKE A SALLET OF ELDER BUDS

Take ye elder buds when first they begin to flower,
before any white appears. gather y^m in bunches, & put
them in a glass or pot, & put to them as strong brine
[as]* will bear an egg. when you use it, boyle it tender
& put vinega[r] & sugar to it. make ye brine of vinegar,
& boyle it not at all.

Pickled elder buds were a popular element of boiled salads; they
were highly regarded for their medicinal qualities (S 254) and they
must have brought a sprightly touch to winter meals. They seem
never to have become popular in American cookery, but recipes
for pickled radish seed pods appear in a number of early American
cookbooks.
        Brine "as will bear an egg" is normally calculated at 6
tablespoons or so of salt for a quart, but when based on vinegar,
which is not to be boiled, 4 tablespoons is more than ample. (For
pickling, see C 159.)

172   TO PICKLE ASHEN KEYS [WOOD
        SORRELL] OR SUCH LIKE THINGS

Put them in water that is boyling &·salt, & let them
boyle till they be tender. y^n put them in a sive that y^e
water may dreyne from them. when they are cold, put

* Written *is*.

173

them in a glass or pot with verges, strow* salt on the top of ye pot, & keepe them close stopt from Ayre.

Keys are a dry fruit with a thin membranous wing, usually growing in bunches. *Ash* (*Fraxinus*) appeared as *aesc* in a glossary of the year 700 (*OED*). Turner, in his *Herball*, 1562, claims that, "the juice . . . of ashen leaves is good to make fatte men leane." Wood sorrel is discussed in S 241. For more on pickling, see C 159.

---

173   TO BARRELL OYSTERS Y^t THEY SHALL LAST 6 MONETHS

First open ye oysters & take ye liquor from them, & put to it a reasonable proportion of ye best white wine vinegar, a little salt, & some pepper; & soe barrell up ye oysters in small casks, covering them all in ye pickle. If you doubt ye long keeping them, you may boyle ye oysters in ye pickle, with some mace & cloves, & then barrell them up as before & they will keepe a long time.

I believe that most of the oysters called for in the recipes of our manuscript are pickled; here is the recipe.

The first version is the ancient fermented preparation of raw pickled oysters. The second, although cooked, shows elements of *ketchup*, from Amoy *kĕtsiap* (or Malay *kĕchap*), meaning brine of pickled shellfish. (Forms of the word appeared in English by 1690, according to *OED*.) The essential difference is that in our recipes the oysters are the important element while in ketchup they are discarded as having given their all. By the early eighteenth century, E. Smith was giving recipes for *English Katchup* and adding it to various dishes with little ado (*The Compleat Housewife*, 1742). And Rebecca Price, who kept a manuscript cookbook from 1681 to 1740, also has a recipe, *To make catchup to be put into any sawces.* These were mushroom ketchups, but pickled oysters appeared under the name of ketchup, as well. Until after mid-nineteenth century, ketchup in American cookbooks was assumed to be of either mushrooms or oysters unless otherwise specified. The earliest published recipe for *tomato catsup* that I know is given by Mary Randolph in *The Virginia Housewife*, 1824, who also gives one for *tomato soy* (a name that became popular), that differs little from the other.

* The *o* is not clear, but *strow* is invariable.

Coming back to our manuscript, I believe that the pickle was added to the cooking along with the oysters and most likely was used instead of vinegar in recipes as the oysters were used. So that the English *katchup* tradition antedated the name.

---

174   TO PICKLE COCKLES AND MUSTLES

Wash y^r cockles clean wth water & salt, y^n put y^m in A kettle wth halfe a pinte of water in ye bottom, on a slow fire. shake y^m often, & w^hn they open, pick y^m out of ye shells. y^n streyene ye liquor, & take to a quart, halfe a pint of white wine & wine vinegar. y^n take large mace, grose pepper, & cloves, a pritty deale of salt, boyle y^m together, & when ye pickle is coold, put it to ye cockles. let y^m stand till ye next day, y^n pot y^m for y^r use. when you dish y^m, put fresh vinegar to y^m, with some of ye pickle.

Cockles properly refers to *Cardium* but it was formerly applied indifferently to many bivalves. The name came unchanged from Old French *cokille*, shell, into Middle English. *Mustles* are, of course, mussels, most likely *Mytilus*. The name comes from Latin *musculus*, meaning mouse but also *muscle*. Mussels used to be eaten a great deal in England, especially by the poor. Langland, in *Piers Plowman*, 1393, says: "A ferthying . . . worth of muscles Were a fest for such folke." But they were not looked down upon by royalty, as evidenced by recipes for *muskels* in *The Forme of Cury*, about 1390. Mrs. Beeton, in 1861, does not so much as list them. *Grose pepper* is cracked pepper.

---

175   [TO] KEEP STURGION

First poure out all the pickle it comes in from beyond sea, then fill it with good white wine till it be covered. & allways as it sowreth, renew it, but put not out ye old. If it be sour before you have it, this will renew it: put in a pinte of basterd white wine, boyled with ye scin of 2 or 3 leamons, till they be soft, y^n take them of & put to them an ounce of bruised pepper & 4 rases of

ginger slyced, & when it is stone cold, put it to y^e
foresayd liquor.

Since common sturgeon abounds in all north European waters,
the fact that this sturgeon came in pickle "from beyond sea" means
that it must have been Beluga sturgeon from the Caspian or Black
Sea; clearly, it came in an unpalatably strong brine and badly
needed refreshing. The charming language lets us in on the routine
concerns of yesteryear: "always as it sowreth renew it" with good
white wine. If it really turns, more drastic measures are called for
and *basterd* is indicated. Bastard seems originally to have been a
sweet Spanish wine on the order of muscatel, but the term came
to refer to any sweetened or honeyed wine, usually with the implication of suspicion of adulteration. It appears as early as 1399
(*OED*) and was still current around 1600; Shakespeare speaks of
"a Pint of Bastard in the Halfe Moone" (*Henry IV*, Part II). A *rase*
is a hand of ginger (S 92).

---

176   TO SOUCE A PIKE

Take water & boyle it with 2 or 3 handfulls of salt, and
binde A bundle of rosemary, burrage, parsley, &
margerum, of each a handfull, and put into the water.
then cut ye pike into what fashion you please, and put
it in & let it boyle untill you think it be enough, then
take it of & let it stand in ye same liquor till it be cold.
then boyle a quart of white wine & another of white
wine vinegar together by themselves A quarter of an
houre, then set it of the fire till it be cold, and then lay
the pike in an earthen pan, and poure on it ye wine
and vinnegar and some of the broth they were boyled
in.

While this souse was not intended to keep the fish indefinitely,
it will keep quite some time, particularly under refrigeration; it
improves on a few days maturing. The fish should be a little undercooked.

---

[177]

On turning a page, the copyist inadvertently omitted
number 177. It is possible that the recipe was omitted as well; in
any event, the index agrees.

178   TO PICKLE MACKRELL [FLOUNDERS]
       SOLES OR SPRATS

Scrape & wash them, then cut of theyr heads and draw
them; notch* them on each side & cut of theyr tayles,
then wipe them with a clean cloth & lay them one by
one, & sprinkle them with a little salt. stir them
alltogether, & soe let them ly 3 hours. then take a cloth
& dry them, & flowre them & fry them in sallet oyle
somewhat yallow. fry such a quantety as a gallon of
liquor will cover. y^n take for ye pickle, a quart of
vinegar, a quart of verges, & a quart of water, put it
into a pipkin wth a few bay leaves, 2 or 3 sprigs of
rosemary, two leamons, pepper beaten gross, with
cinnamon, mace, cloves, & nutmegg. boyle these
together for A quarter of an houre or whilst ye fish is
frying; but ye pepper you must not boyle with ye other
spice, but put it in raw. when your fish is fryde, take
them out with a scummer & lay them on plats that y^e
oyle may run from them. then lay them in an earthen
pot one by one & cover the pot with a dish to keep it
warme, but first, after they are all in, poure in y^e
seething pickle, and If they want Liquor to cover them,
after all ye liquor is in and cold, then fill it up with
unboyled vinegar. for sprats, they neede not be drawn,
but other fish must.

We have here a classic *escabeche* recipe, presented in great detail.
This may be an early English recipe for the dish, although there
had long been recipes for soused fish. The characterizing note of
escabeche is the frying in olive oil before pickling; the light corning
and dusting with flour are also typical. *Escabeche*, a Spanish word,
comes from the Arab *iskebêŷ*, which referred to pickling with
vinegar (Corominas).

The Anglicized term *caveach* became current in mid-eighteenth century. In the 1750 edition of *The Compleat Housewife*, E.
Smith gives a recipe for *Mackrell to caveach*; the same recipe appears

* Written *nocth* because of a wrongly inserted *t*.

in the first American edition, 1742, as *To pickle Mackrel*, following classic escabeche procedure. Elizabeth Raffald gives a number of recipes to caveach fish in *The Experienced English Housekeeper*, 1789, and Hannah Glasse gives a recipe under the title of: "The Jews way of preserving Salmon, and all Sorts of Fish" in *The Art of Cookery*, 1796. This last is particularly interesting; it is possible that the Jews, fleeing the Inquisition, brought with them the recipe from Spain. However the recipe came to England, it was a useful one in the days before refrigeration; indeed, fish is far superior when kept this way for several days than as a cadaver on ice.

Caveach came to the colonies and a recipe appears in Mary Randolph's *The Virginia Housewife*, 1824, for example. The dish unaccountably fell from favor towards the end of the century and disappeared from American cookbooks. Recently, as *escabeche*, it has been "discovered" and presented with much fanfare as an item in gourmet exotica.

You will most likely be substituting excellent vinegar for the verjuice (C 4). Since it is no longer primarily a question of preservation, you may make the pickle as light as you please. A few days maturing improves the dish. The note about not boiling the cracked pepper is a remarkably perceptive one; I have always felt that boiling pepper draws out a slightly acrid taste and vitiates the aroma.

---

179   [TO] SOUCE AN EELE

Take a great eele & cut it down ye back & take out the back bone, then wash it clean & take nutmegg & ginger, or cloves & mace, or what spice you please, & season ye inside thereof. then roule it up in cloaths as you would doe collers of brawne, then boyle it in white wine vinegar, white wine, & water, of each a like quantety. put in some salt in ye boyling & any sort of sweet hearbs, quartered nutmegg, whole mace, & ginger. when ye Eele [is]* tender, take it up & throw it into cold water, & when ye pickle is cold, then take of ye cloaths & put ye fish into ye pickle & it will keepe 10 days.

* Written *it*.

Great eele is likely conger eel, but the recipe could equally apply to a large ordinary eel. Collaring is rolling a strip of meat (most often flank as in C 34) into a neat coiled bundle for easier handling. Eel takes especially well to souse. See C 4 and 176 on *souse*.

---

180   TO SOUCE AN EELE ANOTHER WAY

Take halfe a pinte of white wine vinegar, as much white wine, & as much water as both of them. put to it some salt, a branch or 2 of rosemary. when these ingredients have boyled a good while, put in ye Eele, & let it boyle till it is enough, then coole ye souce drink, & after let ye Eele ly in it 3 dayes. & when you serve it up, put to it vinegar and oyle, and strow upon it parsley and ounion and margerum shread small together, and allsoe you must strow on it the juice of an orringe and pepper grosely beaten. serve it up in A handsome dish, which you must garnish with salt, green hearbs, & ounions minced with ye orreng pill.

This is an interesting recipe and quite old, I believe. The garnish is remarkable: salt (quite likely coarse), herbs, and onions minced with orange peel in addition to the strewing of vinegar and oil, parsley, onion, marjoram, the juice of a bitter orange, and cracked pepper. All of that requires some skill to harmonize, but I find it appealing. If you have only sweet orange, I suggest spiking the juice with a little juice of both lemon and grapefruit to suggest the Seville orange.

---

181   TO STEW AN EELE

Cut ye Eele in pieces ye length of y^r finger & put them in a pipkin or dish with halfe water & halfe vinegar, as much as will cover it. then put in a littl salt, some nutmegg, mace, & currans. soe let it stew untill it is browne & tender. put in allsoe a bunch of sweet hearbs. then take it up with ye broth, & put in A little melted butter & the youlks of 2 eggs well beaten, & soe serve it up.

The eel is to be gently stewed until the liquor has reduced to an aromatic, almost medieval sauce. I find the egg yolk liaison unnecessary here but if you use it, observe all the customary precautions (C2).

---

182   TO STEW OYSTERS

Take y^r oysters, open & pick them very clean, & save ye liquor that comes out of them when you open them. set on a scyllet of water, & make it boyle, but not to fast, then put in y^r oysters & make them boyle up. y^n take them up & put them in a cullender, & poure cold water on them. this is to plump & keepe them from shrinking. then set* them a stewing in theyre owne liquor & as much water as will cover them, or put to ye liquor white wine in ye roome of water. put in a whole ounion, some whole pepper, & whole mace. when you serve them up, put in butter & garnish y^r dish with beaten & sifted ginger.

It is to be remarked that this cook understood very well the technique of blanching; it is the cold plunge *after* the scalding that fixes color and texture. Where I would quarrel with the recipe is in the subsequent stewing, which does odd things to the texture of an oyster; perhaps English oysters are different. I would suggest, instead, reducing the oyster liquor and white wine with the seasonings without the oysters, quickly heating them in the broth just before serving. The butter is stirred into the sauce off the fire, and will give a beautifully light liaison. The dusting of ginger is interesting.

Roome is used in an archaic manner; Shakespeare so used it, and it is difficult to find any but poetic use of the word in this sense.

---

183   TO BUTTER SHRIMPS

First take y^r shrimps after they are boyled, & set them on coles till they are verry hot, then melt y^r butter, & beat it very thick & poure it on them when they are served up, & strow on some pepper.

* I excised a repeated *then set.*

This typically seventeenth-century sauce is what later came to be known as *drawn butter*. While it does not have the elan, the elegance of French *beurre blanc* (warm whipped butter with shallots and a memory of vinegar), it does provide a lovely richness, uncomplicated by anything but a good whiff of freshly ground pepper, just what shrimps need. Above all, there is no flour to sludge things up, nor have I found flour in a butter sauce in English cookbooks until the eighteenth century, when recipes started appearing for *melted butter*, which is essentially butter, flour, and water brought not quite to the boil, stirring constantly; *drawn butter* is nothing but melted butter whipped into the consistency of a sauce, often with a little water added.

---

184   [TO STEW] LAMPERIES

Scin them, then take out ye string, & gut them, but [do]* not wash them; then season them with pepper, salt, & nutmegg. then cut them in pieces ye length of your fingar & put them in A pipkin with as much water as will cover them. put in an ounion. when they are stewed tender, then take out ye ounion, & put them into A dish with butter & verges & ye youlks of 2 eggs beaten up thick together, & soe serve them up.

The lamprey, while superficially resembling an eel, is quite different biologically and gastronomically; its flesh is finer than that of an eel. The name comes from Old French *lampreie* and so appeared in Middle English (*OED*). The English evidently regaled themselves on lamprey at one time; there are two recipes for it in the royal *Forme of Cury*, about 1390, and the cookery manuscripts of the fifteenth century usually have several recipes. After Tudor times, however, the popularity of lamprey gradually declined. Americans never took to lamprey. The first cookbook published in America, *The Compleat Housewife* by E. Smith, 1742, does not give a recipe and American writers followed suit; neither Amelia Simmons nor Mary Randolph mention lamprey, for example. For that matter, it virtually disappeared from English cookbooks, as well. Lamprey is still regarded as a great delicacy in France; we are the poorer for ignoring this valuable resource of our waters.

There is more character and interest to this recipe than might at first be apparent; the interplay between the finesse of the lamprey, the richness of the egg yolk and butter liaison, and

* Supplied.

the tartness of the verjuice, should be subtle and delightful. As always, you may substitute lemon juice or good vinegar for the verjuice.

---

185   TO STEW A CARPE

First wash your carpe very clean, then take faire water, vinegar, & verges, & salt, as much or more then will halfe cover it. Let it stew between 2 dishes & put into it slyced ginger, & slyced nutmegg, a little rosemary, & some parsley chopt, an anchovie or 2, a good piece of butter, & some pickld cockles with their liquor, If you have them. turne ye carpe 2 or 3 times in ye stewing, & before it be to soft, serve it up with sops & sippets layd about ye dish. If you doe not sale,* it is ye better.

In the last sentence, the writer counsels us not to salt the dish, and she is right; the brine of the cockles (C 174) and the anchovies make it prudent to wait on the salt. She is also right about not over-cooking the carp; it tends to turn mushy. The covering of the carp when setting it to stew refers to the liquid, of course. *Between 2 dishes* and *sippets* are discussed in C 1. You will surely want a few turns of the pepper mill for this dish.

---

186   TO MAKE A BROTH FOR A CARPE
        OR PIKE

Take old yeast & a pinte of white wine, & a handfull of currans, some whole blades of mace, some sweet hearb[s], & a good piece of fresh butter, & some sugar. boyle all these together with a little water & a little salt. then drayne y^r fish well from ye water after it boyled in water & salt. and lay it in a dish & poure ye broth all over it.

Recipes calling for yeast in cooking, as differentiated from baking, are quite rare, and old, stemming from a time, I believe, when broth and brewing (and bread, for that matter) were far more closely associated, even linguistically. Two recipes in Dawson's

---

* The *e* is pristine. It is either a scribal error or an unrecorded form deriving from French *saler*, to salt.

The Good Huswifes Jewell, 1586, call for straining "sweete breade" (clearly broth) into a pot and boiling meat therein. A recipe for *Ballok broth* with eels in Harlieian MS. 4016, about 1450, has you add *faire berme* (yeasty ale, see S 151) to the broth, as well as wine. Dawson calls for adding a little strained yeast to the broth of *Lambes Head and purtenance.* A. W. gives in *A Booke of Cookrye,* 1591, a recipe *To seeth A dory or a Mullet* that starts: "Make your broth light with yest, somewhat savery with salt, and put therein a little Rosemary." The fish is seethed "very softly" in that broth and then served with another broth with "new Yest," currants, mace, verjuice, dates, gooseberries, sweet butter, and sugar in it. Despite the extended list of fruits, the recipes are structurally identical. I cannot recall ever having encountered such recipes in seventeenth-century sources.

The use of ale continued in English cookery, frequently half and half with wine (see C 22). If you are sufficiently curious, you may make up some *ale yeast* (C 92, but I do not propose dry yeast for this purpose); I suggest plain imported ale, perhaps a cupful.

It must be understood that the fish is poached separately in plain salted water, then served with the separately made yeasty broth. To reduce the danger of burst skin, a large fish is placed in tepid liquid, which is then gradually brought to an imperceptible simmer.

---

187   TO BOYLE A CARPE [IN ITS] BLOOD

Take a well growne carpe y^t is a melter, beeing alive; wipe it clean, then cut of his head & let him bleed in a dish wherein is a little white wine. when he hath blead as much as he will, cut of his tayle at his belly, & cut ye midle piece in 2 & chine the back bone. then take out his intrayls, from whence take his gall & ye end of his great gut. he beeing thus alltogether in his blood, sprinkle him with A handfull of salt & boyle him in A pinte & halfe of white wine, wherein put a branch of rosemary, A nutmegg grated, & as much ginger cut in bigg pieces, & an ounion cut in ye midst. then put in ye head a little before ye rest, for it requireth longest time of boyling. then put all ye rest in & cover it with a small dish to keepe it in. because of ye little liquor, as it boyles over, coole it twice by putting in a little white wine, & when it is boyled, keepe it warme while you take out all ye liquor. If it be to much, boyle some of it away y^t it be not too thin, & in ye boyling, put in 10 oysters. & upon a chafing dish of coles dissolve 5 or 6 anchovis in a little white wine & butter, y^n put it to ye other liquor as it simpers, & as much more butter as will amount to halfe a pound. when you think it is boyled enough, poure it on ye carpe in a large dish, & garnish it with leamon & barbaries.

This is an ancient recipe, well worked out and well presented. The combination of ginger, nutmeg, anchovies, oysters (most likely pickled, C 173), white wine, the blood of the creature, and the garnish of fresh lemon and barberries, is fascinating; we can fairly judge the effect because quite precise measures are given. While the nutmeg is typically a bit much, the seasonings are not so garish as might be supposed; for one thing, the carp was undoubtedly very large, perhaps 10 pounds, and carp has little flavor. Also, the lavish use of butter would soften the effect of the spices. The cook shows awareness of culinary technique and her use of the word *simper* to describe the correct simmering temperature is telling, related of course to the French *sourire*. "As it boyles over" here means as it threatens to boil away; the addition of more liquid only as necessary is nice braising technique and her reminder that it may be necessary to reduce the liquor to a sauce is another sign of a good cook.

A *milter* is a male fish, especially in spawning season. *Melt* was the current form from the fourteenth to sixteenth centuries, but did continue in dialect (*OED*). To *chine* a beast is to split it down the back bone.

188   [TO] ROSTE A CARPE

First salt ye carpe, then wash it very well & take out all ye insyde of it, & fill ye belly of ye carpe whith grated bread & a pritty deale of time, minced very small, & put in halfe a pound of fresh butter. then sow up ye belly & ty it to ye spit with 2 laths for an houre, in which time it will be roasted. then rip up ye belly & let out ye sauce & mingle it with some more melted butter

& some minced leamon & capers; mingle all well
together, then pour it on y^r carpe being laide in a
handsome dish, & garnish it with ginger.

This recipe may be used with any fish of suitable size for roasting;
if you lack the equipment, you may simply bake it. (Cover it loosely
with cooking parchment and baste with butter.) I think it would
be more attractive to present the roasted fish entire, garnished
with grated or sliced green ginger, diced fresh lemon, and capers,
as suggested, and carry out the saucing at table.

---

189   TO BOYLE A TROUT

Cut ye trout in pieces, then boyle it in white wine, sum
butter, as much salt as will season it, & a little
rosemary, some grated or slyced ginger. when it [is]*
boyled, serve it up with sops layd in ye bottom & sydes
of ye dish.

This is a delightful recipe, one that can be used for virtually any
fish. It should be understood, however, that the fish is to be
poached, not boiled. For small fish or fillets, the liquid should be
boiling when the fish is placed therein; the heat must then immediately be turned down. The liquid must never actually be allowed to bubble. For fillets, I take the pan off the heat; the retained
heat is sufficient. For *sippets*, see C 1.

---

190   TO BOYLE ROACHES

Take ye fattest roaches you can get, boyle them in faire
water & a good deale of salt, a little vinegar, 2 or 3
leaves of mace, some time, & parsley. & when they
boyled enough, lay them in a dish, & mince ye hearbs
and put in ye liquor with a good piece of fresh butter,
beat thick in, & poure it on ye roches & serve them up
with sippets.

The roach is a freshwater fish of the carp family, common in the
rivers of northern Europe; this recipe may be applied to any small
fish. Because the poaching liquid is to serve as the base for the
sauce, I suggest using as little water as is feasible; keep this in

* Supplied.

mind when adding seasoning. (See C 189 on poaching.) When you have carefully lifted out the poached fish, reduce the liquid if indicated, and off the fire whisk enough butter into your sauce to give the desired richness and consistency. I see no reason why you cannot chop the herbs before adding them. The vinegar must be of excellent quality.

---

191   TO DRESS A PIKE CA[RPE JUB] OR LARGE TROUT

Take your fish & scale it & slyt it alive, & wash it with white wine; & take ye blood & as much white wine as will cover it, putting a fish plate in ye bottom of y^r kettle, & some large mace, with a bund[le] of sweet hearbs, as time, parsley, & sweet margerum. let it have one boyle, then take it of and let it stew leasurely. then bone 6 anchovis & put into ye liquor. then take 3 quarters of a pound of good fresh butter, & let them stew together a little while. then take up y^r fish & shake up your butter, anchovis, & broth alltogether & poure it on y^r fish & dish it up with sippets.

This is an excellent recipe and an old one. "Slyt it aliue" is undoubtedly meant to be taken literally; people were far more finicky about the freshness of their fish those days. (*Slyt* is a fifteenth-century form, according to *OED*.) The sauce is well constructed; one might wish to cut down on the anchovy a bit, but the large amount of butter can balance a fair amount of seasoning. Whisking in the butter at the end, as in the previous recipe, results in a fluffier and finer emulsion.

    Jub, which comes from the scribe's index, is *chub*, a river fish of the carp family (*OED*). I could not find *jub* in any source, but *j* occasionally replaced the initial *ch* in popular forms of other words.

---

192   TO DRESS WHITEINGS CODLINGS OR HADOCKS

First set on y^r water with pritty store of salt, 2 or 3 nutmeggs quartered, & 2 or 3 ounions cut in halves. when it boyls, put in ye fish on a plate, & against it is

enough, make y^r sauce wth gravy, white wine, & an
anchovie or 2 melted in it. put in store of butter beaten
up thick, barbaries, capers minced, pickld cockls or
oysters, a little juice of orring or leamon. y^n take up y^r
fish & lay ye tayls up together as high as can [be]* in a
large dish & poure all ye sauce on y^m & garnish y^r dish
[with]* leamon slyced, barbaries, & capers.

I suppose this to be a recipe for poached fish, although the placing
of the fish on a platter could conceivably indicate some sort of
steaming arrangement. Perhaps the plate was perforated so that
it functioned like a fish kettle. (See C 189.)

"Against it is enough" can best be translated as mean-
while, with the clear implication that the sauce is to be ready when
the fish is. The *gravy*, as always, is the running juices of roast
meat (C 3); the idea of mixing meat and fish did not trouble epicures
of the day, although I believe that it was becoming old-fashioned
by the end of the seventeenth century except for certain classic
combinations such as chicken and oysters, and the use of anchovy.
The orange is the bitter Seville orange; use lemon juice or add a
bit to the orange. Note the elaborate presentation, one more common—and more effective—with crisply fried fish.

---

193   [TO] MAKE A CARPE OR TENCH PIE

Take a carpe [or]† tench & take out ye guts, lungs, & all
that is within it. Lance or clip it on ye back & lard it
with bacon. rub your fish well with salt & spice, & put
some within ye belly. and on ye bottome of y^r pie Lay
in butter cut in slyces, & season ye milts & rones well,
& lay them on ye sydes of y^r fish, but first perboyle
them & your fish. & put in good store of parsley, time,
& other sweet hearbs shread small, oysters, capers,
hearty‡ choak bottoms cut in pieces, mushrumps, A
pritty quantety of muton gravie. when y^r pie is halfe
baked, take it out of the oven & put in some butter &
vinegar with ye milke of sweet almonds, 2 or 3

* Supplied.
† Written *ot*.
‡ There is an apparent attempt to cross out the *e*.

spoonfulls, wch you must reduce to milke with a little
vinegar, & 2 or 3 ounces of almonds will serve. you
must allsoe add harde youlks of eggs cut in quarters, &
set y^r pie in the oven againe.

This is a fascinating recipe. The presence of almond milk (see page
9) and the *olio* character of the pie (C 53 and 199) mark it as being
very old. The drawing of the almond milk with vinegar is especially
interesting.

Perboyle means to cook through, but in view of the long
baking, I do not understand the necessity of this operation in
regard to the milt and roe. The artichoke bottoms, however, should
be cooked until just tender; the mushrooms, which would have
been the wild field variety, most likely, should be parboiled or
sauteed. For *gravy*, see C 3.

The fish would have been baked in a suitably sized oblong
coffin; see C 48 for the proper pastry.

The dish, with its faintly medieval aura, would make a
most unusual and handsome main dish.

Rone is a Northumberland form of *roe*, according to Halliwell; the more usual old form was *rown*. The tench is a lake fish
allied to the carp (*OED*).

---

194   TO FRY SOLES

First gut y^r soles, & wash or wipe them clean. then fry
y^m well in hoggs larde, & when they are fryed, take out
ye longe bones y^t goes downe ye back. & you must
have some anchovis made ready before, with theyr
scinns taken of & theyr back bones pulled out, y^n put
them in ye places from whence ye back bones were
taken of ye soles, and squeese into y^m some juice of
leamon or orringe. soe stew them over ye coles in a
dish, wth white wine, verges, water, & butter.

The idea of masking the excision of the back bone of a sole with
strips of anchovy makes an amusing presentation. I personally
find its presence a jarring note with the delicately flavored sole,
but the dish is typical of seventeenth-century cooking. Taking out
the backbone of a fried fish neatly is quite a trick, all the more
taking into account the curiously inconsistent texture of the various
flat fish that masquerade as sole in America. The idea of frying or

broiling a fish before simmering strikes us as a bit much, but it was, again, quite typical. For the orange, see C 192; for *verges*, see C 4. I suggest whisking the butter into the sauce just before serving.

---

195   TO DRESS A DISH OF [MUSHRUMPS]

Take y^r firme mushrumps & pill ye scin from them & scrape away all ye red y^t grows on ye insyde of them, & pill y^r stalks likewise. If you finde them firm, throw them as you doe them into faire water & let them ly 3 or 4 hours, then take them out of ye water & set them on ye fire in a pan. theyr owne liquor will stew them. put in an ounion cut in halves and often shake them. as ye water rises, cast it still away till you finde them allmoste dry. then take out the ounion & put in a little sweet cream y^t is thick & shread in some time & parsley, & put in some grated nutmeg, & a little grose pepper, & a little salt, & soe let them boyle, shakeing them well together. & put in A piece of fresh butter, giveing them another shake, & soe dish them up.~~~

this is aproved, but ye yolks of too Eggs with a [?] cold Creem and thick y^m wth it.*

Soaking mushrooms in water shocks me, but wild mushrooms cooked in heavy cream is one of the loveliest dishes imaginable. Judging by the directions, these were field mushrooms, but morels or *cèpes* would be just as delightful. *But do know your mushrooms.* Cultivated mushrooms are scarcely worth the trouble. A memory of scent and flavor can be suggested by the mixing in of a few imported French or Italian dried mushrooms; little can be done with the unappealing texture of the mass produced ones.

The reading of the later addendum is difficult but the meaning is clear: 2 egg yolks are mixed with some cream to affect a liaison; I find it a needless complication.

* Added in a different hand.

189

195

To dress A dish of

Take ye firme mushrumps & pill ye scin from them
& scrape away all ye red yt grows on ye insyde of
them & pill yr stalks likewise, If you finde them firme
throw them as you doe them into faire water & Let them
ly 3 or 4 hours, then take them out of ye water &
set them on ye fire in a pan, theyr owne liquor
will stew them, put in an ounion cut in halues and
often shake them, as ye water rises cast it still away
till you finde them allmoste dry, then take out the
ounion & put in a little sweet cream yt is thick &
thread in some time & parsley, & put in some grated
nutmegg & a little grose pepper & a little salt &
soe let them boyle, shaking them well together &
put in A piece of fresh butter giueing them another
shake & soe dish them up
this is aproued but ye yolks of two eggs with a little vinegar beaten and thick is ye best

To keepe neats tongues
& dry them

196

First, take water yt will make meate look red
& make a strong pickle yt will bear an egg halfe of
bay salt & halfe of white, y{n} put in ye tongues & let ym ly
a weeke, y{n} make a new pickle in wch they must ly another
weeke y{n} hang them in a chimney 2 yerds from ye ground keep
ym with a continuall fire for a moneth of saw dust If you can
get it or else wood, but then you must hang them 3 or
4 yerds high, after hange them on ye outside of a chim
ney, where a continuall fire is kept & you may spend ym presen

196 TO KEEPE NEATS TONGUES
& DRY THEM

First take water y^t will make meate look red & make a
strong pickle y^t will bear an egg, halfe of bay salt &
halfe of white. y^n put in y^r tongues & let y^m ly a
weeke. y^n make a new pickle in wch they must ly
another weeke. y^n hang them in a chimney 2 yerds
from ye ground. kee[pe] y^m with a continuall fire, for a
moneth, of saw dust If you can get it or else wood, but
then you must hang them 3 or 4 yerds high. after
hange them on ye outside of a chimney, where a
continuall fire is kept, & you may spend y^m presen[t]ly.

Water that will make meat look red is that to which saltpeter has
been added, as explained in C 197. (Red sanders would have been
specified; see C 58.) The importance of the quality of salt used in
pickling can hardly be exaggerated, and when getting through the
winter depended on the proper preservation of food, women perforce became well aware of differences in quality. Hannah Glasse,
in *The Art of Cookery*, 1796, says firmly: "The salt which is commonly
used hardens and spoils all the meat . . . Yorkshire is famous for
hams; and the reason is this: their salt is much finer than ours in
London; it is a large clear salt, and gives the meat a fine flavour.
I used to have it from Malden in Essex, and that salt will make
any ham as fine as you can desire . . ." Elizabeth David, in *Spices,
Salt and Aromatics in the English Kitchen*, spends several pages discussing this most important article, notes that that bay salt, obtained by spontaneous evaporation of sea water, is to be preferred
for curing meats. Both English and French sources often give recipes with bay salt and common salt in proportions similar to those
given in our recipe; one must suppose that it was to eke out the
more expensive bay salt. Modern table salt is so full of driers and
other adulterants that it is unfit for pickling, or for human consumption. ". . . and if the salt be once unsavery what can be salted
ther with? it is thenceforthe goode for nothynge but to be cast oute
at the dores and that men treade it under fete" (Matthew 5, translated by William Tyndale, the Martyr, 1526.) Sea salt is increasingly
available. The instruction in our recipe to make a new pickle is
wasteful and it was more customary to simply boil up the brine,
as in C 197, if deemed necessary.
Neats tongue is beef tongue.

197   [TO M]AKE TONGUES RED

Take pumpe water & make brine as salt [as] will bear an egg. boyle it & let it stand all night, y^n put in y^r tongues, rubing ye rootes well with salt before you put them into ye brine, & stop into ye roots a little salt peeter. Let them ly in ye brine a week, then take ye same brine & boyle it againe, letting it stand all night, & ye next morning put in y^r tongues & let them ly a weeke longer, & then hang them up. If you would have them look black on ye outsyde when you boyle them for eating, you must not pull of ye outward scinn at all, but rub them on ye out syde with lampblack or charcole beaten small and sifted. you must rub it on whilst they are hot, & when they are cold, rub it of well with a corse cloth. soe likewise, you may make a gammon of bacon black like a west fallia ham.

Whatever the harmful effects of saltpeter in nutrition may be, its use in the pickling of meats is ancient and widespread. Without it, corned meats are a sodden grey; with it, the color ranges from rosy pink to deep mahogany. It assists in preservation as well, but in so doing it toughens the meat fibers unless this effect is counteracted with the addition of sugar. Salt also toughens meat, but to a lesser extent. The balancing of the various elements of the curing process to assure preservation and yet achieve palatable results is an art. In this connection, it is interesting to examine a typical recipe for pickling tongue given by the estimable Eliza Acton in 1865: 2 gallons of water, 3 pounds of bay salt (5 pounds of common salt may be substituted, "but the meat will not be so finely flavoured"), 2 pounds of coarse sugar (most likely unrefined), 2 ounces of saltpeter, and 2 ounces of black pepper. It would thus seem that less saltpeter was used at the time of our manuscript than came to be used later, since no mention whatsoever is made of sugar in our recipes.

The toughening effect of saltpeter can be unacceptably unpalatable with beef but with pork, it is another matter. In Audot's *La Charcuterie*, 1818, we find that the critical difference between various French hams and *Jambon à l'anglaise* is the presence of sugar in the curing brine of the English-style ham, resulting in the mild tender meat typical of English and American sugar-cured hams in contrast to the celebrated *Jambon de Bayonne*, for instance, which must be sliced paper thin to be fully appreciated.

So if you do use saltpeter, you must use barely enough to impart an appetizing blush of color, no more than a teaspoonful for a good-sized tongue, perhaps less. (This is a tiny fraction of commercial formulas.) Westphalia hams are normally rubbed with wood ashes.

This recipe is considerably later than that presented in C 196 (which see for discussion of salt).

---

198   TO STEW A DUCK THE FRENCH WAY

First halfe roste her, then cut her up & lay her in a stew pan with a little salt & water, as much as will cover it. y^n take a little time, margerum, winter savory, rosemary, & an ounion cut in 2, a blade of mace & 2 or 3 pepper cornes, some clarret wine, & soe let y^m stew together. when it is allmoste enough, put in a piece of butter, y^n beat ye youlks of 6 eggs wth a spoonfull or 2 of clarret, & mix wth beaten butter. y^n put y^m to y^r ducks after they have had a walme or 2 together. y^n shake y^m & serve them up.

The construction of this dish is faulty. The technique of green roasting, dismembering, and simmering of the bird, much as for a *salmis* (which requires wine), is promising. But the French customarily approach the challenge of the duck's fattiness with more flair. Here, the problem is compounded with a rich liaison of 6 egg yolks and beaten butter; the claret cannot balance all that richness.

If you would try the recipe, I suggest the following procedure for the sauce, which is not made until the duck is tender. Simmer about a pint of good white wine with the suggested aromatics, with the addition of a little salt and 1 or 2 spoonfuls of best white wine vinegar, if you wish. When reduced by about a third, strain it and thicken it with 4 or 5 egg yolks beaten with a little white wine, observing the customary precautions (C 2). Then, off the fire, whisk in as much sweet butter as you deem necessary to harmonize the sauce (which depends on the wine), perhaps about 3 or 4 tablespoons, and verify the seasonings. Pour it over the duck, which has been very well drained, give a shake, and so serve it up.

The claret here must surely be white; red would combine with the egg yolks to give a curious color. See *clarret*, C 22.

---

199   TO MAKE THE PASTY [ROYALL]

Take A large legg of muton & stryp of ye scin, and take out ye bones & ye sinnews. then beat ye flesh to mortifie it, then cose it to be well chopt, & as you do chop it, season it with salt & spices very well. y^n take a good handfull of suet shread small, & put to y^r shread meat* a reasonable proportion of chestnuts halfe rosted, & about halfe a pound of bacon cut in small pieces. moreover, you must line ye bottom & sydes of y^r pastie pan with slyces of fat bacon, & when you have put all these in to y^r pasty pan, cover all with slyces of fat bacon. & If you pleas, put in a good quantety of sweet hearbs shread small with ye shread meat. this pasty will take a good time of bakeing, & y^r oven must be close shut. you must take it out of ye oven, or to ye ovens mouth, 2 or 3 times to supply it with strong broth and gravie, wch you must put in with a tunnell, above halfe a pinte at a time, beeing well heated. when this pasty is halfe enough, draw it & cut it up, or take of ye lid whole, & put therein sweet breads, lamb stones, & kidneys slyced, & neats tongues slyced, youlks of eggs rosted & cut in quarters, mushrumps, a clove of garlick, & some white wine vinegar. & put some marrow amongst y^r sweetbreads with some harty choak bottoms, grapes, & sparragus. If these be not in season, take capers & other pickles, & oysters, cockles, & sassages. & put in a pound of fresh butter cut into slyces. after all this, put your pasty againe into ye oven, & let it be well baked. y^n take out ye clove of garlic, & fasten ye lid, & serve it up.

This is another of those great *olio* pies with strong medieval traces.

* I excised a confusing &.

A Booke of Cookery

There is one puzzling omission, and that is sugar; it may be inadvertent. Much of the discussion of the pie of *seuerall things*, C 53, applies here as well. (Also, see C 193.) If the last copyist had been more conscientious, this recipe would have appeared alongside.

Properly speaking, a pasty is not baked in a mold, but I wonder if *pasty pan* might not be another word for *coffin*; if not, it refers to a dish or mold. *Pasty, coffin,* and suitable pastries are discussed in C 48. It should be noted that *paste royall,* C 148, is suggested for pasties, but the coffin would be more suitable.

In cooking, *mortify* is an obsolete term for hanging meat to develop flavor and tenderness, but in this case, it means to tenderize by bruising, reverting to its literal meaning.

This is the only mention of chestnuts in the manuscript. What is stranger is that the first citing in *OED* is 1519. The chestnut is thought to have been introduced to northern Europe "within historical times" from Asia Minor. It is difficult to believe that it was unknown in England before the sixteenth century, but it is true that it is not mentioned in early cookbooks. Gerard, in 1597, devotes a good deal of space to it, including what the ancients had to say about it, and in the 1636 edition, Johnson discusses the American chestnut, claiming that it was sweeter and generally superior to the European varieties.

I am not sure that the bacon called for was smoked. In any event, modern bacon is so full of preservatives and has such a stinging taste that I would prefer to use thin sheets of pork flare. *Grauie* is running juices of roast mutton; a *tunnell* is a funnel. Oyster and cockles are pickled (C 173 and 174), as is neats tongue (C 196). One little clove of garlic is to perfume the entire great pie, then removed. There are two fine sausage recipes, C 25 and 26. Artichoke bottoms are to be parboiled; the egg yolks are from hardcooked eggs.

---

200   [TO BO]YLE A LEGG OF MUTON
THE FORC'D WAY

Take a large legg of muton, & take forth ye leane &
mince it very small with a pound of suet, & put to it a
handfull of sweet hearbs shread small, halfe a pound of
currans, & halfe a pound of sugar, 6 egge youlks, mace,
cloves, & nutmegg beaten, a good handfull of grated
bread, & a little salt. worke all these together with y^r
hand, & put halfe of it into ye scinn of y^r legg of

195

muton. & make 20 or 30 little balls of what you leave
out, & role ye rest in 2 rouls. role them in grated bread,
& after in youlks of eggs & bake them. & wrap ye legg
in a cloth & boyle it. take 10 or 12 of ye balls; & when
ye legg is allmoste boyled, take allmoste a quart of y^e
broth & streyne it into a deepe dish, & poure ye liquor
into it out of y^r bakt forct meate. & take ye rest of y^r
balls and & put them into this broth, set them on a
chafing dish of charcole, & make it boyle; & put in 3 or
4 hard eggs shread, 4 youlks of eggs beaten with 4
spoonfulls of vinegar; put in some parsley shread small,
& stir all these together, & put in a little sugar. then lay
y^r legg in a large dish, & poure ye sauce all over it. lay
in sippets. and cut ye bakd balls in halves, and lay
them about the dish with tostes fry'd in eggs, and
parsley fryed, and hard youlks of eggs, and barbaryes.
& soe serve it up. ye youlks of eggs you lay about y^r
dish must alsoe be cut in halves.

This is an elaborate and ancient dish. The currants, the cup of
sugar, and the vinegar all add up to the medieval *egerdouce* and
the complex presentation has retained many medieval characteristics, as well.

The recipe for the stuffing, or forcemeat (C 13), is straightforward enough. Considering the eventual reconstitution of the
leg of mutton, the skin must be taken off with great care so that
it may be stuffed; it is then wrapped in cheesecloth and gently
simmered. We now come to the meat balls. Somewhere, I lost
count, or perhaps it was the scribe. I cannot say with certainty
how many are to be *endored* (gilded with egg yolk) and baked and
how many are to be simmered in the special little broth. Little
matter, the main lines are clear enough. Out of the remaining
forcemeat, using your hands, make meat balls the size of hard egg
yolks, from 20 to 30 of them. Roll half of them in fine bread crumbs
(of homemade bread), then in egg yolks beaten with a spoonful
or so of water, set in a buttered pan, and bake in a moderate oven.
This *endorement* was one of the most prized conceits of medieval
cookery.

The directions for the sauce are fairly clear: the remaining
meat balls are simmered in nearly a quart of the mutton broth,

further enriched by the pan juices of the baked meat balls. When all is cooked, the chopped hard-cooked eggs and herbs are to be added to this broth, and then the raw egg yolks beaten with the vinegar (having first stirred a little of the hot broth into the egg mixture), stirring well and not allowing it to overcook. The *tostes fry'd in eggs* were apparently elegant sippets prepared much as we would *pain perdu*, or French toast (C 72), but using only beaten egg. I would prefer proper *sippets* (C 1).

Arrange everything as prettily as you can around the leg of mutton, and so serve it up. There is a certain principle of symmetry that is to be observed in the presentation of these grand dishes, not unrelated to the principle of chopping for a specific Chinese dish. (And what does one of with all those extra egg whites? The recipe does not say.) It is a prodigious amount of work, much of it having to be executed at the very last moment.

---

201   TO MAKE A MARROW PIE

Take a quarter of a pound of beefe marrow, one kidney of veale, one or 2 calves tongues, shred pritty small, & put to it some powder sugar, & ye youlks of 2 or 3 eggs beaten, a little salt, some currans & rayso[ns], ye rinde of a leamon pill shread, A spoonfull or 2 of cream, some naple bisket & mackroons quartered. ye bisket must be grated, & ye leamon pill must be candyed. put in 2 spoonfulls of grated white bread. mix all these together, & when y^r pie is allmoste enough, poure in some rose water & sugar.

This recipe should have been tucked in among the other sweet mince meat pie recipes, beginning with C 63. Pies and pastry are discussed in C 48. *Powder sugar* is simply beaten sugar, finely sifted, and has nothing to do with confectioners' sugar as is often written. (The same error is made translating from French *sucre en poudre*.) For *naple bisket*, see C 143; for *mackroons*, S 184.

---

202   TO MAKE EXCELLENT FRITTERS THE
        FRENCH WAY

Take a pinte of flowre & add thereto some cheese curd broaken small, & 6 eggs beaten, & about ye biggness of

an egg in marrow shread small. mix these well with
halfe a pinte of white wine, & some sugar, & a little
salt, & add to these some apples shread, & preservd
leamon pill, & other suckets. then melt some fresh
butter in a frying pan, & fry them in little lumps about
ye biggness of a wallnut or less. & strow on them when
they are servd up some sugar, & cinnamon, If you
please.

For other fritter recipes, see recipes C 98 and 99. You may make
cheese curds as suggested in C 106. *Suckets* are discussed in S 93.
It is prodigal to fry fritters in fresh butter and folly to attempt it;
at the least, it should be clarified butter. (Historically, clarified
butter was in favor for such cooking in Elizabethan times, having
largely replaced the lard and olive oil of medieval times. Beef suet
from around the kidney was still in use and serves admirably; it
is a nuisance to render. I have little use for peanut oil and less for
the various commercial frying oils.)

---

203 TO MAKE WHITE BROTH

Take a capon with whole mace, cloves, sinamon, &
boyle curran[s] & raysons in a cloth, & when y^r broth is
enough, take out your capon & put in as much cream
as will make it white. y^n blanch & beat almonds &
strayne y^m with cream. y^n beat & strayne as many eggs
as will make it thick enough, put in a little sack, & set
all on a slow fire, & keepe it stiring till it is thick
enough.

This is a more classic *white broth* than the one presented in C 113;
it is closer to its ancestor, the medieval *blank manger*, to use Chaucer's name. Many recipes for *blanc manger* (white food) from early
English court cookery have come down to us from fourteenth- and
fifteenth-century manuscripts. The most consistent elements were
minced or pounded capon and its broth, raisins and currants, and
almond milk, and it was usually sweetened. Sometimes rice was
added and there were versions based on fish. As the dish evolved,
it took two separate paths: the *blanc manger*, a sweet dish characterized by almond milk until sometime in the eighteenth century,
when it began to be made with sweetened milk and arrowroot or

cornstarch—the ignominious end of a noble dish. Its end was lingering however; there are delightful nineteenth-century American recipes for it (see the related *white leach,* C 127). The other path was our white broth, which by Elizabethan times, at least, usually boasted an entire capon. Markham, in 1615, gives several bases, including one with fish. The dish began to be old-fashioned in the eighteenth century but Eliza Leslie, in *Directions for Cookery,* 1837, gives a splendid version called *Rich White Soup* that harks back to the early versions: pounded capon and its broth, pounded almonds and bread crumbs, egg yolks, a quart of cream, and all; it lacks only the dried fruits that were so characteristic.

In our recipe, I believe that the currants and raisins are to be boiled in separate water. For the liaison, whisk egg yolks with sherry and follow the procedure outlined in C 2. Salt to taste.

---

204   [TO M]AKE A WHIPT POSSET

Take A quart of cream, & a pinte of rennish wine, & halfe a pinte of sack, & 3 quarters of a pound of sugar. mix them alltogether in An earthen pan with a sprigg of rosemary, & A piece of leamon pill, then whip it with a clean whiske till it riseth with a froth. then take it of by spoonfulls & put it into y^r glasses.

This recipe demonstrates the difficulty of defining the difference between a *posset* and a *syllabub*; a posset was most often made of ale and served warm while a syllabub was most often made of wine and served cool. (See C 110 through 120.) Actually, you will have something more like fluffy curds than posset.

The rosemary and lemon zest add a delightful note and the mixture would make a charming dessert. The sugar amounts to 1½ cups, which is pretty sweet.

---

205   TO MAKE PEPPER CAKES THAT WILL
           KEEP GOOD IN Y^e HOUSE FOR A
           QUARTER OR HALFE A YEAR

Take treakle 4 pound, fine wheat flowre halfe a peck, beat ginger 2 ounces, corriander seeds 2 ounces, carraway & annyseeds of each an ounce, suckets slyced in small pieces a pritty quantety, powder of orring pills one ounce. worke all these into paste, and let it ly 2 or

3 hours. after, make it up into what fashions you please in pritty large cakes about an intch and halfe thick at moste, or rather an intch will be thick enough. wash your cakes over with a little oyle and treacle mixt together befor you set them into ye oven, then set them in after houshould bread. & though they be hard baked, they will give againe, when you have occasion to use it,* slyce it & serve it up.

As the reader must have noticed, this is a recipe for gingerbread. Pepper entered into a number of baked confections, harking back to a time when its use was not as differentiated from that of other spices as it later came to be; there is pepper in the *gyngerbrede* recipe from about 1430 mentioned in S 186, for example. Various European pepper cakes survive to this day, especially in Danish and German baking. There is, however, no pepper in our pepper cakes; the omission may be inadvertent.

As discussed in S 186, the medieval gingerbread made with bread crumbs silently left the scene early in the seventeenth century. (I should note that ancient versions appeared intermittently through the century, particularly in succeeding editions of earlier works; for the most part, however, they were less archaic in character than that represented by S 186.) About the same time, I believe, recipes for the new-fangled baked gingerbreads began to be recorded in English cookery manuscripts, antedating by decades their appearance in printed books. There is a recipe for *Gingerbread* given in the 1705 edition (significantly, not in the 1696 edition) of *The Family Dictionary* by William Salmon that really differs from C 205 only in detailing the amounts of specific candied peels; Salmon claims that: "This was made for King Charles II [1660-85]." But baked gingerbread had been made in France for centuries (S 186), the only basic difference being that treacle, rather than honey, came to characterize the English baked confection. I found one honeyed version in *The Lucayos Cook Book,* a transcription of a manuscript kept from 1660 to 1690 "by a noble family of Elizabethan England," followed a little later by one calling for treacle. From the language and context, I believe these recipes to have been entered in the 1660s, but I must note that the provenance is scanty. In the manuscript kept by Gulielma Penn, who died in 1694, we find a recipe for *Ginger-Breed* that differs from our own primarily in calling for ½ a pound of sugar—a later development, I believe—in addition to 3 pounds of *treckell.* As Evelyn Benson, editor of the

* There was no punctuation here.

manuscript remarks, the recipes "should be associated with a mid-seventeenth century date rather than with the relatively late transcription date [1702]." As discussed in the section dealing with the history of our own manuscript, I cannot with certainty narrow down the date of this fair copy further than sometime in the latter half of the seventeenth century. While I am convinced that no recipe dates from later than mid-century, its position as penultimate entry, tacked on in what I call a caboose section, makes me reluctant to more than suggest an earlier date. I do feel that this is perhaps the most modern recipe in the manuscript.

All of these recipes represent early examples of the use of *treacle* referring to the uncrystalized syrup produced during sugar refining; the first citing by *OED* is "molassus or common Treacle," 1694. Molasses was the earlier term in England, having been in use for well over a century at that point, and was brought to the colonies, where it persisted. (Technically, molasses is the uncrystallizable drainings, but the difference is largely ignored in popular usage on both sides of the Atlantic.) As explained in S 284, molasses replaced honey in the medicinal *London treacle*, as it was to replace honey in baked gingerbreads in England. But in one of several recipes for gingerbread given by E. Smith in the first American 1742 edition of *The Compleat Housewife*—and quite likely in earlier English editions, as well—she specifies *London treacle*. If one remembers the early history of gingerbread (S 186), this curious use of medicinal treacle becomes more understandable. Indeed, I am led to wonder if perhaps some of these seventeenth-century recipes for baked gingerbread with *treacle* might not have been made with *London treacle*.

Most eighteenth-century English gingerbreads were enriched with butter, eggs, and occasionally cream; they were often rolled thin and cut into fancy shapes, baking up into crisp but tender cookies. Americans took to gingerbread early and with enthusiasm. Amelia Simmons gives five recipes for it in her little book, *American Cookery*, 1796, already showing certain peculiarly American traits: one is for "Soft Gingerbread to be baked in pans" (perhaps the earliest printed recipe for what came to be the preferred form in the States, although it is not dark), one is for "Molasses Gingerbread," and two call for *pearl ash* (potassium bicarbonate). Mary Tolford Wilson writes in her introductory notes to the Oxford facsimile edition that American women were routinely using this chemical (made at home of wood ash) in their baking and that this is the first cookbook to record it. Soda bicarbonate later replaced it, followed by various baking powder mixtures. It should be noted that with stiff doughs, these baking powders do not so much leaven the dough as render the finished cake some-

201

what porous in texture, an effect achieved in our own recipe above by allowing the dough to ferment a few hours, and without imparting a chemical aftertaste.

For half a peck of flour, start with 16 cups (see C 92); 2 ounces of powdered ginger amounts to about 6 tablespoons; an ounce of anise seeds is about 3 tablespoons; as for *suckets*, other period recipes proportionately call for amounts of mixed candied peel varying from 4 ounces to 2 pounds. (See S 93.)

---

206 TO MAKE ALMOND [BUTTER ?]

Take a pinte of cream & ye youlks of 15 eggs & beat them well together. then let them boyle, and stir them continually till they are thick. then put them in a cloth & hang them up to let ye whey run from them, then take halfe a quarter of a pound of almonds & beat them well in 3 spoonfulls of rosewater. then take ye butter out of ye cloth & heat ye almonds therwith upon a soft fire with a quarter of a pound of beaten sugar.

This recipe is not listed in the scribe's index. I call it a butter because it is so referred to in the body of the recipe and there is precendent (see C 129). It is properly a recipe for curds with almonds, however, as in C 136. The amount of sugar is ½ cup.

Part II

INTRODUCTION TO
A BOOKE OF SWEETMEATS

A Booke of Sweetmeats starts out with the clarification of sugar and the successive stages of syrup, takes us through over 200 recipes for the preserving of fruits and flowers, and ends with some 90 distilled medicinal waters and preparations of various kinds; in short, an archetypical still-room book. In fact, most of the recipes in the book, even those for *marchpane*, were considered salutary and had specific medicinal virtues, a happy pretext to some extent, but one sanctioned by the medical profession.

Nowadays, most of us find *A Booke of Cookery* more appealing, and more useful. We can understand the need to conserve the fruits at a time when it represented the only way of having fruits out of season, but with modern pharamacopoeia available at the corner drug store, it is perhaps difficult for us to appreciate that for the women who used these books, it was quite likely the *Booke of Sweetmeats* that was the more precious. Markham, in *The English Hus-wife*, 1615, after piously admonishing women ever to "be of chaste thought, stout courage, patient, untired, watchfull, diligent, witty, pleasant, constant in friendship, full of good neighbor-hood, wise in discourse but not frequent therein, sharpe and quicke of speech, but not bitter or talkative, secret in her affaires, comfortable in her counsailes [counsel], and generally skilfull in all the worthy knowledges which doe belong to her vocation," writes that "it is meet that shee have a phisicall [healing] kind of knowledge, how administer many wholsome receits or medicines for the good of their [families'] healthes." These women *Phisitians*, as Gerard admiringly called them, gathered the herbs, bought the exotic sugar, spices, and *treacles* (panacean electuaries) at the apothecary, decocted and distilled the medicinal waters, and administered them.

To better understand the nature of *A Booke of Sweetmeats*, or *A Booke of Cookery*, for that matter, it is necessary to have some understanding of the underlying philosophy of popular medicine and dietary rules as practiced in sixteenth- and seventeenth-century England.

Medieval European medicine was based on the precepts of the famed medical school of Salerno. Legend has it that *Schola Salerni* was founded in the seventh century by a Saracen, a Greek, a Jew, and a Roman Christian. Be that as it may, by the ninth century it was flourishing in a Benedictine monastery where principally Arab and Jewish physicians taught and practiced a medicine whose principles had been enunciated by Hippocrates, the "father of medicine" (c.460-370 B.C.), Aristotle (384-322 B.C.), Dioscorides, Greek physician from Asia Minor (first century A.D.), and Galen, Greek physician of Pergamum (A.D. c.130-200), whose works had been preserved and considerably elaborated upon by the Arabs. (It is apropos to note that a number of women physicians are said to have practiced there, as well: Costanza, Abella, Trotula, and Rebecca, among others.) It became the medical center of Europe, and popes and kings journeyed to Salerno to undergo treatment.

Much oversimplified, the basic theory is this. Health of mind and body is the perfect equilibrium among four humors: choleric, hot and dry, characterized by a bilious complexion and a fiery temperament; phlegmatic, cold and moist, characterized by a pale complexion and apathy; melancholic, cold and dry, characterized by sullenness and depressed spirits; and sanguine, hot and moist, characterized by a ruddy complexion and great appetites and capacities. (These humors corresponded to Aristotle's four elements: fire, water, earth, and air, respectively.) Anything that disturbs this precarious balance results in illness; health can be restored only by bringing the humors back into equilibrium. Drawing on Aristotle's concept that every living thing had its unique form, its psyche, an entire body of medicine was built up around the observed attributes of every plant and animal then known to man. Each plant, for example, was assigned heating or cooling and moistening or drying attributes up to the fourth degree. Other specific attributes, often based on acute and sustained clinical observation, were also assigned to each plant, such as improving vision, inducing sleep, quickening of the senses, bringing down the menses, binding or loosening of the digestive tract, or increasing lust. Inevitably, the entire system of thought became entangled with all manner of mysticism, errors, pious nonsense, and just plain old quackery. In this regard, it differed little from all systems of thought, including modern medicine. And considering the continued use of quinine, a bark discovered by the Indians to be helpful in treating malaria, the use of penicillin, a mold product, in fighting infection, or the difference in the effect on human skin of poison ivy as compared to that of almond milk and rose water, for instance, it behooves us not to scoff too loudly. The fact is that each plant has a specific biochemical formula and it is altogether likely that certain preparations were efficacious. I suspect that in many respects, physicians of the day were more perceptive on the relationship of diet and health than they are today; certainly the dietitians in modern hospitals would do well to study the composition of the wonderfully comforting broths that were recommended for those with wasted bodies and low spirits. This said, I hasten to add that in no wise should this be construed as recommending any of the medications detailed in this book.

The medical profession in medieval times studied Dioscorides and Galen, along with *Circa instans*, the pharmacopoeia from the School of Salerno (S 186), and other works. But popular acquaintance with these ideas came about principally through *Regimen Sanitatis Salerno* (Salerno health regimen), prescribed, it is thought, for Robert, Duke of Normandy, son of William the Conqueror, on his way home from the First Crusade, about 1100. It is written in medieval Latin doggerel and it is the principal source of the dietary works that came to be so popular in England, those of Andrew Boorde and Thomas Cogan being perhaps the best known.

Many of our commonest and happiest food combinations are derived from the principles set forth in this regime. Excessively cooling foods were thought to lead to death; soporific plants were classified as cold, for example, with the deadly nightshade being classified as cold in the fourth degree. (Fear of the dread chilling effect of the tomato, also a *Solanace*, delayed its use as a food in England for many centuries in spite of the fact that Gerard, for example, reported in 1597 that the people of "Spaine and those hot Regions" ate *Apples of Love* avidly. Some of the same fear attached to the related white potato but it was accepted considerably earlier, in part because it had been confused with the sweet potato from the beginning [see C 53], and also because it was filling, I suspect.) Lettuce was considered cold and moist, for example, so it was desirable to balance it by adding olive oil (hot and moist), pepper (hot and dry), and vinegar (cold and dry); cresses and other hot and tonic herbs were also considered salutary additions. Conversely, by the same reasoning, if a person were suffering from a fever, it was considered sound medical practice to give cooling foods in quantities that might otherwise have been considered unwholesome. Hot and dry spices such as ginger (to the third degree) and mustard (to the fourth degree) were much used to counteract phlegm and overly cooling foods. Elizabeth David, discussing ginger in *Spices, Salt and Aromatics in the English Kitchen*, 1970, says that in her childhood, "it was customary to hand round a bowl of powdered ginger when melon was served . . . to counteract [its] chilling effects." It is interesting to note that many Danes serve pepper with melon, and that the Italians brilliantly team it with peppered ham, customs surely stemming from that same belief. Vinegar, much used in food preservation, caused concern because it was cooling; it was also thought to "make leane" and engender melancholy, so pepper corns, coriander seeds, and other cheering herbs and spices were always added. Thyme, parsley, rosemary, mint, and tarragon were among those hot and dry tonic herbs that entered many dishes for dietary reasons; the most congenial combinations from a gastronomic point of view survived.

(The study of these congenial combinations is the study of comparative cuisine. The case of French and English cuisines is especially fascinating because from the time of the Norman Conquest until say the fifteenth century, the cooking of the royal households and many of the noble households in the two countries differed but little. Indeed, the English royal house was French, and English cookery manuscripts of the period were little more than translations from the French. Now the French were as influenced by the precepts of the Salerno regimen as the English; to this day, the medicinal *tisanes* [herb teas], *apéritifs* and *digestifs* [originally medicinal waters] hold sway. Yet ideas on what constitutes ideal food combinations could hardly be more different in the two countries. Variations in soil and climate are primordial, but I suspect that the differences are due in large part to the compelling presence of wine in France, whose influence in forming the French palate has been incalculable.)

It is difficult to overemphasize the extent to which these dietary-medical ideas had penetrated popular consciousness; the works of Chaucer and Shakespeare, both masters of the vernacular, abound in references that make this clear. In the *Prologue* to the *Canterbury Tales*, for example, Chaucer introduces us to the *Doctour of Phisik* (healing), who "knew the cause of every maladye, Were it of hoot, or cold, or moyste, or drye, And where they engendred and of what humour," and he rattles off names of Greek and Arab physicians down through the ages, serene in the knowledge that their names would be recognized by his readers. And most of his characters are introduced with a description of their humors and complexion. (Also, see S 70.) I have cited Shakespeare in this regard a number of times (C 21 and C 53, for example); many of his jokes and allusions come to life only if we understand, as his audiences did, the putative medicinal virtues of certain plants. There was nothing arcane in Shakespeare's plays in his day; rosemary for remembrance was not just a poetic thought but a popular medical prescription.

The herbals described the herbs and listed their virtues. As noted earlier, it was the housewives who gathered the herbs and decocted them into medicinal waters. A certain amount of this lore must have been part of an earlier oral tradition, possibly stemming in part from monastaries and convents, since literacy was not widespread before the day of the printed word, even among the upper classes. Some of it may antedate Norman times, as suggested by early Saxon manuscripts and it is possible that there are traces of native *leechcraft* (healing) in English herbal medicine, particularly among the more humble practitioners. The precepts of the School of Salerno held forth in the printed herbals, however, complete with impressive citations from the works of Dioscorides and Galen. Interestingly, there were a number of high-born women famed for their success in ministering to the sick. *A Choice Manuall, of Rare and Select Secrets in Physick and Chirurgery: collected, and practised by the Right Honourable, the Countesse of Kent, late deceased,* 1653, indicates that the Countess was a healer; a medication on the order of Doctor Gascoyn's powder (S 307) bears her name and so entered English pharmocopoeia. In *The Queens Closet Opened,* 1655, there are some 15 ladies, including a countess or two, credited with prescriptions and this number increased in succeeding editions. While some of this may have reflected name-dropping, there is reason to believe that many ladies took their good works seriously. In *English Cookery Books,* 1913, Oxford quotes from the preface of *The Widdowes Treasure,* 1595, indicating that the prescriptions were written down "at the earnest request . . . of a Gentlewoman in the Country for her private use, which by these singular practices hath obtained such fame, that her name shall bee remembered for ever to the Posterity." Oxford primly adds that "it is difficult to believe that a gentlewoman could have treated or even described so plainly some of the diseases mentioned," forgetting that Elizabethan and Victorian mores could hardly have been more distinct.

As may be seen by the numerous recipes, the distillation of spirits, oils, and waters was largely carried out at home in the still room. Indeed, the book of sweetmeats was often called the still room book. The process of distillation, along with the alembic (see *limbeck,* S 269), was brought to Europe by the Arabs. The basic principle is simple: each substance volatilizes and condenses at specific temperatures. Alcohol and oils, for example, vaporize at lower temperatures than does water, so that one can extract the spirit or essence of a substance by applying this principle.

The accompanying diagram, based on a sketchy drawing from *Divers Chimicall Conclusions concerning the Art of Distillation,* 1594, by Hugh Plat, shows a schematic home still of the day. The substance to be distilled is placed in vessel *A,* usually made of brass or copper. As it is heated, the vapors rise (by alphabetical progression) to the alembic proper (usually made of pewter), where

they are trapped and cooled by fresh water flowing over the outside walls so that they condense, whereupon the condensed spirits flow into the blown glass receiver C. The art of distillation consisted of judging and maintaining the correct temperatures, no mean feat with such rudimentary equipment; one can understand the instruction in a number of recipes to *lute,* or seal, the joints. Nevertheless, a great deal of successful and potent distillation was carried out in these simple home stills. Any reader wishing to follow the recipes involving the use of a still is advised to consult technical works on the subject. Later in the seventeenth century, recipes began to appear for "a very good Cordial water without a Still" (a title from the "inner pages" of our manuscript), which simply called for steeping the various herbs and spices in brandy for several weeks, then straining off. It is a system that works perfectly well. (The appearance of the recipes would indicate a decline in home distillation and the increasing commercial availability of brandy and other spirits.)

I have quoted extensively from *The Herball* by John Gerard, using the 1597 edition for the most part; occasionally I used citations from the additions and emendations by Thomas Johnson as given in the 1636 edition and have so attributed. I chose Gerard over other herbalists primarily because I felt that the state of knowledge reflected in his herbal most nearly represented that of most of the entries in our manuscript. Also, his was the first popular herbal to detail products from the New World, and fine drawings preclude any contemporary misapprehension of the text. Honesty compels me to report, in sorrow, that scholars, beginning with the

210

above Doctor Johnson, show convincingly that Gerard lifted the greater part of his book, in many sections word for word, from *Pemptades*, a work by Rembert Dodoens as Englished from the Dutch by a Doctor Priest, who had conveniently died on completing the translation. This lamentable circumstance does not diminish the value of the work as a measure of what the people of Elizabethan and Jacobean England knew and believed concerning the various herbs and remedies with which they dosed themselves.

I should note that in my annotations all scientific names, with but few exceptions, are those given in the *Oxford English Dictionary*. The problems of classification and nomenclature are complex and troublesome and I did not propose to become entangled therein. The early botanists occasionally disagreed among themselves and since their time, Linnaeus and the modern botanists have rearranged scientific classification a number of times; even today, they are not always in agreement. I am trained neither in medicine nor in botany; I am a housewife, and had I lived in those times, I would perforce have acquired "a phisicall kind of knowledge," and learned how to choose, decoct, and administer the healing herbs. In tracing the identity of many herbs, charming corruptions of the old Latin names and variants on the popular names that appear in our manuscript often made the chase a merry one; in a few cases, there was simply no way of telling exactly which herb had been meant by the original writer of the recipe. Since the medicinal recipes are in no way intended for use today, this was only an exercise in scholarship, a highly absorbing one, which I followed insofar as I was able. I make no pretense of definitive findings; I am not sure that it was always possible, given the material. I would like to think that I have opened a door to the past through which readers may enter and so better understand the attitudes of the people of sixteenth- and seventeenth-century England in regard to their diet and what they expected of their medications. These attitudes came to the Colonies and persisted through the seventeenth century, and longer, in spite of the medical discoveries of William Harvey and others, so that these beliefs are part of American history as well.

211

THE INDEX

* A leaf is missing from the index. All titles from number 101 through 150 are taken from the recipe titles themselves. Although there are often minor differences, I have not considered it necessary to place all these titles in brackets.

215

* This marks the last of the recipe titles entered on the missing leaf; with
No. 151, we pick up the scribe's index.

* The first letter *e* has been corrected from *a*, or vice versa.

* Corrected by the scribe from *Aquimirabelis*, or vice versa. In the recipe titles, it is a clear *Aquimirabelis* in all cases.

* This and the following number were written 390 and 391 in error.

A BOOKE OF SWEETMEATS

A: Booke. of Sweetmeats

1

To know how to Clarefie your Sugar

Take a pinte of faire water & beat ye white of an
egg into it, to a froth, then put a pound of sugar in
to it, & set it boyle uery fast, & there will rise
a black scum on ye top of it, as it riseth take it
of till it is uery clean, & then streyne it thorough
A Jelly bagg or wet cloth, & soe use it as you plese
to euery pound of sugar as you clarefie, you must
put a pinte of faire water, & ye white of an egg.
ye white of one egge will clarefy 2 pound of sugar
as well as one pound.

2

To know when Sirrup is thin, or that your sugar is brought to a thin Sirrup

After you haue clarefied yr sugar, set it to boyle
againe, & as there did rise a black scum in ye clarefi
ing, soe there will rise another scum which will be
white, wch you must take of uery clean as it riseth,
& when there will rise noe more, it is in a thinn
sirrup, & it will look thin & pale cullored. & soe
you may use it as you please.

3

To know when yr sugar is in A full Sirrup

After yr sugar is in a thin Sirrup set it to boyle
againe, & in ye boyling it will change its culler and
looke high cullored like strong beare, & then it is
in a full sirrup, & soe you may us it.

1   TO KNOW HOW TO CLAREFIE YOUR
     SUGAR

Take a pinte of faire water & beat ye white of an egg
into it to a froth. then put a pound of sugar in to it, &
let it boyle very fast, & there will rise a black scum on
ye top of it. as it riseth, take it of till it is very clean, &
then streyne it thorough A Jelly bagg or wet cloth, &
soe use it as you plea[s]. to every pound of sugar as
you clarefie, you must put a pinte of faire water, & y^e
white of an egg. ye white of one egge will clarefy 2
pound of sugar as well as one pound.

Our *Booke of Sweetmeats* opens with the traditional section on the
clarification of sugar and the various heights or stages of syrup.
While sugar was regarded as having medicinal virtues of its own—
chiefly that of tempering harsh qualities of other substances and,
as Gerard put it, putting away "hoarsenesse, the cough, and all
sourenesse and bitternesse"—its main use was in the preservation
of fruits and making medications more palatable and more efficacious. This had been the peculiar contribution of the Arabs to
medicine; it was they who brought the art of working sugar, along
with the name *sukkar*, to Europe. (*OED* says that the relationship
between Persian *shakar*, Prakrit *sakkara*, and Greek *sakcharon* is unclear.) Sugar is thought to have originated in India, apparently in
prehistory. Sugar is not cited as appearing in English before the
late thirteenth century (*OED*), but since Latin was the language of
the apothecaries, this is not conclusive. (See pages 11 and 12 for
further discussion of sugar.)

   The economical note at the end of this recipe was clearly
tacked on by an interim hand as the result of the user's experience.
She was right: 1 egg white suffices to clarify 2 pounds of sugar.
Sugar is highly refined nowadays, and it is rare to find such directions, but for fastidious work it is well to follow them. It is not
necessary for ordinary preserving, however.

   While the *pinte* measure varied from one region to another, it may be considered as having been equivalent to 16 fluid
ounces (about 454.4 cc.), the old English wine or ale pint, which
is mentioned several times in our manuscript. And in S 236, we
find: "a pound of Juice, which is a pinte." The imperial pint of 20
fluid ounces was not adopted in Britain until 1826; United States

retained the old measures the colonists had brought with them, so that liquid measures in our manuscript need not be translated and the pint equals 2 U.S. cups. This works out in practice, as well. (The passage in S 236 also indicates that ordinary scales, *avoirdupois*, were used in the kitchen.)

---

2   TO KNOW WHEN SIRRUP IS THIN,
         OR THAT YOUR SUGAR IS BROUGHT
         TO A THIN SURRUP

After you have clarefied y^r sugar, set it to boyle againe, & as there did rise a black scum in ye clarefying, soe there will rise another scum which will be white, wch you must take of very clean as it riseth. & when there will rise noe more, it is in a thinn sirrup, & it will look thin & pale cullered. & soe you may use it as you please.

Syrup comes from Arabic *sharāb* by way of Old French *sirop*. (All the forms used in the manuscript were current in the fifteenth and sixteenth centuries.) One of the early citations, *surypes*, is in Trevisa's monumental medical work, *De Proprietatibus Rerum*, 1398 (*OED*). In *The Forme of Cury*, about 1390, it appears as *cyrip*, so that its two chief functions, that of serving as a vehicle for medications and of preserving fruits, were recorded in English before the end of the fourteenth century.

---

3   TO KNOW WHEN Y^r SUGAR IS IN A
         FULL SIRRUP

After y^r sugar is in a thin sirrup, set it to boyle againe, & in ye boyling it will change its culler and looke high cullered like strong beere, & then it is in a full sirrup. & soe you may us[e] it.

---

4   TO KNOW WHEN YOUR SUGAR IS AT
         MANUS CHRISTI HEIGHT

When y^r sugar is at manis Christi height, it will draw betwixt y^r fingers like a small thrid, and before it comes to that height, it will not draw. & soe use it as you

have occasion.

It has been suggested by Barbara Scott that the name for this stage of syrup comes from the testing gesture, which is the same as that of *manus Christi* (literally, hand of Christ), the Blessing of the Host and Chalice. It is an ingenious and delightful explanation that I have not encountered elsewhere. It is also possible that it was named after *manus Christi*, the confection (S 107), but that required a much higher syrup. With the Reformation, the Latin term fell into disuse in this sense and I have not found the term used in directions for syrup in seventeenth-century books. Curiously, the name was later applied to a sweet cordial.

The temperature of this stage is 215°F.

---

5   TO KNOW WHEN YOUR SUGAR IS AT CANDY HEIGHT

When y^r sugar is at a candy height, which is the second

height it comes to, it will draw between your fingers in

great flakes like bird lime, and then it is at a just height

eyther to candy or for any other things.

Candy comes directly from French *candi* but before that there was Arab *qandi*, meaning candied, Persian *qanda* meaning crystallized sugar, and Sanskrit *khanda* meaning sugar in crystalline pieces, from *khand*, to break (*OED*).

Bird lime is a viscous sticky substance prepared from the bark of holly and used to catch small birds. In Old English it meant any adhesive, but now it is only poetic (*OED*). At the time of original entry of the recipe, the substance must have been familiar to the women of a household.

The temperature of this syrup is 220°F.

---

6   TO KNOW WHEN YOUR SUGAR IS AT A CASTING HEIGHT

After you have clarefied ye sugar as in ye first receipt,

& boyled it to a candy height, let it boyle still, &

sometimes swing your stick from you, and when your

sugar is at a casting height, it will flie from your stick in

great flakes like flakes of snow, or like fethers flying in

the Ayre, and till it is at a casting height, it will not fly

A Booke of Sweetmeats

in flakes. and this is the last and greatest height you can boyle your sugar too except you will have it to burne. and soe you may reserve it for your use. Manus Christy is accounted the first of the heights y^t sugar may be boyled too, Candy height ye second, & casting height the last of all.

This is perhaps the clearest recipe for cooking sugar to *grand souffle* or feather stage, I have seen; it is certainly the prettiest. The temperature will register at 232°F. It is interesting to note that caramel, the next stage, was considered burnt. Burnt sugar cakes were a feature of nineteenth-century American cookbooks but directions make it clear that it was caramel stage.

Receipt showed up as a word for recipe in the sixteenth century.

---

7   TO PRESERUE QUINCES

To every pound of quince take a pound & A quarter of refined sugar. then core y^r quinces & put them in boyling water, there let them boyle leasurely till they are tender. shift them once in ye boyling least they be too high cullered, & be sure both ye waters boyle before you put them in. & as soone as they are tender, take them out of ye water & pare them, & to every pounde of quince, take a wine pinte of faire water, & half ye sugar ye quinces weighd put into ye water. then set it on a quick fire, & make it boyle very fast till ye sirrup be ready to Jelly. then put ye quinces into ye sirrup with ye other halfe of ye sugar, then let them boyle as fast as is possible. & when you perceive ye syrrup Jelly, take them of, & put them into glasses, for every quince a glas[s]. keep out halfe ye syrrup till ye quinces be cold in ye glasses, & then cover them over with ye rest.

The quince is the hard, acid, yellowish pear-shaped fruit of *Pyrus cydonia*, pear of Cydonia, Crete. Properly speaking, quince is the plural of *quine* or *quyne* from Old French *coyn* (*OED*) but that long ago fell into disuse. From a culinary point of view, it is not a grateful fruit: astringent and rather difficult. The English took to the quince and this manuscript is typical; there are no fewer than 22 recipes calling for it in our manuscript. For one thing, it was regarded as being highly medicinal; Gerard says: "They strengthen the stomack, stay vomiting, stop lasks and also the bloudy flix," and gives recipes for *Cotiniat* and *Marmalad* (S 14 and 198) noting that Dioscorides prescribed quinces.

This is the first of 13 recipes for preserved quinces and quince marmalade. Some of the recipes are redundant but there are, nevertheless, certain differences. Women of the day took a pride in their preserving which is difficult for us to comprehend today. To be sure, it was more necessary, but the art of preserving fruits so that they be golden yellow, a fine white, clear as amber, a true green, red like ruby or cornelian, or of the *orient culler* (the brilliant flush of dawn), was of great importance to them. Quinces were particularly challenging and rewarding in this regard because of the palette of colors offered by ingenious variations in cooking technique and time of harvesting, but apples and plums also served to show off the preserver's skill. By reading the entire section, you will often find a bit of puzzling procedure cleared up in another recipe.

Several recipes in this section call for egg white and refer to the clarifying of sugar (S 1). This is unnecessary with modern sugar in the making of preserves.

To *shift them once in yᵉ boyling* means to shift them in a perforated ladle to another pot of boiling water.

---

8   TO PRESERUE QUINCES WHITE

Take 2 pound of yellow pear Quinces, core & boyle them in faire water (unpared)* till they be tender. when they are cold, pare them, & make sirrup for them with 2 pound of brazeele sugar, beeing clarefied with a pinte & halfe of faire water, & yᵉ whi[te] of an egg. soe let yʳ quinces boyle a while in yᵉ sam sirrup till you can put a straw thorough yᵐ. then take yᵐ up & boyle yʳ sirrup till it comes to a Jely, & wh[en] they [be co]ld, Pot them.

Brazeele sugar was imported from Brazil (see *sugar*, page 11). For quinces, see S 7.

* Scribe's parentheses

9   TO PRESERUE QUINCES WHITE

Boyle y^r quinces in faire water till they be soe tender y^t
a rush will goe thorough* them. wash them in cold
water, after core & pare them. & to a pound of quince,
put a pound & a quarter of sugar & a quart of water.
clarefy ye sirrup with the whites of eggs. take y^e
kernells & lay them in a little water, & they will make it
Jelly, then streyne it out into ye sirrup before it be
clarefyed & y^t will make it thicke. then put ye quinces
into ye sirrup & make them boyle apace for a little
while, y^n take them up & put them into glasses.

Not only do the kernels contain pectin, but the jelly made using
them was considered effective against fevers. For quinces,
see S 7.

10   TO PRESERUE QUINCES YALLOW

Take 2 pound of quinces beeing pared & coared. boyle
them very tender in faire water, & take 2 pound of
sugar & a pinte & halfe of faire water, & ye whites of 2
new layd eggs, with which you must clarefy your sirrop
very clear. when it is come to a perfect sirrup, put in
your quinces & let them boyle till they be soe tender
that A straw will goe thorough them. then take them
up & boyle y^r sirrope a little thicker by it selfe. then put
all together and the quinces will look yellow.

11   TO PRESERUE QUINCES RED

Take yellow faire ripe quinces, core them at ye top with
a small knife, then parboyle them in a kettle of fayre
water till they be a little tender, & put into ye kettle y^e
quince kernells & 2 or 3 cut quinces. then take out y^e
quinces & when they are cold, pare them as thin as you

* Written *thorought*.

can, & weigh them. & to every pound of quince, allow
a pound pare weight of sugar, & to every 2 pound of
sugar, put 4 pintes of y^t water you boyled y^r quinces in
cold. & for every pound of sugar, put in ye white of an
egg well beaten to a froth with cold water, & beat & stir
it well into ye water & sugar. & when ye sugar is well
melted, set it on a good fire of coles, & let it boyle well
up till ye eggs have raysed up all ye scum, & y^t y^e
sirrup be clear. then streyne it thorough a thick wet
napkin, then put in y^r parboyled quinces, and boyle
them gently till ye sirrup begins to thicken. then boyle
them a good pace, still keeping them close covered, &
now & then shake and scum them till ye quines be of
A curnelian culler, and the sirrup will Jelly. then put
every one in a little pot or glass that will fill it and
keepe some of the Jelly to put over y^m when they are
cold. & then paper them up.

Pare weight I suppose to mean scant or barely, as opposed to *downe weight* (S 16). Cornelian is a variety of chalcedony, most typically of a deep, dull red. Quinces do turn a surprisingly deep color. See S 7. This recipe is rather more modern than many of the others.

---

12   TO PRESERUE QUINCES RED

Take 2 pound of faire Quinces, pare & core them. then
take 2 pound of sugar & 2 quarts of faire water, & y^e
whites of 2 eggs, with which clarefy your sugar very
perfectly. then put it in A preserveing pan with your
quinces. soe boyle them very tender, & keepe them
close covered, which will bring them to theyr orient
culler, & turne them often to keepe them from spotting.
when they are tender, take them up, & let y^r surrup
boyle for a while after very fast. then pot y^r quinces, &
put y^r sirrup to them, & they will keepe all ye yeare.

Orient culler refers to a brilliant or sparkling color. See S 7.

231

13   TO MAKE RED MARMALET OF QUINCES

Take faire water & small quinces & boyle them together
close covered till ye liquor is somewhat red. then take 3
quarts of it, into which put 4 pound of good sugar.
boyle it on a very quick fire & scume it clean. then take
3 pound & A halfe of quinces, beeing very clean pared
and coared & cut in halves. put them into ye liquor,
and then make them boyle very fast till they are tender.
then break them with a spoone & stir them very well
for fear of burning too. when it will cut, it is boyled
enough. then take it up & put it in glasses, or boxes,
but lay it not s[m]ooth on ye top.

Marmalet comes from Portuguese *marmelado*, so named because it
was made with the *marmelo*, a kind of quince. The first citation in
English is from 1524 as *marmalade* (*OED*). I do not know when
marmalade ceased to be made exclusively of quince, but it was
early. The marmalade recipe presented in S 20, for example, was
published in 1608 and quite likely dates from the 1550s. Recipes
for *Marmalade of Oranges* were commonplace by the time of Markham, 1615. In time, of course, marmalade came to refer almost
exclusively to that made with oranges or other citrus fruits.

To *scume* is to remove scum, and is an old form. The word
comes from Old French *escumer*, and the spelling here may give
us a clue to the pronunciation. *Burning too* means burning, of
course, but it can also mean simply sticking or in danger of burning.
The usage is common in our manuscript.

It should be noted that these marmalades were far stiffer
than those to which we are accustomed. For quince, see S 7.

14   TO MAKE RED MARMALET OF QUINCES

Take y^r quinces & cut of all ye hornyness & pick out all
ye blacks. then put them in spring water & lay a
wooden dish over them in ye pan, & when they are
soft, take them up, & pare & core them, & save y^r
pareings & cores, & boyle them* in y^t water till it is
very strong of ye quince. then take to every pound of

* Scribal repetition of "& boyle them" is excised.

quince a pint of y^t water strayned clear, & to every
pinte of y^t water A pound of ye best loafe sugar. soe
boyle them in a preserving pan close covered, stiring it
sometimes. & put some of ye seeds in a lawn ragg,
which you must boyle with ye quinces for halfe an
houre. If you would not have y^r marmalet lumpie, take
it up with a spoone & break it in a dish. If not, break it
as it boyls. when it comes clear from ye preserving pan,
it is enough.

The scribe absentmindedly used the negative in both cases, making
the directions for not having lumpy marmalade unclear. One can
mash cooked quinces more thoroughly off the fire, certainly, but
marmalade tends to be lumpy unless the quinces are pounded, as
in S 16, or strained. She also neglected to tell us to set the quinces
on the fire in the second sentence.

Loafe sugar refers to the blocks in which sugar reached the
consumer. For the use of the seeds, see S 9. Lawn is a kind of fine
linen. For quinces and marmalades, see S 7 and 13.

---

15   TO MAKE ORDINARY QUINCE
      MARMALET

Pare, core, & quarter y^r quinces, & to every 3 pound of
them, put a pound of loaf sugar. then put them both
into a silver or earthen basin & let them stand 2 or 3
days till ye sugar be all melted. then boyle them, and
when they begin to be tender, break them with a
spoon, and cover them sometimes with a dish, & when
it comes from ye pan, it is enough.

---

16   TO MAKE WHITE MARMALET OF
      QUINCES

Take quinces, core & scald them soft in fayre water.
then take of ye softest of ye quince and grinde it in a
stone morter. then take a pound of sugar to a pound of
quince downe weight, and set them together on ye fire
to boyle. take a little of it in a spoon to coole, & if it be
stiff, it is enough.

Downe weight signifies full weight, enough to down the weight, not just to balance it. It is the quinces that are so weighed.

---

17 TO MAKE WHITE MARMALET OF QUINCES

Core y^r quinces & scald them till they are tender, then put them into pippin water as fast as you pare them; & to every pinte of water, take 3 quarters of a pound of sugar. when they are mixt, boyl them up as fast as you can. take ye weight of y^r quinces in sugar, & to every pound of quince a pinte of pippin water will serve.

Pippin water is that in which apples have been poached (see S 27). The last sentence may be an addition by an interim hand; the proportions do not jibe. For each pound of quince and pint of water, the first formula calls for ¾ pound of sugar (1½ cups), the other calls for 1 pound (2 cups).

---

18 TO MAKE WHITE MARMALET OF QUINCES

Boyle your quinces till they are soft, then pare & scrape them, & to a pownd of y^t pulpe take a pound of ye finest sugar & clarefy it. in ye mean time, set y^r scraped quince in a dish against ye fire, set it sloping to dreyne. y^n put it into ye sugar & stir it till it be fit to box. be carefull ye fire be not too hot to change ye culler.

---

19 TO MAKE WHITE MARMALET OF QUINCES

To a pound of quince, take full 3 quarters of a pound of ye best loafe sugar. then pare, core, & quarter ye quinces, & as fast as you pare them, have ye sugar ready beaten, & strow [it]* on them. then let them stand 3 hours for ye sugar to melt, & when it is any thing moyst (for it will not be thin† till it comes to y^e

* Supplied.
† The scribe mistakenly closed parentheses here.

fire), then boyle them as fast as you can, & break it small, or in lumps is ye fashion. halfe an houre will boyle it If ye fire be quick.

The childish signature of Frances appears, upside down, at the top right corner of the page. I believe it to be that of Frances Parke. (See appendix 2, page 460.)

Due to inattention on the part of the copyist, one sentence does not read but I think the meaning is clear. Note that lumpy marmalade was in fashion (see S 14).

---

20   TO MAKE A MARMALET THAT WAS PRESENTED TO Y^e QUEENE FOR A NEW YEARS GIFT

Take a pound & halfe of sugar, boyle it with a pinte of water till it comes to manus Christi. then take 3 or 4 quinces; A good orring pill preserved & finely beaten; 3 ounces of allmonds blanch'd & finely beaten by themselves; oringo roots preserved, 2 ounces & a halfe. stir these with ye sugar in a bason over a chafing dish of coles till it will come from the sides of ye bason, & then put in A little muske & ambergreece dissolved in rosewater, of each 4 greyns; of cinnamon, ginger, cloves, and mace, of each 3 drams; & put in 2 drops of oyle of cinnamon. this beeing done, box it up, & present it to whome you please.

This is one of the few recipes for which I found a direct source: *A Closet for Ladies and Gentlewomen, or, The Art of preserving, Conserving, and Candying. With the manner howe to make divers kinds of Syrups: and all kind of banqueting stuffes*, 1608. The recipe is entitled: "To make an excellent Marmelate which was given Queene Mary for a New-years gift," and it differs from the recipe at hand only in minor details. (It is *Eringus* roots rather than *oringo*, for example.) The most interesting aspect is the evocation of Queen Mary, who reigned from 1553 to 1558. Elizabeth died in 1603 so that, at the time of publication, James I was on the throne. Until I found this recipe, I had naturally thought that the said *Queene* was Elizabeth; it now appears that the recipe dates from the time of Mary, nearly 50 years earlier. The little book is full of precisely the sort of recipe that we find in our own *Booke of Sweetmeats*. In other words, it is taken from a similar family still room book, complete with *divers soveraigne Medicines and Salves*. There is no other explanation, and we have seen how these family manuscripts were pillaged, without attribution, for the greater glory and profit of male authors and publishers, it not being seemly for *Ladies and Gentlewomen* to be in the market place of ideas—a right exercised only by the courageous even today. Furthermore, they may not have realized the value of their little manuscripts. (It is entirely possible, of course, that the two recipes come from a common source; an editor's hand would perfectly explain such differences as exist between them.) One cannot help but wonder why the name of Mary was expunged from our manuscript; perhaps the family became Protestant; perhaps they did not, and found it prudent not to refer to her; perhaps it has no significance whatsoever.

As for the recipe itself, it has elements of the "restorative" marmalade, of which there is a good example, S 70. The eryngo roots, highly regarded as an aphrodisiac, and all those spices, were not so much for flavor as for exuberant good health and success for those engaged in the *sports of Venus*.

Almond (*Amygdalus communis*) comes directly from Old French *almande*, and so appears in English by 1300 (*OED*). Gerard says that "there is likewise in the almonds an opening and concocting [digesting] quality, with a certain clensing faculty, by which they are medicinable to the chest and lungs, or lights, and serve for raising up of flegme and rotten humors." Five or 6 bitter almonds, "being taken fasting do keepe a man from being drunke." They were imported from Spain (see S 162 and 166).

Ambergris is the morbid secretion of the sperm whale. The name comes from Arabic *anbar* by way of *ambre gris*, grey amber. Originally, *amber* retained the original meaning, referring only to the secretion, and old recipes, especially in pharmacopoeia, still used *amber* for ambergris. But after its extension to the resin, first called *ambre jaune*, yellow amber, the secretion more and more came to be called *ambre gris* to distinguish them. The various forms of *grease* are an attempt to account for *gris*, the meaning of which had been forgotten, and the substance is waxy (*OED*). Culpeper, in *Pharmacopoeia Londinensis*, 1654, says: "*Ambergreese*, strengthens the brain and memory, the heart and vital Spirits, [and] warms cold stomaches . . . It provokes lust, and makes barren women frutful." It also "resists pestilence." It is now used only in perfumery (see C 76).

Eryngo roots are treated in S 34, 35, 89, and 90; *manus Christi* in S 4. A *dram* may be either ⅛ or 1/16 of an ounce (see S 70).

21   TO PRESERUE PIPPENS

First pare ye pippins very thin, then cut y^m in halves, &
weigh & put them in faire water. & put to every pound
ye full weight in sugar, & mingle halfe ye sugar with a
pinte & halfe of faire water. set on ye water with y^e
pippins & put in 2 spoonfulls of rose water. let them
not boyle to fast at ye first, but set them on a very
gentle fire for halfe a quarter of an houre. w^{hn} you
think they are soft, & more then halfe done, then strow
in ye rest of y^r sugar by little & little, & squeese in a
leamon by degrees, & take ye rinde of an orringe after it
hath boyled in 2 or 3 waters, slyce it in thin slyces &
put it in halfe an houre before ye pippins are enough.

Pippin refers to any of numerous varieties of apple raised from
seed. The word comes from Old French *pepin*, pip.

This is the first of a group of recipes for preserving pippins. They differ from the quince recipes in flavorings and technique (see S 7). Preserved fruits, as differentiated from fruits conserved with sugar in other ways, are left as whole as possible in
a thick jellied syrup and appearance is very important.

There are a number of English pippin varieties, of green
or golden hue, for the most part. The choice of apple in America
is a vexing one: whether the tree be a seedling or a grafting is not
the issue, I think; the problem is flavor and the characteristic of
holding its shape. Greenings, Gravensteins, Winesaps, and Granny
Smiths are possible candidates. There is no point whatsoever bothering with Golden Delicious, a picture book apple devoid of taste.

Starting the apples on a gentle fire is nice technique, designed to reduce the danger of their disintegrating. (Also, see S
25.) I suppose the given amounts of rose water and lemon juice
to be for a pound of apples. A most important point in preserving
is to work with small quantities; even when small quantities are
not explicitly mentioned, it is always assumed. The action of heat
on sugar is quite different with varying sizes of batch, intensity of
heat, etc.

---

22   TO PRESERUE PIPPINS RED

Take y^r best cullerd pippins & pare them, then boare* a
hole thorough each of them with a piercer. then make
as much sirrup as will cover y^m and let them boyle in A
broad preserving pan. put into them a cinnamon stick
& let them boyle close covered very leasurely. you must
turne them very often, else they will spot & ye one
syde will not be like ye other. Let them thus boyle untill
they begin to Jelly, then take them up & put them
eyther in galley pots or glasses, & they will keepe all
the year.

Gallipots are small earthen glazed pots (*OED*). *Galley* most likely
harks back to their having been brought to England in galleys; that
is, from the Mediterranean.
For *pippins*, see S 21.

---

23   TO PRESERUE PIPPINS WHITE

Take faire large pippins though it be after Candlemass.
pare & boar a hole thorough each of them, as you did
for ye red ones, then make a weak sirrup, in which
they must boyle till they are tender. then take them up
& let y^r sirrup boyle a little higher. then put them in a
galley pot & let them stand all night, & the next
morning, then boyle ye sirrope againe to its full
thickness. soe pot them up & they will keep all ye year.
If you pleas, you may put in a grayne of muske, & a
drop or 2 of chymicall oyle of cinnamond.

The weight of a grain is 1/7000 of a pound avoirdupois, the weight
of a grain of wheat. (*Greyne*, from Old French *grain*, was in use
from the thirteenth to sixteenth centuries—*OED*.) However, since
musk comes in sticky particles, it is likely that a small particle is
indicated (see S 113).

* A blot over the *a* could represent a deletion, but see S23.

Gerard says that, "The oyle [of cinnamon] drawne chim-
ically prevaileth against the paines of the brest, comforteth the
stomacke, breaketh windiness, causeth good digestion . . ."
Candlemas is February 2.

---

24   TO PRESERUE PIPPINS GREEN

Take pippins when they are small & green, fresh from
ye tree, & cut 3 or 4 of ye worst to pieces. then boyle
them in a quart of faire water till they be pap. then let
ye liquor run from y^m as you doe from quidony into a
basin.* then put in to them a pound of clarefied sugar,
& as many pippins unpared as y^t liquor will cover. soe
let them boyle softly till they are as tender as a codling.
then take y^m of & pill of ye outermost[e] white scinn, &
then y^r pippins will be green. then boyle them in y^e
sirrup againe till ye sirrup be thick, & soe you may
keepe y^m all ye year close tyed [in] glasses or gally pots.

The syrup of the preserved apples (see S 21) is to be thickened
with the pulp of the *worst*, or least presentable, apples. A *quidony*,
or quiddany, is a conserve of quince, from Old French *codignac*
(see S 198). A *codling* is a cooking apple (C 67).

---

25   TO PRESERUE GREEN PIPPINS

First coddle y^r pippins when they are green, but let
them† stand noe longer on ye fire then they will just
pill. then pill them & put them in a posnet of fayre
water, & let them stand some two hours close covered,
over a soft fire, but let them not boyle for then they will
break all to pieces. put to A pound of apples A pound
and a quarter of sugar, and A pinte of water. when
your syrrup is boyled and scumed, put in your apples
with A spoone, but very softly least they break, and
take them of the fire when you turne them. and when
the sirrup is boyled pritty thick, take the apples out and

* The *i* is apparently corrected from an *o*.
† I excised a repeated *them*.

give it A walme or 2 after. then poure it scalding hot
upon your apples, and soe let them stand till ye next
morning. then boyle it againe with the apples till the
sirrup be of A good thickness. this last boyling makes
them keepe all the year. you must get the right winter
pippen, else they* will be apt to goe to water, and you
must choose them large, else they will shrivell to
noething. and when they are preservd thoroughly, put
them up in glasse or pots and tie them up very close.

This is a carefully presented recipe of a perceptive cook, the same
cook, I believe, who gave the recipe for the *Frykecy* in C 2. There
are certain turns of phrase common to both but above all, it is her
way of anticipating pitfalls and of giving reasons for the more
important instructions.

Coddle means to lightly poach (see C 67). A *posnet* is a
three-footed pot (see S 125).

---

26   TO PRESERUE PIPPINS GREENE OR
        PLUMBS

Take 2 scillets of water & set y^m on ye fire. when it
[be]† scallding hot, put in ye green apples or plums.
keep them covered but not boyle, & let y^m remaine
there in till they have lost theyr culler. y^n put them in
ye other scillet of water, beeing as hot as ye former.
there let them rest till ye little scins rise, which must be
pilled of. y^n take y^m out & put y^m into ye first water
which must be kept hot, & there let them remaine till
they are perfectly green. then ty y^m up severally in
pieces of tiffany. when you have weighed them, boyle
y^m up in sirrup, adding more sirrup to y^m then you
comonly use to other preserves. y^n tie a little musk in
tiffany & put in If you like it. y^n take y^m up & pot
them, & boyle ye sirrop a while after. ye tiffanies are
used to preserve them from breaking.

* Written *the*.
† Supplied in lieu of confusing *here*, apparently corrected from *hear*.

This is another thoughtful recipe, although not well presented. The wrapping of each apple in tiffany is noteworthy. For musk, see S 113.

Tiffany may be either a thin transparent silk or a transparent gauze muslin. The name is apparently from Epiphany silk (*OED*). The skillet, a large shallow pan, was usually footed and long-handled for easy use in fireplace cookery (see S 310).

---

27 TO MAKE PIPPIN MARMALET

Take pippins & boyle them A good while. then streyne it, & to a pinte of y^t water & a little more, put a pound of sugar. then slyce candyed orringe pills & put them into ye sirrup. boyle it very fast, & when it is allmoste enough, put in some juice of orringes & leamons, more or less according to y^r taste. after, boyle it fast a little, and then glass it up. & if you like it, you may put in s[ome am]ber.

The directions for this marmalade indicate that only the cooking water is used, providing an apple jelly basis for the addition of candied orange peel and the juice of Seville oranges and lemons. Nothing is said of the fate of the cooked apples, but straining does not normally imply pureeing, and the use of the word water seems specific enough (see S 17 and 32).

For marmalades, see S 13. *Amber* is ambergris (S 20).

---

28 TO PRESERUE ORRINGES AND LEAMONS

Take orringes or Leamons and lay them a night in water. then boyle them till they be tender. shift them 8 or 9 times in the boylling into severall waters. put into ye first water a handfull of salt, & let every water boyle before you put y^m in. take as much sugar as they weigh, & as much water as will make A sirrup to cover them. then boyle them halfe an houre very softly. the longer y^t you boyle an orringe in sugar, ye harder it will be. y^n take up your orringes & boyle ye sirrup untill it

To preserue Pippins Greene or Plumbs

26

Take 2 scillets of water & set y^m on ye fire, when it heee scalding hot put in ye green apples or plums, keep them couered but not boyle & Let y^m remaine therein till they haue lost theyr culler yⁿ put them in ye other scillet of water beeing as hot as ye former, there let them rest till ye little scins rise which must be pilled of, yⁿ take y^m out & put y^m into ye first water which must be kept hot, & there Let them remaine till they are par- fectly green. then ty y^m up seuerally in pieces of tiffany, when you haue weighed them, boyle y^m up in sirrup adding more sirrup to y^m then you comon ly use to other preserues, yⁿ tie a little musk in tiffany & put in if you like it, yⁿ take y^m up & pot them, & boyle ye sirrup a while. after ye tiffa- nies are used to preserue them from breaking.

To make Pippin Marmalet

27

Take pippins & boyle them a good while then streyne it & to a pinte of y^r water & a little more put a pound of sugar, then slyce candyed orringe pills & put them into ye sirrup boyle it uery fast, & when it is allmost enough put in some iuice of orringes & leanons, more or less according to y^r taste after boyle it fast a little and then glass it up. & if you like it you may put in some amber.

will button on a dish syde. when they be both cold, put
them in a glass together.

We now come to a group of recipes for preserved oranges and
other citrus fruits. As explained in S 21, preserved fruits are kept
as whole as possible, so that in these recipes, the general effect
will be that of Chinese preserved kumquats, and indeed, they will
do very well in these recipes.

What may seem an inordinate emphasis on shifting of
many waters in these recipes is due to the fact that they were
dealing with the bitter Seville orange, *Citrus bigaradia*, according
to *OED* but *Citrus aurantium* in *The Oxford Book of Food Plants* (see
S 94). The recipes, though of uneven quality, show a solid grasp
of the techniques of preserving. Citrus fruits must be cooked tender
in water before being put to syrup; as the recipe admonishes, they
harden in boiling syrup, so take care. I like the jelly test: "it will
button on a dish syde."

It is thought that all oranges (genus *Citrus*) originated on
the northern frontier of India. *Orange* comes directly from Old
French *orenge*; before that there was Arabic *narānj* (whence Spanish
naranja), late Sanskrit *nāranga,* and Hindu *nārangī*. The dropping
of the initial *n* in French was perhaps due in part to its absorption
by the article *une,* and in part to a confusion with various forms
of *or* (gold) because of the deep golden color of the orange. (Robert,
however, says it comes from Italian *melarancia,* in turn from the
Arabic.) The forms in our manuscript are sixteenth-century forms
(*OED*).

I do not know exactly when the sweet orange came to
England, but at the time of our manuscript there is question only
of the Seville orange; to this day, it is preferred for marmalades,
and in meat cookery it is far superior (see C 14).

For lemons, see C 1.

---

29   TO PRESERUE ORRINGES AND
      LEAMONS

Take thick rined orringes or leamons, chipp y^m & cut
them in halves or quarters, & take out all theyr meat.
then boyle & shift them in severall waters till they are
tender, which will take away theyr bitterness. every
water must be first warmed before you put y^m in. y^n
take as much sugar as ye pills weighs, & make as much

sirrup as will cover them. there let y^m boyle till* y^e
bitterness be gon. then make another stronger sirrup &
boyle it to a good thickness, in wch you must† put y^r
pills in galley pots to keepe all [ye year].

This recipe is not well presented and some details remain unclear,
particularly the fate of the flesh of the oranges. There may be
missing phrases towards the last which would have elucidated that
detail.

---

30   TO PRESERUE ORRINGES

Pare y^r orringes very thin, & rub them with salt, & put
them in water for halfe an houre. y^n set on 2 new
pipkins full of fayre water, & when your water is hot,
cut your orringes in halves & take out a little of y^e
meat, or cut A hole in ye top & take out ye seeds. & put
ye pills in one of ye pipkins, & let them boyle A good
while till ye water be bitter. then take them out & put
them into the other pipkin, & soe shift them 5 or 6
times, till they are very tender. then take them out of y^e
water, & lay them one‡ by one on a clean cloth. wipe
them or let ye water run clean from them. then take to
every pound of orringe A pinte & quarter of water, & 2
pound of sugar to make y^r sirrup. then take 6 whites of
eggs & beat y^m well with a little water, & put halfe y^e
eggs into ye water & sugar before it boyle. & ye rest,
put in by little & little as it boyles. when it hath boyled
a good while, take it from ye fire & let it stand a little.
take of ye scum, y^n strayn it thorough a cotten strayner
& poure it hot upon y^r orringes. & let y^m stand soe 2
dayes, then set them on ye fire agayne. & let y^m boyle
an houre & halfe. y^n take y^m of & let y^m stand till they
are allmoste cold. y^n set y^m on ye fire againe, & put to
y^m halfe a pinte of renish wine, & a good piece of dry

* I excised a repeated *till*.
† Written *musts*.
‡ Written *on*.

sugar. let y^m boyle on a soft fire till theyr sirrup is pritty thick, y^n take y^m up & boyle ye sirrup till it will Jelly. y^n put ye orringes in & let them warm[e.* y^n take] y^m of ye fire & let y^m stand all night. ye next day pot y^m.

In the transfer from pipkin to pipkin, the water is changed each time (see S 28). New pipkins are occasionally recommended because earthenware has a way of absorbing old flavors.

The egg whites have to do with clarifying the sugar, an unnecessary operation nowadays in preserving.

I suppose that *warme* is the correct reading. *Warp* means to spurt, which is precisely what happens when you put cool preserves on the fire; it would be used much as "give it a walme or two," elsewhere.

---

31   TO PRESERUE LEAMONS OR CITRONS

Take ye thickest rined leamons you can get, pare them as thin as you can, & then rub them well with salt. lay them to soak in faire water for a night, y^n shift ye water, & after, you must boyle y^r leamons in faire water till they are tender, still filling them up with water whilst they are thus boyling. clarefy ye sirrup & boyle it very thick against ye leamon be tender. then put them out of ye water into ye sirrup. to a pound of leamons, put a pound & halfe of sugar, & a pinte & halfe of water. when ye leamons have been a while in ye sirrup, to every pownd streyne in 5 spoonfulls of leamon Juice. when you think they are halfe done, take them of & cover them till ye next day. then preserve y^m out, & leave out some sugar to strow on in theyr last boyling.

For preserving citrus fruits, see S 28. I believe some words were omitted by the copyist at the last. For citrons, see S 33.

* Because of damage, the *m* is doubtful; I first read it as *warp*.

32   TO MAKE MARMALET OF ORRINGES

Lay y^r orringes in water 9 dayes, y^n boyle them whole
in 3 or 4 waters till ye bitterness be gon. y^n pare them
& take onely ye pills & beat them in a morter, y^n take
halfe a pound of it & halfe a pound of ye pap of scalded
pippins. mix y^m together & dry them in a dish over a
chafing dish of coles a quarter of an houre, & stir y^m
well. then take a pownd & halfe of sugar & as much
rose water as will wet it, then boyle it in a dish on coles
till it is allmoste sugar agayne. then mingle ye orringes,
ye pippin pap, & sugar alltogether & dry it in ye dish
againe over a chafing dish of coles, till it is stiff enough.

This is a curious marmalade recipe, and the instructions are by no
means clear. See S 28 and 13. Oranges and pippins seem to have
been a fairly common combination.

Recipes S 29 and 31 more nearly resemble modern English
marmalade.

33   TO PRESERUE POMCITRONS

Take a pound & halfe of pumcitrons, & cut them, some
in halves & some in quarters. take ye meat out of them
& boyle them tender in fayre water. then take 2 pound
of sugar, beeing clarefied, & make sirrup for them in
which they must boyle a quarter of an houre very
gently. then take them up & let y^r sirrup boyle till it be
thick. then poure it on your citrons & they will keepe
all ye year.

Of pomecitron (*Citrus medica*) Gerard says: "The rinde of the Pomecitron is good against all poysons, for which cause it is put into
treacles and such like confections." It is also good "against a stinking breath," he claims.

The pulp is rarely used. Citron has fallen into disfavor;
one seldom encounters it except in fruit cake. (See S 237.)

34   TO PRESERUE ORINGO ROOTES

Take a pound of fayre oringo roots y^t are not knotty.
wash them clean, & boyle them tender, then pill of y^e
outermoste scin, but break them not as you pare them.
put y^m in cold water, till they be all finnished, y^n take
to every pound of roots 3 quarters of a pound of
clarefied sugar. boyle it allmoste to ye height of sirrup.
then put in y^r roots & let them boyle very gently
together, & stir them very little for fear they break. w^{hn}
they are enough, pot them up, & soe keep them.

Eryngo roots are sea holly (*Eryngium maritimum*). Gerard says: "The
roots condited or preserved with sugar . . . are exceeding good to
be given to old and aged people that are consumed and withered
with age and which want natural moisture; they are also good for
other sorts of people that have no delight or appetite to venery,
nourishing and restoring the aged, and amending the defects of
nature in the yonger." This explains the line in *The Merry Wives
of Windsor*: "Let the skie raine Potatoes . . . haile kissing-Comfits,
and snow Eringoes." Provokers of venery, all. (Also, see S 89, 90,
and 197.)

Gerard says that it "grows by the sea side," and that he
has found it "growing plentifully at Whitstable in Kent," and other
places, "from whence I brought plants for my garden." Its popularity waned steadily during the seventeenth century and is all
but unknown today.

For additional details, see also S 35.

35   TO PRESERUE ORINGO ROOTES

Seeth them till they are tender, then pill them & put y^m
in a cullender, till they have dropt as much as they
will. then have a thin sirrup ready, & put them in
beeing colde. let them stand 3 days in ye sirrup. then
boyle it, adding more fresh sirrup to it, to supply what
ye roots drink up. at 3 days end, boyle the sirrup
againe, without any more addition. boyle it to ye full
height of a preserving sirrup, then put it to y^r root[s, &
soe keJepe them.

36   TO PRESERVE PEACHES

Take a pound of ye fayrest & best cullered peaches you
can get, wipe of theyr white hore with a clean linnen
cloth, then parboyle them in halfe a pinte of white
wine, & a pinte & half of running water. then pill of
their white scin, & weigh them, & to a pound of peach,
take 3 quarters of A pound of refined sugar. dissolve it
in a quarter of a pinte of white wine & boyle it allmoste
to ye height of a sirrup. then put your peaches, and let
them ly in the sirrup for more then a quarter of an
houre If they require it. then pot them up & keepe
them all ye year; they must have A little quick boyle in
ye sirrup till they Jelly.

In this long preserving section, we now come to a group comprising
peaches, apricots, cherries, plums, gooseberries, raspberries, and
barberries. For notes on preserving, see S 21.
    This is an excellent recipe. The white wine must be good,
however, or it will be better to use water.
    Peach (*Amygdalus persica*) comes from Latin *Persicum malum*,
Persian apple, by way of Old French *pesche*. The *hore* is the fuzz
of the peach. *Hore* was the North Midlands form of *hair* in the
fourteenth and fifteenth centuries. More likely, however, it is the
related word *hoar*, meaning white hair, from which *hoar frost* derives, although I found no specific reference (*OED*).

37   TO PRESERUE MALAGATOONES

Take malagatoons, stone and parboyle them in water, &
take of ye outer scinn. you need not fear theyr breaking
for they will boyle a very long time. when they are
boyled tender, make sirrup for them with ye same
weight in sugar, & to every pound of sugar take a wine
pinte of faire water, & clarefy your sirrup. then put in
your mallagatoones and boyle them very fast till they
Jelly. then pot them and keepe them for your use.

A melocoton (*melum cotoneum*, Cydonian apple) is a peach grafted
to a quince tree (*OED*). (There seems also to have been a variety

of peach so named, but the hardness of the fruit indicates the grafting.) The English corruption of the Spanish *melocoton* to *malagatoone* suggests that the English imported the stock from Spain. The fruit was cultivated in England and was popular during Elizabethan times and through the seventeenth century.

Peaches could be substituted in this recipe, exercising due caution in the boiling of this more tender fruit. A *wine pinte* corresponds to a U.S. pint (S 1). I would use the poaching liquid as part of the water for making the syrup.

---

38   TO PRESERUE APRICOCKS

Take yᵉ fayrest apricocks you can get, & to a pound, take 3 quarters of a pound of double refin'd sugar. stone & pare yᵉ apricocks, & beat yᵉ sugar finely, & put on them. let them stand all night, & in the morning set them on yᵉ fire without any water, & boyle them softly, & they will Jelley. then put them up in glasses.

The apricot (*Prunus armeniaca*, prune of Armenia) may have been brought to Europe by the Arabs. At least the name comes from Arab *al-borcoq* or *al-burquq*, most likely by way of French *abricot*. However, the classical Greeks knew it and thought that it came from Armenia. It seems to have been slow in coming to England; *OED* does not cite it before early in the sixteenth century. *Apricock* was a common sixteenth- and seventeenth-century form (*OED*).

Paring an apricot is a trick and quite unnecessary, but apparently was a nicety of the day. It is a fine recipe. For preserving, see S 21.

---

39   TO PRESERUE APRICOCKS

Take a pound of apricocks & a pound of sugar, & clarefy yʳ sugar with a pinte of water. then put it into a preserving pan, & put yʳ apricocks into it (first being pared & stoned),* & let them boyle gently till they be allmoste enough. then boyle them fast till yʳ sirrup be very thick. soe put them in glasses & keepe them. in like manner, you may preserve a pearplum.

For apricots, see S 38; for preserving, S 7. The *pear plum* was one

* Scribe's parentheses.

of several varieties of plum, so named because it was somewhat pear-shaped. The shape and description (see S 119) make me wonder if it might not be the same as the *great white wheat plum* of S 47, where plums are also treated.

---

40   TO PRESERUE APRICOCKS

You must first scald y^r apricocks over a soft fire, & when they be tender, pill ye scins of & stone them. then lay them in a skillet without water. then take theyr weight in suger & strow some of it on them. after, set y^r skillet on a slow fire, & as y^r sugar melts, strow on more, till it is all on. you may ges when they are enough by the sirrups beeing thick & th[eyr] falling to ye bottom.

---

41   TO PRESERUE APRICOCKS

Take a pound of ye fayrest fresh gathered apricocks you can get; let them be full ripe. pare y^m very thin, & as fast as you pare them, put them into a bason of faire water, then wipe them wth a clean cloth. after, take a pound of double refined sugar fine beaten, strow some of it on the bottom of a sillver bason,* & lay y^r apricocks one by one into it. y^n strow on them ye rest of y^r sugar & let y^m stand till it is pritty well melted. y^n set y^m on a gentle fire, & let them boyle a walme or 2. turne them often in ye boyling. y^n take them of ye fire againe, & let y^m stand till ye next day. turne y^m often till they be colde. then cover them, & ye next day, set them on againe, & make them hot but not boyle. use them as before. doe thus every 24 hours till ye sirrup be thicke enough, y^n pot y^m.

I believe this to be a recipe of our friend of the *Frykecy* (C 2). In any event, the cook shows the same perceptiveness and care. The apricots must be fresh gathered and full ripe, and the technique

* The *o* is an ink blot.

of gradual permeation of the fruit by sugar is an excellent one that is very old.

Please do not use fine silver; the scribe is warning us against brass and iron, to which I would add aluminum—they all discolor fruit. Nostradamus, in his recipes for preserved fruits, made a point of earthenware for this reason. I like copper, but pans lined with stainless steel are fine.

---

42   TO PRESERUE CHERRIES

Take 2 pound of fayre cheries, & pull out ye stones at ye top with ye strigs. & take one pound of cheries with ye stones, & bruise & streyne them thorough a canvis strayner, to which Juice take 2 pound of loaf sugar, & when it is melted, boyle in it ye other cherrys untill the sirrup will Jelly, and then put them up in pots or glasse, & tie them up close.

This recipe makes use of a fairly common technique of the day, that of preserving whole fruit in a syrup fortified with crushed fruit, usually of the same variety. For preserving, see S 21. See also recipes 43 through 45.

Cherries (*Prunus cerasus*) comes directly from Old Norman French *cherise* (with some confusion over thinking it a plural form), but they were known in England long before that; *OED* cites *ciris* in a manuscript of about 1000, and Anne Wilson says that the Romans brought the cultivated cherry to England.

The *strig* is the stem or stalk. *Canuis*, sometimes called cushion canvas because it is of an open regular lattice-work weave used for embroidery, was much used as a sieve. Finer ones were of lawn or silk. They all made excellent sieves but tended to pick up odors.

---

43   TO PRESERUE CHERRIES

Take a pound of cherries & stone them, y^n take a quarter of a pound of sugar beaten fine & strow it on them & put y^m in a preserving pan, strowing first a little sugar on ye bottom of y^r pan. y^n set y^m on a moderate fire & put 2 spoonfulls of water to y^m & let y^m simper till they be thoroughly tender, but not boyle.

y^n take up ye cherys & lay y^m in ye bottom of a sive, & when they are well drayned, set y^m into a warme oven on a tin plate, or earthen pan. y^n take ye liquor they were in & to every pinte, put a pound of sugar. boyle & scum it well. If it be* ordinary sugar, clarefie it. & when it is allmoste cold, put in y^r cherries which are for preserving, & boyle them pritty fast. when they are tender, take them up, & when y^r sirrup is thorough cold, put in y^r cheries, & pot them up.

The use of *simper* for not quite a simmer is delightful; just so the French use *sourire*, to smile. See S 42.

Siue was in use from the fourteenth to seventeenth centuries; *sieve* sppeared in the sixteenth. An eleventh-century form was *sife* and is from the same stem as *sift*.

---

44   TO PRESERUE CHERIES

Put to y^r cheries their weight in sugar, & in the bottom of a scillet lay some of ye sugar, then A lay of cherries, & then sugar againe, & upon every lay of cherries put 4 cherries bruised to pieces. soe set them on ye fire & let them seeth halfe an houre. then take them of & scum them clean, & shake & turne them sometimes in ye boyling least they burne. y[ou may stri]p ye strigs short & leav ye stones in or take y^m [out].†

---

45   TO PRESERUE CHERRIES

Take 2 pound of faire cherries & clip of the stalks in ye midst. then wash them clean, but bruise them not. then take 2 pound of double refind sugar, & set it over ye fire with a quart of faire water in ye broadest preserving pan or silver basen as you can get. Let it seeth till it be some what thick, y^n put in y^r cherries, & let them boyle. keepe allwayes scumming & turning them gently

* I excised a repeated *be*.
† Supplied.

with a silver spoon till they be enough. when they are
cold, you may glass them up & keep them all the year.

---

46   TO PRESERUE GREEN APRICOCKS
        GREEN PEACHES OR GREEN ALMONDS

Take y^r green almonds, peaches or green apricocks
when they are soe tender y^t you may put a pin
thoroughly ye stones, then take faire water & ashes &
boyle them together, & strayne ye water from ye ashes
& put y^r fruit into it, & let them ly in it 3 dayes & it
will draw of all ye ruggedness & scurf from them. then
boyle them very tender in faire water, & clarefy 2
pound of sugar & boyle it to a full sirrup, & put y^r
apricocks, peaches, or almonds into it, & let them boyle
very leasurely till they are very tender. then set them to
cool, & 3 dayes after, boyle ye sirrop by it self [& a little
w]hile after* put it to your fruit.

The soaking of acrid fruits—green olives, for example—in water
in which ashes have been boiled is an old trick to leach out any
bitterness or "ruggedness." (Lye would be used nowadays.) *Scurf*
is a scaliness or roughness. For almonds see S 20.

---

47   TO PRESERUE PLUMS GREENE

The plum which will be green when preserved is y^e
great white wheat plum, which is ripe in wheat
harvest. gather them about ye midle of July, or sooner
or later as you see y^m in bigness, for If you let them
grow till they begin to turne yellow, they will never be
a good green when they are preserved. when they are
gathered, put them in water ye space of 12 hours, but
first weigh them & cut of their stalks, & set 2 scillets of
water on ye fire, & when one of them is allmoste
scalding hot, put in ye plums & take y^m from ye fire &
cover them. & soe let them stand for a quarter of an

* Written *ater*.

houre, then take them up & when ye other skillet of
water boyles, put them into it, but let them stay in but
a very little. & let ye first skillet wherein they were first
put, be set on ye fire againe & made to boyle. then put
them into it as before, & when they shrivel all over, y^n
scrape of ye thin scin, & have a care they break not.
weigh them, & to every pound of plums, put one
pound & 12 ounces of double refind sugar, very finely
beaten. then set a pan on ye fire with a little faire
water, & when it begins to boyle, put in ye plums, & let
them boyle leasurely for about half an houre till they*
grow green. then take them of ye fire & cover them, &
let them stand about a quarter of an houre, then take a
handfull or 2 of y^r weig[hed] sug[ar & lay] it in y^e
bottom of y^r pan, & put in y^r p[lums] ye water beeing
drayned from them as clear as you can, & put ye rest of
their weight upon them. then set y^r pan on a moderate
fire of charcole, letting them boyle continually, but very
softly for fear of breaking. in 3 quarters of an houre, or
a little more, y^r plums will be ready, wch you may
perceive by ye greenness of y^m & thickness of ye sirrup,
which If it be boyld enough it will Jelly. when it is cold,
take up y^r plums & put them in a galley pot. boyle y^r
sirrup a little higher, & when it is little more then bloud
warme, poure it on ye plums, but cover not ye pot till
they are thorough cold. let them be preserved in such a
pan as they may ly one by another for fear of breaking,
& give them as much roome in ye last water. when they
have layd 5 or 6 dayes in ye sirrup, if it be not thick
enough, take it from ye plums & boyle it higher. this
way, you may doe ye pippin, peach, or pearplum,
saveing ye pippin & peach must have [one]† or 2
scalldings & then boyling to bring ye culler, & ye plum
must have 3 scalldings & a boyling.

* Written *the*.
† Supplied.

This well-detailed recipe, replete with preserving technique, heads a group of recipes for preserving plums. It is long winded and there is a contradictory passage (as well as a damaged portion) but I think that no real difficulties are presented. In spite of advice to the contrary, I believe that the long soaking comes before the rest of the procedure; see S 48.

The plum (*Prunus domestica*) has long been popular in England; it is mentioned in a manuscript from around 725, and was quite likely gathered long before. The word comes from Latin *prunus*; the earliest recorded forms in English (in common with other Northern languages) already involve *plum* or *plom* (*OED*).

This "great white wheat plum" may possibly be what *The Oxford Book of Food Plants* calls *White Magnum Bonum* or *Yellow Egg Plum*, described as an old parent variety of a greenish-yellow family. The green gage seems not to have been introduced from France (the *Reine Claude*) until the eighteenth century.

---

48   TO PRESERUE ANY GREEN PLUMS

Take y^r plums when they are green, & scalld them in hot water, & let them stand in ye water till it be sucked into them & they will loose theyr greenness & be pale. then put y^m into cold water, & let y^m ly in it 3 dayes, & it will draw all ye sappiness & redness from y^m, & when they come to be boyled in ye sirrup they will turne to theyr perfect greenness. then clarefy 2 pound of sugar, & let them boyle leasurely till they be very tender. then set y^m to coole, & 3 days after, boyle ye sirrup by it selfe & scum it. & then put it to your plums againe.

---

49   TO PRESERUE DAMSONS OTHER PLUMS
      OR APRICOCKS TO KEEP ALL Y^e YEAR
      IN A QUACKEING JELLY

Take a pinte of apple water & boyle 2 pound of sugar in it, till it is thoroughly dissolved & is in a perfect sirrup. then take 2 pound of y^r fairest & ripest plums, & put into it, & let them boyle very leasurely till they

are very tender. then set them to coole, & let them
stand in ye sirrup 3 days. then take them out & boyle
ye sirrup by it selfe, & as it riseth, scum it of very clean,
& put to it y^r plums, or y^r plums to it, & they will keep
all ye year very well, & ye sirrup will be in A quacking
Jelly.

Damsons (*Prunus damascena*) are a variety of plum introduced very
early into Greece and Italy from Syria, whence they spread. It is
a dark blue cooking plum of a luscious intense taste. It showed up
as *damasceyne* in English by the fourteenth century; the modern
form followed shortly (*OED*). Also see C 70.

Apple water is that in which apples have been poached
(see S 122, for example); for preserving of plums, see S 47.

It should be noted perhaps, because of an ink blot just
where the *c* most likely is, that the *c* of *Quackeing* in the title is
justified by the text. *Quack* is a fourteenth-century form of quake
(*OED*).

---

50   T O P R E S E R U E A N Y K I N D E O F P L U M S
        T O K E E P I N A P E R F E C T S I R R U P A L L
        Y^e Y E A R

Boyle a pound of sugar & clarefy it into A casting
height, & put a pound of y^r plums to it boyling hot, &
ye strength & heat of y^r sugar will binde y^r plums from
slipping theyr skins, & the liquidness of y^r plums will
turne ye strength of y^r sugar into a thin sirrup againe.
boyle them as leasurely as you can, till you may feele y^e
stones of them. then set them to coole, & let them
stand in ye sirrup 3 days. then boyle ye sirrup by it
selfe till it hangs to y^r stones. scum them clean & then
put ye sirrup to your plums again in A pot or glass. soe
paper them up & keepe them for your use.*

For preserving of plums, see S 47; *for casting height*, S 6.

* This was an especially clear example of the archaic use of *v* for *u*; see
facsimile, page 257.

To Preserue Damsons other plums or
Apricocks to keep all ye year in A
Quaeking Jelly

49

Take a pinte of apple water & boyle 2 pound of
sugar in it, till it is thoroughly dissolued & is
in a perfect sirrup, then take 1 pound of y^r fairest
& ripest plums, & put into it, & let them boyle
uery leasurely, till they are uery tender, then set
them to coole & let them stand in ye sirrup 3 days
then take them out & boyle ye sirrup by it selfe,
& as it riseth scum it of uery clean, & put to
it y^r plums or y^r plums to it, & they will keep
all ye year uery well, & ye sirrup will be in A
quaeking Jelly

To preserue any kinde of Plums to keep
in A perfect sirrup all ye year.

50

Boyle a pound of sugar & clarefy it into A
casting height, & put a pound of y^r plums to it
boyling hot, & ye strength & heat of y^r sugar will
bind y^r plums from slipping theyr skins, & the
liquidness of y^r plums, will turne ye strength of y^e
sugar, into a thin sirrup againe, boyle them as
leasurely as you can, till you may feele ye stones
of them, then set them to coole & let them stand
in ye sirrup 3 days, then boyle ye sirrup by it
selfe till it hangs to y^r stones, scum them clean
& then put ye sirrup to your plums againe
in A pot or glass soe paper them up & keepe
them for your use.

51   TO PRESERUE WHITE PEARPLUMS

Take pear plums when they are allmoste ripe, & slit
them with a penknife on ye side, & cut out or thrust
out ye stones with a bodkin. & put them in hot water &
let them stand A little. then take them out & lay them
in a faire cloth, & dry ye water clean from them. then
take a pound & allmoste halfe of sugar to a pound of
plums. make a sirrup & put them in & make them
simmer. then take them of, & ye next day set them on
againe. soe doe 2 or 3 dayes, & never let them boyle for
fear of breaking. then take up ye plums, & give y^e
sirrup A little quick boyling, & when it [is]* allmoste
cold, put it to your plums.

For *pearplum*, see S 39; for preserving of plums, see S 47. A *bodkin*
is a small pointed instrument for piercing holes; originally, it was
a weapon.

52   TO PRESERVE DAMSONS

Take damsons, prick & weigh them, and take their
weight in sugar. then take some of your sugar and put
it in y^r pan, & put in as much water as will wet it. then
lay your damsons in that & cover them with the rest of
your sugar. then set them on A softe fire, and let them
boyle as gently as you can, till they are allmoste
enough. then make them boyle fast till they are quite
enough. then take them of, and put them up in glasses
or pots, & when they are quite cold, tie them up with
papers. you must be careful to choose y^r damsons that
they be fresh, faire, & free fr[om blemish (?)] & not to
ripe, least they break.

For damsons, see S 49; for preserving plums, see S 47.

* Supplied.

258

53   TO PRESERUE DAMSONS

Take large faire & well coulered damsons, but not
thorough ripe, for then they will be apt to break. pick
them clean & wipe them one by one, then weigh them,
and to every pound of damsons take a pound of good
barbary sugar, & dissolve it in more then halfe a pinte
of fai[re] water. boyle it allmoste to ye height of a
sirrup, then put in y^r damsons, & keep them with
continuall stirring, y^t is, turning & scumming with a
silver spoon. let them boyle till they be enough on a
gentle fire, then take them up & pot them.

For damsons, see S 49; for preserving plums, see S 47. *Barbary
sugar* was that imported from the Maghreb, particularly Morocco.
(See discussion of imported sugar, page 11).

54   TO PRESERVE DAMSONS OR OTHER
PLUMS

Take a pound of damsens, & their weight in sugar
beaten & melted, with 2 or 3 spoonfulls of water. then
set it on ye fire to boyle, & scum it clean. for want of
double refin'd sugar, take of ye best lofe sugar &
clarefie it with ye white of an egg well beat. scum y^e
egg very clear, then streyne it thorough a Jelly bagg. &
when y^r sirrup is a little warme, put in y^r plums, letting
them boyle very softly. when they are halfe boyld, take
y^m of, & let y^m stand till ye next day, y^n boyle them
softly till ye sirrup will Jelley. put all kinde of plums in
y^r glasses betwixt hot & cold, & reserve some of y^r
sirrup till ye next day. y^n put it to y^m, beeing neyther
hot nor cold. cover not y^r plums till all y^r sirrup is in &
thorough cold. whilst you are boyling any plums, take
y^m of y^e [fire 3 (?)] times for a quarter of an houre, to
keep y^m from [breaking].

For damsons, see S 49; for preserving plums, see S 47.

The refining of sugar is unnecessary nowadays. "Betwixt hot & cold" means "neyther hot nor cold," or lukewarm. Because of damage to the manuscript, it is impossible to know how many times you are to take off the plums; perhaps three times? It is good technique.

---

55   TO PRESERUE GRAPES

Take ye fairest ripe grapes, soe soone as they look clear. slit them in ye side & take out ye stones. weigh them against double refin'd sugar beat very small, then put to it 2 or 3 spoonfulls of faire water, & soe let stand till it be melted. then set it on ye fire & when it boyls, scum it clear & take it of ye fire. & when it is allmoste cold, put in y^r grapes, & set them on ye fire & let them boyle prity fast. & when you see them shrink & ye sirrup grow pritty thick, take out ye grapes & put them in your glasses you intend to keepe them in, & put in a little of ye sirrup to them. & ye next day, boyle ye remainder to a Jelley, & pour it on y^r grapes thorough a coten cloth, & they will keep very green all ye year.

Most grapes, whether they be wine grapes, dessert grapes, or those grown for drying, belong to *Vitis vinifera*, according to *The Oxford Book Of Food Plants*. There is no clue given as to the variety here, except that they are white. The word grape comes from Old French *grape*, meaning bunch (see C 156).

For more on preserving, see S 21.

---

56   TO PRESERUE GOOSBERRIES

Take ye fairest you can get, & doe but halfe a pound at a time. take their weight in sugar, & when they are stoned, lay some sugar in ye bottom of y^r preserving pan, & then put in y^r berries, & then more sugar, & soe doe till they are all in. y^n put in 3 or 4 spoonfulls of water, & set them on ye fire, & shake them often till ye sugar be melted. y^n make them boyle apace y^t you cannot see one of them. take of ye scum as it riseth, &

when y^r berries are clear, they are enough, y^n put them up. when you stone y^r goosberries, put y^m into water & set y^r sugar with y^t water, which will m[ake them the] better.

We now come to a group of gooseberry recipes. The advice to do only a small amount of preserves at a time is sound; the heating period is shortened, the taste will be truer and fresher, the fruit will be less liable to disintegrate, and there is less danger of sticking and burning. That said, it is entirely feasible to do at least a pound at a time if you have a proper preserving pan. (See preserving, S 21.)

Gooseberry (*Ribes grossularia*) is not cited by *OED* before 1532, which is surprising for this popular fruit. One theory of the name proposes that French *groseille*, currant, became a hypothetical *grossberry*, then *gorseberry* by transposition, and finally *goosebery* by the common English habit of substituting a familiar word of similar sound for one they no longer understood, as happened with asparagus and *sparrow grass*. I should note that *OED* is unimpressed.

I believe that gooseberries early became associated with goose cookery in England, replacing the acidy fruits and vegetables of medieval recipes, where goose was often stuffed with green grapes or served with green sauce of sorrel and other greens, sharpened with verjuice. Hannah Woolley, in *The Gentlewomans Companion*, 1682, gives two recipes for *green Geese*: "Take the juice of Sorrel mixed with scalded Goosberries, beaten Butter and Sugar, then serve it on Sippets [with the geese]. Or fill their Bellies [of the geese] with Goosberries, and so roast them, then take them out, and mingle them with Sugar, Butter, Vinegar, Cinnamon, and served on Sippets." This theory is entirely conjectural on my part, but it seems reasonable and the cookbooks support it. Just so, gooseberries are called *groseilles à maquereau* in France because of their association with the cooking of mackerel.

---

57   TO PRESERUE GOOSBERRIES

Take of ye fairest goosberries y^t are & thoroughly ripe, & pick of all ye stalks, wash them clean. then take a pound of them & set on ye fire till they be hot, y^n take them of & let ye liquor run from them. then take 10 ounces of hard sugar & 4 ounces of white sugar candy & clarefy it with a pinte of water & ye white of an egg,

& boyle it to a thick sirrup. y^n put y^r berrys in & let
them boyle a walme or 2. y^n between hot & cold pot
them up, & keep them all ye year.

It is quite unnecessary to clarify sugar nowadays for preserving.
Normally gooseberries take their weight in sugar. "Between hot
& cold" means neither . . . nor. For gooseberries, see S 56; for
preserving, see S 21; for candy, see S 100.

---

58   TO PRESERUE GOOSBERRIES

Put y^r goosberries into a pottle pot with a pinte of
water, & set it into a kettle of seething water and boyle
y^m leasurely, till they be tender. then strayn out their
liquor thorough a cullender into a bason. y^n put into it
a pound of clarefied* sugar, & let it boyle to a thick
sirrup. y^n put in y^r berries & give y^m 2 or 3 walms on a
chafing dish of coles. then pot them up. you must slit
y^r berries on ye sides, & take out ye seeds, & they must
be large & green.

This *bain marie* method of cooking the gooseberries was to assure
the wholeness of the preserved fruit, a nice touch. See S 56
and 21.

A *pottle pot* has a capacity of two quarts. *Cullender* is still
given as current in *OED*. The word is related to *cullis* (from French
coulis), which can be anything strained but most typically was a
strong broth. Both words come from French *couler*.

---

59   TO PRESERUE GOOSBERRIES OR
       CURRAN BERRIES

Take y^r berries fresh from ye trees & pull them from
their stalks, y^n clip of ye stalks & ye little black beards.
then weigh them, & to a pound of any of them, take a
pound of ye best lofe sugar. then stone ye fruit & put to
ye sugar Just as much water as will wet it. then boyle it
to a candy height, or till it begins to hare, then put in
ye fruit & let it boyle very fast. then try with a spoone if

* Written *clarefies*.

it will Jelley, & when it will [do so, pot] it up. thus you may doe both red & white curans.

Currants, or *raisins of Corinth* (C 11) had been known to the English at least since the Crusades, but the first mention in English sources of what later came to be known as English currants, *Ribes rubrum* (because they grew in England while the others came from Greece), seems to be in Lyte's translation of Rembert Dodoens' *Niewe Herball* in 1578, where they are called *Beyond sea Gooseberry* and Bastard Corinths (*OED*). They quickly became popular, threatening to preempt the name of currant. The white currant is a sub-variety of the red.

There is a recipe for preserved currants, S 215, mistakenly tucked among the jelly recipes; there is also a *Quidony of English Currans*, S 205, and two more jelly recipes. See also S 21 and 56.

---

60   TO PRESERUE RASBERRIES

You must take to y^r rasps their weight in sugar & strow on them, & let them stand a while to melt. & put to them 2 spoonfulls of red currans & 2 spoonfulls [of]* rasps, but none of ye pound. then set them on & let all boyle as fast as you can, or els ye rasps will be hard. ye Juice of currans will make them Jelley. you may put it in when ye rasps are boyling If you pleas.

The first mention of raspberries (*Rubus idaeus*) in English seems to be by Boorde in 1542 when he referred to a wine, "respyce, the whiche is made of a bery." (But see S 255.) Any number of forms, mostly variants of *rasps*, preceded and coexisted with *rasberry*; curiously, the modern form did not show up until the eighteenth century, according to *OED*. In 1548, Turner listed them under *Rubus idaeus*, called them *raspeses* in English, *framboise* in French, and said that "they growe in certayne gardines of Englande." Gerard in 1597 refers to the raspberry as the *Raspis* or *Framboise bush* and discusses it under the bramble, or blackberry (see S 253). He cites Dioscorides as saying that the virtues of the plant are the same as those of the bramble. (For the most part, its use in external medicine is discussed: a lotion made of the leaves, for instance, was a remedy for healing sores of the mouth, eyes, *fundament* [buttocks], etc.)

It seems curious that the raspberry came so late to Eng-

* Written *or*.

263

land. The word *framboise* appears in French by 1306; Robert says that the word comes from Frankish *brambasia* as *frambeise*, and this seems to have happened by the twelfth century. The relationship between *brambasia* and *bramble* seems evident. Perhaps the bramble and the raspberry were simply not well differentiated (this is supported by Gerard's grouping them together), but remembering French influence in England over the centuries, this is difficult to understand as well. It is interesting to note that the more formal name, *rasberry* is used in the titles but the homier *rasps* in the text.

The recipe is awkwardly presented. The mystifying "none of ye pound" refers to the understood fact that preserves were made in batches of a pound of fruit and that this was in addition. The combination of currants and raspberries is a remarkably successful one. The currants intensify the flavor, improve the color, and, as the recipes indicates, have lots of pectin, facilitating the jelling.

---

61   TO PRESERUE RASBERRIES

Take faire & well cullered rasps & pick them very clean, & wash them, but with care, y^t you bruise them not. then weigh them, & to every pound of rasps, take 6 ounces of hard sugar & 6 ounces of white sugar candy, & clarefy it with halfe a pinte of faire water & 4 ounces of raspe Juice. beeing clarefyed, boyle it to a weak sirrup, then put in y^r raspis, stir them up & downe & boyle them till they are enough, & pot them when they are almoste cold.

It is not necessary to clarify sugar nowadays. See S 60 and 21. For sugar candy, see S 100.

---

62   TO PRESERUE RASBERRIES

Take a pound of clarefied sugar with water & ye white of an egg, & set it on a charcole fire, & put into it a pound of red raspes. let them boyle till they be tender, then pour them into a cullender, & boyle ye sirrup againe till it is thick, & it will Jelly. & when it is cold, pot ye rasps, & p[aper] them.

The language is clear enough, but surely the egg white is part of the clarifying procedure (unnecessary now); perhaps a phrase has been omitted. For more on preserving, see S 21 and 60.

---

63   TO PRESERUE BARBERRIES

Take* well cullered barberies & pick out every stone of them, then weigh them, & to every ounce of barbaries, take 3 ounces of sugar & with halfe an ounce of pulp of barbaries & one ounce of red rosewater. you must dissolve y^r sugar, then boyle it to a sirrup. after, put in y^r barbaries, & let them boyle a quarter of an houre very fast, then take them up. & soe soon as they begin to be cool, pot them up & they will keepe theyr culler all ye year.

Barberries (*Berberis vulgaris*) are oblong, red, sharply acid berries. *OED* says that the etymology and history of the barberry is unknown—the first mention in English seems to be as *Barbaryne* about 1400—but it seems safe to say that while apparently it does not come from Moorish sources, the English *thought* that it did; the popular form is *barbaries*, and even the Latin name reflects this belief. In any event, it came to be used as a substitute for pomegranate in cookery, about which they had learned from the Arabs; *poumgarnet* appears as early as 1320 and is called for in many recipes from fourteenth- and fifteenth-century manuscripts. They must have been very expensive.

Gerard says that barberries are cold and dry and that both leaves and berries are used to season and garnish meat. They are good "against hot burnings and cholerick agues . . . and also profitable for hot Laskes, and for the bloudy flix." He adds that, "A conserve made of the fruit and sugar performeth all those things before remembered, & with better force and successe."

In the recipe, I believe that the ½ ounce of barberry pulp is in addition to the ounce of whole barberries given in the proportions. Three ounces of sugar make 6 tablespoons; 1 ounce of rose water is 2 tablespoons. See recipes S 21, 64, and 65. I don't know why cranberries could not be substituted in all these barberry recipes; certainly they would be different, but they should work.

The barberries so frequently called for as a garnish in our recipes I believe to be preserved according to recipes C 168 and 169.

* I excised &.

64   TO PRESERUE BARBARRIES*

Take ye full weight of your barberys in sugar finely
powdered, & as you stone them, strow on some of y^e
sugar on them. & to halfe a pound of barberies, you
must put 5 spoonfulls of barbaries Juice, & with y^t
make your sirrup, keeping out a spoonfull of sugar. put
in your pickt barbarys into ye sirrup & boyle them
leasurely a quarter of an houre, & take of ye scum, with
the back of A spoon. then take your barberies out one
by one in A dish, then boyle up your sirrup with that
spoonful of sugar that was kept out, & scum it as
before. then put it in a dish till it be cold. before that,
you put it into your barberries. & then you may pot
them & tie them up.

65   TO PRESERUE BARBERIES

Take a few loose barbaries, & put a little water to them,
& boyle them till ye water look red. then take as much
of that water as will wet ye sugar, which must be twice
ye weight of y^r barbaries. then you must boyle it apace
& scum it, & then put in your barbaries & boyle them
as fast as you can till they be done.

66   TO PRESERUE RED ROSE LEAUES

Take of ye leavs of ye fairest buds of red roses halfe a
pound. sift them clean from ye seeds, y^n take a quart of
fair water, & put it into an earthen pipkin, set it over y^e
fire, till it be scalding hot. then take a good many of
other red rose leavs & put them in ye scallding water
till they begin to look white, y^n strayn them. thus doe
severall times till ye water looks very red, y^n put to it a
pound of refined sugar small beaten, & ye halfe pound

* Inexplicably corrected from *Barberries*; the *e* is barely visible.

of red rose leavs before mentiond, & let y^m boyle together. you may know when they are enough by takeing some of y^m in a spoon as you doe cheries & letting it coole; It it will scarce run out, it is enough. y^n take y^m of & when they be thorough cold, pot them & keep them close.

We now come to a group of recipes for flowers. For most of us, rose water from the Middle East, candied violets from France, jasmine tea from China, and tales of great-grandmother's rose petal jam, perhaps constitute our acquaintance with the use of flowers as food. But at the time of our manuscript still, the gathering and conservation of vast amounts of flowers was a routine part of household summer routine. Many were dried for their scent (there are a number of recipes for perfumes and cosmetics toward the end of the manuscript), a few are largely medicinal, but the greater part of them were for eating and garnishing food. They all had medicinal virtues ascribed to them; since sugar was considered to enhance these virtues—and in any event, was a vital element in preservation—there is always the suspicion that such virtues were a happy pretext. Perhaps. But they did believe.

We have here three types of flower preparation: preserving, where they are kept whole in a heavy syrup; conserving, where they are pounded with sugar; and candying, where they are glazed. (Later, we have recipes for pastes and syrups of flowers and in *A Booke of Cookery*, we have recipes for pickled flowers.) Today, many of these preparations will have only the nostalgic charm of yesteryear, but some of them are genuinely delicious and deserve to be revived. A WORD OF CAUTION: beware of insecticides.

The most beloved of all flowers was the rose (genus *Rosa*). The recipes of the earliest English manuscripts read almost like Arab recipes of the same period; rose petals and rose water in some of the most surprising dishes, and rose water continued in sweet dishes until it was displaced by vanilla in, roughly, the early part of the nineteenth century. Gerard says: "The distilled water of Roses is good for the strengthning of the heart, and refreshing of the spirits, and likewise for all things that require a gentle cooling. The same being put in junketting dishes, cakes, sauces, and many other pleasant things, giveth a fine and delectable taste." (The cooling is a medicinal quality.) Also, see S 298.

(As a sidelight, it is interesting to note that at least by mid-fifteenth century, *junket* referred to various curd and cream dishes, originally formed in rush baskets (*OED*); it must have been so much earlier, because *jonquette* in Norman patois has the same meaning.)

Rose leaves are the petals. The fairest buds are to be preserved in the red rose syrup.

---

67   TO PRESERVE ROSE BUDS AND GILLEFLOWRS

Take a pound of roses & a pinte of water, & boyle ye roses in it till it be soft. y^n take 3 times ye weight in sugar & boyle them till they be thick enough to [jelly. (?) y^n] take y^m of ye fire & pot y^m up. thus in like ma[nner you may do gi]lleflowers.

The gillyflower is what we know as the clove-scented pink, or carnation (*Dianthus caryophyllus*). *Gilly* comes from French *girofle*, clove (S 273). It is pronounced *jilly*, and most likely always was as evidenced by forms *jellyflowers* and *July flowers*; both are fine examples of the substitution of a word of known meaning for an unknown one of similar sound. (Actually, the term has been occasionally applied to other clove-scented flowers as well, especially stock.) Gerard says: "The conserve made of the floures of the Clove Gillofloure and sugar, is exceeding cordiall, and wonderfully above measure doth comfort the heart, being eaten now and then."

For roses, see S 66.

---

68   TO PRESERUE ANGELICO STALKS IN APRILL

Take angellico stalks & boyle them in water till they are tender, then scrap of ye strings on ye outside, & crush ye water out of them. then take to a pound of sugar, a little more water then will wet it. boyle it pritty thick, then put your stalks into it & let it stand halfe a day, covered, on hot coles but not boyle. then take it of & let it stand 3 or 4 dayes covered in ye sirrup. y^n set them on ye fire till ye sugar be melted of them, then take them up & scrape ye sugar of them into ye pan. y^n boyle y^r sirrup to a great height, but not to sugar. then put your stalks into ye sugar & let it stand A little while on ye fire. turne them, & twist or plat them, & lay them on plates, & set them in a stove, in which put a chafing dish of coles twice a day, till they be dry.

Angelica (*Angelica archangelica*) is a highly fragrant herb that is still used, principally as a decorative element in confectionery and pastry making. Gerard says that it is "a singular remedy against poyson, and against the plague . . . It attenuateth and maketh thin, grosse and tough flegme . . . and is right beneficiall to the heart." In short, the angelic herb.

A *stove* is a closed chamber or box, so arranged that it can be heated for the purpose of drying out herbs and confections, or other gentle heating. Any oven that can be kept below 150°F will do very well, one with a pilot light being perfect.

Here, *plat* is to plait or braid.

---

69   TO PRESERUE ANGELICO STALKS & DRY THEM

Take ye stalks in aprill, & cut y^m in what lengths you pleas. then set on some water, make it boyle, & put them in & let them boyle till they are pritty tender, & will both pill & string, which when you have done, put them into ye water againe, & there let them boyle till they are very tender. for 2 pound of stalks, take a quart of ye water they were boyled in, & make a sirrup with a pound of sugar. scum it, & then put ye stalks in and cover it. soe you may eyther boyle them up presently & pot them, or let y^m stand a week in y^t sirrup, now & then setting them on coles, till it be allmoste consumed. y^n take halfe a pound of sugar & boyle it to candy height, & dip in y^r stalks till th[ey are candied.(?)] If you lay them on a glass & they stick not, they are [enough (?)].

---

70   TO MAKE A RESTORATIUE MARMALET

Take ye purest green ginger, 6 drames; citron & oringo roots, of each an ounce & halfe. beat these finely &

dragg them with a silver spoon thorough a hare sive. take of nut kernells & almonds blanch'd, of each an ounce; cocks stones, halfe an ounce; all steeped in honey 12 hours, then boyled in milke & beaten & mixed with ye rest. then take ye powder of ye seeds of red nettles & rochet, of each one dram; plantan seeds, halfe a dram; of ye back & belly of a fish called scincus marinus, 3 drams; of diaseterion, 2 ounces. beat these finely, & with ye other powder mix it, & a pound & halfe of fine sugar dissolved in rosewater till it comes to sugar againe. mingle ye powder & all ye rest of ye things, & put in 6 leavs of gold & 2 drams of prepared perle, & oyle of cinnamon, 6 drops. when these thus done & well dryed, box it up, and use it as you have occasion.

Effectively, this marmalade is a homemade *treacle*, an elixir or panacea, differing from the various pharmaceutical formulas more in texture than in composition (see S 284). This marmalade is like a confection. Medicinal virtues, mostly tonic and aphrodisiac, are ascribed to the several ingredients.

On apothecaries' scales, a *drame* (a fifteenth-century form) amounts to a weight of 60 grains, or ⅛ of an ounce. (On common scales, a dram is only 27 ½ grains, or about 1/16 of an ounce; since the ingredients in question were purchased from an apothecary, they were most likely weighed there.)

Citron was more often called *pomecitron* at the time (S 33). It is the preserved rind that is wanted. The *oringo roots* (S 34) were also preserved and the green ginger (S 92) must have been as well, judging by its position and the structure of the preparation. You are to *dragg* or push the mixture through a fine sieve made of horse hair.

Nut kernells are walnut meats (S 72). *Cocks stones* are the testicles of the rooster. Culpeper, in *Pharmacopoeia Londinensis*, 1654, reports that they "refresh and restore such bodies as have been wasted by long sickness . . . [and] help such as are weak in the sports of *Venus*." Honey, according to the same source, "is of a gallant and clensing quality."

Red nettles would appear to be what Johnson calls *Urtica rubra*; they are assigned the same attributes as other stinging nettles. Gerard says: "The seed of Nettle stirreth up lust. . . . It is good for such as be sick of the inflammation of the lungs . . . and also against the troublesome cough that children have, called the Chin-cough." It seems also to have been a remedy against hemlock, mortal mushrooms, quicksilver, henbane, and the bites of serpents and scorpions. I make no promises for nettles to stir up lust, but I repeat an interesting suggestion for abating it. Boorde, in *The Dyetary of Helthe*, 1542, says: "*Erection of the yerde to synne.* A remedy for that is . . . to put Nettles in the codpeece about the yerde and stones.*" (If you think of a yard stick, you will better understand the use of *yerde* as a popular name for the phallus.) Fleeing "from al maner of occasions of Lechery" was also counselled.

Rochet is rocket (*Eruca sativa*). Gerard describes it as a good "sallet herbe," and goes on to say: "The use of Rocket stirreth up lust, especially the seed." *Plantan* is plantain (*Plantago major*). Gerard says "The root of Plantaine with the seed boiled in white wine and drunke, openeth the conduits or passage of the liver and kidnies, [and] cures that jaundice."

The *scincus marinus* is an elusive creature, not a fish at all but a small lizard of the Sahara and Red Sea littoral, *Scincus officinalis*, used in medicine for millennia. The *Papyrus Ebers*, a medical work written in Egypt about 1500 B.C., and thought to be based largely on practices centuries older, includes lizard in its pharmacopoeia; significantly, it was considered restorative. Dioscorides, the great Greek physician of the first century A.D., in *Materia Medica*, as Englished by John Goodyear in 1655, likens the *Skinkos* to a small earth crocodile and says that it comes, preserved in salt, from Egypt, India, Libya, and Mauritania. He goes on to claim that, "that part of it which lyes about ye kidnies . . . is a great provocative to lust . . . It is also mixed with Antidots." Pliny, at about the same time, in *Historia Naturalis*, recommends the addition of Satyrion and rocket seed to heighten its aphrodisiac virtues; we now have the core of our recipe.

The attributes of the skink remain unchanged down through the ages until we come to seventeenth-century England, when faith in its nearly magical powers was on the wane; medical writers, even the prolific and prolix Culpeper, mention it only in passing as an ingredient in ancient prescriptions such as *diasatyrion* (see below) and *Mithridate*. (Its use persisted longer on the continent, however.) As with all exotic pharmaceuticals, less costly substitutes were sought, and found. The commonest was the newt, clearly described in the two oldest extant manuscripts of *Circa instans*, for example. (One dates from the twelfth century, the other from the thirteenth; they constitute an important part of our legacy from the famed *School of Salerno*. See page 206.)

But how did a desert reptile who assiduously avoids water come to be tagged *scincus marinus*, or sea skink? After much searching, the answer was found in *The Herbal of Rufinus*, written in Genoa around 1190, where he describes *scincus ultramarinus*, the shink from *across* the seas, as being the most efficacious. Clearly, some later scribe omitted *ultra*, leaving us with *scincus marinus*. Since it arrived in European apothecary shops skinned and salted, the continuing error is perfectly comprehensible. The name *scincus marinus* in our manuscript indicates the imported one; what the apothecary may have had in stock is another matter. By 1719, Quincy says that *scincus* is no longer found in the shops. (For unearthing the more arcane facts in this passage, I am indebted to Frank J. Anderson; it represents original research on his part.)

Diaseterion, diasatyrion, is an electuary whose characterizing ingredient is the herb Satyrion (*Orchis*), named in reference to its putative aphrodisiac powers; its popular names included *Dogs Stones, Serapias stones, goats stones.* (The bulbous root growths do suggest the shape of testicles and illustrate the signature theory of healing virtues.) Gerard says: "Our age useth all the kindes of stones to stir up venery," and he cites Dioscorides as reporting: "That if men do eat of the great full or far roots of these kinds of Dogs stones, they cause them to beget male children," Neither vouches for this, to be sure. The compound was the sovereign aphrodisiac of the day; it not only excited lust, but assured triumphal performance. Who could resist?

In speaking of the virtues of gold, Culpeper claims that, "it strengthens the heart and vital spirits . . . and resists mellancholly, faintings, swoonings, feavers, [and] falling sickness." But Chaucer, in the Prologue to *The Canterbury Tales*, ends his introduction of the *Doctor of Physic* with these bitterly skeptical lines:

And yet he was but esy of dispence.
He kepte that he wan in pestilence;
For gold in phisik is a cordial—
Therefore he lovede gold in special.

(I remind the reader that in the fourteenth century, *physic* meant healing or medicine, and *cordial* meant good for the heart, literally. These meanings continued through the seventeenth century; only gradually did the figurative meaning of *cordial* completely take over. Chaucer, of course, is saying that doctors put gold in medications to justify the price.)

Perle is a fourteenth- to sixteenth-century form (*OED*). See S 308 for its use in medicine.

(This recipe and the five that follow are interlopers among the flower recipes, inexplicably out of category.)

71 TO MAKE MARMALET OF MULBERIES OR RASBERIES

Take to a pound of mulberies or rasberies, halfe a
pound of sugar, which must be well wet with rose
water & boyled to a great height. then let your berries
be strayned & put ye liquor into ye sugar. stir it well, &
then take it of ye fire before it seeths, & stir it tilll it be
allmoste cold, & then box it.

Mulberries (*Morus nigra* and *alba*) shows up as *murberien* about 1265;
in 1398, Trevis called them *mulberies* in his medical lexicon (*OED*).
Gerard says: "The Mulberrie trees grow plentifully in Italy and
other hot regions, where they do maintaine great woods and
groves of them, that their Silke wormes may feed thereon," but
adds that they "grow in sundry gardens in England." The black
mulberry seems to be indigenous to Europe; the white one came
from China along with the silkworm, and is said to have been
introduced into England in mid-fifteenth century in an attempt to
establish a silk industry. The black mulberry was valued for its
coloring properties (murrey-colored), but otherwise, the two seem
to have been treated much the same in medicine. Gerard says:
"Of the juyce of the ripe Berries is made a confection with sugar,
. . . in the manner of a syrrup, which is exceeding good for the
ulcers and hot swellings of the tongue, . . . or any malady arising
in those parts." They were regarded as medicinally cooling.
    This recipe belongs in the marmalade section starting S
13, which see.

72 TO PRESERVE WALLNUTS SOLITURE

Take wallnuts between whitsontide & midsumer when
they are a little bigger then nutmeggs. set them on y^e
fire in a pritty quantety of running water (which must
boyle before you put them in),* where they must boyle
till they are soe tender y^t a rush will goe thorough
them. then take a quart of ye liquor they are boyled in,
and add a pound & quarter of sugar to every pound of
wallnuts from ye tree. soe boyle them leasurely till y^e

* Parentheses supplied

sirrup be thick, & then pot them up. you must prick y^e
wallnuts full of holes with a pin before you put them
into ye first water.

We call them English walnuts (*Juglans regia*), as distinguished from
American black walnuts, but etymologically, we find that *wal-*
means Gaullish, Celtic (Welsh), or Roman; the word appears as
walh-hnutu in Old English by about 1050, according to *OED*. (The
English shared with the Normans the habit of substituting *w* where
the French used *g*; see *gaufre* and *wafer* in C 143.)

Gerard says of them: "The greene and tender Nuts boyled
in Sugar and eaten as Suckad, are a most pleasant and delectable
meat, comfort the stomacke, and expell poison,"

Whitsontide is the seventh Sunday after Easter, which occurs the first Sunday after the calendar full moon after the spring
equinox. (If these calculations seem pagan, know that the festival
originally honored the dawn goddess, *Austrôn*, and bears her name
in English.) The writer is thus indicating the month or so preceding
midsummer as the time to gather the nuts.

I was unable to find any reference to *Soliture*, and I find
it difficult to justify proposing any connection with any of the
various meanings of solitaire.

---

73   TO MAKE HONEY OF ROSES

Take a pinte of honey, boyle it & scum it. y^n add as
many bruised leavs of red roses buds (ye whites beeing
cut of)* as you may easily stirr it. then cover it close &
boyle ye pot in water till you think ye goodness of y^e
roses is in ye honey. then change ye roses once or twice
in ye same manner, & at ye last, strayn out ye roses
clear.

We are back to flowers again for a rose recipe. Both honey and
roses had medicinal virtues, making this mixture cooling, cleansing
(gently laxative), and generally salutary. (See S 66 and 70.) The
concoction was undoubtedly enjoyed for its own sake, as well.

Our scribe did not notice that this identical recipe is repeated in S 249. Also, see page 452.

* Scribe's parentheses.

74 TO PRESERUE APPLES FOR A TART

First coddle y^m in faire water, y^n take halfe thei[r] weight in sugar, & make as much sirrup as will cover ye bottom of ye pan you intend to preserve y^m in. ye rest of ye sugar strow on y^m as they boyle, wch must be ve[ry softly,] & turne y^m often y^t they burne not too.

This recipe is hopelessly out of category; see C 67.

75 TO MAKE MARMALET THAT WILL KEEPE 2 OR 3 YEARS

Take y^r best apple quinces & lay them in a dish one by one. then set them into an oven after the bread is drawn; there let them bake like an apple. when they are well baked, take of their scin & scrape ye pulpe from them. you must take ye best of it, but not too neer ye core. then take ye full weight in sugar & boyle it with ye quince, but not to much. then box it.

This recipe belongs with the other marmalades, beginning S 13, which see. *Apple quinces* are the fruit of a quince graft on an apple tree; sixteenth- and seventeeth-century gardening manuals abound in such grafting instructions.

We have here a different technique, and a very interesting one. Baked fruits develop a far more intense flavor than stewed ones and is most marked with apples and apricots. I have never tried it with quince.

76 TO MAKE CONSERUE OF BARBERRIES

Take barberries which are very red & ripe, & pick them from ye stalks. then wash & put to them A pritty deale of fayre water & set them on ye fire in an earthen pan, & scalld them thoroughly. pulp them thorough A searce, & to every pound of pulpe, take a pound of powdered sugar, & boyle them together till it will cut like marmalet, & then box it.

We have here a conserve of fruit. While I can find nothing in the dictionaries to support this, my reading of cookbooks leads me to believe that a conserve differed from a preserve in that it was pounded. (See S 21.) In *A Booke of Cookrye* by A. W., 1591, we find in a recipe *To preserue Orenges* the customary care to keep the fruit whole, but in *To make Conserue of Orenges,* we are instructed to "beat them small." Certainly the recipes in our manuscript follow this distinction. I do not know how long this obtained.

A *searce* is a sieve or strainer. The Middle English term was *saarce,* from Old French *sass;* the word is now historical only (*OED*).

Powdered sugar is fine granulated sugar; it has nothing to do with confectioners' sugar. (The same error is often made in translating from the French, where *en poudre* has been retained to designate sugar that is simply more finely sifted.)

---

77   TO MAKE CONSERUE OF BUGLOSS FLOWERS

Take buglos flowers, pick them clean & weigh y^m & to every ounce of flowers, take 2 ounces of hard sugar & one ounce of sugar candy. beat them together till they be exceeding fine, then set them on the fire to dissolve the sugar, & when you have soe done, pot it up for your use.

We are back to flowers again. For *conserve,* see S 76; for sugar candy, S 100; for flowers, S 66.

Bugloss is any of several plants of the order Boraginaceae (to which borage belongs), especially *Anchusa arvensis.* Some of the lines were pretty hazy but since *Prickly Ox-tongue* is included as a bugloss, the old *lang de boef* (variously spelled) was quite likely included as well. Gerard says that "modern physicians" were giving bugloss instead of borage to "drive away sorrow & pensivenesse of the minde, and to comfort and strengthen the heart."

---

78   TO MAKE CONSERVE OF SUCKORY FLOWERS

Take suckory flowers y^t are fresh gathered, for If they lie an houre or 2, they will loose theyr culler. therefore, weigh them presently, & to every ounce of flowers,

take 3 ounces of double refind sugar, & beat them
together with A wooden pestle in an alleblaster morter.
ye better ye flowers & sugar is beaten, ye better your
conserve will be. when they are thoroughly brayed, but
them into A chafer clean scoured, & set them on the
fire till they be thoroughly hot, & then pot them.

All the forms of succory (*Cichorium intybus*) are alterations of old
forms of chicory. (Chicory, escarole, and endive are garden relatives of succory.) It has bright blue flowers; the "blue endive" of
the poets is succory. Both garden and wild succory have, according
to Gerard, "vertue to coole the hot burning of the liver, to help
the stopping of the gall, yellow jaundise, lack of sleep, stopping
of urine, and hot burning fevers."

Alablaster was a common sixteenth- and seventeenth-century form for alabaster; it was apparently confused with the word
for crossbowman, *alablaster*. Alabaster comes from the Greek and
was said to have been the name of a town in Egypt.

To *bray* is to pound to a powder, usually in a mortar; it
is from Old French forms of *broyer*, of the same meaning. A *chafer*
is a pan, perhaps one designed specially to fit on a *chafing dish of
coles* (C 15).

For conserves, see S 76; for flowers, see S 66.

---

79   TO MAKE CONSERUE OF ROSEMARY
      FLOWERS

Take rosemary flowers fresh & good, pick them very
clean from ye green husk, then weigh them, & take to
every ounce of flowers 3 ounces of white sugar candy.
beat them very fine, & use them in every respect as you
 ·   doe your other conservs.

The Latin name of rosemary (*Rosmarinus officinalis*) simply means
sea dew; *ros*, dew, became assimilated to rose, and *marinus* to the
Virgin. The present form was set in the sixteenth century (*OED*).
Gerard says: "The Arabians and other Physitians succeeding, do
write that Rosemary comforteth the braine, the memorie, the inward senses, and restoreth speech unto them that are possessed
with the dumbe palsie, expecially the conserve made of the floures
and sugar, or any other way confected with sugar, being taken
every day fasting." The same Arabs also write that it "is good for
the cold rheume which falleth from the graine."

For conserves, see S 76; for flowers, S 66; for sugar candy,
S 100.

---

80   TO MAKE CONSERUE OF ROSES

Take ye buds of red roses & clip of all ye whites at y^e
bottom & a little of the tops. & pick out all ye seeds.
then take treble their weight in good loafe sugar, beat
them together in an alleblaster morter, & strow in y^e
sugar by degrees. b[eat it v]ery finely, & then pot them.

For roses, see S 66; for conserves, see S 76.

---

81   TO CANDY ROSE LEAUES TO LOOK
      FRESH

Take of ye fayrest rose leavs, red or damask, and
sprinkle them with rose water, & lay them one by one
on white paper on a hot sunshiney day. y^n beat some
double refind sugar very small, & sift it thinly on y^e
roses thorough a fine laune sive. & they will candy as
they ly in ye hot sun. then turne ye leaves & strow
some rose water on the other side, & sift some sugar in
like manner on them. turne them often, sometimes
strowing on water, & sometimes sifting on sugar, till
they be enough. then lay them in boxes betwixt clean
papers, & soe keep them all ye year.

This is the first of a group of candied flower recipes; appropriately,
we start with the beloved rose. (For *candy*, see S 5.)
     The damask rose is supposed to have originated in Syria.
It may have been the *Rosa gallica*, variety *damascena*, a semi-double
pink or light red rose cultivated in the East for attar of roses. *OED*
says that it has undergone much change. The damask rose was
the most highly regarded of all the roses. Gerard describes it as
being in other respects "like the white Rose; the especiall difference
consists in the colour and smell of the flours: for these are of a pale
red colour, of a more pleasant smel, and fitter for meat and medicine."
     For the virtues of the rose, see S 66. The sieve is made of
lawn, a fine linen.

82   TO CANDY ANY FLOWERS FRUITS OR
SPICES WITH Y^e ROCK CANDY

Take two pound of barbary sugar, great grayned, and
clarefy it with ye whites of 2 eggs. and boyle it allmoste
to the height of manus Christi. then put it in A pipkin
that is not very rough, then put in your flowers, fruits,
or spices. & then put your pipkin into A still, and make
A little fire of small cole or charcole under it. and in the
space of 12* days your fruit, flowers, or spice will be
rock candid.

This is a recipe in which I have little confidence; it is effectively,
sugar candy with flowers. (See S 100.) *Manus Christi* syrup is explained in S 4; for flowers, see S 66.

83   TO CANDY MARYGOLDES

Take ye green from y^r marrygolds & open y^m abroad.
then take ye white of an egg & dip them into it, then
take them out, & beat some sugar candy pritty small, &
strow it on ye one syde, then lay them to dry. ye next
day, dip them againe with egg as you did before, but
beat your sugar candy not soe small. strow in on
likewise, & let them dry, & then box them.

Marigolds (*Calendula officinalis*) were much used in cookery and
medicine. Gerard says: "Conserve made of the floures and sugar
taken in the morning fasting, cureth the trembling of the heart and
is also given in time of plague or pestilence, or corruption of the
aire." For use of marigolds, see C 32; for flowers, see S 66; for
candy, see S 100.

84   TO CANDY MARRYGOLDS IN THE
SPANISH FASHION

Take ye fairest marrygolde flowers, 2 ounces. shread &
dry them by ye fire, then take 4 ounces of sugar &
boyle it to ye height of manus Christ[i]. then poure it

* Apparently corrected from *10*.

on a wet pie plate, & betwixt hot & cold, cut it into wedges. then lay them on A sheet of white paper, & set them in A stove to dry & scrape sugar on them.

For working with flowers, see S 66; for marigolds, S 65; for *manus Christi*, see S 4; and for *stove*, see S 68.

---

85   TO CANDY FLOWERS IN THEYR NATURALL CULLER

Take ye flowers with theyr stalks, & wash them in rose water, wherein gum arabeck is dissolved. then take fine searced sugar, & dust it over them. & set them A drying in a sive, set in an oven. & [they will] glister like sugar candy.

Gum arabic is exuded by certain species of *Acacia*; it is soluble in water. See the candy recipes preceding this one. Also, for working with flowers, see S 66. A *searce* is a sieve (S 76).

---

86   TO CANDY VIOLET FLOWERS

Take violets which are new & well cullered. weigh them, & to every ounce of flowers take 4 ounces of very white refined sugar, & dissolve it in 2 ounces of water. soe boyle it till it turn to sugar againe, & scum it very often that it may be very clear, then take it of & let it coole. after, put in y^r violet flowers, stiring them together till ye sugar grow hard to ye pan. y^n put them in a box & keep them to dry in a stove.

Violet flowers (*Viola odorata*) may be purplish blue, mauve, or white. The word violet appeared in the fourteenth century (*OED*). Gerard says : "the floures are good for all inflammations, especially of the sides and lungs; they take away the hoarsenesse of the chest, the ruggednesse of the winde-pipe and jawes, allay the extreme heate of the liver, kidnies, and bladder, mitigate the fiery heate of burning agues, temper the sharpnesse of choler, and take away thirst." Violet flowers were classified as cold and moist.

For working with flowers, see S 66; also refer to other candied flower recipes.

87   TO CANDY ROSEMARY FLOWERS

Take rosemary flowers ready pickt, & weigh them, & to
every ounce of flowers take 2 ounces of hard sugar, &
one ounce of sugar candy. dissolve them in rosemary
flower water, & boyle them till they come to sugar
againe. then put in y^r rosemary flowers. when the
sirrup is allmoste colde, soe stir them together till they
be enough. then box them & set them in a stove.

For rosemary, see S 79; for sugar candy, S 100; for *stove*, S 68. Also,
see other candied flower recipes.

88   TO CANDY BURRAGE FLOWERS

Take burrage flowers & pick them very cleane. weigh
them, & use them in every respect as you did rosemary
flowers, except y^t when they be candied, you must set
them in a still. soe keep them in A sheet of white
paper, putting in every [day]* a chafing dish of coles
into ye still. & they wi[ll be candied] in a short time,
then box them.

Borage (*Borago officinalis*) has bright blue flowers, and the stem and
leaves are covered with prickly hairs (*OED*). Gerard says: "Those
of our time do use the floures in sallads, to exhilerate and make
the minde glad . . . The leaves and floures of Borrage put into
wine make men and women glad and merry, driving away all
sadnesse, dulnesse, and melancholy, as *Dioscorides* and *Pliny* affirme." Conserving them in sugar only intensifies these delightful
virtues. Borage was the characterizing ingredient of the *cool tankard*
and the *claret cup*.
    For working with flowers, see S 66. Also see preceding
candying recipes, especially S 82.

89   TO CANDIE ORRINGO ROOTS

Take fresh gathered oringo roots, set on A ketil of
spring water. let it seeth, then put in ye roots & make

* Supplied.

them boyle as fast as A parsnep. then cut them in y^e
midst & pick out theyr pith with A knife, then pill &
throw them into A bason of faire water. then wring
them out of ye water & dry them with a clean cloth.
place them 3 or 4 together, & tie them at each end with
A thrid. then take as much sugar as they weigh, & as
much rose water & faire water together as will make A
sirrup to cover them. then set them over ye fire & dry
them, after they are boyled in ye sirrup till it allmoste
all boyled away & shaked in the bason to worke in y^e
sirrup. then dry them by ye fire, & box them for all y^e
year.

Eryngo roots are discussed in S 34. It is useful to go over the
preceding candying recipes. The penultimate sentence is awkward,
but it does make sense.

---

90   TO CANDY ORINGO ROOTES

Take oringo rootes ready for preserving and weigh
them, and to every pound of roots, take 2 pound of y^e
purest sugar you can get. & clarefy it with the whits of
eggs, that It may be as clear as cristall. and beeing thus
clarefied, you must boyle it to the height of manus
Christie. then put in your roots, two or three at once,
till they be all candied. and after, put them in A stove
to dry. and then box them and keepe [them for your]
use.

See the previous recipe; for *manus Christi*, see S 4. It is no longer
really necessary to clarify sugar for this work.

---

91   TO CANDY ELICOMPANE

Take of y^r fayrest Elicompane roots preserved, take
them clean from ye sirrup, wash ye sugar of them & dry
them againe with A linnen cloth. then weigh them, &
to every pound of roots, take a pound & 3 quarters of
sugar, clarefie it well, then boyle it to ye height of

manus Christi. then dip in y^r roots, 3 or 4 at once, &
they will candy very well. soe stove them & keepe
them.

Elecampane (*Inula helenium*) has very large yellow flowers and bitter,
aromatic leaves and root. Popular names included *Scab-woort* and
Horse-heale, according to Gerard. He also says that the root "is
marvellous good for many things, being of nature hot and dry in
the third degree," and that, preserved, it "is given to purge and
void out thicke, tough, and clammy humours, which sticke in the
chest and lungs." It was also used against cramps and convulsions
and for those who had "any member out of joint."

This recipe starts with already preserved root; I refer you
to eryngo roots, S 34; also to preceding candying recipes.

---

92   TO CANDY GINGER

Take faire & large ginger, pare it & lay it in water A
day & a night. then take double refined sugar & boyle
it to ye height of sugar againe, & when it beginneth to
be cold, take y^r ginger & stirr it well about till y^r sugar
is hard to y^r pan. then take it out rase by rase, & lay it
by ye fire for 4 houres. then take a pot & warme it &
put the ginger in it, then ty it very close & every
second morning, stir it about roundly, and it will be A
rock Candy in A very short space.

Ginger is the rhizome of *Zingiber officinalis*. Old English took *gin-
giber* directly from Late Latin, which goes back to Sanskrit *çrngavēra*,
with Dravidian and Malayan traces beyond that. The modern form
has been with us since the fourteenth century (*OED*). Originally,
ginger was supplied to Europe from the East Indies, but the best
is now thought to come from Jamaica. Gerard says: "Ginger, as
Dioscorides reporteth, is right good with meat in sauces, or otherwise in conditures. . . . It is to be considered, That canded, greene,
or condited Ginger is hot and moist in qualities, provoking Venerie;
and being dried, it heateth and drieth in the third degree."

Ginger enters into an extraordinary number of recipes in
fourteenth- and fifteenth-century English cookbooks; there are
traces of this in our manuscript. It seems that green ginger was to
be had more easily in medieval and Tudor England than today
outside of Oriental communities. Perhaps, as some write, cooks
often had to make do with dry roots, but this recipe is specific and

several recipes make sense only if it be green, particularly in the fish recipes.

The use of ginger started to decline in the last years of the reign of Elizabeth. Markham, for instance, in 1615, calls for ginger only in the older recipes, but this may have been partly due to personal taste; or perhaps changing trade patterns affected its use. The English predilection for ginger continued in sweets (preserved and in gingerbread, for example, C 205), and ginger beer and ale, vestiges of medicinal waters.

A *rase* is a hand of ginger, from French *racine*, meaning root. Also, see S 106.

---

93   TO CANDY SUCKETS

Take your sugar & put as much water to it as will wet
it. seeth it till you see an hayre will flie from ye spoone,
then take it of ye fire & dip your preserved orringes &
leamons into it. then dry them in A stove.

Suckets are candied sweetmeats made of all manner of fruits and vegetables. Oranges were doubtless the most popular, and are occasionally called for in our manuscript.

See S 6 for the cooking of the syrup; preserved orange and lemon recipes start with S 28. *Stove* is explained in S 68, and previous candying recipes may be useful.

---

94   TO CANDY ORRING PILLS

Take Civill orringes & pare them very thin. then cut
them in little pieces, & lay them in faire water a day &
a night, & shift them evening and morning. then boyle
them, & shift them when the water is bitter into
another water, & continew this till the water & boyling
hath made them soft & y^t theyr bitterness be gon. then
dreyne ye water from them, & make a thin sirrup, in
which boyle them a pritty while. then take them out &
make another sirrup a little stronger, & boyle them a
while in y^t. then dreyne ye sirrup from them, & boyle
another sirrup to candy height, in wch put them. then

take them out & lay them on plats on[e]* by one. when
they are dry, turne them & then they are done.

Civill orringes were bitter oranges (see S 28). *Ciuill* was a common
sixteenth-century form for Seville, yet I have found it glossed as
civil, purportedly meaning of the best quality. In these recipes, it
will be helpful to refer to preceding candying recipes.

Whether *plats* refers to *plates* (flat dishes) or *plats* (sheets
of metal), the word was already nearly archaic, except in dialect,
by the seventeenth century (*OED*). In most cases in our manuscript, *plates* refers to what we would call baking sheets or pans.

---

95   TO CANDY GOOSBERRIES

Take faire goosberries, but not to ripe. wipe them very
clean with a linnen cloth & pick of all theyr stalks.
weigh them, & to every ounce of berries, take 2 ounces
of refined sugar & halfe an ounce of sugar candy.
dissolve ye sugar in an ounce or 2 of rosewater, boyle it
to ye height of manus Christi, then let it cooll. after, put
in y^r berries, beeing preserved before. If you put them
in hot, they will shrink, stir them round with a wooden
pestle till they [be candied (?)], then take them up &
stove them.

For gooseberries, see S 56; for *manus Christi*, S 4; for sugar candy,
S 100; for *stoving*, S 68. Some of the preceding candying recipes
might be helpful.

---

96   TO CANDY ANGELICO

Take your angellico when it is young, & cut of ye root
ends & any place where it is red, & put it in a kettle of
water uncovered,† & boyle it till it be tender. then take
it up & string it, & put it into ye same water againe.
when you have strung it all, put a pewter dish on y^e
top of it, but not to touch it. then make a paste to paste
it downe y^t none of ye steem may come out, & set it on

* Written *on*, a common form of *one*.
† Written *uncoued*.

a moderate fire, y^t it may not boyle but scalld for halfe an houre. then take it up, & dreyne it from the water. after, weigh it, & take weight for weight in sugar, finely beaten, & let your angelico ly in it all night, reserving halfe of the sugar till the next day. then take up the angellico and let it be dreynd well from the sirrup, and then put in the remainder of your sugar & boyle it to a candy. but before it be to high, draw all the stalks thorough it. when your sugar is allmoste candy height, put in all your angellico and take it up as fast as you can againe, least it burne too. when you take it out, strip it two or 3 times thorough your fingers, which makes it look green. the stalks you brayd, must be slit in two, then lay them on glasses, & put them in a stove to dry. to make any candy, take halfe a dosin spoonfulls of water & put it to y^r sugar well [beaten. then] boyle it till it be sugar againe.

Angelica is discussed in S 68; *candy height* in S 5; *stove* in S 68. The stalks were often braided before being laid out to dry; the instructions here are elliptical but see S 68 and 97. (*Brayd* is a fourteenth- to sixteenth-century form, according to *OED*.)

---

97   TO CANDY ANGELICO STALKS

About A weeke in aprill, take of ye stalks of Angelico,* & boyle them in faire water till they be tender. then pill ye thin scin of them & squees them betwixt 2 plates till all ye water be out. then brayd them If you like it, & boyle them to A candy in sugar as other roots be done. then dry them in a stove.

I refer the reader to S 96; the stripping of the stalks is somewhat more clearly expressed here, however.

* Written *Agelico*.

98   TO CANDY ANGELICO ROOTES

First boyle them in water, pritty tender, then make a
sirrup, or 2 If you will be at ye cost, & boyle y^m in both
sirrups. but ye last sirrup must be stronger, in which
you must boyle them to ye full height you will have
them candyed.

There is need whatsoever to have two pots of syrup, even though
you may well be able to afford it. After the first immersion, simply
boil the syrup to a *candy height* (S 5) and continue. See S 96
and 97.

99   TO CANDY GREEN APRICOCK CHIPPS

Take your Apricocks, pare them and cut them into
chipps, and put them into running water with A good
handfull of green wheat, before it be eard. then boyle
them a little, after take them from the fire, and put
them in a silver or earthen dish with a pritty quantety
of good white sugar finely beat[en]. then set them over
the fire till they be dry, and they will look clear and
green. then lay them* on glas[ses & put] them in a
stove A while, & then box y^m.

Green wheat, like any grass, stains whatever it touches with an
intense green; it was a common coloring matter. As noted, it must
not have started to ear, and it is to be strained out once the color
has been leached out.

100   TO MAKE SUGAR CANDY

Take refined sugar & boyle it to A Candy height, then†
pour it into a deepe earthen pot y^t is narrow & put into
it a stick & stop it up close. then set it in a warme oven
or stove, & soe let it stand 3 weeks. your pot must have
A hole at the bottom stopt with a cork to let out all the
sirrup that will run from it. then let it stand A week

* Written *then*.
† Written *the*.

287

longer, allways keeping it warme. then break y^r pot, &
dry y^r sugar Candy.

This is the sugar candy called for in a number of preserving and
candying recipes. I do not altogether understand the need for it.

These candy jugs, with the narrow neck and draining hole
at the bottom, must have been fairly common because I have seen
other recipes.

---

101   TO DRY PLUMS

First stone your plums, then weigh them and to 6
pound of plums, take 3 pound of sugar. then make a
sirrup of halfe that sugar, & put your plums into it
when it is scallding hot. then cover them & soe set
them of till they are tender & not break theyr scins. let
them stand in that sirrup A day & A night. then pour
away ye thinest of it, after add ye rest of ye sugar to y^e
sirrup,* and boyle it A little. y^n put in y^r plums againe.
soe let them ly A day & a night or 2 days, turne them
now & then. y^n put them in A new sive to dreyne y^e
sirrup from them, then lay them on dry sives & often
turne them, & dry them in A warme oven. & when
they are allmoste dry, wet a cloth in warme water &
wipe them one by one all over.

We come to a group of recipes for drying fruit. Actually, except
for the pippins, these fruits are not so much dried as glazed, or
perhaps dry glazed.

---

102   TO DRY PLUMS

Take halfe [ye weight]† of y^r plums in sugar, & make
sirrup of it, & scum it. then poure it to ye plums in a
gally pot, & let them stand above halfe a day. then
pour ye sirrup from them againe & boyle it. soe doe 3
or 4 times. then preserve them halfe up, & after dreyn

* I excised *to it*, made superfluous and confusing by an inserted correction.
† Supplied.

them clean from ye sirrup in A cullender, & lay them in a stove to dry upon plates or glasses.

Preserving recipes for plums start with S 47. The alternation of simmering and standing assures a thorough permeation of the plums with sugar and assists in keeping them beautifully whole. For *stove*, see S 68.

---

103   TO DRY APRICOCKS OR OTHER FRUIT WITH SUGAR

First preserve all your fruit, but boyle them not to tender. then take them out of ye sirrup & wash them in scallding water, then dry them on ye bottom of A sive in an oven after ye bread is drawn. then take halfe a pound of double refind sugar and boyle it to a candy height. then draw your fruit thorough y^t sirrup, then lay* them on A wicker & set them in A stove, & set A chafing dish of coles into ye stove till they are thorough dry.

For preserved apricots, see S 38. Also see other fruit drying recipes in this section. *Stove* is explained in S 68.

---

104   TO DRY PEARS OR WARDENS

Pare them & put them in a pipkin, & put to them any old sirrup, or else some clarret wine, sugar, and water. soe set them in the oven, and flat and dry them, [taking y^m out of] ye sirrup upon plates or sive bottoms.

Wardens are an old variety of baking pear. They first appear about 1380 as *wardon peryz*. *OED* says that the origin of the word is obscure, but I am convinced by their suggestion that it comes from Anglo-French *warder*, French *garder*, to keep, making *warden* a keeper. (On this consonant shift, see *wafer*, C 143 and *wallnut*, S 72.) Palsgrave, in 1530, defines *wardon* as *poire de garde*, or keeping pear. They have been described as brownish and hard. (See C 71.)

* I excised a repeated *then lay*.

The pears are to be cooked until barely tender, then laid out flat and stoved. Even if you do not dry them, oven cooking is the ideal way to cook almost any fruit; the flavor is intensified and the fruit remains whole. See preceding recipes for drying fruit.

---

105   TO DRY PIPPINS

Take pippens & put them in sives, & set ye sives into ye oven upon sticks after ye bread is drawn. y^n stop ye oven up for 24 hours. If they be soft enough to flat at ye first time, then flat them. If not, heat ye oven againe a little, & stop them up as before. then set them in A warme stove to dry upon plats or glasses, & If you pleas, dust some sugar on them as they dry.

For *pippins*, see S 21. No hint is given as to preparation, but I suppose the apples to be cored and perhaps peeled and quartered as well. With modern ovens, it is only necessary to bake them at say 200°F for a few hours; for the *stoving*, see S 68.

---

106   TO MAKE GREEN GINGER

Take ginger, pare it, & lay it in soack 2 days in white wine. then take ye weight in sugar, with which let it boyle leasurely halfe a day at ye least, & then pot it up.

See S 92. The *soack* is the steeping liquid.

---

107   TO MAKE MANUS CHRISTI

Take halfe a pound of refined sugar and some rosewater, & boyle them together till it comes to sugar againe. then stir it about till it be allmoste cold. then take leafe gold and mingle with it as much as you shall think fit. then cut it in round goblets, and soe keepe them.

This confection should have the texture of old-fashioned mint cakes; the size would be about right, that of a quarter. Gold leaf is used in Persian cookery to this day; in the West, it survives, to my knowledge, only in *goldwasser*, an ancient medicinal *cordial water*. As a form of conspicuous consumption, it can hardly be improved upon, but that was not the purpose, or not the only one (See S 70 for the virtues of gold in medicine; also of pearl, which occasionally replaced gold in *manus Christi*.) *Manus Christi* survived as a *cordial* confection into the seventeenth century, but more and more, the Latin name was replaced by others (see *Lozenges*, S 110, and *manus Christi*, a stage of light syrup, S 4), and, of course, faith in the cordial properties of gold ebbed.

It is an ancient confection. In a shopping list in *Le Ménagier de Paris*, about 1392, we find *manus-christi* among the *dragées* (candied almonds) and other confections. There is also a sacerdotal connection for which I can find no entirely satisfactory explanation. Du Cange, in *Glossarium . . . Latinitatis*, 1845, defines it as *massa quaedam saccharo condita* (a patty of sugar confection). He cites an item from dispense accounts of Nîmes, 1334: "Pro duobus pixidibus sive massapanis, unum de Mana Christi, et alim de confiegs, etc." Translation: For two consecrated wafer boxes [pix], or reliquary caskets, one for *Manus Christi*, and the other for confections, etc. (*Confiegs* were usually sugar-coated fruits and nuts, but could include any product of the *confiseur*, or confectioner.)

It would thus appear that in medieval times, in France at least, the consecrated wafer, the body of Christ, may have been candy. The justification is slender, perhaps, but it explains the otherwise mysterious name of the confection, and also the persistence of the traditional form, that of a small wafer, as late as our recipe. I should add that the addition of precious substances was surely a profane one, stemming from medieval medical practices, as noted above.

Goblets are gobbets or morsels. This is such a rare usage that *OED* suggests a misprint when Palsgrave, in 1530, defines *Goblet* as "lumpe or a pece." *Gobbet* was becoming archaic by the end of the sixteenth century and became increasingly and self-consciously so as as time went on.

---

108   TO MAKE LOSSENGES OF ANGELICO

Take halfe a pound of green roots of Angelico, clean washed & pickt. boyle them in faire water till they be very soft, then beat them to pulpe & strayne them thorough A clean strayner. then put to them 2 pound of sugar finely powdered, & 2 ounces of rosewater, in which dissolve 2 ounces of gum tragacant. soe mingle all these well together & make it up into tablets.

Lozenge takes its name from its diamond shape, that of a rhomb, according to *OED*. The word, which comes by way of Old French *losenge*, has a long history in English cookery; there are several recipes involving *loseyns* in *The Forme of Cury*, about 1390, one of which gives specific directions for making nothing other than *lasagna*: "seep thinne foyles [leaves] of past" in broth and serve them with "Chese ruayn grated." (*Ruayn* refers to the seasonal deeper color, not to Rouen. Just so, in the same period, cheese *brie*, from Old Norman *brier* [modern French *broyer*], means that it should be pounded, not that it comes from Brie as is too often written.) And in Douce MS. 55, about 1440, we find: "Cut hem in the maner of losenges." There appears to be no etymological connection between *losenge*, which Robert says comes from Gaulish *lausa*, meaning flat stone (forms of which are still current in patois for roofing stone), and *leche*, meaning thin narrow slice (see *leach*, C 127), tempting as that is. Thus it appears that *lechyngys*, in Harleian MS. 279, about 1430, is a curious form of *losenges*, not *lechings*, although the cook may have used the terms indifferently. (Austin glosses *lechyngys* as long thin strips in the text but corrects it in his collation with Ashmole MS. 1439, of about the same date, where it appears as *Lozenges* in a parallel recipe.

Those *loseyns* of paste seem not to have survived the fifteenth century in England. *Lozenges* survived only in confectionery and medicine; they are now nearly invariably wafer shaped, and this is not recent. In the twelfth-century Baghdad manuscript translated by Arberry, there is a recipe for a confection that bears the name of *lauzīnaj*, which he says is the origin of the lozenge. The confection calls for spreading marchpane (pounded almonds, sugar, and rose water) on paper-thin bread, rolling it like a jelly roll, slicing it into thin round wafers, which are then soaked in syrup and rose water. This could well account for the name persisting in confectionery, as well as the later wafer shape.

But Battisti, in *Dizionario Etimologico Italiano*, says that *lasagna*, which appeared only in the fourteenth century and thence passed into French (citing an Occitan form, *lazanho*), finally derives from Greek *lasanon*, meaning a three-footed cauldron. This connection seems tenuous to me, even if one were to accept the premise that this shape of pasta was the only one in early times. What seems more likely to me is that we have here the same sort of popular association of similar but unrelated words, varying from country to country, as we find with *marchpane* (S 158).

Tragacanth is a gum obtained from a Persian shrub, *Astralagus*. The word comes to us by way of French *tragacante* (*OED*). One of the popular names was *gum draggon*, which appears in our manuscript. For *Angelico*, see S 68.

109   TO MAKE ORRINGE LOZENGES

Take preservd orringe & leamon pill minced small, of
each one ounce; sugar candyed, ye quantety of A
nutmegg; ye powder of ye lesser cardemones &
carraway seed, of each ye weight of 2 pence; musk &
civit, of each ye weight of 2 graynes; fine sugar
dissolved in rosewater, 5 ounces. mingle these well
together over ye fire, then spread them on a silver plate
& cut them into lozenges, & soe let them coole.

Elettaria cardamomum, from Malabar, was the more highly prized;
Amomum cardamomum was known as the lesser cardamom; both
were considered to have the same properties. Cardamom was revered in ancient China, India, and Chaldea for its medicinal virtues
(principally carminative, diuretic, and cardiac) and *Elettaria* is still
used in British pharmacopoeia, according to *OED*. Lagriffe, in 1968,
says that it was brought to Europe by the Arabs, who called it
cordumeni. Gerard treats *Elettaria*, *Ammomum*, and *Meleguetta* (grains
of Paradise) all together. "They also comfort and warm the weake
cold and feeble stomack, help the ague, and rid the shaking fits,
being drunke with Sacke," he claims.

The twopence is an old English silver coin. If it weighed
two pennyweight, it amounted to 48 grains (about 3 grams or $\frac{1}{9}$
ounce). For *graynes*, see S 23; for *lozenges*, see S 108; for sugar
candy, S 100.

110   TO MAKE AROMATICUM LOZENGES

Take fine sugar, halfe a pound, boyle it in red rose
water till it come to y^e height of lozenges. y^n gild them
& cut them square with a knife for y^t purpose. If y^r
gilding will not stick on, wet them gently with a little
rose water, but not too much. w[hen they are] dry, box
them.

This recipe is identical to *manus Christi*, S 107, except that the gold
leaf is used for gilding rather than being incorporated. Note how
much more modern the recipe sounds: we are instructed to cut the
mixture into squares (most likely elongated diamond-shaped
ones), not *gobbets*, for example.

111   TO MAKE PASTE OF APRICOCKS AND
       PEARE PLUMS

> Take a pound of Apricocks or pear plums, & put them
> between 2 dishes with a little rosewater & let y^m boyle
> till they be tender. then strayn them, & dry them on a
> chafing dish of coles. then take as much sugar as they
> weigh, being boyled to candy height; put them together
> & stir it, & fashion it on a pie plate in what fashions
> you pleas. then stove them, & keep them when they
> are dry for y^r use.

This is the first of a long section of recipes for fruit paste confections. Apricot leather and Turkish delight are among the fruit pastes that have survived into modern confectionery, especially in Europe, where they are more popular. Except for slight differences in technique involved with varying fruits, the recipes differ little. You must stir the paste very well with a wooden spatula as you cook it; it sticks and burns if you so much as bat your eyelashes. The technique of first cooking the sugar to *candy height* (S 5), as called for in this recipe, is an excellent one. After drying the cut-up pieces in a *stove* (S 68), you may roll them in granulated sugar, if you wish. I like the coarse sugar used by confectioners for this purpose, but it is not easily obtained in America, something I am unable to understand.

    Cooking *between 2 dishes* is explained in C 1. For apricots, see S 38; for *pear plums*, S 39. Do not use aluminum or other metal that might discolor the paste. I see no reason why all of these pastes could not be made by pureeing the fruit in a food processor; the blender is less successful.

---

112   TO MAKE PASTE OF PEACHES

> Take peaches & boyle them tender, as you did your
> apricocks, & strayne them. then take as much sugar as
> they weigh & boyle it to candy height. mix y^m together,
> & make it up into paste as you doe y^r other fruit. soe
> dry them and use it at your pleasure.

For peaches, see S 36; for pastes, S 111.

113   TO MAKE PASTE OF RASPASES

Take rasps & bruis them in an alleblaster morter, with a
spoonfull or 2 of rosewater & A grayne or 2 of muske.
then draw them thorough A piece of cushion canvis.
then dry it, & take as much sugar as it weighs & make
it up into paste on what fashion [you please].

Raspases are raspberries; see S 60. *Alleblaster* is alabaster; see S 78.
For canvas, see S 42. Pastes are discussed in S 111.

Musk is an odiferous, reddish brown substance secreted
in a gland by the male musk-deer. Its powerful and enduring odor
was highly prized; in medicine it is a stimulant and anti-spasmodic.
The ultimate source of the word is Sanskrit *mŭska*, meaning scro-
tum; the path was the usual one, by way of Persian *mŭsk*, Arabic,
Latin, and French (*OED*). I understand that the possession of musk
is illegal in the United States for fear of anthrax. Under no circumstances should you use any of the various substitutes, as they are
not meant to be ingested.

114   TO MAKE PASTE OF GOOSBERRIES

Take goosberries & cut them one by one, and wring y^e
Juice from them till you have as much as will serve y^r
turne. then boyle it a little y^t it may be the thicker, then
take as much double refin'd sugar as ye Juice will
sharpen. mix them together, then dry it & beat it to
powder againe. then take as much gum tragacant
steeped in rose water as will bring this sugar into a
perfect paste. beat it in an alleblaster morter, then take
it up & print it. dry it in a stove & not by the fire. then
gild it. this is excellently good for one y^t hath a weak
stomack.

The note about this paste being "good for one y^t hath a weak
stomack" reminds us that most of these confections were coun-
tenanced because of their ascribed medicinal qualities. See fruit
pastes, S 111.

Wring means to press or squeeze. If first appears in Old
English as *wringan* in 890. *Turne* means requirement or purpose,
an archaic usage. *Print* is to mold, a reminder that printing was

once done this way. They had charming alabaster (S 78), wooden, and metal molds for pastes and gingerbreads. The gilding is literal, with gold leaf. For *stove*, see S 68; for molds, S 166.

---

115   TO MAKE PASTE OF GOOSBERRIES

Take ripe large goosberries, & boyle them betwixt 2 dishes till they are tender, then strayne them & take as much sugar as they weigh, & boyle it to a candy height. then make paste of them as you doe of your respas. soe stove them, & when they are dry, box them.

For these pastes, see S 111 and 114; for paste of *respas*, S 113. *Betwixt 2 dishes* is discussed in C 1. For *candy height*, see S 5.

---

116   TO MAKE PASTE OF GENOA

Take a pound of ye pulpe of quinces & as much of peaches. streyn & dry it in a pewter dish over a chafing dish of coles. then boyle as much sugar as it weighs to ye height of manus Christi. y^n put them together & fashion it on pie plates, & dry it in a oven. [then gild th]em with gold, & box them.

In English and French cookbooks, Genoa is often credited with recipes for fruit paste. Actually, they were much older; the Arabs, and the Persians before them, had been making them for centuries. In Europe, however, Italy early became preeminent in pastry and confectionery and quite likely confectioners came to England from Genoa, bringing the art with them. (The Arabs first brought the art of working sugar to Spain; one may speculate that early refugees from the Inquisition, who are known to have fled to Genoa, may have been responsible for this center. We know, for example, that this was the case with the introduction of chocolate into Bayonne, France. However, cooks did a surprising amount of travelling from one royal house to another in Europe.)
    For these pastes, see S 111; for *manus Christi* syrup, S 4. For *chafing dish of coles*, see C 15; do not use pewter as not all alloys can take such heat. For quinces, see S 7; for peaches, S 36.

117   TO MAKE PASTE OF GENOWAY

Take mallagatoons or peaches, & boyle them very
tender in faire water, & strayne them thorough A sive.
& put to y^r mallagatoon or peach halfe A pound of y^e
pulpe of quince. then clarefy A pound of sugar & boyle
it to a candy height, & put y^r quince, mallagatoone, or
peach into it & keep it stiring over ye fire till it come
clean from ye bottom of y^r pan. then lay it on plates
and dry it.

For these fruit pastes, see S 111. *Mallagatoons* are treated in S 37;
peaches in S 36; quince in S 7.
    Genoway, meaning of or pertaining to Genoa, is an ob-
solete form which came from Old French *genoueis* (from Italian
Genovese). It was frequently used, wrongly, as the name of the city
(*OED*). See S 116.

118   TO MAKE PASTE OF PIPPINS OF THE GENOWAY FASHION

Take pippins, pare & cut them in quarters. then boyle
them in faire water till they be tender, then streyn &
dry them in a dish on a chafing dish of coles. then
weigh it, & take as much sugar as it weighs, & boyle it
to manus Christi. & put them together, then fashion
them on pie plates, & set them in an oven haveing
been very slightly heat, & ye next morning turne them
& put them of ye plates on sheets of paper. lay them*
on a hurdle, & set them into an oven of like heat, &
there let them remaine 4 or 5 dayes, putting every day
a chafing dish of coles into ye oven. & when they are
thoroughly dry, box them.

For fruit pastes, see S 111; for *Genoway*, S 117. *Pippins* are treated
in S 21; *manus Christi* syrup in S 4; *chafing dish of coles* in C 15. For
oven, see S 68.
    Heat is the old past participle; *heated* appeared in the six-

* Written *then*.

teenth century, but the old form lingered and appears elsewhere in our manuscript.

A *hurdle* is a frame, interwoven or wattled with hazel or willow shoots (*OED*).

---

119   TO MAKE OF PLUMS PEARS OR APRICOCKS A PASTE Y^t SHALL LOOK CLEAR AS AMBER

Take white pear plums or faire yellow Apricock[s]. pare & stone them, then boyle them on a chafing dish of coles till they be tender. then streyne them & dry the pulpe in a dish. then take as much sugar as ye pulp dos weigh, & boyle it to a candy height, with as much rose water as will wet it. then put your apricocks or pear plums into ye sugar, & let them boyle together & keep it stirring. then fashion it upon A leaf of glass into halfe apricocks, & put ye stone into ye syde. then put them into a stove or warme oven, & ye next day turn them, & close 2 of them together, & then put ye stones into them betwixt ye hollows. soe dry them out, & box them.

An interesting and elaborate conceit. The stones would have been put into only half the total number of "half apricots." For fruit pastes, see S 111; for *pear plums* (the title is in error), S 39; for apricots, S 38.

---

120   TO MAKE PASTE OF QUINCES

Put quinces in faire cold water, & set them on ye fire till they are ready to boyle. Coddle them soe long till ye meat will come from ye core. make it very fine with ye back of a spoon, then take their full weight in sugar finely beaten, and mingle it with the pulp, & set it over ye fire in a silver vessell till it be well incorporated, fit for paste. then worke it into what shapes you please, and dry them in A stove, & then box them.

For fruit pastes, see S 111; for quinces, S 7. To *coddle* is to cook under a simmer; see C 67.

---

121   TO MAKE ANY KIND OF RED PASTE OF DAMSONS CHERRIES BARBARIES OR OTHER RED PLUMS

Take your fruit when they are thorough ripe, & put them into a pan, & keepe them stiring over ye fire till they are thorough hot. then streyne them thorough A sive, & put to a pound of ye Juice y^t comes from them A pound of ye pulpe of pippins. then clarefy 2 pound of sugar & boyle it to a casting height, & put your pulp into it, & keep it stirring over ye fire till it come clean from ye bottom of your pan. y^n lay it on Plates, what fashion you pleas, & dry it, & keep it for your use.

The copyist doubtless intended to write "or other red fruit" in the title. *Pippins* are treated in S 21; damsons in S 49; cherries in S 42; barberries in S 63. For fruit pastes, see S 111; for *casting height*, S 6.

---

122   TO MAKE ANY GREENE PASTE

Take your apples or pippins, & pare them & take out their cores (when they are very green),* & cover y^m over in a pot with faire water. then cover ye pot & set them by a soft fire for 3 hours, & make them ready to boyle, & the heat of ye water will draw out all ye redness & sappiness from them. y^n boyle them very tender & streyne y^m thorough a sive. then clarefy a pound of sugar & boyle it to a casting height, & put a pound of your apples into [it], & stir it over ye fire till it will come clean from ye pan bottom. then lay it on plates & dry it for [your use].

The parenthetical phrase was an afterthought and is misplaced. Read: "Take your apples or pippins when they are very green, & pare them . . . "

* Parentheses supplied.

299

The apples are to sit at a constant scald for three hours; culinary logic demands that the poaching water, along with its "redness & sappiness," be reserved for another use. (See S 49, for example.) For fruit pastes, see S 111; for *casting height*, S 6.

---

123   T O   M A K E   P A S T E   O F   P I P P I N S   L I K E
              P L U M S ,   W I T H   S T A L K S   &   S T O N E S

Take 2 pound of pippins, pared & cut in pieces. boyle them tender & streyne them, then take as much sugar as the pulpe doth weigh, & boyle it to a candy height with as much rosewater as will wet it, & then put in y^r pippins. let it boyle a while together, then fashion them on pie plates. some like whole fruit. & some like halfe fruit. & dry them in an oven after bread is drawn. ye next day, turne them, & close your halfe plums together, & put plum stones in ye midst of y^m & stalks at ye ends. then put them into ye oven or stove till they are fully dry. & then you may box & keep them all ye year, & they will look like naturall green plums. If you would have them look green, you must make y^r paste when y^r pippins are green, but If you would have them red, you must mix preserv'd barbaries with them, & it will give them a good sharp taste as well as a tincture. you may make them all the year, If you keep your stuff in Galey pots as thin as starch, and season it with sugar, whether it be of plums, pears, or els pippins. & you may allsoe keepe the stones of plu[ms to] put in ye midle of them.

See S 119 for a similar conceit. Reading the other pastes of pippin apples in this section may be helpful; for fruit pastes, see S 111. For preserved barberry recipes, see S 63 on; *candy height* is given in S 5; *galley pots* in S 22.

124 TO MAKE PASTE OF ORRINGES OR
LEAMONS

Take orringes or leamons, & rase ye outward scin with
a rasp of Iron, or pare them as thin as you can with a
knife y^t is very sharp. cut them in halves & take y^e
meate out of them, then lay them in water 3 dayes & 3
nights. then boyle them tender, & to take away theyr
bitterness, boyle them in severall waters. when they are
tender, stamp them in a morter & strayne them, then
dry them in a dish over a chafing dish of coles. take as
much sugar as they doe weigh, & boyle it to a candy
height, & put it to y^r pulpe. then fashion it in branches
on a pie plate. soe stove them in an oven after bread is
drawn. when it is dry, box them up & they will keep all
ye year as yellow as amber.

We have here a group of three orange or lemon fruit pastes. (See
pastes, S 111.) As always, these are Seville oranges (S 28). I do not
understand why the aromatic zest is to be *rased*, or scraped, off
while the especially bitter pith is retained; perhaps it is badly expressed, and you are to discard the white pith.
   Branches must refer to a branch-like figured pattern intended for embroidery or other ornamental work; it is an obscure,
archaic definition with only one citation from 1606 (*OED*).

125 TO MAKE PASTE OF ORRINGES &
LEAMONS

Take orringes, prepared as before, & boyle them in
water, & beat them in A wooden boule or morter with
a wooden pestle. then streyne ye pulpe thorough a thin
canvis strayner. then take as much sugar as it weighs,
& put into it as much water as will wet it. boyle it to a
candy height, then put ye pulpe into it & stir it often.
boyle it till it will stand on a pewter pie plate even as
you lay it. then fashion it, & dry it as ye paste of genoa.
If you will make marmalet of this sirrup, boyle it till it
will [come away] from the bottom of ye posnet.

As the recipe directs, see S 124. A *posnet* is a small metal pot having a handle and three feet. The Middle English form was *possenet* from Old French *poçenet* (*OED*). The paste of Genoa recipes start S 116. For *candy height*, see S 5.

---

126   TO MAKE PASTE OF ORRINGES OR LEAMONS

Take orringes or leamons & lay them in water 2 or 3 dayes, then boyle them in severall waters [that] they be soe tender that you may strayne them. when you have streyned them, put to halfe a pound of ye pulp of orringe pills, halfe a pound of ye pulpe of pippins, & mix them well together. then clarefy a pound of sugar, & boyle it to candy height. then put y^r paste into it & keepe it stiring over ye fire till it comes clean from ye pan. then lay it on plates what fashions you please, & dry it.

See S 124 and 111; for *pippins*, S 21.

---

127   TO MAKE PASTE OF EGLANTINE OF Y^e CULLER OF RED CURRALL

Take eglantine berries, otherwise called hipps, & stamp them in a morter with gum tragacant & rose water, & streyn it thorough a streyner. then take halfe a pound of refined sugar, beaten & searsed, & work them together into paste. & print it with moulds, then stove it, & after gilde it.

Rose hips are an extraordinarily rich source of vitamin C, and they have been gathered from eglantine, sweet briar (*Rosa canina*), for millennia. See recipe C 68, as well.

For fruit pastes, see S 111; for *tragacant*, see S 108. *Searsed* means sifted; see S 76. To *gilde* is to cover with gold leaf. Historically, the name *red coral* belongs to an arborescent species found in the Red Sea and the Mediterranean, prized since antiquity for its beauty (*OED*).

128   TO MAKE PASTE OF VIOLETS

Take fresh gathered violets. pick & bruise them in an
alleblaster morter, & wring ye Juice from them. & put
as much sugar in fine powder to it as ye Juice will wet.
then dry it, & powder it againe. y^n take as much gum
tragacant steeped in rosewater as will bring this sugar
to a [perfect pa]ste. then print it & dry it in a stove, &
[?   &] guild it.

For violets, see S 86; for pastes, S 111.

129   TO MAKE PASTE ROYALL

Take a pound of refined sugar. beat it & searce it, &
put into it an ounce of cinamon & ginger with a grayne
of musk. soe make it up into paste, then print it with
your moulds. then gild it, & serve it up.

Recipe S 130 is rather more helpful in procedure. Also see other
sugar pastes, S 107 through 110. For musk, see S 113; for molds,
S 166.

130   TO MAKE WHITE PASTE ROYALL

Take a pound of refined sugar, beaten & searsed, & put
it into an alleblaster morter with an ounce of gum
tragacant steeped in rose water. If you see y^r paste be
too moiste, put in more sugar; If too dry, put in more
gum with a drop or 2 of oyle of Cinnamon. you never
need stand upon quanteties when you may thus order
it. beat it into perfect paste, & then print it with y^r
moulds, & when it is dry, gild it. & soe keepe it.

131   TO MAKE CAKES OF ORRINGES

Take ye freshest orringes you can get, & pare the
outsydes as thin as you can possible. y^n quarter y^m &
take out their meat, & boyle them in severall waters till

they be very tender. then mince them small & streyn some of ye Juice on them, which will bring them to theyr culler againe. y^n take ye weight & halfe of y^r orringes in fine sugar, & boyle it to a candy, after, put y^r orringes in & let them stand a while to dry on ye fire. then drop them into cakes, & dry them in [a stove].

This is the first recipe of a long section of cakes made of fruit. The difference between the composition of these cakes and the pastes is an elusive one. In some cases, the fruit seems to be more carefully pounded and more finely strained for the cakes (in some cases, juice is used), but by no means consistently. There is no clear pattern in composition, only in form, one that we would call a cookie or a patty.

In this recipe, if I understand correctly, both zest and pulp are included in the paste, the inner tough white membrane being discarded. For Seville oranges, see S 28. Some of the preceding pastes for oranges might be helpful.

---

132   TO MAKE APRICOCK CAKES

Take Apricocks, pare them & cut them in halves. & put them into a pewter flaggon, & set them in a pot of boyling water and let them boyle till they are tender. then poure a little of ye Juice from them, then crush them thorough* a cloth till you leave allmoste noething in ye cloth. you must streyn them into a glass, in which you must weigh them. & to a pound of them, take a pound & quarter of double refind sugar, & boyle ye sugar to a candey height. then stir in your apricocks, & let it stand on ye fire till it be ready to boyle. then put it into dishes of what thickness you will, & when it is cold, put it into a stove till it is hard candied over, then turne them upon plates & let them stand 3 or 4 days before you cut them. then cut them into what fashions you please. soe dry them up, & after box them.

* Written *thoroug.*

See recipe S 111 for apricot paste; also S 131. A *flaggon* is a large
bottle-shaped vessel of 2 quarts capacity that may be well closed.
Pilgrims originally carried wine in such jugs (*OED*). A stoppable
Pyrex vessel could be used.

---

133   TO MAKE CLEAR CAKES

Take raspis & stew them in a pot. & take a pinte of
their sirrup from them, y^n take their weight and halfe
in beaten sugar, & put as much water to it as will just
wet it, & boyle it to sugar againe. y^n mingle y^r raspas
Juice (beeing kept warme)* with y^r sugar, & keep it
stirring on ye fire till it be ready to boyle. then take it
of, & make cakes of it upon a plate, but first let it dry
in little glasses, & after dry the [cakes upon (?)] a plate.

For raspberries, see S 60; for these cakes, see S 131. This is a
beguiling recipe.

---

134   TO MAKE CAKES OF RASBERRIES OR
       GOOSBERRIES OR ANY PLUMS

Take raspis or goosberries, & put them in a stone Jugg
& set them in a pot of seething water. & as it doth
dissolve, poure ye liquor thorough a strayner, & take a
pinte of that liquor & put it in a postnet with as much
faire water† as will wet it. boyle it to a candy, & boyle
ye other liquor, then put them hot together. after, put
them in glass plates made like marmalet glasses, or
boxes. then set them in a warme oven, & let them
stand a fortnight. then turne them & set them in
againe, or in a stove where a little continuall fire of
charcole is kept. after they are turned, set them in again
till they be dry. & they will be candyed without any
moystness within. thus you may make cakes of any
plums.

* Scribe's parentheses.
† A passage has been omitted.

Directions for the amount of sugar were inadvertently omitted. Following the proportions given in S 133, I suggest for a pint of juice, 1½ times its weight in sugar (making 3 cups), set to boil with "as much faire water as will wet it," boiling it to candy stage (S 5). For the *stove*, see S 68; for these cakes, see S 131; for raspberries, see S 60; for gooseberries, S 56; for *posnet*, see S 125.

---

135   TO MAKE RASBERRY CAKES OF Y^e SEEDS

Take their downe weight in lofe sugar, & a quarter, then make a candy, & when your candy is very high, put in ye seeds of your rasberries after som of ye Juice is strayned out, but they must not be too dry. let them boyle together till you disserne them to grow thick. y^n drop them into y^r moulds. but for want of moulds, take a back board, sifting some wheat flower upon it, & soe drop them [on] it. after a day, you may turne them on a she[et of glass (?)].

This is the answer to the leftover seeds from clear raspberry cakes (S 133). *Downe weight* signifies good or full weight (S 16). Also see S 131.

The *back board* was surely a backgammon board. It could also have been what was called a *lap board*, a sort of tray. However, we know from *table man* in S 159 that backgammon (called *tables* until the seventeenth century) was quite likely played in this household; it was popular in Tudor England.

---

136   TO MAKE VIOLET CAKES

Take a quarter of a pound of sugar, & put to it 2 or 3 spoonfulls of water, & boyle it to sugar againe. then take fresh gathered violets & clip ye green from them, & shread them very fine. then mingle them with your sugar on ye fire & give them a walme or 2. then drop them on a plate, & they are made.

It is of interest to compare this recipe with that for violet paste in S 128. I should perhaps remind the reader that all these confections were thought to have medicinal virtues; for the violet, see S 86.

137 TO MAKE VIOLET, COWSLIP, OR MARRIGOLD CAKES

Beat y^r sugar very fine & put to it 2 or 3 spoonfulls of rosewater, or faire water, & boyle it to a candy. then shread y^r flowers & put them in, but it must not boyle after ye flowers are in. y^n take a back board & sift some fine flowre upon it & drop them on, & make them about ye biggness of a 6 pence or bigger, If you like them soe.

Cowslip (*Primula veris*) comes from Old English *cù-slyppe*, which might be translated as cow slobber; a fifteenth-century form was *cow slop*. Also known as the primose, it is a wildflower with drooping umbels of fragrant yellow flowers (*OED*). Gerard says: "A conserve made with the flours of Cowslips and sugar prevaileth wonderfully against the palsie, convulsions, cramps, and all diseases of the sinues."

Violets are treated in S 86; marigolds in S 83. For these cakes, see S 131. *Back board* is explained in S 135.

138 TO MAKE CAKES OF ROSES

Take roses & cut the whites from them after they are pluckt, then stamp & streyne them with damask rose water & ye Juice of leamons. then put it in a skillet with as much sugar as your Juice will wet. then set it on a soft fire, & let it boyl softly till it be pritty stiff. then drop it on a plate, & If it stand, it is enough. then drop it in litt[le cakes an]d set them in the sun to dry.

See preceding cake recipes, starting S 131. For roses, see S 66.

139 TO MAKE MARGERUM CAKES

Take a pound of fine sugar & about an ounce of sweet margerum powder, dryed & finely beaten & sifted with ye sugar. then dissolve gum arabeck in rosewater, with which wet ye end of a pestle ever as it drys, & in a Prittye time, ye sugar & margerum will be paste, with

beating & often dipping the pestle in this water. keep
out halfe of ye sugar to strow into ye water as you beat
it. it must be beat 3 or 4 hours, till you finde it [not]*
gritty when you tast it. then dry them, but not in an
oven.

Marjoram (*Origanum majorana*) is still a common herb in cookery.
Here, its use is primarily medicinal, I believe. Gerard says: "Sweet
Marjerome is a remedy against cold diseases of the braine and
head, being taken any way to your best liking . . . it provoketh
urine . . . and is used in medicines against poyson . . . It easeth
. . . such as are given to overmuch sighing." It was considered to
be hot and dry in the second or third degree, according to the
authority.

The use of *prittye* here is a charming archaic one meaning
a pretty long time; 3 or 4 hours, as is indicated farther on. I imagine
that a food processor would make short work of it.

An ounce of dried marjoram would be about 5 or 6 tablespoons. For *stoving*, see S 68.

---

140   TO MAKE MINT CAKES

Take a pound of sugar finely beaten, & put to it 3 or 4
spoonfulls of mint water, & boyle it up to a candy. then
take some mint & shread it small & put it to y^r candy
and drop it as you did the rose cakes, & set them in y^e
sun or a stove to dry.

Mentha viridis, garden mint or spearmint. Gerard says: "Mint is
marvellous wholesome for the stomacke, it stayeth the Hicket,
. . . vomiting, and scouring in the Cholericke passion, if it be taken
with the juice of a soure pomegranat." (Normally, sugar was
thought to enhance medicinal virtues.) Later he says: "Garden
Mint taken in meat or drinke warmeth and strengthneth the stomacke, and drieth up all superfluous humours gathered in the
same, and causeth good digestion." (It was also used externally:
"*Dioscorides* teacheth, That being applied to the secret part of a
woman before the act, it hindreth conception.") See *Spirit of Mint*,
S 301.

This recipe is precisely for after-dinner mints. Candy stage
of syrup is explained in S 5; also see S 131 and succeeding recipes.

* Supplied.

141 TO MAKE HUNNY COMBE CAKES

Take halfe a pound of beaten sugar & 2 spoonfulls of
rose water, 2 spoonfulls of orring flower water, & 2 or 3
spoonfulls of faire water. boyle these to a candy height,
& mince a little orring pill & put to it. y^n poure it out
into little papers, sliked, & made into ye fashion of
dripping pans turned up at ye syde, and they are
made. you may make them onely with faire water, but
they are not soe good.

Hunny combe refers to the texture of these little cakes, as there is
no honey. The Old English was *hunicamb*.
 This is the only use of orange-flower water in the manuscript, and this accurately reflects the situation in English cookbooks. Rose water appears in perhaps a quarter of all the recipes,
virtually all the sweet dishes aside from preserved fruits. The reason, of course, is largely one of climate; roses thrive in England
while the orange tree does not.
 I refer the reader to S 131 and succeeding recipes for little
cakes. For *candy height*, see S 5.

142 TO MAKE SUGAR CAKES

Take 3 ale quarts of fine flowre, & put to it a pound of
sugar, beaten & searced; 4 youlks of eggs, strayned
thorough a fine cloth with 12 or 13 spoonfulls of good
thick cream; & 5 or 6 spoonfulls of rose water; A pound
& a quarter of butter, washt in rose water & broaken in
cold, in bits. knead all these ingredients well together.
after, let it ly A while, covered well, to rise. then roule
them out & cut them with a glass, & put them on
plates (a little buttered) in an oven gently heat. all these
kinde of things are best when ye sugar & flower are
dryed in an oven before you use y^m.

We now come to a section of baked cakes, starting off with what
Americans would call cookies. This is an excellent recipe for sugar
cookies, really sand tarts. The dough will not actually rise, but

even a short period of rest permits a maturing and fermentation that improve texture and flavor.

Approximate quantities for a quarter batch are: 3 cups of natural pastry flour, unbleached (see *flours*, page 18); ½ cup of granulated sugar, 1 egg yolk, scant 4 tablespoons of fresh heavy cream, 2 scant tablespoons of rose water, 10 tablespoons of sweet butter. Flours vary in absorption; what is wanted is a nice rich cohesive dough. I suggest an oven of 375°F. (For use of word *heat*, see S 118.)

In all of these baking recipes, blond raw sugar (not too molassessy) will give delicious results that I suspect are also more authentic. It has a coarse grain, which can be remedied by whirling in a blender for a few moments, sifting it through a fine strainer, if that seems indicated.

A note on the word *flour*. It comes from French *fleur de farine*, flower of meal—we would be more liable to say cream of meal. Strictly speaking, only white flour, the finest bolting, should be called *flour*; whole wheat flour is more properly called wheat meal, and this distinction is preserved in Britain. (Old French recipes call for *fleur*, but that was sloughed off quite early and it is now *farine* for all grades.) *Flour* and *flower* were not differentiated until the eighteenth century (Samuel Johnson, in 1755, did not, for example); all forms were used indifferently for flour and blossoms, as is amply illustrated in our manuscript.

---

143   TO MAKE SUGAR CAKES

Take 2 pound of flower, & one pound of sugar, & yᵉ youlks of 2 eggs, & a spoonfull of sack, & a spoonfull of rosewater, & make it up into paste with melted butter. & roule it out pritty thin, & cut them with a beer glass, & put them on plates & set them in an oven* meanly hot with yᵉ stone downe.

Another fine recipe for little cakes; see S 142. A pound of flour amounts to about 3 cups of American flour so that approximate quantities for half a batch are: 3 cups of natural unbleached pastry flour, 1 cup of sugar, 1 scant tablespoon each of sherry and rose water, and melted butter; I propose 12 tablespoons or so, suggested by the proportions of S 142. The butter should be melted over hot water. Flours vary, so be prepared to adjust a little.

* Appears to be *oueun*.

310

144   TO MAKE SUGAR CAKES

Take a pound of fine flower, & a pound of sugar finely
beaten, & mix an ounce of cinamon finely beaten &
searc'd with them, & 3 quarters of a pound of butter, &
a little sack, 4 whites of eggs. mingle all these & make
it into paste. make them round cakes or what fashion
you [please. bake] them in a temperat oven, y^t they be
not [burnt. ye butter m]ust be rubd in cold with y^r
hands.

Approximate quanitities: about 3 cups of natural unbleached pastry
flour, 2 cups granulated sugar, 4 tablespoons of ground cinnamon
(use your discretion as this may be an error), 1 ½ cups sweet butter,
a little sherry, and 4 egg whites.
See S 142 for further suggestions.

145   TO MAKE CLEER CAKES OF ANY FRUIT

Take y^r rasps or other fruit, & put them in a pot &
cover them close with a cloth. then put ye pot into a
pot of seething water. If it be white fruit, then as it
boyles, for fear of growing red, take their liquor from
them. then weigh ye cleerest, & take a little more then
their weight in sugar. If ye liquor be thin, as of some
fruit it will, then boyle your sugar to sugar* againe &
let y^r sirrup boyle by it selfe, & then put it into y^r sugar
& let y^r sugar be well melted, but let it not boyle when
it is together, for then it will never candy. soe poure it
out in glasses, & dry them in a stove. & when they are
candyed on ye one side, turne them on ye glasses to
candy on ye other, & will be moist in ye middle.

Not only is this recipe out of category (it belongs with S 133, which
see) but it is presented awkwardly. There is, however, considerable
knowledge of technique.

* Badly corrected.

146   TO MAKE CARRAWAY CAKES

Take 2 quarts of flowre & 2 pound of butter. rub y^r
flowre & butter together, then take 6 eggs & beat them,
& 6 spoonfulls of yeast & 6 spoonfulls of cream. knead
these well together, & then mix A pound of carraway
cumfits with them & set y^r paste before ye fire to rise
for halfe an houre. after, make it into little [cakes, or
else bake(?)] it all in one, as you pleas. an houre
[? will bake it].

Caraway (*Carum carui*) is an umbelliferous plant bearing aromatic
seeds. The name comes directly from medieval Latin *carui*, before
that Arabic *al-karawiyā* (*OED*). Gerard says, "The seeds confected
or made with sugar into Comfits, are very good for the stomacke,
they help digestion, provoke urine, asswage and dissolve all windiness." They were regarded as hot and dry in the third degree.
Caraway had become naturalized in England early on, but Gerard
cites Dioscorides as saying that it grew in Caria, "whence it tooke
his name." Caria was in what is now Turkey; actually, its native
habitat was infinitely more far flung.

   Cumfits, comfits (from Old French *confit*, preserved), were
small fruits, bits of aromatic root or rind, or seeds, preserved with
a sugar coating. Caraway comfits were especially popular. Also,
see S 196.

   This is a version of English seed cake, and a most excellent
one (see also S 150). As for comfits, I have never tried candying
seeds, but I should think it not too difficult. If it should turn out
to be more of a praline, put it through the coarse blade of a Mouli;
you will still get the benefit of candied sugar and toasted seed.
You might substitute about 1 cup of sugar (see S 142) and ¼ cup
of seeds, but know that the results will not be as interesting.

   We must once again confront the vexing problem of flour
measures. The old 2 quart flour measure is 56 ounces (about 10 ½
U. S. cups). I have not tried the recipe, but I believe that the ale
quart was used in home kitchens (C 92); I suggest 8 cups of natural
unbleached flour. Six *spoonfuls* of yeast usually work out to be 3
ounces of fresh yeast, but this is a great deal whatever the flour
measure may have been; 2 ounces will be ample. (Four scant teaspoons of dry preservative-free yeast is the make-do equivalent.)

   As noted in the recipe, the cake may be baked in a single
large loaf or in smaller ones (see S 151). I suggest a 350°F oven; the

baking time may be an hour and a half but will depend on the size of your cake, in any event.

---

147   TO MAKE SHROWSBURY CAKES

Take 4 quarts of flower, 3 pound of butter, & breake it in little pieces, & worke them well together. then take a pownd & halfe of powder sugar, halfe an ounce of cinamon, a little cloves & mace, 3 whites of eggs, a little rosewater & sack, & work it up with warme cream, & soe bake it.

Shrewsbury Cakes are described by *OED* as flat, round biscuit-like cakes, a specialty of Shrewsbury in Shropshire. Under *strew*, the same dictionary explains that it was often pronounced to rhyme with *so*, and *strow* with few; this must explain the spelling of *Shrowsbury* and of *strow* (which is invariable) in our manuscript.

It is instructive to compare this recipe with that given in S 148; both are for *Shrewsbury Cakes*, but the proportions and flavorings are quite different, and S 148 tells us a good deal more about the traditional appearance. The amount of butter is not given in S 148, but in most versions, the proportion varies from about three parts to four of flour to equal parts, by weight, varying somewhat with the amount of cream. (Hannah Glasse, in 1755, calls for no butter, but it may be an error because she calls for only a little cream.) An interesting difference concerns the use of egg yolks in S 148. Yolks give a richer, more tender texture; the whites give a more cohesive texture and, if well handled, an attractive crispness.

Eighteenth-century cookbooks abound in recipes for *Shrewsbury Cakes* and they came to America; Amelia Simmons gives a recipe in *American Cookery*, 1796: 1 pound butter, ¾ pound sugar, 1 pound flour, 4 beaten eggs, and a little mace. It is a most excellent recipe. Mary Randolph also gives a fine one in *The Virginia Housewife*, 1824, but the cakes did not survive the century.

So for half a batch, approximate amounts are: 8 cups of natural unbleached pastry flour (see S 146 on measures), 3 cups of sweet butter, 1 ½ cups of granulated sugar, 1 tablespoon powdered cinnamon (but use your discretion), cloves and mace (¼ teaspoon each), 2 small egg whites, a little rose water and sherry (say a tablespoon each), and enough fresh heavy cream to make a good paste. I suggest an oven of 400°F. See S 148 for appearance. (I also refer the reader to S 142 and 151 for various bits of information.)

148 TO MAKE SHROWSBURY CAKES

Mix a pound of searced sugar & a pound of flowre well together. then beat & searce some sinamon, nutmegg, & ginger, & put in 2 egg youlks. worke all these to paste with sweet butter, & roule it about halfe an incth* thick. cut them round, & flowre y^r papers, & soe bake them. & when they looke Ised over, they are enough.

Shrewsbury Cakes are discussed in S 147, which see. The proportions here will be approximately: 2 cups of granulated sugar, 3 cups of natural unbleached pastry flour, powdered cinnamon, nutmeg, and ginger (perhaps a scant ½ teaspoon of each), and 2 egg yolks. I suggest a pound, or 2 cups, of sweet butter.

149 TO MAKE EXCELLENT CURRAN CAKES

Take 2 pound of butter & wash it in rose water, casting ye water out. then take 2 pound of flowre & 2 pound of sugar, mix ye flowre & sugar together, deviding it into 2 parts, & putting in some into a dredging box. & shake it into a trey till halfe be shaked in, beating ye butter all ye while with y^r hand. y^n take 6 eggs to a pound of sugar & flowre (takeing out 2 of ye whites),† 6 spoonefulls of rose water, some mace beaten. y^n put in ye other halfe of ye sugar & flowre, & 2 pound of currans, picked & rubbed ver[y clean. y^n bu]tter y^r panns & fill them halfe full, & set [them in a moderate (?)] oven.

This is a pound cake; mace is still the traditional flavoring but rose water gives this cake a lovely nostalgic seventeenth-century air. The total number of eggs for 2 pounds each of flour and sugar should be 12; the directions are confusing. The proportion of egg is a little light even so, but the rose water supplies the liquid. (Discarding the rose water in which the butter is washed is prodigal, even when one remembers that they made their own.)
Approximate quantities then are: 4 cups of sweet butter,

---

* In error for *intch*, the more customary form.
† Parentheses supplied for clarity.

6 cups of natural pastry flour (unbleached), 4 cups of granulated sugar, 12 eggs with 4 whites removed, 6 tablespoons of rose water, powdered mace (say a teaspoon), and 2 pounds currants (which could be reduced somewhat without harming the cake). The mixing directions are awkwardly expressed but clear enough, I think; a standard recipe for pound cake should solve any difficulties. It helps to have all ingredients at room temperature. Oven temperature should be moderately low, 325°F.

---

150   TO MAKE AN ANNYSEED CAKE

Take 6 pound of fine flowre, & to it put 3 pound of

melted butter and one pound of annyseed comfits.

mingle these together, & make it up as fast as you can,

and soe put it into ye oven.

I find it difficult to believe that this dough is to be baked in one cake, as is implied. Perhaps it is an error and small cakes are intended. I have not tried the recipe. For *annyseed*, see S 240; for *comfits*, S 146. *Annyseed comfits* could be substituted for the *carraway cumfits* in S 146.

Proportions for one-third of a batch: 2 pounds (about 6 cups) of natural pastry flour; 1 pound of butter, melted; and ⅓ pound of anise seed comfits.

---

151   TO MAKE A GREAT CAKE

Take a peck of flowre & put to it 10 eggs beaten; take

out 3 of ye whites. put in nutmegg, cinamond, cloves,

& mace, of each a quarter of an ounce; A full quart of

Ale barme, & mingle with ye flowre two pound of fresh

butter. when it is allmoste kneaded, put 6 spoonfulls of

hot water to it, & 10 pound of currans, & halfe a

pownd of sugar beaten. let it ly a while by ye fire to

rise, & then bake it.

This is the first of four recipes for *Great Cake*. These remarkable cakes more nearly resemble various European enriched breads, such as Polish Easter Bread or *Panettone*, than the feathery *brioche*, for instance. Of these, I have tried only S 152, which see.

Those who have had any experience at all in handling yeast dough will encounter no difficulty; it is largely a matter of

315

feel. Still, the recipes are from another day, and I urge those who would try any of them to read carefully all four recipes and the notes. Some of the suggestions given in S 146, and other baking recipes, concerning old flour measures and the use of raw blond sugar, for example, are pertinent here.

Barm is the froth that forms on top of fermenting ale and has been used as leavening down through the ages. I have excellent results working with the formula I give under *ale yeast*, C 92. As always when working with yeast, cutting down the size of the batch entails increasing slightly the proportion of yeast.

Approximate quantities for one-quarter batch are: 8 cups of natural unbleached flour (see S 146); 3 eggs, removing 1 white; scant ¾ teaspoon each of nutmeg, cinnamon, clove, and mace (preferably freshly ground); 1 cup barm (1 ounce of fresh yeast liquified in 1 cup liquid at blood temperature, using imported ale, water, or a mixture); 1 cup sweet butter; 2 tablespoons hot water; 2 ½ pounds currants; ¼ cup granulated sugar. I add 1 teaspoon of sea salt.

I find that setting the barm to 2 cups of the flour so that the yeasts can get a good start while I am working the butter into the bulk of the flour (see S 152) and going about other preparations (such as plumping the currants in hot water and drying them), is good procedure. (*In extremis*, 2 or 3 scant teaspoons of preservative-free dry yeast may be used instead of fresh, in which case the sponge system assumes more importance.)

I like to use a small proportion of whole wheat flour to approximate the less efficient bolting of the day (1 or 2 tablespoons of each cup) and I find that the ale in the barm mixture also lends a fine seventeenth-century richness.

Certain details of mixing and baking become clear only on reading all four recipes, and further illumination is cast by Markham (1615) in recipes for *Spice Cakes* and *Banbury Cake*. (I shall deal here only with characteristics common to all; see S 152.) In the first, he makes a point of working the dough "good and stiffe that you need not worke in any more flower after," and after working in the currants, "bake your Cake as you see cause in a gentle warme oven." For the *Banbury Cake*, he says to "worke [the ingredients] all together an houre or more: then save a part of the Past, and the rest breake in peeces and worke in your Currants: which done, mould your Cake of what quantity you please, And then with that Past which hath not any Currants cover it very thinne both underneath and aloft. And so bake it according to the bignesse." (I find 10 minutes of kneading sufficient.)

There is in none of these recipes a hint of baking the cakes in molds, nor even of using the cake hoops that became so popular in manuscripts and cookbooks beginning about mid-seventeenth century. So that the cakes must have been cast in large round loaves directly on the floor of the brick oven, just as bread was. The wrapping of the *Banbury Cake* in a sheet of plain paste is an ingenious solution to the problem of burnt currants. Both the Markham recipes could otherwise be part of this series of *Great Cakes*.

I counsel baking the cakes in molds. If you cast the cakes, the dough must be stiff enough to hold its own; with molds there is more latitude. I prefer earthenware, but not everyone does; molds specific to airier descendants of this sort of cake (*Gugelhupf*, for example) work very well. Butter the pans well and fill them no more than ⅔ full, cover loosely, and allow to rise as usual. I propose a preheated oven of 350°F. Watch that the currants do not burn; lay a sheet of plain paper or foil over the cakes toward the end, if indicated. Baking time depends on the size of the cakes but will be nearly an hour at least. (See *oven management*, page 19.) If you would like to ice your cake in period style, see S 155.

---

152   TO MAKE A GREAT CAKE

Take a peck of flowre, 8 pound of currans, A pinte of barme, 3 pound of butter; you must not melt ye butter but rub it into ye flowre with your hands. allsoe put in A pound of sugar, & 12 spoonfulls of rosewater. then take A quart of cream & make a tender possit of it with ale, it must not be clear. put in cloves, mace, & nutmegg as you pleas. it must not be wet with any thing but ye possit.* when you goe to heat ye oven, you must goe about to make your cake, for [you must] not keepe it long out least it be heav[y].

This recipe produces a delicious cake that is a little like certain very old recipes for wedding cake. (I should note that it in no way resembles the cake that Martha Washington is claimed to have made for the wedding of Nellie Custis, her granddaughter. See page 463.) The crumb is rather dense (which permits thin slicing) compared to our puffy cakes, and the crust is particularly fine, with an attractive texture that survived even freezing and thawing. (As with the resurrection of any baked goods, its life is then fleeting, so freeze appropriately sized pieces in hermetically sealed plastic.) Perhaps the most interesting comment to be made is that

* The letter *e* was corrected to *i*, or vice versa.

this *Great Cake* is actually less sweet than many so-called breads today; the intense flavor and fruity sweetness of the currants are set off by the buttery richness of the cake in a highly satisfactory manner.

Approximate amounts for one-quarter batch are: 8 cups or so of natural unbleached flour (of which ½ cup or so may be whole wheat flour); 2 pounds of currants; ½ cup barm (1 ounce fresh yeast liquified in ½ cup imported ale, water, or a mixture, at blood temperature); ½ cup sugar; 3 or 4 tablespoons rose water; a *posset*, made with 1 cup fresh heavy cream, ½ cup imported ale, and 3 eggs, taking out 1 white; ½ teaspoon each of cloves, mace, and nutmeg, preferably freshly ground. I add 1 teaspoon of sea salt, not to forget ¾ pound butter.

I adhered as closely as possible to the recipe. I did feel that the dough was underleavened in view of the short rising time and by comparison with other recipes of the day and so fortified the barm with additional yeast (see S 151). There is no way of knowing precisely how active their barm was, hence how light these cakes were expected to be, but it must be remembered that their remarkable keeping qualities are an aspect of their relative denseness.

I mixed the posset, but saw no need to actually make it (see C 110); it is to be "tender," or undercooked, and it must be cooled to blood temperature before proceeding. The use of a posset as the liquid in a cake marks this recipe (and S 154) as being very old. (Elizabeth David also remarked on the venerability of this practice.) Markham, 1615, for example, in the recipes cited in S 151, makes no mention of posset. He does call for setting the cream "on the fire till the cold bee taken away," but it is to be "somewhat cold" before being mixed with eggs or other ingredients.

The dough is soft and rich; if you would cast this cake, you may need to add a little more flour. (Perhaps there were to be fewer eggs in the posset; there wasn't a clue.) For discussion of baking procedures and other details, see S 151.

---

153   TO MAKE A GREAT CAKE

Take a peck of flowre, 4 nutmeggs grated, halfe an ounce of cloves & mace, & as much cinnamon, & as much carraway seeds beaten, 3 quarters of A pound of sugar mingled with 7 pound of currans pickt clean & rubd clean with a cloth, A pinte of good ale barme, & allmoste A pinte of lukewarm water, 3 pound of butter

melted. first strow in a little salt upon ye flowre. then
mingle all ye spice together, & strow into ye flowre, &
strow in y^r water, barme, & butter. when all is well
mingled, knead it up & let it ly an houre by ye fire
covered close with a cloth. mingle ye currans & sugar
with ye dow. 2 hours will bake it.

I give approximate quantities for one-quarter batch: 8 cups or so
of natural unbleached flour (of which ½ cup or so may be whole
wheat flour); 1 nutmeg grated (about 2 teaspoons); a good teaspoon
each of cinnamon, clove, mace, and carraway seeds; ⅓ cup sugar;
1 ¾ pounds currants; ½ cup barm (1 ounce fresh yeast liquified
in ½ cup imported ale, water, or a mixture, at blood temperature);
½ cup warm water; ¾ pound butter, melted.

Again, I felt that the dough was underleavened and increased the yeast. See other *Great Cake* recipes, particularly C 151.

Dow is a form that lasted from the fourteenth to eighteenth
centuries; *dough* appeared in the sixteenth. It comes from a pre-
Teutonic word *dhigh*, to knead, related to Sanskrit *dih-*, to daub.
A common dialect pronunciation in England is *duff*, as *rough* (*OED*).

---

154   TO MAKE AN EXCELLENT CAKE

Take a peck of flowre, 10 eggs beaten, 2 nutmegg, A
quartern of cloves & mace, 2 pound & halfe of fresh
butter, one pound of sugar, 6 pound of currans. wash,
dry, & pick them very well. then take halfe a pownd of
candyed orring, leamon, & citron pill, & mince it small.
& make a possit with good cream, halfe A pinte of
sack, & as much Ale. & put halfe of y^r butter into y^e
posset & ye other halfe with some good ale barme. put
in to ye flowre & break it in, into small bits, & strow in
some rose w[ater, juice of lea]mond, & sack as you
mingle & knead up. [If you please, you may put (?)] a
little ambergreece in ye Jack.*

Approximate quantities for one-quarter batch: 8 cups or so of natural unbleached flour (of which ½ cup or so may be whole wheat
flour); 2 or 3 eggs, beaten; ½ nutmeg, grated; about ½ teaspoon
each of clove and mace; 1 ¼ cups butter; ½ cup granulated sugar;

* *Jack*, perhaps in error for *sack*, but see S 229.

1 ½ pounds currants, 2 ounces candied orange, lemon, and citron peel (in all, I believe); a *posset*, made of 1 cup fresh heavy cream, ¼ cup sherry, and ¼ cup ale; ½ cup barm (1 ounce fresh yeast liquified in ½ cup ale, water, or a mixture, at blood temperature); a spoonful or so of rose water, lemon juice (it could hardly be anything else), and sherry; ambergris (S 20).

The making of the posset is unnecessary (see S 152). No measures were given for cream or barm; I was guided by general proportions of previous recipes, which see, especially S 151.

---

155   TO MAKE LITTLE CAKES

Take A pound of wheat flowre twice sifted, a pound of currans, A quarter of a pound of sugar, A little nutmeg grated, A little saffron, ye whites of 14 eggs beaten, A little salt, some rose water. mingle ye flowre with a little sweet & thick cream, & put it into y^r saffron, eggs, & sugar finely beaten. when ye paste is made, beat it well with a rouling pin, & roule out part of it thin. then take your currans, nutmegg, & rosewater, & lay them on your paste, & strow on them a little fine sugar. then roule out ye other piece of paste thin, & lay it on the top. then close it together, & cut ye superfluous paste with a Jagg. thus you may make y^r paste all into one, or into severall little cakes, according to y^r pleasure. when they are baked, you may Ice them over with A little sugar & rosewater wash'd over on ye top, & ye white of an egg beaten with it, & after set them a little into ye oven againe. & soe you may Ice your great Cakes.

This is a filled cookie, a "currant newton," if you will. The whites are whisked only until foamy, I believe. The beating of the dough is for tenderness, exactly as for our Southern beaten biscuit. Whatever size you want to make these cakes, keep in mind that they must be transferred to the baking sheet. I suggest rolling out a large rectangle with half the dough, placing dabs of the currant mixture, rather as if you were making ravioli, covering it with the rest of the rest of the dough rolled thin, then cutting through with your *jagg* (jagging-iron) or pastry wheel, and baking. Diamond-shapes are easy and can be justified historically (S 108).

The rose water glaze is delightful. I suggest a good table-spoon of rose water and about 3 tablespoons or so of fine granu-lated sugar whisked with an egg white until all is well amalgam-ated; paint the top surfaces of your baked cakes and return to the oven until glazed.

A pound of flour amounts to about 3 cups of American flour; ¼ pound sugar is ½ cup. I suggest an oven of about 375°F.

---

156 TO MAKE ALMOND CAKES

Take halfe a pound of searsed sugar, 2 ounces* of fine
flowre, halfe a pound of almonds blanched in
rosewater, 2 whites of eggs well beaten. as you beat y^e
almonds, strow in ye sugar & flow[re, & then y^e] eggs.
& [bake] them in litle cakes.

Half a pound of sugar is 1 cup; 2 ounces of flour is about 6 table-spoons. It is difficult to know just what is meant by "well beaten" with regard to egg whites as efficient whisks were as yet unknown; I would say beaten so that they are good and foamy but not stiff. For more on almond cakes, see S 157.

---

157 TO MAKE ALMOND CAKES

Take 4 new layd eggs & beat them, halfe a pound of
loaf sugar, & beat it well into ye eggs. take a quarter of
a pound of almonds, blanched in well water, & beaten
in rose water, then take a quarter of a pound of fine
flowre, well dryed against ye fire. beat it well together
with ye egge & sugar mixed & beating them all together
with ye almonds. put in a grayne of muske, then set y^r
plates in the oven to warme. after, fill them halfe full,
& let them have an indiffrent quick fire.

Half a pound of sugar is 1 cup; ¼ pound flour is about ¾ cup; for musk, see S 113. *Plates* are probably pie plates; preheating them makes a remarkable difference in the crust. They must be buttered. There is no clue as to the size of these pans, but my impression is that the cakes are to be fairly thin. I think it fair to translate "an indiffrent quick fire" as about 375°F.

* Written above *pound*, which is crossed out.

158   TO MAKE MACHPANE* CAKES

Take almonds & blanch them in warme water. then
beat them very fine in a stone morter and put in a little
rose water to keepe them from oyling. then take y^e
same weight in sugar as you doe of almonds, & mingle
it with them when they are beaten very small & short,
onely reserveing some of it to mould up ye almonds
with all. then make them up in pritty thick cakes, &
harden them in a bakeing pan. then make a fine clear
candy, & doe it over your marchpanes with a feather.
soe set them in y^r pan againe, till ye candy grow hard.
then take them out, & candy ye other side. set them in
againe, & look often to them. keepe a very temperate
fire, both over & u[nder them,] & set them in a stove to
dry.

March payne showed up in the fifteenth century; *marchpane* followed
shortly, but because so much of it has been imported from Ger-
many and Austria, *marzipan* has become a current form (*OED*), very
nearly displacing the English word.

The word has long posed a beguiling etymological puzzle.
Liger, in *Dictionaire du Bon Ménager de Campagne et de Ville*, 1715,
calls it *Marsius panis* and claims that it was the creation of an Italian
pastry chef by the name of Marco. In the same vein, it has been
proposed that it derives from Saint Mark's bread; no authority is
offered and I am unable to find a reference suggesting such an
association in any primary source or serious work. More difficult
to dispose of is the existence of the Medieval Latin *massapanis*, a
small reliquary casket in which reposed fragments of Christian
martyrs. In actual practice, at least in France, they frequently seem
to have contained consecrated bread and even various confections,
presumably also consecrated. (See S 107.) Then, *OED* notes an
ingenious theory involving *mauthabān* (meaning seated king), the
Arabic name for a Venetian coin which bears the figure of a seated
Christ. It is an enticing if fanciful construction; it accounts for the
earlier wafer shape and even takes into account the manifestly
Saracen origin of the confection. (It should be noted that the *mas-*

* Possibly in error for *marchpane*; I find no evidence for forms without
an *r* in English. However, she repeats this form in S 175; perhaps French
massepain was of influence in this regard. (See *sale* for salt, C 185.)

sapanis contained holy wafers and that the word could be construed as literally meaning something like a wafer.)

But Amado Alonso, in *Revista Filologia Hispanica*, 1946, shows that the various forms of the word could not have evolved from *mauthabān*, and cites the appearance of an Arab word *mašsipan*, designating the confection, in a twelfth-century manuscript of Cordoba by Ben Quzman. (The Arab š sound is an explosive one rather like *ch*, that would account for the *marchpane* and *marzipan* forms.) This antedates the Venetian coin by some time and is more direct. Corominas, under *mazapan* in *Diccionario Etimologico de la Lengua Castellana*, confirms the Arab confection (phoneticizing it as *mahšabân*) but thinks that the word may somehow have been connected with the packaging of madeira for export, citing Italian *marzapane* of 1340 and Low Levantine Latin *marzapanus* of 1202 in this regard. Yet another confusing factor.

The precise relationship among *mahšabân*, an infidel confection, *manus Christi*, a consecrated confection, and *massapanis*, a Christian reliquary casket often holding consecrated wafers (to say nothing of *marzapanus*, madeira packaging), is probably lost in time. I imagine that the same sort of accidental popular etymology of association of somewhat similar but unrelated words, such as we found with *asparagus* and *sparrow grass* (C 157), obtained here. Corominas says as much when he also suggests an influence from *masa*, paste, and *pan*, bread. This observation would also apply to French *massepain*.

In the Arab document of 623/1226, translated by A. J. Arberry as *A Baghdad Cookery-Book*, there is a recipe for a confection called *makshūfa* that calls for equal parts of pounded sugar, pounded almonds (or pistachios), honey, and sesame oil, all cooked until "almost set" and flavored with rose water and saffron. While there are tantalizing similarities, there are problems, both philological and culinary.

The oldest certain recipe for the confection is from a fourteenth-century Catalan manuscript, *Libre de Totes Maneres de Confits*. It is called *Mersepa* and differs from our own recipe only in being more explicit in such details as the drying of the almonds after blanching; proportions and basic procedures are the same. Massialot, in *Le Confiturier Royal*, 1676, gives no less than eight different recipes, considerably more evolved and elaborated in technique. The most interesting differences involve cooking the sugar to *feather* (S 6) before mixing it with the pounded almonds and cooking the paste over a gentle fire until "it leaves the sides of the pan." The French seem always to have preferred orange-flower water and lemon flavorings to the more classic rose water.

Marchpane became tremendously popular in England for those who could afford such luxury and recipes appeared in virtually all cookbooks from Elizabethan times on through the first part of the eighteenth century, including the 1742 American edition of *The Compleat Housewife* by E. Smith. But from then on, recipes were pretty much relegated to confectionery books; there is none in *The Art of Cookery* by Hannah Glasse in 1755, 1798, nor the first American edition of 1805, nor in such editions of Elizabeth Raffald and Susannah Carter as I have at hand. One must suppose that it was no longer being made in the home to any extent. Marchpane never became as popular in the United States as in England and on the continent.

Medicinally, marchpane was considered to be a restorative. Morellus Petrus, as Englished by Culpeper in *The Expert Doctors Dispensatory*, 1657, also claims that it is good for all "affections of the lungs," and is "convenient for people that are leane."

Marchpane recipes in our manuscript run through S 170, interspersed with instructions for making fantastic Tudor-style conceits, the glory of what was called *banquetting stuffe* (showy sweets, mainly).

The French food processor makes successful marchpane in seconds; be sure that the almonds are powdered before you slowly add the sugar, dribbling in the rose water as necessary to counter oiling. Stop when it forms a "perfect paste." A good blender will do an acceptable job on the almonds but bogs down on the paste. I highly recommend the French procedure of cooking the paste (see S 170); it cuts the drying time immeasurably and allows you to set things right if you add too much rose water. Use a wooden spatula and stir constantly as it scorches while you blink your eyes. For the stoving, the oven should at no time be more than 200°F; I suggest 150°. (See *stove*, S 68.)

Recipe S 160 is rather more informative on the pounding process and S 159 is more helpful on shaping. If you wrap the finished paste in plastic and store it for a day or two in the refrigerator, it will be more tractable. An individual wooden butter mold (soaked in cold water beforehand and rinsed between printings) makes a pretty form and is easy, but you are limited only by your imagination and skill. If the paste remains sticky, you most likely used too high a proportion of sugar; try working in additional powdered almonds. Early French recipes often call for only three parts of sugar to four of almonds, by weight; for special purposes, it was often one part sugar to two of almonds, as in S 162. For this purpose, super-fine granulated sugar is best; 1 pound amounts to 2 cups. For the candy glaze, see S 5, quite different from the glaze in S 159.

159   TO MAKE MARCHPANE CAKES

Take your marchpan paste & roule it out about a
quarter of an intch thick, & cut them in little round
cakes about ye biggness of a table man. cut them some
3 & some 4 square, & some like a hart, & what other
fashion you pleas. then lay them on papers or* pie
plates & dry them. then take ye white of an egg, & beat
searsed [sugar]† into it till it is something thick, & Ise
ye one side of them over with it & dry them againe in a
warme oven for a quarter of an houre, then turne them
& ice ye other side of them in ye like manner, & they
will be very white with smooth sides. & soe keep them
for y^r use.

The *table man* is a "man" or piece in any game played on a board,
especially backgammon, which was then called *tables* (see *back
board*, S 137). *OED* cites *Tabylle man* from 1483. The various suggested forms are: a heart, a square, and an isosceles triangle.

    For *marchpane* and details on drying, see S 158. *Searsed*
sugar is simply sifted (see S 76); use super-fine sugar.

160   TO MAKE MARCHPANE PASTE

Take a pound of almonds, blanch & wash them very
clean. then put to them A pound of sugar and beat
them together the space of an houre and it will be in A
perfect paste. and If you see your paste begin to grow
oylie, put A little rosewater into it, and beat it together
& it will take away the oyliness from it. and soe you
may make A marchpane with it, by printing it with
your moulds or makeing the premention'd cakes, or
useing it any other way as you pleas or have occasion.

See S 158, where a slightly different technique is suggested.

    * I excised a confusing *a*.
    † Supplied.

159   To make marchpane Cakes

Take your marchpan paste & roule it out about
a quarter of an inch thick & cut them in Little round
cakes about y⁰ biggness of a table man, cut them
some 3 & some 4 square & some like a hart & what
other fashion you pleas, then lay them on papers
or a pie plates & dry them, then take y⁰ white of
an egg, & beat seated into it till it is something
thick & ise y⁰ one side of them over with it &
dry them againe in a warme oven for a quarter
of an houre, then turne them & ice y⁰ other side,
of them in y⁰ like manner & they will be very white
with smooth sides, & soe keep them for y⁰ use.

160   To make marchpane Paste

Take a pound of almonds blanch & wash them
very clean, then put to them A pound of sugar
and beat them togother the space of an houre
and it will be in A perfect paste, and If
you see your paste begin to grow oylie put
A Little rosewater into it, and beat it toge-
thor & it will take away the oyliness from
it and soe you may make A marchpane
with it, by printing it with your moulds
or makeing the prementiond cakes, or use
ing it any other way as you pleas or have
occasion

161   TO MAKE A MARCHPANE

Take wafers & make a round bottom of them. then
roule out y^r marchpane paste upon them, about a
quarter of an intch thick & cut [wth] a round compass,
with A voyder, or A dish at ye biggness y^t you will
have it to be. & then set an edge to it of ye same paste
& nip it with y^r fingers. then take 2 or 3 spoonfulls of
rose water & beat searsed sugar in it till it be something
thicke, then set it on papers & Ice your marchpane
within, with it, & bake it. & then take long cinnamon
comfits & stick in it, with some other conceits, & gilde
it [for]* your use. then for to gild it, cut y^r gold & wet
ye place that must be gilt with some gum water, & soe
lay ye gold upon it.

This is an extravagant conceit. See S 158 for discussion of marchpane. The final effect of the marchpane here is that of a large very
shallow tart with pinched edges. The use of the *wafers* is better
described in S 162, which see. The marchpane paste works up
surprisingly easily. Gold leaf is laid on with gum arabic dissolved
in water. For *wafers*, see C 143.

A *uoyder*, voider, is normally a vessel into which refuse
is emptied, part of the table service. However, there is an archaic
usage applying the word to a large plate, especially one of ornamental design, for handing round sweetmeats, and this is clearly
the intended meaning. (The word comes from Old French *vuideur*,
to empty.)

162   TO MAKE MARCHPANES

Take 2 pound of Jordan almonds, blanch & beat them
in a stone morter till they come to fine paste. put in it
now & then a spoonfull or 2 of rose water to keep it
from oyling. then beat with them A pound of fine sifted
sugar till it comes to perfect paste. then roule it out thin
& as bigg as a charger & cut it by it, & set an edge
about it, & A bottom of wafers under it. y^n bake it in

* Supplied for an indecipherable character.

327

an oven or baking pan, & when you see it hard or dry, take it out & Ice it with rose water & sugar, & set it in againe. & when you see it ri[sing], take it out & garnish it wth dry sweet meats [and long (?)] comfits stuck upright & small ones strowed [about]* and gild it.

This is same basic conceit as given in S 161 (which see) except that the proportion of almonds is twice as high; see S 158 for marchpane and the question of these proportions. For *wafers*, see C 143.

The Middle English term for *Iordan almond* was *jardyne almaunde*, apparently from French or Spanish *jardin*, garden (*OED*). In the 1636 edition of *The Herball*, Johnson says that among the almonds brought to England there was "a large sweet Almond, vulgarly termed a Jordon Almond; and a lesser, called a Valence Almond." This was in addition to the bitter almond. They all came from Spain. (See S 20.)

A *charger* is a large platter for carrying a joint of meat. The word most likely comes from Old French *chargeoir*, utensil for loading (*OED*).

---

163   TO MAKE ALL KIND OF FRUTAGE HOLLOW

Take moulds being made of alleblaster, every mould beeing made in 2 pieces. & being watered, y^r sugar must be boyled to candy height. & fill one halfe of ye mould with ye sugar, & turne ye mould round with y^r hands & ye fruits will be hollow. then put them into their naturall cullers.

Hollow sugar fruits were a popular conceit. Clearly, after filling half the alabaster mold with syrup (S 5), the other half is clamped down.

---

164   TO MAKE ARTIFITIALL FRUIT

Take y^r sugar plates & print them hollow in your alleblaster moulds & dry them. then take a little of y^r sugar paste & temper it something thin, and set your fruit together with it, & dry them againe & then culler them after the life, as ye receipt following mentions.

* Supplied.

The recipe for *sugar plate* is given in S 172. These fruits are to grace the marchpanes in S 161 and 162.

---

165   TO CULLER YOUR ARTIFICIALL FRUIT AFTER THE LIFE

> To culler y^r artifitiall fruit: If it must be a light red, take vermillion & grinde it with gum water. If it must be a dark red, culler it with lake, ground in gum water in a brass morter or on a marble stone. & If it must be green, take sap green & steep it in gum water or else ye Juice of spinnage or green wheat. If it must be yellow, take white rose leaves & beat them in a morter wth a little roach allome, & then strayne ye Juice out, which will be a perfect yellow; or else steep saffron in [rose]* water. these are all the cullers y^t you need to [culler artific]iall fruit withall.

I would suppose the artificial colors are available from art supply stores; they are not meant to be eaten, for the most part, and I suggest that vegetable colors only be used, particularly where there are children to be considered. See S 169 for uses.

Uermillion, or cinnabar, is the red crystalline form of mercuric sulphide. *Lake*, rather *lac* or gum-lac, is the dark red resinous incrustation produced by certain tree insects. It is used in the East as a scarlet dye. The word is from Hindustani *lakh*, Sanskrit *laksha*. *Sap green* is one of various expressed vegetable juices of a viscid nature used by painters. *Roche alum*, or rock alum, is used in dying (*OED*).

---

166   TO MAKE BIRDS & BEASTS

> Take a pound of vallentine almonds & blanch y^m & beat them in a morter till they come to perfect paste, then put to them a pound of searsed sugar. soe beat it alltogether A little while, & then you may make y^r conceits by hand, & print some in moulds. soe gild them, & stove them before the fire.

* *Rose* water is suggested by S 169.

This is, of course, marchpane; see S 158. *Vallentine* almonds are from Valencia. *Valentian* was a common form for *Valencian* (*OED*); the corruption to *vallentine* becomes clear. See S 162.

These birds and beasts, and those of the following recipes, are to stand in the marchpanes of recipes S 161 and 162.

Molds are discussed in S 167, 169, 198, 200, 203, and 209.

---

167   TO MAKE ALL KINDE OF BIRDS AND BEASTS WHICH MUST BE CAST IN MOULDS

Take halfe a pound of double refin'd sugar, & put to it 6 spoonfulls of faire water; soe let it boyle till it comes to ye height of manus Christi. then take your double moulds, beeing layd in water 2 hours, dry them well with a cloth. then put your hot sugar into them & let them stand till they are cold. then take them out & gild them. they are used to garnish marchpanes withall.

See S 166 for birds and beasts; S 4 for *manus Christi*. Further conceits continue through S 170.

---

168   TO CAST BIRDS AND BEASTS TO STAND ON THEYR LEGGS

Take barbary sugar & boyle it to the height of manus christi, then pour it into your moulds, they beeing seasoned as for Quidonies. let them stand A quarter of an houre and they will be cold. then you may take them out and gilde them and [let the]m stand upright on theyr feet in your [marchpane].

See S 166.

---

169   TO CAST ALL KINDE OF FRUTAGE HOLLOW IN TURN'D WORKE & TO PRINT THEM

Take your double moulds and wet them in cold water, then tie 2 of ye greatest peeces together, & poure y^r sugar into them, & clap them one upon another quickly.* then put ye third piece upon ye holes & turne ye moulds round in y^r hands, & your fruits will be hollowed. then take them out of the moulds & culler them. A leamon or an old pippin must be cullered with saffron & rosewater together. for A pear, amber, for a green apple, indien lake, & for A cowcumber, say† green.

I have never seen such molds; apparently they differed from those in S 167. See S 165 for more on colors; for molds, see S 166.

---

170   TO MAKE MARCHPANE CONCEIPTS

Take a pound of almond paste made for marchpane, & dry it in a dish, on a chafing dish of coles till it wax white. then print some with moulds & some wth hands or what fashion you pleas, then gild them and stove them.

See marchpane recipes beginning S 158; for molds, see S 166.

---

171   TO MAKE WALLNUTS

Take A piece of white paste royall, beeing beaten with gum tragacant, & mixed with A little searced cinnamon. then drive it thin and cut it in pieces, and put the pieces into the halves of your moulds, in eyther halfe a piece. then put musk cumfits or what you pleas into ye middle, then close them & dry them, & they are made. [(?)] some of this paste square, & roule it up [(?)in cin]namon.

We are still in *banquetting stuffe* (see especially recipes starting with S 163). For *white paste royall*, see S 130; for *comfits*, S 146. Here the mold was evidently made to resemble a walnut and was to be rolled in powdered cinnamon. *Drive* means to spread out or beat thin; it is still a technical term in painting.

* Written *quicly* with inept effort to correct. Immediately following, I excised an inadvertent second *then*.
† Surely in error for *sap green*.

172   TO MAKE SUGAR PLATES

Take an ounce of gum tragacant & lay it in steep in rosewater, till it is in A Jelley. then strayne it thorough a cloth & beat it in a morter till it looks very white. then beat searsed sugar into it by degrees, till it is soe stiff y^t you may take it out of ye morter. then worke more sugar into it, after you have taken it out, till it be A stiff paste. then roule it out & print it in y^r moulds. dry it or use it othe[r] wise as you pleas.

This is very much the same recipe as that for *white paste royall*, S 130. For *tragacant*, see S 108; for other conceits, see recipes beginning S 158.

173   TO MAKE NIMBLESSES

Lay gum dragon in steep in rosewater, then strayn it thorough a cloth, & beat it in a stone morter with ye white of an egg till it looks very white. then beat & searse double refined sugar & beat it into your gum & egg by degrees, till it is soe stiff y^t you can take it forth of y^r morter. then beat in the morter 3 or 4 greyns of muske after ye paste it out, which you must beat with searced sugar. then work it up into y^r paste. then roule out your paste about the thickness of A pie lid, and take marchpane paste and roule it out, and round like an arrow, and wrap it within your other paste. then cut them and [tie] them into knots, and bake them upon [papers. & kee]p them for your use.

The marchpane is rolled into long pencil-slim strips, wrapped in thin sheets of the sugar paste, cut into suitable lengths, and tied in knots, as for *jumbals*, S 191. Finally, they are filled *Gentlesses* (S 174) and quite likely of the same origin. They are to be baked the same way.

174   TO MAKE GENTLESSES

Take of ye white sugar paste you make y^r nimblesses
on & roule it out round, about the biggness of an
arrow. then cut them into lengths & make y^m into
knots as you doe Jumbals & set them upon papers &
bake them & they will rise very light & white, & will be
hollow within. & soe use them as you pleas.

Fynes Moryson writes in his *Itinerary*, Part III, 1617, of how the
Italians would often break their fast "with a bit of cake-bread or
sweet bread (called vulgarly *pasta reale*), ciambolini, and generally
gentilezze, and a cup of sweete wine, and so abstain from dinner."*
We are not given the composition of these little cakes, but if the
shape indicated by our recipe is authentic, this would make *gentilezze* related in form to *ciambolini* (see *jumbals*, S 191). *Gentlesses*
never became popular in English cookery, probably because the
name *jumbals* absorbed all similarly shaped confections (see *rosquillions*, S 175). The *Leamon Jumbals* of S 192 are structurally identical to these *gentlesses*; only the flavoring is different. (Moryson's
description of *pasta reale* makes it unlikely that it was the *Paste
Royall* of sugar in S 129; the name often simply indicated a regal
version of any pastry or confection.)

Our *gentlesses* are made of the paste given in S 173, tied
into knotted loops, and baked on parchment paper or plain white
paper. (Never use waxed paper.) I suggest an oven of 325°F.

175   TO MAKE ROSQUILLIONS

Take A pound of fine flowre, & a quarter of a pound of
sugar & work them together ye space of an houre, & it
will be a perfect paste, haveing first put in to ye flowre
& sugar halfe a pinte of warm milke, 2 ounces of sweet
butter melted, & ye youlks of 2 eggs. make it up into A
stiff paste & then roule out y^r paste about ye thickness
of a pie lid. then take of y^r machpanet paste & roule it
out like an arrow & about ye thickness of an arrow, &
wrap it within y^r other paste & cut & make them into

* With thanks to Elizabeth David.
† *Marchpane.* See S 158.

knots. & put them on papers & bake & keep them for
y^r use. you need not worke y^r past an houre as
prementiond, for y^t was a mistake.

Rosquillions are a pastry from Spain; it was Elizabeth David who
pointed that out to me. Neither of us knows of another example in
English cookbooks and we are left to speculate as to how the recipe
turned up in an English family manuscript.

Corominas says that *rosca* is peculiar to the Iberian pen-
insula; it very early designated a circular object, especially bread,
but later meanings referred to spiral or coiled serpent shapes. This
brings to mind *m'hencha* (the serpent), the splendid Moroccan
coiled pastry. The recipes are by no means identical, but their
relationship is undeniable, the most striking common characteristic
being the filling based on marchpane. In *m'hencha*, the wrapping
is *warka* (resembling phyllo leaves) and the pastry is one continuous
coil while in our recipe, the wrapping is a cookie dough and individual pastries are knotted into loops. (Paula Wolfert gives a
recipe for *m'hencha* in *Couscous and Other Good Foods from Morocco.*)

Among old Spanish recipes, I do not find a close parallel
to our *rosquillions*. But in *Libro de Guisados* by Maese Ruperto de
Nola, 1529, there is an exceedingly elaborate *Rosquillas de Fruta* that
involves a *rosca* of biscuit, fruit paste, honey, almonds and other
nuts, and *mazapān*. *Rosquillas* are still made in Spain but the recipes
that I know are rather ordinary pastries, their sole connection with
the early ones being their ring-shape, often cut like a doughnut.
(Also, see S 191.) They early came to Mexico, and Diana Kennedy
tells me that *roscas* are frequently local specialties. In one version
in her *Recipes from the Regional Cooks of Mexico*, they are twisted
ring-shapes.

Approximate equivalents: about 3 cups of unbleached
pastry flour; ½ cup sugar; 1 cup milk; 4 tablespoons butter; 2 egg
yolks. For marchpane, see S 158. The dough should be lightly
worked, as the scribe belatedly recognizes.

---

176 TO MAKE BISKET BREAD

To a pound of flowre take a pound of sugar, 6 youlks
of eggs, 8 whites. beat y^m 2 hours before you strow in
ye flowre, & then beat y^m 2 hours longer. y^n put in 1
ounce of [anny]* seeds, A few corriander seeds, 2

* There is a shadow of a *y*.

greynes of musk. [put it in (?)] to y^r pans & bake them
in an oven no[t too hot].

We leave the more fanciful conceits of *banquetting stuffe* and turn
to *biskets*. The word comes from Old French *bescoit*, cooked again,
but I have the impression that most biscuit recipes are Italian in
origin. There are in this series, three basically different pastries
whose only common characteristic is either a second baking or a
prolonged drying out in a slow oven, although this is not always
made clear. They also all lack shortening, so that crispness or
tenderness is achieved in varying ways, which will be noted in the
appropriate places.

The first three recipes (also S 183) represent the technique
of beating the dough for tenderness. *Bisket* recipes not too different
from these continued in England well into the eighteenth century;
those given by E. Smith in *The Compleat Housewife*, first American
edition, 1742, illuminate a number of puzzling details posed by
elliptical directions here. In spite of the popularity of English cookbooks in the colonies, these particular sweet crisp *biskets* never
seem to have become very popular here. There are a number of
biscuit recipes in *American Cookery* by Amelia Simmons, 1796, and
in *The Virginia Housewife* by Mary Randolph, 1824, but they show
signs of the softness that was to characterize these American quick
breads, later made with baking powder. In spite of a real difference
in composition (and the improbable Indian name for an English
bread), it is only in Mrs. Randolph's recipe for *Apoquiniminc Cakes*
(actually Southern *beaten biscuits*, a designation I do not find until
after the Civil War) that I find the same ferocious beating for tenderness, accomplished with a wooden bat exactly as directed by
Dawson in his recipe for *bisket bread* in 1586. For the English, a
biscuit was to remain a flat round crisp cake, what we Americans
might call a cookie, a cracker, or a rusk, depending on type.

The technique represented by these first recipes has long
since evolved into what might be called variations on the meringue
or sponge cake technique, which was made possible by more efficient whisks. Elizabeth Raffald gives several such recipes in *The
Experienced English Housekeeper*, 1789, where eggs and sugar are to
be beaten very well indeed, but tells us to "whisk in your flour
gently," when making *Drop Biscuits*. These are really *biscuits à la
cuiller*, or what we call lady fingers, and what Mary Randolph calls
Naples Biscuits (see C 143), except that the latter ones are properly
dried out so that not only are they airy and fragile, but they keep
well and hark back to the original meaning of biscuit.

The passing of the biscuit represented by this recipe
should not be mourned; its interest is more historical than gas-

tronomic, and the labor is prodigious (although excessive in some of these recipes, by all other sources). In a recipe that differs in no significant detail, Markham in 1615, calls for "very neere an houres beating," and this accords with other recipes. (This first recipe calls for 4 hours in all.)

However, the machine does make it possible, once again, to make these *biskets*. I tried the first two recipes, abbreviating the beating time in line with Markham and with regard for the greater efficiency of the machine; I used as my criterion the blistering noted in S 177. Only a heavy duty machine should be used. I switched to the batter attachment when I added the flour. The French food processor does not do eggs properly, but should do the paste efficiently.

Approximate equivalent amounts are: 3 cups of un-bleached pastry flour; 2 cups of sugar; 6 egg yolks and 8 whites; ¼ cup of anise seeds; a few corriander seeds (surely pounded). For musk, see S 113.

Because the dough was heavy enough to be baked exactly as drop cookies, I followed E. Smith in regard to what she calls *dropt biskets*. I dropped them on buttered parchment paper, allow-ing for moderate spreading. The sugar-flour dusting called for in S 177 (plain sugar in most sources) is practically obligatory and gives a nice finish. An oven of 350°F encourages the nicest puffing but produces a higher color than English sources thought proper. An oven of 325° gives the requisite paleness but a denser texture. After baking, I transferred them to racks and finally back to the oven, at 150°F, for drying out, allowing them to finish by the heat of the pilot light. (The necessity for thorough drying is not always made clear.) These *biskets* are not expected to be delicate, I think, but if they are hard, it is because you did not beat long enough, the puff was insufficient or not well set, or the *biskets* were not well dried. Half a batch gives about 4 dozen *biskets* of cookie shape and size.

If the *biskets* were to be baked in molds, there is little in the way of informative detail in these recipes. *Plates*, for example, could as well refer to baking sheets. Markham refers to "buttered Bisket panes," and they may have been pans with round inden-tations, rather like shallow muffin tins. Massialot, in *Le Confiturier Royal*, 1676, in a virtually identical recipe for *Biscuits communs*, plainly says that the mixture is to be put into individual molds, even allowing paper ones. The problem is that virtually every recipe I know, including later ones for both *dropt biskets* and molded ones, call for 1 pound of flour, 1 pound of sugar, and 8 eggs; occasionally, a couple of whites or yolks are subtracted, but this is often compensated for with rose water, for example (see S

178, the one recipe that departs from this classic proportion, but by very little, in actuality). The length of the beating varies, but the pattern is constant. In short, it is not consistency that determines the baking procedure. See recipe S 183 for more discussion on the consistency of the batter. I should note that I have tried baking *biskets* in molds; they must be very shallow or you will inevitably fill them too full and have a thick *bisket*.

---

177   TO MAKE BISKET

Take a pound of fine flowre of wheat, A pound of sugar, 4 whites of eggs & 8 youlks, & 4 spoonfulls of rosewater. ye longer you beat it ye better it will be. then put to it eyther annyseeds or carraway seeds or corriander seeds. you must beat it till it will bubble. then poure it into your plates. then take some sugar finely beaten, & a little flowre, which you must put in a piece of tiffany (y^r sugar must be thrice as much as your flowre)* & with this dust your plates of bisket before they are set into the oven.

See S 176. For *tiffany*, see S 26; use a fine sieve.

---

178   TO MAKE BISKET BREAD ANOTHER
        GOOD WAY

Take a pound and halfe of flowre & as much sugar, 8 eggs beaten, 10 spoonfulls of rosewater, & A few annyseeds. dry the flowre in a dish on A chafingdish of coles, and beat the eggs, rosewater,† and sugar by themselves. when you are allmoste ready to set into the oven, mingle the flowre with the rest of the ingredients & beat them A while together, and then bake them, & be sure your oven be not too hot. mingle allsoe with them 2 or 3 spoonfulls of sack, in which you may infuse A little Ambergreece If y[ou please].

For a discussion of these *bisket* recipes, see S 176. A pound and a

* Parentheses supplied.
† Final *r* missing.

half of flour amounts to about 4 ½ cups; the rose water, I believe, is 10 tablespoons. In the context of *bisket* recipes, it is difficult to say how long one is to beat after the flour is added, but the recipe clearly represents a step in the direction of the evolved technique discussed in S 176.

---

179   TO MAKE FRENCH BISKET

Take halfe A peck of fine flowre and bake it in ye oven, then mingle with it A quarter of a pound of annyseeds. then make it up with as hot water as you can, & 5 or 6 eggs. knead it into paste as you doe for manchets, then make it into a longe roule & soe bake it. and when it is a day ould, pare it and slyce it, & sugar it with powder sugar. then bake it againe for an houre. after that, take it out, & when you see it is dry, hard, & cold, y^n take double refined sugar beaten & searsed, & rub it well with your hand over every slyce of your bisket, & it will keep it white as any flowre on ye outsides. then box them up & they will keep 2 or 3 years.

This recipe is for a sweet rusk, thus adhering more closely to the original meaning of *bisket* than some of the other recipes in this section (see S 176).

I cannot see making this enriched bread without yeast; surely it was omitted inadvertently. The *Cinamon Bisket* of S 182, a similar recipe, pretty much confirms this. If you opt for the yeast, the water must be blood warm. See *manchets*, C 95.

Approximate equivalent quantities are: 16 cups of unbleached flour; 5 or 6 eggs; water (flours vary, as do eggs, but nearly 5 cups should be right); I suggest 1 ½ ounces of fresh yeast (3 scant teaspoons of preservative-free dry yeast, *in extremis*). I also suggest a scant tablespoon of sea salt.

What is wanted here are long sausage-shaped loaves, or *baguettes*, so that they may be sliced into even round slices for the second baking.

---

180   TO MAKE BISKITTELLO

Take halfe a pound of double refind sugar, beeing beaten & searsed, & put to it ye weight of two groats in

annyseeds powderd. soe beat it up to paste with a little
gum tragacant steeped in rose water, with 2 grayns of
musk.* then make it up into little loves ye fashion of
manchets, & about ye biggness of eggs. then put A
piece of paper† under every one of them, & bake them
in A bakeing pan, & they will keepe good all ye yeare.

These two recipes for *Biskittello*, manifestly Italian in origin, are
related to *Nimblesses* in S 173 and clearly belong there rather than
with *biskets* (see S 176).

The coining of the *groat* (equal to fourpence in value)
ceased in 1662; it weighed ⅛ of an ounce (*OED*), and ¼ ounce of
anise seeds, or about 1 tablespoon, seems reasonable. Half a pound
of granulated sugar is 1 cup. The language favors *paper* in the
recipe, but wafers are called for in S 181. For *wafers*, see C 143.

---

181   TO MAKE BISKITTELLO

Take 4 ounces of double refind sugar, beeing beaten &
finely searced with 2 greyns of musk & one of
ambergreece. beat all these to perfect paste with a little
gum tragacant steeped in rose water, & ye white of an
egg. then make it up into little loves like manchets, &
put wafers under them. bake them in an oven & they
will be very white & light as A puff. when they be
thorough dry, you may box them & keep them all the
year for your use.

---

182   TO MAKE CINAMON BISKET

Take halfe A peck of fine flowre, and two ounces of
cinnamon finely beaten, 2 ounces of corriander seeds,
and halfe an ounce of anny seeds, 3 eggs, & 3
spoonfulls of Ale yeast, and as much warme water as
will make it thick as paste for manchets. make it in long
rouls and bake it in an oven for ye space of an houre.
when it is A day old, pare it, and slyce it, and suger it

* Written *must*.
† Corrected from *wafer*, or vice versa.

339

all over with searced sugar, then put it againe into y^e
oven, & when it is dry, take it out & sugar it againe,
[and so box (?)] it.

See recipe S 179. The approximate equivalent quantities here are:
16 cups of unbleached flour; 8 tablespoons of powdered cinnamon;
8 tablespoons powdered coriander seeds; 2 tablespoons of anise
seeds; 3 eggs; 1 ½ ounces of fresh yeast (see *ale yeast*, C 92); and
perhaps as much as 5 cups or so of water. The spicing is rather
heavy; use your better judgment.

---

183   TO MAKE PRINCE BISKET

Take A pound of fine flowre, & as much sugar finely
beaten & searced, & an ounce or 2 of annyseeds clean
pickt. & put to these 8 eggs & a spoonfull of muskadin.
beat all these into batter as thick as for fritters, beat it in
a boule for an houre. then putt it into y^r coffins of plate
or frames of wood & set it into an oven, & let it
remaine there an houre. you may slice some of them
when they are a day old, & dry them on wickers. you
may allsoe take your loves & wash them over with a
fether diped with ye youlk of an egg beaten in
rosewater, & before it is dry, cast carraway comfits & a
little white sugar candy beaten on them. then spot
them with gold & they are made, or you may omit y^e
gold If you pleas. in their bakeing, take ye oven stone
downe sometimes to keepe them from burning or from
cullering too fast.

This *Prince Bisket* belongs with the first recipes of this series, beginning with S 176.

There is a problem of proportion here. Flours vary, to be
sure, but I obtain excellent results using an equivalency figure of
3 cups of American flour to 1 pound of English flour (most writers
call for 3 ½ cups and even more). So that the instruction, "batter
as thick as for fritter," must be in error because a spoonful of
muskadin (see C 54) simply will not supply sufficient liquid; perhaps
a fair amount of rose water has been omitted. If the recipe intrigues
you, I suggest using sponge cake procedure (see S 176) and proceeding with these sweet rusks as directed.

Approximate quantities are: 3 cups unbleached pastry flour (this is important); 2 cups fine granulated sugar; 4 to 8 tablespoons of anise seeds (use discretion); 8 eggs; a spoonful of muscatel wine.

Coffins were more often of paste (C 49); *plate* usually refers to silver, but Hugh Plat in *Delightes for Ladies*, 1608, speaks of "Coffins of white plate." Pyrex loaf pans are fine. *Frames of wood* are, in effect, wooden spring pans. The bottom was usually carved in a decorative pattern and the sides can be unlatched. The forms must be well buttered. *Wickers* are a wicker frame; use a cake rack. Taking "ye oven stone downe sometimes" was a way of cooling the old brick ovens. For the baking, I suggest an oven of no more than 350°F. For the drying of the rusks, see S 179.

---

184   TO MAKE MACKROONS

Take a pound & halfe of almonds, blanch & beat them very small in a stone morter with rosewater. put to them a pound of sugar, & ye whites of 4 eggs, & beat y^m together. & put in 2 grayns of muske ground with a spoonfull or 2 of rose water. beat y^m together till y^r oven is as hot as for manchet, then put them on wafers & set them in on A plate. after a while, take them out. [y^n when] y^r oven is cool, set [y^m in] againe & dry y^m, & [keep them for your use (?)].

Cotgrave, in 1611, translates French *macarons* as *macarons*, describing them as "compounded of Sugar, Almonds, Rosewater, and Muske, pounded together, and baked with a gentle fire," so that there must have been recipes abroad for some time. The word comes from Italian *maccarone*; the connection with the pasta is not altogether clear, *OED* says. Finally, as can be seen, they are simply baked puffy marchpane.

The French food processor makes short work of the preparation. (For musk, see S 113.) Bake the macaroons on parchment paper, or plain white paper, if you have no *wafers* (see C 143). I suggest a preheated oven of 325°F so that they will puff nicely. After about 10 minutes or so, turn the oven down to "stoving" temperatures of about 150°F. The idea is to dry them rather than bake them really; they are to remain as white as possible. You will never again buy commercial macaroons.

185   TO MAKE ORRING BISKET

Take Candyed orring or leamon pills, & lay them two
dayes in water, then beat them in a marble morter very
well, then take sugar beat & searsed, & strow a
handfull on ye pills, beat* it together till you have
brought it into a paste, & a grayne of muske, If you
pleas, beat amongst it. when it is well beaten, make it
into little cakes & dry them.

This recipe is related to *orringe Lozenges* of S 109, which see.

186   TO MAKE GINGER BREAD

Take a gallon of ye purest honey & set it on ye fire till it
boyle. then take it of & put into it allmoste halfe a pinte
of good white wine vinegar, & it will make the scum
rise y^t you may take it of very clean. & when it is
scumed put into it a quart of strong ale, & set it on the
fire againe. then put in halfe a pound of ginﬅer, halfe a
pound or more of good licorish, halfe a pound of anny
seeds, 6 ounces of red sanders. let all these be finely
beat & searced and mingle them well together, and let
ye spice boyle in it. then put in A peck of grated bread
by little and little, and worke it well in. & then mould it
in searced cinamon, of which you must allow halfe a
pound to this proportion. when yo[u have worked(?)] it
well together, then print [it in molds] or make it into
what fashion you pleas.

The name and basic composition of medieval gingerbread come
to us from medicine, not cookery. We find *gingibrati* in the records
of Robert Montpelier, apothecary to Henry III of England, for the
year 1242/43;† this was probably not gingerbread but a common
name for *Diazinziberios*, a medicinal electuary based on ginger.
(Confusingly, *gingibrati* was occasionally applied to conserved gin-

---

* Written *bet*, possibly in error, although *bet* was a recorded form through
the sixteenth century (*OED*).
† G. E. Trease, *Spicers and Apothecaries of the Royal Household*.

ger, as well.) The formula for *Diazinziberios* is given in *Le Livre des Simples Medicines*, taken from a thirteenth-century French translation of an earlier treatise on pharmacopoeia:* "take very well cooked parsnips, mince them and cook them with clarified honey until all the honey is absorbed, stirring well so that the mixture does not stick to the vessel; then put in aromatic powders, *gimigibre*, pepper, nutmeg, and galingale; and cook together to a candy" [my translation from Old French—K.H.]. It is now fairly clear what happened: gradually, bread crumbs replaced the parsnips, most likely due to a mistaken association of *brati* with bread. The first citation of gingerbread in *OED* is given as *Gingerbrar* from 1299; *OED* feels that it refers to conserved ginger and, curiously, does not mention the ancient electuary. By 1351/52, we find *Gyngebrede*; the assimilation of *brati* to bread is complete.

The earliest recipe I know for what is called gingerbread appears in Harleian MS. 279 about 1430, under *Leche Vyaundez*. (A *leche* is that which can be sliced, to oversimplify; see *leach*, C 127. *Vyaundez* is meat in the medieval sense of food.) It is for *Gyngerbrede* and starts out much as ours does: "Take a quart of hony, & sethe it, & skeme it clene . . . " It has the grated bread and substantially the same spices, including *Saunders*, but no ginger; the omission can only be inadvertent. (Occasionally, the name of a medieval dish would linger after the characterizing element had fallen into disuse in that context: *rosee*, rose petals; *murrey*, mulberries; and *tansey*, C 101. But ginger was in its heyday and *Gyngerbrede* was on the rise.) But in the Arundel MS. 344, about 1400 but manifestly copied from an older manuscript, we find a recipe for *Leche Lumbarde* which calls for honey, vinegar, bread crumbs, and a number of spices, among which are *saundres* and *pouder of ginger*; gingerbread in all but name. (Note *Leche Vyaundez* above.)

(In *Libre de Sent Sovi*, the Catalan manuscript of about 1324, we find *gingebrade* applied to a sweet-sour leach based on pounded almonds, honey or sugar, lemon or orange juice, rose water, and ginger, to be served with roast fowl or hare. Grewe notes that the *sapore bianco* of medieval Italy was a similar preparation. I might

---

* Paul Dorveaux, ed., *Le Livre des Simples Medicines* (1913), purports to be a translation of *Liber de simplici medicine dictus Circa instans*, the great work on pharmacopoeia that constitutes the major part of our legacy from the School of Salerno. Frank Anderson, who is doing an annotated edition of the treatise, says that it is not. Those who have studied it, he says, conclude that the French work is a translation of another ancient work, quite likely stemming from the medical school at Montpellier, which was founded by adherents of the School of Salerno in the tenth century. After the sacking of Salerno, Montpellier became the medical center of Europe and its fame lasted into the seventeenth century.

add that the memory of these sweet-sour gingered sauces lingers in a number of European dishes, notably the German *sauerbraten*, where ginger snaps and cream are made to do for ginger and almonds. The ancient characterizing name seems not to have survived in any of these sauces.)

Markham, in 1615, gives a recipe for gingerbread differing in no structural way from the preceding recipes or from those in our manuscript, but it already looks archaic and this is the last important appearance of this medieval confection (see C 205). I find no gingerbread in *A True Gentlewomans Delight*, 1653, attributed to the Countess of Kent, for example. Its omission must mean that it was considered out-of-date, particularly since the book is patently based on a manuscript much like our own in many ways. The presence of five such gingerbread recipes in our manuscript is a mark of the sixteenth century.

So much for early English sources. French sources attribute the origin of gingerbread to the Chinese. In *Le Pain d'Epice de Dijon*, for example, Martine Chauney says that by the tenth century, the Chinese were eating *Mi-Kong*, literally honey bread, and that it was made of wheat flour, honey, and spices all kneaded together and baked in the oven, apparently in large loaves. (The *melitounta* of classical Greece was spread with honey after baking and did not contain ginger, I believe.) It is said to have been included among the rations for the followers of Genghis Khan. The Arabs adopted it and inevitably it came to Europe by way of the Crusaders. (No documentation is given and I am unable to find mention of such confections in K. C. Chang's *Food in Chinese Culture*, although other sorts of honey cakes are mentioned. All the elements, including wheat flour, have been in use for millennia in China, however, and the Chinese predilection for ginger makes it all seem reasonable.) What is a matter of record, according to Chauney, is that in 1571, the bakers of *pain d'épice* in Reims won the right to have their own guild, separate from the *pâtissiers*, marking the attainment of considerable power that must have been based on long standing. (*Le Ménagier*, about 1393, reports that powdered ginger was kneaded with flour and eggs into *gros bastons* the size of *andouilles*, large fat sausages, then baked between irons by *gauffriers*, waffle makers. No mention is made of honey.) In Reims and Paris, small cakes, often formed in wonderfully carved wooden molds, were permitted to weigh as little as 12 to a pound and large loaves of various forms as much as 20 pounds. In *Le Thresor de santé, Ou Mesnage de la vie Humaine*, Lyon, 1607, there is a recipe for *pain d'épice* that calls for 4 pounds of flour, 1 pound of cooked honey, 2 ounces of cinnamon, ½ ounce of ginger, and 2 drams each of pepper and clove. The recipe fits the description of much older versions and its inclusion in a book on health is consistent with the entire early history of gingerbread.

The wonder is that this form of baked gingerbread seems not to have come to England until some time in the seventeenth century, and for the most part, *treacle* came to replace the characterizing honey. (Nor do I find any trace of the bread crumb type of gingerbread in French sources.) This type, new to England, is represented in our manuscript by a recipe for *Pepper Cakes*, for which see C 205, where the history of gingerbread is continued.

Licorish or *licorice* is the rhizome of *Glycyrrhiza glabra*. The name comes from Old French *licorice*; in the meantime, the French adopted a metathetic form, *reglisse* (*OED*). Gerard says: " . . . moreover, with the juice of Licorice, Ginger, and other spices, there is made a certaine bread or cakes called Ginger-bread, which is very good against the cough and all infirmities of the lungs and brest."

In the 1636 edition of Gerard's *Herball*, Johnson says of red sandalwood (*Pterocarpus santalinus*): "Red Saunders have an astrictive and strengthning faculty . . . [and] are used in divers medicines and meates both for their faculty and pleasing red colour." Ginger is discussed in S 92.

I hardly expect that anyone will be interested in actually trying these recipes, although they are feasible. (A peck equals 2 gallons.) Four more gingerbread recipes follow, some containing elucidations of murky details in this recipe, including the thickness of the cakes.

---

187 TO MAKE CULLER'D GINGER BREAD

Take 2 pound and A halfe of dryed bread crums
searsed very fine, one pound of beaten cinnamon
searced, A third part of ginger, and the same quantety
of cloves, nutmegg, mace, licorish, and anny seeds.
then take A gallon of clarret wine & 6 pound of good
loaf sugar beat very small. then mix your spices very
well together with as much sanders as will make them
of a good culler (which you may disserne by mixing a
little in a spoon),* with a little claret wine. soe put your
spices into the wine with your sugar, and set them on
the fire in A pan or pot that will not brase. and when

* Parentheses supplied for clarity.

they are well boyled together, and begin to grow pritty thick, keeping of it stird continually, then put in A pinte of sack, and halfe of your bread crums. when you have cullerd it well, take it of the fire, and strow some crums in the bottom of the boule you intend to put it into. then poure it out of your pan as fast as you can, and then strow in the remainder of your bread crums, and knead them well in with your hands. when it is pritty coole, roule it out & put or sprinkle a little cinamon on y^r prints, which you must reserve out of your beaten cinnamon. and soe print them up.

In the recipe for *white Ginger Bread*, S 189, we are told that the colored gingerbread is "commonly made allmoste halfe an Intch thick or a quarter of an intch at ye least." White and colored gingerbreads, by the way, continued as late as *American Cookery* by Amelia Simmons, 1796 and later editions.

Brase means discolor. The scribe was cautioning against brass or iron; for the same reason, do not use aluminum. For a discussion of gingerbread, see S 186.

---

188   TO MAKE CULLER'D GINGER BREAD

Take stale white bread & pare it & cut it in thin slices, & dry it in a dripping pan, & beat & searce* it fine. to a pound of these crums take 1† ounces of annyseeds, 2 ounces of licorish, 1 ounce of mace, 1 ounce of cloves, 2 ounces of nutmeggs, 3 ounces of ginger, 2 ounces of cinamon. dry these spices, beat & searce them fine. then steep 6 pennyworth of turnsell over night in halfe a pinte of white wine vinegar. y^n take 3 pound of sugar, & as much clarret wine as will make it of a pritty thickness, like pancake batter. then set it on the fire and boyle it, stiring of it continually. then put in your spices and turnsell, and If you see it is not of a good culler, put in three penny worth of sanders searced.

* Written *seace*.
† Corrected from 2.

and when it is boyled as stiff as one can stir it, take it
up and lay it on a table to coole. then make it up with
cinnamon finely beaten and searced, and soe make it
into prints or rouls as you like them best, or cakes, but
prints is moste used after the second course in
christmas. be sure you boyle it in a brass or Iron pot,
and not in a pan, for If it be boyled in A brass pan, it
will loose its culler.

Another medieval gingerbread; see S 186. Prints, or pretty molded
forms, were more elegant than cakes or rolls and so more suitable
for Christmas. The last passage makes no sense unless there was
some difference between the finish of a pot and pan that escapes
me. Neither brass nor iron nor aluminum should be used with
food of any acid content whatsoever.

Turnsole is a violet-blue or purple coloring matter from
Crozophora tinctoria. The word comes from French *tournesole*, turns
toward the sun. *Turnsell* is a sixteenth-century form (*OED*). I have
no idea how much one got for 6 pence.

---

189   TO MAKE WHITE GINGER BREAD

Take halfe a pound of blanched allmonds, 2 ounces of
cinnamon, & put in ginger to y^r taste, a pound of
searced sugar, A penny loafe grated of white bread, &
dry it & searce it over night. & put some gum dragon
to steep in rose water, then beat y^r almonds in a
morter, & now and then put in a spoonfull of y^r spices,
sugar, & crums of bread, and sometimes sprinkle in a
little sack. and toward the latter end of your beating,
put in some of your gum to binde alltogether. and
when it is well beat & mixed in the morter, you may
make it into roles or print it according to your pleasure,
but it is best to roule it out & print it. the prints of
white ginger bread are used much thinner then the
cullerd, which is commonly made allmoste halfe an
Intch thick, or a quarter of an intch at ye least.

See the previous recipes for gingerbread, beginning S 186. For
penny loafe, see C 85. The most helpful bit of information is the

thickness of the prints. If I read correctly, white gingerbread was to be appreciably less than a ¼ inch in thickness, while colored gingerbread was at least that thick.

---

190   TO MAKE GINGER BREAD ROYALL

Take well blanchd almonds according to ye quantety you make, & beat them to a paste with a little rose water & sugar. then take dates & raysons of ye sun & let them be well picked, stoned, & shread small, then beat them with y^r almonds. then season them with sugar, sinnamon, & ginger beaten & finely sifted. then put some sack in, mingled with sirrup of clove gilly flowrs or clove gillyflowers themselves. & [when they] are well beaten, roule them out in differe[nt forms (?)].

This confection hardly qualifies as gingerbread; it is more of a fruited spiced marchpane. See gingerbread recipes, S 186 on.

---

191   TO MAKE IUMBALS

Take a pound & halfe of fine flowre & a pound of fine sugar, both searced & dryed in an oven, 6 youlks & 3 whites of eggs, 6 spoonfulls of sweet cream & as much rose water, fresh butter ye quantety of an egg. mingle these together & make it into stiff paste. work it a quarter of an houre then break it abroad, & put in as much annyseeds or carraway seeds as you shall think fit, & put in A little muske & ambergreece. roule them into rouls & make them in what forms you please. lay them on pie plates thin buttered, & prick them with holes all over. then bake them as you doe diet bread. If this quantety of eggs will not be enough* to wet ye flowre & sugar, put in 3 or 4 more, but noe more cream, butter, nor rosewater.

We have here four recipes for *jumbals*. The word derives from Latin *gemel*, twin; *gimbel* (one of several forms not well differentiated) is

* Written *enought*.

a curious double-finger ring popular in the sixteenth century. So that early jumbals quite likely were not simple circlets as they later came to be. This is confirmed by Phillips in 1678, who describes them as "wreathed in knots" (*OED*).

Jumbals existed in Italy as *ciambelline* and in France as *gimblettes*, all manifestly related words. The pastry may have originated in Italy, but I believe that Favre is in error when he assigns *ciambetta* (*échaudé*, scalded) as the etymology of *gimblette*. He also gives what he claims to be an ancient recipe from Albi which calls for parboiling the *gimblettes* after "pricking them well," then baking them; also, some old recipes for *échaudés* call for ring shapes. The first citing of *jumbal* in *OED* is from Markham, 1615, but Dawson gives a recipe in 1585, *To make Jombils a hundred*, in which the following instructions are given: " . . . and make it in little rowles beeing long, and tye them in knots . . . then put them into a pan of seething water," where they are to have one walm before being taken out, dried, and baked. Also, in *The Accomplisht Cook*, 1671, Robert May gives recipes for *Jemelloes* and *Jamballs*, where he directs us to "boil them in fair water like simnels" before baking them. This makes jumbals originally related in technique to other ancient cakes such as *cracknells* (C 144) and to the breads pretzels and bagels, for that matter. *Gimblettes, ciambelline*, and even jumbals, are still made to some extent; their only present link is their ring shape. Their recent history thus parallels that of *rosquillions* (S 175).

Markham gives two recipes for *jumbals*, very similar to those in S 191 and 193; neither is scalded, so the technique was not invariable. Jumbals became highly popular and in due course came to America, where recipes appeared in most early cookbooks. Fannie Farmer did not include one in 1896, but recipes appeared sporadically down through the years.

Approximate quantities: 4½ cups unbleached pastry flour; 2 cups sugar; 6 egg yolks and 3 whites; 6 tablespoons each of fresh heavy cream and rose water; about 4 tablespoons of butter; anise or carraway seeds as you please. (Of all the recipes, this is perhaps the closest to the Dawson recipe in composition.)

The *rouls* are pencil-shaped ones to be entwined into such knots as you have patience for. I have the impression that a figure eight may have been a common shape, conforming to a current meaning of the name. The instruction concerning "workes" in S 192, gives an impression of elaboration. Prick them well (note the same direction in the Albigensian recipe), and bake in an oven of about 350°F. (*Diet bread* seems to have been of varying composition, but one early type calls for a batter resembling that for lady fingers, mentioned in C 143, and does indeed require a moderate oven.)

192   TO MAKE LEAMON IUMBALS

Take double refined sugar finely beaten & searced, A
little gum dragon steeped in rosewater, ye froth of y^e
white of an egg, a little ambergreece. mingle these well
in a stone morter with a little Juice of leamon. soe beat
them well together, and If you see cause, put in more
Juice of leamon as tis beating. make y^r paste stif
enough* to worke into Jumbals. then lay them in
workes on pie plates, & set them in [to ye oven after]
manchet is drawn.

See preceding recipe for *Jumbals*. The composition is more that of
a meringue; it is the design that makes it jumbals. The oven should
be at 325°F.

193   TO MAKE ALMOND IUMBALS

Lay some almonds 2 dayes in cold water, & then blanch
them, & beat them well in A little rosewater to keep
them from oyling. then mingle them with musk, sugar,
& ambergreece, & roule y^m out as you doe other
Jumbals. lay them on papers, & set them in A stove
with coles, & ye next day, glase them with ye froth of
ye white of 2 new layd eggs beaten with sugar, as much
as will make it thick as pap. then spread it with A knife
as thin as you can on the Jumbals. then let them stand
in the stove againe 5 or 6 hours. then glase the other
side & set them to dry in the oven.

Effectively, this is marchpane in the shape of jumbals. See marchpane, S 158 on, and *jumbals*, S 191.

194   TO MAKE JUMBALS† OF BARBARIES

Put y^r barbaries into an earthen pot & set them into an
oven or pan of water & let them‡ boyle a good while.

* Written *enonough*.
† A *J* is written over an *I*; in the text, the scribe reverted to *Iumbals*.
‡ Written *the*.

then streyne them thorough a thin cloth. then put to it
after it is cold, double refined sugar finely beat &
searced, & strow it in with a spoon till it be stiff paste.
then make it up into Jumbals or little cakes, & dry them
on A paper & strow sugar on ye paper before you lay
them on. & If you put in muske or ambergreece into
the barbaries, it will give them [a very ple]asant taste.

Jumbals of fruit paste were fairly common, and in French cookery,
as well, emphasizing the importance of the shape. For *jumbals*, see
S 191; for barberries, see S 63.

---

195   TO MAKE PIES COLLOPS & EGGS

Take halfe a pound of marchpane paste & make some
of it into pies, & fill these little pies with little pieces of
marmalet, preserved cherries, apricoks, or what other
sweetmeats you please. & strow on ye top of them
some carraway comfits, & then gild them. then you
may make some of y^r paste like collops of bacon, If you
culler some of it with A little sanders or red roses, then
lay a little piece of red & then white together, then red
& white againe. then cut it in slyces & it will shew* like
larded bacon. & cut y^r white paste round for ye eggs, &
culler ye middle with A little saffron streynd with
rosewater.

Collops & eggs are bacon and eggs. At one time, *collop* referred to
an egg fried on a rasher of bacon; this is the meaning of *Collop
Monday* (*OED*). But by 1542, Boorde speaks of *coloppes and egges*,
showing that by then collop referred to the rasher of bacon (also,
see C 4).

This dish, pretentious and silly as it may seem, is solidly
in tradition. In *The Forme of Cury*, about 1390, there is, for example,
a recipe for *Lete Lardes*; the materials are altogether different and
it is not a sweetmeat, but the idea is the same: mock bacon. For
a conceit to be successful, it seems to me, it has to be witty; this
is fairly heavy-handed.

* Possibly *show*, but I think not; see S 147.

196   TO MAKE MUSKE CUMFITS

Take 2 pound of double refind sugar, beat & searced.
y^n take gum tragacant steeped in rose water & beat
them together with 7 grayns of muske in an alleblaster
morter, & it will be white as snow. then roule it on a
sheet of white paper till you can see a knife thorough
when it is put under. y^n cut it like diamonds & in long
pieces. then dry y^m on papers before ye fire & then box
them.

Cumfits, properly comfits, are discussed in S 146; for musk, see S
113. There is nothing to keep you from using vanilla bean in the
same fashion, but know that it is unauthentic. For drying, see
stove, S 68.

Except that *comfit* came to be almost another word for
confection, this is not a typical one and actually, along with S 197,
belongs with the *Lossenges* starting with S 108.

197   TO MAKE MUSKADINE COMFITS

Take halfe a pound of muske sugar, beaten & searsed,
y^n take gum tragacant steeped in rose water, & 2
grayns of muske. beat them in an alleblaster morter till
it comes to perfect paste, then roule it very thin & cut
[it like] diamonds, and cut sume with a rowell [in long
pieces (?). y^n] stove them & box them.

A *muskadine* is a sweetmeat perfumed with musk. The word comes
from Italian *moscardino* by way of French *muscardin* (*OED*). John
Murrell, in *A Daily Exercise for Ladies and Gentlewomen*, 1617, gives
a recipe entitled: "Muscadinoes, commonly called kissing-Comfits," thus explaining Shakespeare's line cited in S 34. They seem
to have been enormously popular in Elizabethan times.

Musk sugar is sugar in which musk has been laid, just as
we now do with vanilla beans. Hugh Plat explains it in *Delightes
for Ladies*, 1608. For this, and other details, see S 196.

A *rowell* is a small stellar wheel with sharp radial points
forming the extremity of a spur (*OED*). There is no reference to
cookery, but it is a *jagg* or pastry wheel. The cutting in long pieces
is suggested by S 196.

198   TO MAKE QUIDONY OF QUINCES

Take 2 pound of yellow pear quinces. pare & cut them
in pieces & put them into a pipkin with a quart of faire
water. soe let them boyle till they be tender, then wring
ye liquor from them thorough a thin cloth into a clean
bason. then put it into a cleane posnet with a pound of
sugar, being first clarefied with a pinte of water & y^e
white of an egge. there let it boyle till it comes to a
perfect culler & thickness, which you may know by
cooling a little of it on ye back of a spoone. then poure
it into y^r moulds, which must be boyled in water before
you print y^r quidony, for y^t will make it cast and come
out well.

We have here a section of ten recipes for *quidony*, now quiddany.
Properly speaking, a quidony differs from other fruit jellies only
in that it is made of quince (see S 24), a distinction that had evidently already disappeared by the time of our manuscript, just as
with marmalade.

I am hard put to point out any distinction between the
quidony recipes and the jelly recipes (S 208 through 219) which
holds true. One reads, for example, that a quidony was not so stiff
as a marmalade (the latter not being strained), but several of these
recipes call for molding and printing. I can say that the jellies seem
to be consistently less stiff than the quidonies and also more pains
are taken to have them clear, although this is not always spelled
out. But the juice for quidony is "wrung," or pressed out, while
for jelly, the jelly bag is specified so that the juice falls through of
its own weight and is much clearer. For more on molds, see S 166.

I believe that pear quinces are the fruit of a quince graft
on a pear tree (*Soyle for an Orchard*, about 1650). Sugar need not
be clarified for preserves.

199   TO MAKE QUIDONY OF QUINCES OF A
RUDDY CULLER

Take 2 pound of quinces, pare & cut them in small
pieces, & put them into a posnet with 3 pintes of faire
water. soe let them boyle till they are tender, then put

into them a pound of sugar & let it boyle till they are
fallen* to ye bottom of ye posnet. then let the liquor run
thorough A strayner into A bason, & put it into a
preserveing pan & let it boyle till it cometh to its perfect
culler and thickness. then print it with your moulds,
being first boyled in water.

---

200   TO MAKE QUIDONY OF A RUDDY
       CULLER

Take 2 pound of pippins, being pared & cut in small
bits, then put them in a pipkin, with as much water as
will cover them, over ye fire and when they are boyled
tender, strayne all ye liquid substance from them. & to
every pinte of liquor put in halfe a pound of sugar, &
let it boyle leasurely, beeing close covered, till it come
to ye culler of claret wine. then uncover it & let it boyle
as fast as you can, till it is as thick as Jeley. you may
know when it comes to its thikness by seeing a drop ly
on the backside of a spoon in stiff Jelley. then take it
from ye fire & coole it a little, then pour it into your
moulds y^t are made of wood, which you must first
boyle. but If they are made of tin, you need doe
noething but wet them. when y^r Jelley is cold, take It
out on a wet trencher, & convey it to y^r boxes, & soe
you may keepe it all ye year.

For *quidony*, see S 198; for *trencher*, C 98; for *claret*, C 22; for molds,
S 166.

---

201   TO MAKE QUIDONY OF APRICOCKS OR
       PEAR PLUMS

Take 2 pound of apricocks or pear plums & put them
into a deep dish with a pinte of faire water, in which
boyle them tender. y^n wring ye liquor from them
thorough a fine cloth into A basin, & put into it a

* Ineptly corrected, with a *d* visible.

354

pound of sugar well clarefied, & let it boyle in a [posnet] till it comes to its full thickness, then [put it in y^r] moulds, & soe box it.

---

202   TO MAKE QUIDONY OF PLUMS

Take 2 pound of plums & put them in A posnet with a pound & halfe of brazeele sugar, clarefied with a pinte of faire water. set them on ye fire & let them boyle till ye plums break. then take it of & let y^r liquid substance run thorough a strayner, then put ye liquor againe into the posnet, & let it boyle till it comes to its full thikness. then coole it, & print it with y^r moulds.

---

203   TO MAKE QUIDONY OF PIPPINS W^{ch} MAY BE MADE ALL Y^e YEAR

Take 2 pound of pippins, eyther green or old. pare & cut them in small pieces, then put them in a pipkin with a quart of faire water. boyle them so tender till they will fall to ye bottom. then take A pound of brazeel sugar, & clarefy it with a pinte of faire water & the white of an egg. after, let them boyle together till all fall to ye bottom, y^t is, all the fruit. then strayne ye liquor from ye fruit, & put ye liquor into A clean posnet & there let it boyle till it comes to its culler & full thickness. then print it with your moulds & box it. your moulds must ly A night in water before you use them, & an hour before you print with them, take them out of the water.

---

204   TO MAKE QUIDONY OF GOOSBERRIES

Take a quart of goosberries & put them into a pottle pot, & put into them halfe a pinte of fair water, & set y^r pot into A seething pot of faire water. there let them boyle till ye fruite be tender, then strayne it thorough a piece of cushion canvis, and wring ye liquor in a basin. then put unto them as much sugar as will make them sweet, then boyle them on a chafing dish of coles in A deep dish, till it comes to its culler & thickness, wch you may know by rouling some of it on the back of a spoone. then print it with your moulds.

---

205   TO MAKE QUIDONY OF ENGLISH CURRANS

Take A pound of english currans & bruise them with ye back of a spoone, & put into the bruising halfe a pinte of faire water. then [streyne]* y^m and put [into]* the liquor halfe a pound of clarified chogar,† & soe boyle it up to its culler & thicknes. then print it with ye moulds. you may make Quidony of all kind of weak fruits, as rasberies, goosberries, mullberries, or ye like, without putting any water at all into them. and you must boyle them quickley or else they will loose theyr culler.

The scribe's mind was elsewhere in transcribing this recipe, but it shows acute knowledge of preserving technique. For all these *quidony* recipes, see S 198. It is not necessary to clarify sugar for preserving. For currants, see S 59.

---

206   TO MAKE QUIDONY OF RESPAS

Take ripe & well cullerd rasps & put them in a dish with 4 spoonfulls of red rose water. mix them together with ye back of a spoon, & wring their liquor thorough a linnen cloth. season it with sugar by y^r taste till it is very sweet, then boyle it on a chafing dish of coles till it is stiff enough. then print it with y^r moulds & box it.

For *quidony*, see S 198; for raspberries, see S 60.

* Supplied.
† Ineptly reworked from an unknown form.

207   TO MAKE QUIDONY OF RASPAS AND
       RED ROSES

Take red raspis & put to them 4 ounces of red roses,
soe bruise them with ye back of a spoon in A dish. then
wring ye Juice from them into a dish thorough a piece
of new canvas. then sweeten it well with sugar, & set it
on a chafing dish of coles. there let it boyle till it comes
to its thickness, then print it with y^r moulds.

208   TO MAKE A DECOCKTION OF QUINCES

Take quinces, pare & cut them in pieces, & boyle A
pound of theyr pieces in a quart of faire water till they
be very soft. then strayne their liquor & put to it a
pound of sugar candy, beaten fine, & let it seeth till
you see it stand like a Jelley. then take it of ye fire &
put therein 4 drops of ye oyle of cinnamon, & 4 drops
of oyle of nutmeggs, & put in 12 leaves of gold. then
stir it together & soe put it in fine christall [glasses &
(?)] keepe y^m all ye year.

This is an elegant jelly, indeed. It is difficult to know whether the
jelly was simply a form of display or whether its putative medicinal
virtues were uppermost. The use of the word decoction (extraction
and concentration of the essence by boiling) tends to support the
latter—quinces (S 7), cinnamon (S 289), nutmeg (S 271), and gold
(S 70), all had medicinal qualities ascribed to them. If so, the presentation in fine crystal is elaborate.

This recipe leads off a section of jelly recipes, going
through S 219. The use of this word has changed not at all; some
of the jellies seem a good deal stiffer than we find attractive today,
but many of the recipes will produce a quivering flavorful jelly of
the requisite sparkling transparency. This assumes that you can
find good fruit. (Also, see *Quidony*, S 198.)

209   TO MAKE IELEY OF PIPPINS OTHER
       APPLES QUINCES OR PLUMS

Take apples & pare them & cut them in pieces, cores &
all, but not the coars of quinces. then boyle them in
faire water very softly till they be tender & sinke to the
bottom. then let the liquor run thorough a cloth &
wring it very hard, then take of that liquor an ale quart,
& put to it a pound of refined sugar. If you would have
it white Jelley, then boyle it apace, and when it is well
boyled, print it. If your prints be made of wood, boyle
them till they sinke to the bottom; after, they are
thrown in water and then they are enuf. when they be
cold, wipe them & put in your Jelley, and cut them
round & put them* up in boxes. but If you would have
your Jelley red, boyle it very softly and cover it till it
comes to its culler that you shall like. then boyle them
apace and box them as before. for plums, put not to
much water in the boyling, but put to them liquor of
greene apples. and for your quinces, boyle them in
halfe quarters, and when you see them grow very
tender, you may take the quinces for paste and the
liquor for quidony or Jelley.

This is almost a master recipe for jelly; it is chock full of bits of
useful information, including treatment of molds. I am, however,
surprised at the instruction to press the straining cloth very hard;
it clouds the jelly badly (see S 198).

---

210   TO MAKE IELLEY OF PIPPINS

Take ye fayrest pippins you can get; pare & quarter†
them & put them in faire water. there boyle y^m till y^e
water is thick & strong of ye apples. then dreyne it
thorough A hare sive, then take to 3 quarters of a pinte
of y^t liquor, a pound of sugar. put them together in a

* Written *the*.
† Written *quarte*.

silver or earthen basin, then boyle it apace. & a little before it be enough, put in ye juice of a leamon. & lay an orring in soak in water, then cut of ye pill about an intch* & halfe long in as thin chips & as narow as you can. then boyle it in 2 or 3 waters till they be tender, then add this orring to ye rest & give it 2 or 3 walmes after it is in. put in a little muske or ambergreece, & soe glass it up.

---

211 TO MAKE IELLEY OF PIPPINS

Take pippins, pare & quarter them, & boyle them in 3 pintes of water till halfe be wasted, then strayne it. & to a pinte of liquor, take a pound of refined sugar, & halfe a pound of tender boyled orring pills. mingle them together before you set them on ye fire, & when they are thoroughly hot, boyle them as fast as you can. & when you see them Jelly, put in ye Juice of 2 orringes & one leamon. soe boyle them a little longer, then put it up thin in glasses or white boxes.

---

212 TO MAKE JELLEY OF WHITE CURRANS

Take your currans when they are full ripe, and pick them from ye stalks, & grind them with a woden pestle in an alleblaster morter. then strayn them thorough A Jelley bagg, & take theyr downe weight in double refind sugar beaten very small. then put to it A spoonfull or 2 of water & boile it allmoste to a candy. but before you put your water to y^r sugar, boyle a piece of Ising glass in the water that is to dissolve ye sugar in. then put in y^r Juce & let it scalld thoroughly and scum it, but let it not boyle for fear of turning yellow. soe let it run thorough A coten Jeley bagg into your glasses. let them stand two or three dayes in ye stove & then paper them up.

* Ineptly corrected.

For currants, see S 59; for *stove*, S 68; for *isinglass*, C 127; for jellies S 208.

---

213   TO MAKE JELLEY* OF RED CURRANS

When your currans are ripe, pick them from the stalks & grinde them in an alleblaster morter. y^n strayne ye Juice thorough A Jelley bagg, & take downe weight of them in double refin'd sugar beat very fine. & put to them 6 spoonfulls of water. soe boyle it up allmoste to a candy, then put in ye Juice, with a good piece of Isinglass. If you disserne y^r currans not to be of a very good culler, you may put in a little soucheneale, but not too much, crushed with ye back of a spoon very small, & it will make it a very fine culler. let it boyle a pritty while, & y^n let [it streyne thorough] y^r Jelley bagg into your glasses.

Soucheneale is cochineal, used here for its brilliant red color; see S 309.

---

214   TO MAKE IELEY OF RASBERRIES

You must make your raspas Jelley eyther red or white, Just as you doe your Jelley of red & white currans, onely strayning them thorough A canvas strayner, but not too dry because you may make cakes of ye seeds.

The red and white currant jellies are S 212 and 213. See S 135 for the cakes of raspberry seeds; the less you press your jelly bag, the prettier your jelly will be and the better the cakes, as well.

---

215   TO MAKE IELLEY OF CURRANS

Take ye weight of your currans in double refined sugar, & boyle ye sugar to A candy. pick ye seeds out of ye currans, & strayne A little of ye Juice to them, & soe put them to y^r candy. rasberries are done ye same way,

* *J* corrected from *I*.

360

onely you must put in ye Juice of curran berries or
goosberries to make it Jelley. ye title page was
mistaken, for this receipt is to preserve & not to make
Jelley.

The copyist was absolutely right; it is indeed a recipe for preserved
currants, and a fine one (see S 7 and 21). Picking out the seeds is
a fastidious and tedious chore, but it is nice. For *candy*, see S 5.

---

216   TO MAKE JELEY* OF QUINCES

First perboyle your quinces A little, then pare & slice
them into an earthen pot. then strayne them after they
are well boyled, and make your Jelley of the liquor that
comes from them, and put A pound of refined sugar to
that liquor, and when it is boyled to a good Jelley, put
it up into glasses.

The recipe neglects to specify the amount of quince liquor to a
pound of sugar; in S 209, it is a quart.

---

217   TO MAKE JELLEY* OF HARTS HORNE

Take to halfe A pound of harts horne, five quarts of
faire water. boyle them softly together, beeing close
covered, till it comes to 3 pintes. then put in A pritty
deal of damask rose water, & let it boyle a little
together. then poure it into a bason & let it stand till it
be settled. then put it into a scillet with some sugar &
ye Juice of leamon & some ambergreece. set it on ye fire
till it simper, then put it into clear glasses. If you would
have it in cullers, then you may put in sirrup of violets
or sirrup of gilliflowers or what culler else you pleas.

Harts horne is a gelatine obtained by rasping or calcining the horn
of the hart, or male deer. As late as the first American edition of
Hannah Glasse's *The Art of Cookery*, 1805, hartshorn jellies were
considered a delicacy. (However, they seem to have been a holdover from earlier editions because they had all but disappeared

* *J* corrected from an *I*.

from other cookbooks by the turn of that century.) The jelly was considered especially suitable for invalids (see S 307). The gelatine dessert continued, using isinglass, which was in use by the latter part of the sixteenth century, and calves' feet. If any of the flavorings in this and the following recipes appeal to you, you could easily adapt them to calves' foot jelly.

---

218   TO MAKE JELLEY OF HARTS HORNE

Take 8 ounces of shavings of harts horne, one ounce of gum arabeck, & 3 pintes* of spring water. let it boyle ye space of 2 hours verry† fast, then strayne it thorough a laune ragg, and squeese in the quantety of 8 orringes, or 4 leamons, and put in some damask rose water, and sweeten according to your taste with sugar, & put it in glasses.

---

219   TO MAKE A FINE IELLEY

Take 8 ounces of hartshorne, 5 quarts of spring water, boyle it in a pipkin up to a Jelley, y^n strayne it thorough a Jelley bagg & put to it ye Juice of 6 leamons, & some of ye pills, and pound of good loaf sugar, A handfull of corriander seeds, & 2 spoonfulls of spirit of cinnamon, 3 tops of rosemary, 2 grayns of muske or ambergreece. boyle all these together uncovered for a quarter of an houre, & then poure it into your Jelley bagg againe. then put it up into your pots or glasses. If you perfume y^r sugar, you need not put in muske or ambergreece.

I believe that the scribe must have intended to write "a halfe pound" but it could have been "a pound," which would be very sweet. Follow instructions in S 217.

* The scribe surely absent-mindedly wrote *pintes* instead of quarts; see S 217.
† Written *uorry*, I believe. *OED* lists *vurry* and *varry* as old forms.

220   TO MAKE SIRRUP OF VIOLETS

Take blew violets, pick & stamp them in a morter very
small, then put them in a glass with as much water as
will make them very moist. soe let them stand a day or
2, then strayn ye liquor clean from them, to which add
as many more fresh violets, & let them stand as long as
ye first. doe this 3 or 4 times, then to every pinte of y^e
liquor, take 2 pound of lofe sugar finely beaten, & boyle
them together till it ropes. then stamp & strayn fresh
violets, & put their Juice into ye boyled sirrup, but let it
not boyle after, for then it will loose its culler, but take
it of & put it [up in a glass bo]ttle.

We now embark on a series of recipes for syrups, running through
S 248. While they were certainly used to make cooling drinks in
warm weather, or to flavor and color clear jellies, for example, they
more clearly belong to the medicinal side of the diet than do the
other preserved fruit preparations. Some of them are entirely medicinal, others are delightful and refreshing in their own right; all
the syrups served as vehicles to make serious medication more
palatable. Sugar was thought to make them more efficacious, as
well.
       There are no less than five recipes for syrup of violets,
each with a small variation in technique. For their medicinal virtues, see S 86. For sugar syrups, see S 1 through 6, with definitions
and instructions on clarifying.

221   TO MAKE SIRRUP OF VIOLETS

Take violets & pick & weigh the flowers, then put them
in a quart of water, & let them stand on hot embers till
ye flowers are turned white, & ye water is blew as any
violet, y^n strayne them, & put to y^t liquor 4 pound of
clarefied sugar. boyle & scum it often till it comes to a
sirrup, & let it boyle on a gentle fire least it loose its
culler, & beeing boyled, put it up.

Note: In all these titles, *Violets* is spelled with a pristine *V*, but in the
text, the scribe reverts to *uiolets*.

To make Sirrup of violets +

220

Take violets & pick & weigh ye flowers then
put them in a quart of water, & let them
stand on hot embers, till ye flowers are turn
ed white, & ye water is blew as any violet y{n}
strayne them & put to ye liquor 4 pound of
clarified sugar, boyle & scum it often till it
comes to a sirrup, & let it boyle on a gentle
fire least it loose its cullor & being boyled
put it up ·

To make Sirrup of violets +

222

Take violet & pick ye leaues of them then stamp
& strayne them, & take ye Juice, & its weight
& halfe in sugar, & put in a glass which you must
not fill by a good daale neyther must you put
in all ye sugar at once but by degrees then set
yr glass in ye sun & stir it up sometimes wth
a stick y{n} let it stand in ye sun till ye sugar be
melted, & it hath done working ·

To make sirrup of violets +

223

Crom in as many pick'd violets into boyling
water as you can thrust into them & to every
pinte a pound & quarter of hardsugar then
boyle it in an earthen pot or glass in water
till noe white skum remains which will be
_____, & then keepe it for your use ·

222   TO MAKE SIRRUP OF VIOLETS

Take violet & pick y^e leaves of them, then stamp &
strayne them. & take y^e Juice, & its weight & halfe in
sugar, & put in a glass, which you must not fill by a
good deale. neyther must you put in all y^e sugar at
once, but by degrees. then set y^r glass in ye sun & stir
it up sometimes wth a stick. y^n let it stand in ye sun till
ye sugar be melted, & it hath done working.

223   TO MAKE SIRRUP OF VIOLETS

Crom in as many pick'd violets into boyling water as
you can thrust into them, & to every pinte, a pound &
quarter of hard sugar. then boyle it in an earthen pot or
glass in water till noe white skum remains, which will
be [seven (?) h]ours, & then keepe it for your use.

This is a *bain-marie* method. The page is damaged and I must warn
the reader that my proposal of 7 hours is based on slight evidence:
the number cannot begin with a letter having an upward stroke;
it is just possible that this beginning letter be an *s*, and *six* is too
short a word for the space. However, it could be "one or two
hours," although that seems not long enough for this slow system.
You shall simply have to wait for the *white skum* to subside. See
S 220.

Crom is a fourteenth- and fifteenth-century form of *cram*
in *OED*; Halliwell, noting that it means to crowd, gives *crom* as a
Northumbrian word.

224   TO MAKE SIRRUP OF VIOLETS

Take as many violets as you can get, pick them clean
from ye whites, then weigh them & take 3 times theyr
weight in lofe sugar. & to every pound of sugar, take a
pinte of water. boyle y^r water & sugar well together &
scum it very well. then beat y^r violets in a marble or
alleblaster morter. when y^r sirrup is clear from ye scum,
put in y^r violets & boyle them till they begin to loose

culler. then strayne it thorough A strayner or thin cloth into an earthen or silver vessell, & when it is cold, bottle it up.

---

225   TO MAKE SIRAP* OF CLOUE
GILLEFLOWERS

Take halfe a peck of clove Jelleflowers,† clean pikt from yᵉ whites, then take 2 quarts of water and put to them into an earthen pot, and set them in A kettle of boyling water, covering of them very close. and when you disserne them to looke pale, strayne them thorough A canvas strayner, and take to every pinte, a pound of loaf sugar & boyle it as fast as you can, & scum it often, & boyle it up to a sirrup.

For gillyflowers, see S 67; for syrups, see S 220.

---

226   TO MAKE SIRRUP OF COWSLIPS OR
IELLEFLOWERS

Take a pound of pickt cowslips or Jelleflowers & put them into a galley pot, then poure into them a pinte of boyling water. then set yᵉ pot into a pot of boyling water till it be could. then some 3 dayes after, strayne it out & put to every pinte of sirrup a pound of sugar, wᶜʰ sugar must be boyled to a candy height or to sugar againe. then put yʳ sirrup into yᵉ sugar & stir them together over yᵉ fire for a quarter of an houre. then take it of yᵉ fire, & yʳ sirrup will have yᵉ perfect culler of yᵉ flowers. you must allways observe to make your sirrup at yᵉ first comming of flowers, which allwayes makes yᵉ [sirrup]‡ be best, for then yᵉ flowers have most vertue in them.

* Pristine.
† In the title, this word has apparently been corrected to *Gille-*, here, to *Jelle-*, but *i* and *e* are both visible in either case; I chose the darker one.
‡ Supplied.

For cowslips, see S 137; for gillyflowers, see S 67; for syrups, S 220. *Could* is a sixteenth-century form for *cold* (*OED*).

---

227   TO MAKE SIRRUP OF ROSES

Take a quart of running water, and put into it halfe a pound of beaten rose leavs of damask roses. set them A stewing on the embers, then strayne it out & put on fresh, twice a day till they be changed 12 times. after this is done, put to every pinte of liquor, a pound [of sugar], & soe boyle it to A sirrup.

We have five recipes for syrup of roses, not including *Honey of Roses* in S 249. For their medicinal virtues, see S 66 and 81; for syrups, see S 220. Remember that rose leaves are petals. For *running water*, see *cundit*, S 242.

---

228   TO MAKE SIRRUP OF ROSES

Take a good quantety of damask rose leaves & pull them, then set a gallon of water on the fire (let it be running water),* & when it is hot, put in ye rose leaves. & when they look white, take them out againe. change them thus 10 times, & then ye water will be red. then strayne them out very clear, & take to every pinte of that liquor, ye white of an egge & a pound of sugar & clarefy it, and boyle it to a sirrup. the thicker it is, the better it will keep all the year.

---

229   TO MAKE SIRRUP OF DAMASK OR RED ROSES

Pick y^r roses clean from ye whites, weigh [y^m]† & take to 3 quarters of a pinte of water 4 ounces of y^r roses. beat y^r roses in a morter of alleblaster. & every day for 3 days together, strayn out y^t water & add ye same quantety of roses. they must be put at first in an

* Parentheses supplied.
† Supplied.

earthen pot, close pasted, & set in a kettle of water at
ye fire end. y^r water must never* boyle. If you disserne
y^r water to waste, ad at ye second time a Jack of water.
on ye 4th day, strayn it, & put to it 14 ounces of sugar,
& boyle & scum it well till it come to a sirrup, wch you
may know by putting a little int a spoon to coole, &
droping it on a [plate]. & If it run not about, it is
enough. y^n bottle it, beeing [cold. do not cork it (?)] but
tie a Paper on it.

The properties of roses are discussed in S 66 and 81; syrups in S
220. The *fire end* would seem to mean to one side, so that it receives
only a little heat. *Iack*, or jack, is an obsolete colloquialism meaning
a whit, or the least bit. In certain regions, however, where a *gill*
is a half-pint (in principle, it was a quarter-pint or 4 fluid ounces
at that time), the quarter-pint is called a *jack* (OED).

---

230   TO MAKE SIRRUP OF DRY ROSE LEAUES

Take of dryed red rose leavs 4 ounces, & infuse [y^m] in
a pinte of faire water on hot embers till ye roses have
lost theyr culler. then take a pound & halfe of sugar, &
clarefy y^r liquor & sugar with 2 eggs. then boyle it to y^e
height of A sirrup, but take heed you set not‡ y^r sirrup
on too hot A fire for then it will loose its culler.

Only the whites are used for clarifying sugar; see S 1 and 3, and
also S 227. (It is not necessary to clarify modern sugar for these
purposes.)

---

231   TO MAKE SIRRUP OF DAMASK ROSES
       WITH RUBARB

Take of y^r best damask rose buds & pick y^m from y^e
whites, & beat 3 ounces of them pritty well but not to
small, & cut in one dram of ye best rubarb pritty small
but not too thin. infuse ye rubarb & roses together in a

---

* Written *neue*.
† An extra *in* excised.
‡ I excised *on*, which had became confusing after a scribal insertion.

quart of spring water, close stoped, one night, till y^e
strength of ye rubarb be in ye water, & then boyle it to
a sirrup with sugar.

Rhubarb is the medicinal root of *Rheum*. The name comes from Latin
Rha barbarum, meaning foreign root, or was thought to. (*Radix* is
Latin for root, but *Rha* was the Greek name for the Volga; since
most of the rhubarb root came from China by way of Russia, there
was long considerable confusion.) By 1400, it was sold by *peny
weght* in England (*OED*). Gerard says: "Rubarb is commended by
Dioscorides, against Convulsions, diseases of the spleen, liver, and
kidnies, . . . pain in the hucklebones [hipbones], spitting of bloud,
shortnesse of breath, . . . the bloudy flix, [and] the laske proceeding of raw humors." He credits the Arab physicians with recog-
nizing the purgative characteristics of rhubarb, saying it "purgeth
away naughty and corrupt humours, and likewise withall stoppeth
the belly." That from China was reputed best, but by 1636, Johnson
appends to Gerard's chapter the fact that *Rha* "is to be found
growing in some of our choice gardens." There is as yet no question
of using the stalks as food. C. Anne Wilson credits John Parkinson,
the herbalist, with introducing modern rhubarb into England from
Italy in the seventeenth century; he thought that the stalks would
be more gently purgative than the root. The major cookbook writers of the eighteenth century do not mention rhubarb; neither
Hannah Glasse, nor E. Smith, nor Elizabeth Raffald, at least not
in editions available to me. In *The American Frugal Housewife*, 1832,
Lydia Maria Child treats it as something novel, saying that it was
also called *Persian Apple*; appropriately, the recipe was for a pie.

For syrups, see S 220; for rose syrups, S 227; for *dram*,
S 70.

---

232   TO MAKE SIRRUP OF BARBERRIES
      OR MULBERRIES

Take y^r barberries when* they are thorough ripe &
stamp them in a marble or alleblaster morter, & strayn
out ye Juice thorough† A canvas strayner, & to every
pinte, take a pound of lofe sugar. boyle it well & scim
it, & when it is boyled sirr[up] height, set it to coole &
when it is cold, bottle [& tie] paper upon it, but not
corke it. [in like manner], make sirrup of mulberries.

* Written *whey* with an unclear effort to correct it.
† Written *thouroug* in error; *thorough* is otherwise invariable.

For barberries, see S 63; for mulberries, S 71; for medicinal syrups, S 220.

---

233   TO MAKE SIRRUP OF MULBERRIES

Take mulberies which are very ripe, & press out ye Juice of them thorough a linnen cloth betwixt 2 sticks. & then to every pinte of Juice, take A pound of sugar, & boyle it to ye height of a sirrup. then keep it all ye year long. & If it wax any thiner a moneth after you have made it, boyle it over againe, & it will keep all ye year.

---

234   TO MAKE SIRRUP OF MULBERIES OR RASBERIES

Take a quart of mulberies or rasberies and set them on a soft fire, and bruise them with A preserving ladle or sillver* spoone, and when they be scallding hot, strayne them thorough a canvis strayner, and put to A pound of sugar this Juice of A pound of Rasberies, or rather, A pinte of this Juice to a pound of sugar. & when ye sugar is well melted in the liquor, set it on the fire, and let it boyle two or three walmes. then take it of and scum it clean, after set it on againe and boyle it to A sirrup, then put it into your glasses. If you take it of two or three times in the boyling and let it stand till it is pritty coole, it will hould culler the better.

The scribe was having a little difficulty; it is, of course, the classic proportion of equal amounts of juice and sugar (weight or volume), or near enough, For mulberries, see S 71; for raspberries, S 60; these syrups, S 220.

---

235   TO MAKE SIRRUP OF LEAMONS

First cut your leamons in 2 & pick out ye stones & prick them well with a knife, & ye Juice will come out y^e

* Written *sillues*.

better. then wring them as long as you can get out any Juice, & to every pinte of it take a pound of sugar. set them on ye fire together & make them boyle as fast as you can, to a thin sirrup, for If you boyle it to much, it will candy presently. It will require a great many leamons to make a pound.

On the medicinal virtues of lemons, Gerard says: "Two ounces of the juyce of Limons, mixed with the like quantity of the spirit of wine . . . and drunk at the first approach of the fit of an ague, taketh away the shaking presently." He cautions, however, that "the Patient be covered warme in a bed, and caused to sweat." For more on lemons, see C 1; for these syrups, S 220. Another syrup of lemons follows.

---

236   TO MAKE SIRRUP OF LEAMONS

Take leamons & cut them in halves & wring out all ye Juice betwixt your fingers, that it may be as clear as you can. then take to a pound of Juice, which is a pinte, A pound & quarter of hard sugar, which is very white, & boyle it to a sirrup.

---

237   TO MAKE SIRRUP OF POUMCITRONS

Take poumcitrons* & cut them in halves & Juice them, but beware you wring them not to hard least they be slimy. then take to every pinte of Juice, 3 quarters of a pound of refined sugar & boyle it in a pipkin till it comes to the height of a sirrup. & take heed y^t your fire be not to violent least it burne. when it is boyled enough, [let it cool (?)] & bottle it up.

For *pomecitron*, or citron, see S 33; for syrups, S 220.

---

238   TO MAKE SIRRUP OF PIPPINS

Take a quart of water & put it in an earthen pot & fill it full of pippins. then set it in a scillet of water on ye fire

* Written *pouncitrons*.

till ye vertue is gon out of them. then change it 6 times.
after, strayne* it clear from ye pippins. then put to
every pinte of liquor one pound of sugar, & put it back
againe into ye pot. there let it boyle againe in ye scillet
of water as before, till it comes to ye thickness of a good
sirrup.

This is a *bain-marie* method; infinitely time comsuming, but it will give clear syrup. You keep putting new pippins into the same water; that is, you change the apples, not the water. For pippins, see S 21; for syrups, S 220.

---

239 TO MAKE SIRRUP OF PURSLANE

Take a halfe a pound of purslane seeds grosely beaten,
2 pound of Juice of endive, 2 pound of sugar, 9 ounces
of vinegar. steep ye seeds in the Juice for 24 hours, then
boyle it with a gentle fire till halfe be consumed. then
boyle ye strayned liquor with ye sugar to a sirrup, &
put in the vinegar when it hath allmoste done boyling.

Raw purslane is "much used in sallades," according to Gerard; raw or boiled it is "good for the bladder and kidnies, and allaieth the outragious lust of the body." The "seed being taken, killeth and driveth forth worms, and stoppeth the laske." Also, see C 164.

Whether it was wild or garden endive, the medicinal virtues were considered to be the same. See *suckory*, S 78; for syrups, see S 220.

---

240 TO MAKE SIRRUP OF LIQUORISH

Take 8 ounces of licorish & scrape it very clean, &
bruise it very well. take of mayden hayre one ounce,
annyseeds & fennell seeds, of each halfe an ounce.
steepe all these in 4 pints of rose water halfe a day.
after, boyle it to a quart, then put in a pound & halfe of
clarefied sugar & boyle with that liquor till it comes to
[a sirrup]. then put it up & keep it for y^r use.

* Or *streyne*.

Mayden hayre refers to certain ferns with fine hair-like stalks *(OED).*
True Maidenhair (Adiantum capillus-veneris) is "a stranger in England," as Gerard put it. It is most likely *English Maiden-haire (Asplenium trichomanes)* that is indicated here. Among its virtues, Gerard says that: "it staieth the laske and other fluxes. Being drunk it breaketh the stone [kidney stone] . . . It raiseth up grosse and slimie humours out of the chest and lungs . . . Moreover, it consumeth and wasteth away the Kings-evill . . . and it maketh the haire of the head or beard to grow." (This last illustrates the signature theory of virtues.)

Annyseeds are anise or aniseeds *(Pimpinella anīsum)* of an umbelliferous plant native to the Levant and cultivated for its aromatic seeds. Gerard says that it "wasteth and consumeth winde, and is good against belchings . . . and stirreth up bodily lust: it stayeth the laske, and also the white flux in women." It also sweetens the breath.

Fennel (Faeniculum vulgare) is another umbellifer. The name comes from a popular Latin form *fēnoclum,* meaning hay, and appeared in Old English by 700 as *finugl;* a popular name was *finkle* *(OED).* Gerard says: "Fennell seed drunk asswageth the paine of the stomacke, and wambling of the same or desire to vomit, and breaketh winde." The entire plant is "very good for the lungs, the liver, and the kidnies . . . and comforteth the inward parts."

For *liquorish,* see S 186; for syrups, 220.

---

241   TO MAKE SIRRUP OF WOOD SORRELL

Take a great quantety of wood sorrell & pick all ye grass & mos from it. then beat it stalks and all, then put it into a canvis bagg & press it in a book sellers press, tying ye bagg very close with 2 choping knives of each side to keep it from ye wood. & set a stone pan or basin under it to save the Juice. then set it shelving in A window where ye sun comes, & put in about 2 ounces of sugar to ye quantety of 2 quarts of Juice. & ye next day clear ye pop* from ye bottom, which will look red, & put it into an earthen pan or silver basin, & set it on A charcole fire, & make it scallding hot. soe scum & strayne it, & put in as much sugar as you please before

* *Pap.*

373

it is set on ye charcole fire. & when it is cold, bottle it up.

Wood sorrel *(Oxalis acetosella),* a low-growing woodland plant *(OED).* Other names were *Wood Sower, Cuckow Sorrell,* and *Alleluia.* It was used in cookery and medicine much as sorrel. Gerard says: "It is a remedy against putrified and stinking ulcers of the mouth, it quencheth thirst, and cooleth mightily any hot pestilentiall fever, especially being made with a syrrup of sugar."

The pap is the sediment and is to be discarded, although the language is not clear. For medicinal syrups, see S 220.

---

242   TO MAKE SIRRUP OF MAYDEN HAYRE

Take mayden haire, 6 ounces; licorish scraped and slyced, an ounce. steep these 24 hours in 4 pints of cundit water, then boyle it to a quart. after, take 2 pound of clarefyed sugar & boyle with that liquor on a gentle fire of charcole till it coms to a sirrup, and scum it very often that it may be clear, and then put it in a glass bottle and [keep it for] your use.

Cundit, a fourteenth-century form, is a conduit, or more rarely, a fountain *(OED).* Ingatestone Hall, from shortly before mid-sixteenth century, had "a piped supply of 'sweet' spring-water in the house and a drinking-tap in the yard," according to Emmison. (He also reports the existence of a well-engineered drainage system.) This was surely not widespread, but running water did exist in some of the great Tudor houses. There are several references to running water in our manuscript. London had a water system, supplied by the *Great Conduit,* by the beginning of the fourteenth century *(OED).* It seems unlikely that London water was of a quality to be specified; spring water was nearly always preferred for such uses.

For maidenhair, see S 240; for licorice, S 186; for medicinal syrups, S 220.

---

243   TO MAKE SIRRUP OF MAYDEN HAIRE

Take a peck of mayden haire, pick it clean and boyle it in 3 quarts of spring water till all the strength be out. & to every pinte, take a pound of lofe sugar, and boyle it to a sirrup, and when it is cold, bottle it.

244   TO MAKE SIRRUP OF HYSSOPE

Take of hysop one handfull; figg, raysons, & dates, of
each an ounce; callemint, halfe A handfull; french
barley, an ounce. boyle these in 3 pintes of water to a
quart, then strayn it & clarefyie it with 2 whites of eggs
& 2 pound of sugar, then boyle it to a sirrup and keep
it for your use.

Hyssop (*Hyssopus officinalis*) is native to Southern Europe (*OED*).
Gerard claims that a decoction of *Hyssope* made with "figges, water,
honey, and rue, and drunken, helpeth the inflammation of the
lungs, the old cough, and shortnesse of breath."

Figes (*Ficus*) appears as early as 1225 in English (*OED*).
Gerard says: "Dry or barrell Figs . . . are a remedy for the belly,
the cough . . . they scoure the kidnies, and clense forth the sand
. . . and cause women with childe to have the easier deliverance,
if they feed thereof for certaine daies together before their time."

Gerard says that sweet raisins have "a temperat and
smoothing qualitie, with a power to clense moderately . . . Moreover, Raisins are good for the liver, as *Galen* writeth." Also, see
C 14.

Dates are the fruit of *Phoenix dactylifera*, and known to the
English as *Dates* as early as 1295 (*OED*). According to Gerard, dry
dates, "stay vomiting, and the wambling of womens stomacks that
are with childe."

Calamint (*Calamintha*) was the principal ingredient of *Dia-
calaminthos*, a decoction which Gerard cites Galen as being "marvellous good for young maidens that want their courses . . . for
in continuance of time it bringeth them down very gently without
force."

For medicinal syrups, see S 220.

245   TO MAKE SIRRUP OF HYSSOPE

Take the distilld water of Hysope & to a pinte of water,
take a pound of white or brown sugar candy. soe give
it A boyle or 2 and let the partie take it for a cold with
A licorish stick slit cross the end. it may be taken night
or morning or any time.

For hyssop, see S 244; for sugar candy, S 100; for syrups, S 220.

246   TO MAKE SIRRUP OF HOREHOUND

Take hore hound, 2 handfulls; coltsfoot, one handfull;
time, penny royall, & callamint, of each 2 drams;
licorish, one ounce & a halfe; figgs & raysons of ye sun,
of each 2 ounces; anny seeds & fennell seeds, of each a
quarter of an ounce. boyle all these in a gallon of faire
water till it comes to a pottle or 3 pintes, then strayn it
& take 3 pound of sugar & 3 whites of eggs & clarefy y^t
liquor, & soe boyle it to a sirrup.

Horehound *(Marrubium vulgare),* is a labiate whose leaves and
stems are covered with white cottony pubescence, whence the
popular name, *hoarhound (OED).* For *hore,* see S 36. Gerard says:
"Syrrup made of the green fresh leaves and sugar, is a most singular remedy against the cough and wheesing of the lungs." He
also claims that wild horehound draws "down the menses . . . as
Dioscorides teacheth."

Coltsfoot *(Tussilago farfara)* has heart-shaped leaves with
a downy underside *(OED).* Gerard says that a syrup made of the
leaves and root is good for a cough and that "the green leaves of
Fole-foot [foal] pound with hony, do cure and heale the hot inflammation called Saint Anthonies fire, and all other inflammations."

Garden thyme *(Thymus vulgaris)* is native to the Mediterranean basin. Gerard says that it is effectual against the cough and
shortness of breath and that "it helpeth the long continued paine
of the head . . . or any disease of melancholy." Thyme is one of
the oldest and most widely used of medicinal herbs. It is listed in
the first pharmacopoeia of which we have record, from Sumer,
toward the end of the third millennium B.C. (see S 309). It continued straight through to modern times, surviving in folk medicine when it lost standing with the medical profession.

Pennyroyal (Mentha pulegium) comes from Anglo-French
puliol real, meaning royal thyme *(pulegium) (OED).* Gerard says:
"Pennie Royall taken with hony clenseth the lungs, and cleareth
the breast from all grosse and thicke humours."

The other ingredients of this cough syrup are discussed
elsewhere. It may well have been an efficacious preparation. A
pottle contains 2 quarts.

247   TO MAKE SIRRUP OF VINEGAR

Take mayden hayre & Issope, of each A little handfull;
one ounce of licorish sliced and scrape[d] thin. boyle
these leasurely in water from A quart to a pinte, adding
to them halfe A pinte of honey. stir & boyle it leasurely
till A fourth part be consumed, & put in soe much
white wine vinegar as will make it taste of it, & boyle it
halfe a quarter of an houre. give of this halfe a
spoonfu[ll] fasting to A childe, & to a grown body a
spoonfull. If it make ye party vomit after it, it is y^e
better, but If not, it will soften & cut ye flame* & drive
it down. this may be taken at 4 a clock† in ye afternoon,
& last at [night], & at other times, upon A licorish stick,
but [only at interv]als (?).

Flame or *fleme* is phlegm. The word comes from the Greek through
Latin *phlegma*, meaning inflammation, or morbid clammy humor
as the result of heat. Latin *flamma*, flame or blaze, comes from the
same root *(OED)*. So that *flame* is not impossible.
   Vinegar was considered drying and chilling. (See page
208.) These medicinal syrups are discussed in S 220. *Issope* is hyssop
(S 244).

248   TO MAKE SIRRUP OF DRY FLOWERS

When damask or red roses, gelleflowers, violets, or any
other flowers are in their prime, before y^t they are to
fully blowne, gather them & cut of theyr whites, & dry
them betwixt papers & not in ye sun. then keep them
in a very dry place till you shall use them. & when you
would make sirrup, put pritty store of them into faire
water and proportion ye quantety of water as you are
stord with flowers. decockt them on embers or a gentle
fire till ye water have drawn out theyr vertue & culler.
then strayn them out clean, & put in more as formerly.

* It is not impossible that this read *fleme.*
† The *a* is pristine.

& when ye liquor is as deep as you desire its culler to
be, strayne it clean, & boyle it up with ye weight in loaf
sugar, If you would keep y^r sirrup long. but it is of
more vertue with less sugar, & made often. If you be
not furnished wth many flowers to dry in summer,
when you pluck them, you may make them with green
flowers, clarefying y^r sugar but little to avoyd candying.

To decoct is to boil so as to extract the soluble parts or principles
of a substance *(OED)*. These medicinal syrups are discussed in S
220. Beware of insecticides and other toxic sprays.

---

249 TO MAKE HONEY OF ROSES

Take a pinte of honey, boyle & scum it, & add as many
bruised leaves of red roses buds (ye whites being cut
of)* as you may easily stir in. y^n cover it close & boyle
ye pot in water, till you think ye goodness of the roses
is in ye honey. then change ye roses once or twice in y^e
same manner, & at ye last, stray[n out ye roses] & keep
it for y^r use.

This identical recipe appears in S 73.

TO MAKE SEUERALL SORTS OF
WINES AND DRINKS

---

250 TO MAKE CHERRY WINE

Take a good quantety of spring water & let it boy[le]
halfe an houre. then beat 4 pound of raysons, clean
pickt & washed, & beat them in a morter to pas[te].
then put them in an earthen pot, & pour on y^m 12
quarts of this water boyling hot, & put to it 6 quarts of
ye Juice of cheries, & put in the pulp & scins of y^e
cheries after they are strayned. & let all these steep
together, close covered, 3 days. then strayn all out & let

* Parentheses supplied.

378

it stand 3 or 4 hours to settle. take of ye cleerest, & run
ye rest thorough a Jelley bagg. then put ye Juice up into
bottles & stop them up close, & set them in sand.

We now come to a group of "wines" and other mildly alcoholic
drinks. Perhaps the purpose of these drinks can best be described
by quoting from the recipe for birch wine (S 257): "this drink is
very pleasant and allsoe physicall [medicinal, healing]," followed
by its virtues. Indeed, I think it fair to say that this is the mood of
most of the sweetmeat recipes in our manuscript. As the section
continues, the recipes become more medicinal in character. Some
of these "wines" have survived into modern times. As explained
elsewhere, all decocting and brewing was the domain of the
housewife, even one of high station.

For cherries, see S 42.

---

251 TO MAKE LEAMON WINE

Take 6 quarts of spring water, then pare and slice 6
leamons into ye water, with a pound of ye best loaf
sugar and A pound of raysons of ye sun, bruised small.
let them stand in steep 2 days, then boyle it pritty well,
& let it stand after y^t 8 dayes to settle in an earthen
pipkin. y^n strayn it thorough a Jelley bagg & bottle it,
adding a lump of loaf sugar to every bottle. you must
put in one leamon pill at first when you [put in your]
leamons.

---

252 TO MAKE GOOSBERRIE WINE

Take 3 quarts of ye ripest goosberries you can get. beat
them to mash in a morter, then take 2 gallons of spring
water & mix them well together. & when they have
stood an houre or 2, let them run thorough a hare sive.
then put to every gallon a quarter of a pound of loaf*
sugar, & put it in a pot & cover it soe close y^t noe aire
can get in to it. make a little hole in ye top of y^r cover,
which stop up close with a corke. then let it stand 2

* I excised a confusing *&*.

days soe close. & at two days end, give it a little vent,
then let it stand 2 dayes longer and give it a little vent
againe. after, let it stand 10 dayes, close covered, and
give it noe more vent. after, take the corke out, & clear
the wine into stone pans. If you dissern any thickness
in it, run it thorough A Jelley bagg. then bottle it up
and put into every bottle a lump of hard sugar. and to
this you may put, If you pleas, two quarts of white
wine, which will make it more quick and brisk and
strong. this is a good way to make wine of rasberries,
mulberries, blackberies, peaches, or any other fruit. but
for peaches, which is a liquid fruit, you may make wine
of their clear Juice without adding [any water] at all.

The gooseberry is discussed is S 56, and the various fruits listed
at the end of this well-detailed recipe are treated under their respective names. See wines, S 250.

---

253   TO MAKE BLACKBERRIE WINE

Take halfe a peck of black berries & stamp them in a
stone morter, & strayne ye cleares[t] of ye Juice
thorough A Jelley bagg. then take a pound of raysons
of ye sun & beat them and put them into 5 quarts of
water, & boyle it very well, then run it thorough A
Jelley bagg, & mix ye Juice with it, & let it stand 2 or 3
days in ye po[t]. then put in about a pound of loaf
sugar, & run it thorough ye Jelley bagg againe. when
they are mixt together, boyle it over againe, & put in y^e
water you boyle ye raysons in, 2 or 3 leamons, slyced.
boyle it with ye raysons & water, & it will make it brisk
& give it a more pleasant taste. then bottle it.

The blackberry is the fruit of the bramble *(Rubus fruticosus* or *ul-
mifolius)*; wild or cultivated, it is one of the commonest fruits in
England. Gerard says that they contain "much juyce of a temperate
heate, . . . [and are] wholesome for the stomacke," and cites Pliny
as reporting that "the berries and flours do provoke urine, and that
the decoction of them in wine is a present remedy against the stone

[kidney stone]." The raspberry and blackberry are discussed by
Gerard in the same chapter; see S 60. Also, see S 250 for wines.

254   TO MAKE ELDERBERRY WINE

Take 3 gallons & a halfe of water & set it on ye fire, &
when it is warme, put to it a peck of elderberries very
rip[e]. bruise them well, & strayne them, & measure
the liquor & set it on ye fire againe, & let it boyle a
quarter of an houre, & scum it very well. & to every
quart of liquor, put a pinte of honey or halfe a pound
of suga[r]. boyle & scim y^m till it will bear an egg, then
take it of, & when it is as cold as ale, put yeast to it &
put to every 2 quarts, A pinte of ale y^t is working. & let
it work a night together, y^n tun it into a runlet. & after
it is done working, stop it up, & at christmas, broach &
bottl[e] [it, & it] will keep a year. this wine is very good
for ye scu[rvy].

The elderberry is the fruit of *Sambucus nigra*. Gerard says: "The
seeds contained within the berries . . . are good for such as have
the Dropsie, and such as are too fat and would faine be leaner."
One of the virtues of the seed was purgative; whether this be lost
in fermentation, I do not know.

    Ale that is still fermenting is virtually unobtainable; per-
haps a light mock *ale yeast* (C 92) might be used. I am unversed in
the arts of brewing and vinification, however, and the reader who
wishes to follow these recipes would do well to consult standard
works on the subject.

    A *runlet* is a cask of widely varying capacity; the word
comes from Old French *rondelet (OED)*. To *tun* is to transfer the
brew into a *tun* or large cask.

255   TO MAKE RASPIE WINE

Take 40 or 50 pound of maligo raysons, pikt from y^e
stalks & stones. put them in a large vate, & put to
every pound of them a quart of water. then cover them
with a thick cloth & stir them once a day. steep them 6
or 7 dayes in ye winter & 5 dayes in ye sumer till y^e

water have soakt out ye strength of ye fruit. then
strayne them & put ye liquor into a convenient vessell,
& set it in ye sun or in ye chimney corner, that it may
stand in some gentle heat to worke for 2 or 3 dayes, &
purge away all ye dross. then bung it up close, & let it
stand in y^r seller, or where else you pleas, for halfe a
year. y^n draw it into bottles & corke it up close. & keep
them for 5 or 6 weeks, & then it may be drunk. you
may put to ye raysons ye same proportion of water y^e
second time & order it just as you did ye first, but this
will not keepe soe long, beeing much smaller then y^e
first. but you may make a good middle wine, by mixing
ye strong & smaller infusions together. when you tun y^r
strongest* liquor, put a gallon of ye Juice of raspas in it,
or rather when you bottle it. put in 6 spoonfulls of y^e
sirrup of rasberies (into every bottle)† made with y^e
Juice, & an equall weight of sugar, boyled a little &
clarefyed. thus you may make Jilliflower wine, baume,
wormewood, or Angelico wine, by hanging in ye barrell
a convenient quantety of the herbs when you tun y^e
liquor up.

This is an interesting recipe from a historical point of view. *Raspie*
would seem to hark back to *Raspis,* which, according to *OED,* is
"kind of wine used in the fifteenth and sixteenth centuries," with
the name possibly deriving from Old French *raspeit* (it rasps); the
last citation is from Thomas Cogan's *The Haven of Health,* 1584. At
about the same time, Florio defines Italian *raspato* as *raspis wine.*
OED feels that Boorde was mistaken in associating it with raspberries in 1542 (see S 60), and that in no case does the context
support the presence of raspberries. I find their argument persuasive and it would explain the curious fact that raspberries play no
role whatsoever in the "vinification," with the raspberry syrup
(S 234) being added only as a flavoring, almost as an afterthought.
I believe that it is an attempt to account for the name which had
become less and less comprehensible with the passing of time,
given the lack of raspberries in the brew. However, I suspect that

* Written *stongest*.
† Scribe's parentheses.

the process had already taken place by the time of Boorde; he was a knowledgeable and observant practitioner and would not have made such a mistake, I think. I believe this to be an old recipe. (Proper raspberry wine would be fermented along the principles given in S 252.)

Maligo raysons are from Malaga. This composition agrees with such reference to *raspis* as I know; it is described as heavy, sweet, and inclining to black in color. *lillyflowers* are discussed in S 67; *baume*, or balm, in S 296; *Angelico* in S 68.

Vate is vat, a great vessel in which ale, cider, etc., undergoes fermentation. *Fate* and other forms occur elsewhere in the manuscript. *Seller* is a fifteenth- and sixteenth-century form of *cellar*, which did not appear until the seventeenth century *(OED)*. *Conuenient* meant suitable.

Wormwood *(Artemisia absinthium)* is proverbial for its bitterness. Gerard says: "If it be taken before a surfeit it keepeth it off, and removeth lothsomenesse, saith *Dioscorides*. . . . Again, Wormewood voideth away the wormes of the guts [and] it keepeth garments also from the moths."

---

256   TO MAKE WINE OF CURRANS

Take 40 pound of currans (or what quantety [you] pleas). infuse them in 10 gallons of water in a [tun] fit for ye purpose. cover it close with a cloth y^t the vapours goe not forth. soe let it heat together 10, 12, or 14 dayes. then poure ye liquor from ye currans into a runlet, & give it time [to] clear & worke. after, stop it up close & broa[ch] it not till it be halfe a year old, & then [you] may bottle it up. now to make a smaller win[e]. put into ye currans y^t came from ye former wine, 3 gallons of water & stirr them very well, & let them infuse together as before. then stray[ne] out ye liquor into a convenient vessell, & after a moneth or 6 weeks, it will be fit to drink. or you may set this vessell of smaller liquor in ye sun & it will make good vinegar. you must observe to stir both ye stronger & smaller liquors every night & morning (with a spatula of wood)

Note: All parentheses are original. Damage along the one edge was such that reconstruction was without complication.

all ye time they are in ye infusion in [y^r] tub. in warme
weather, it will be quickly ready & sharp before y^e
vertue of ye currans be in ye water, so y^t it is not to be
made when ye weather is very hot or very cold, for
then it will not come to perfection at all. but spring or
fall, you may make it in. when it beginneth to wax
sharp, it is ripe enou[gh], & then you may put it up.

I believe this to be related to the *Raspie* of S 255 except that it is
here made of dried currants rather than raisins. The technique is
not that of working with fresh fruit, and the perceptive instructions
concerning the weather confirm this, since English currants would
be made into wine at the time of gathering. I believe this to be an
old recipe. For *currants*, see C 11.

---

257   TO MAKE BIRCH WINE

First make an incission & an hole thorough ye bark of
one of ye largest birch tree bows, & put a quill therein,
& quickly you shall perceive ye Juice to distill. you may
make incision into severall bowes at once, which water
receive into whatever vessill you pleas. it will continew
running 9 or 10 dayes, & if y^r tree be large, it will
afford you [many] gallons. boyle it well, as you doe
bear,* but first put to every gallon, one pound of white
powdered sugar. when it is well boyled, take it of the
fire, & put in A gilefate with yeast, as y^u doe to ale or
beere, & it will worke in the same mannor. after 4 or 5
dayes, bottle it up in the thickest bottles you can get,
for fear of bursting. & then at 8 or 9 weeks end, you
may drink it, but it is better if you keep it older. this
drink is very pleasant and allsoe physicall, first for
procuring an appetite, & allsoe it is an antydote against
gravell and the stone. this liquor must be procurd &
made up in march, which is ye onely time, and not at
the latter end of march neyther, for then the trees will

* *Beer.*

not run soe well & freely as at ye beginning of the moneth.

Birch wine is prepared from the sap of *Betula alba*, the common European birch, as here explained. Curiously, Gerard has little to say about the birch, but recipes for this drink are popular, especially in seventeenth-century sources; as the recipe claims, it was thought to be efficacious in treating urinary tract obstructions. Birch wine crossed the Atlantic, where it was made using the sap of American varieties. *Bow* is a thirteenth- to seventeenth-century form of bough.

A *gilefate* is a vat for brewing ale or beer (see *vate*, S 255) *Gill* was popularly used to mean ale or beer, especially attributively, as in *gill-house*. (This is possibly because *gill* is an old ale and wine measure—see S 229; *OED* does not speculate. *Gile* is given as an obsolete form under a different meaning.) It is curious that *OED* gives nothing on this compound word; perhaps it was not common, but Markham uses *Guil-fat* in just this way, under *Brewing and Bakerie* in *The English Hus-wife*, 1615.

Physicall means medicinal or curative. *Grauell* is an aggregation of urinary crystals; the *stone* is a hard, morbid concretion in the kidney or urinary tract *(OED)*.

---

258   TO MAKE HIPPOCRIS

Take 4 gallons of french wine, & 2 gallons [of] sack, & 9 pound of powder sugar, & 12 ounces [of] cinnamon, 9 ounces of ginger, one ounce of nutm[egg], one ounce of corriander seeds, halfe an ounce of cloves, & 2 quarts of new milk. put ye wine & 2 pound of sugar into a clean tub, & bruis[e] all ye spices, but not small, & strow them on [the] top of ye wine. & let it stand close covered [24]* hours, then put in ye rest of ye sugar & ye mil[k], & stir them well together. then put into a cle[an] coten bagg, & let it run twice thorough it into a clean pot. & when it is clear, bottle it up for y^r [use]. these spices will make ye same quantety againe. [If] you would have it red, culler it with red wine.

Hippocras, a sweet spiced wine, is the wine of Hippocrates. The

* Only the 2 is visible, but see S 259.

great physician has been credited with a recipe for spiced wine; since spices were always considered medicinal and wine was a convenient vehicle, why not? In any event, the principle is ancient. In this connection, the bag used for filtering such mixtures since antiquity is called *Manica Hippocrates*, the sleeve of Hippocrates, and is also credited to him. The oldest English recipe that I know of appears in *The Forme of Cury*, about 1390; it is couched in a most curious Anglo-French, is entitled *Pur fait Ypocras*, and is a list of spices and their proportions. The list is rather longer than ours, but it starts with ginger and cinnamon just as ours does. The wine is understood, and there is no milk; I am not sure that Hippocrates would have approved and I believe the milk to be rare. Recipes for hippocras seem to have pretty much stopped appearing in cookbooks by the eighteenth century but clearly, mulled wine, Swedish *glögg*, and other such spiced wine drinks all trace a direct line back to this ancient medication. See also S 259.

French wine is an unhelpful appellation in Tudor recipes. Here, it would seem to be white, judging by the last sentence. I cannot recommend red wine with milk. *Powder sugar* only means finely sifted.

---

259   TO MAKE HYPPOCRIS

Take 3 quarts of sweet wine & one quart of swee[t] sack, 2 pound of lofe sugar, 2 ounces of cinnamon, halfe an ounce of ginger, halfe an ounce of corriander seeds, 4 numeggs, beat y^r sugar ve[ry] well, but ye other* spices must be onely crusht. y^n put ye wine in an earthen pot, & all ye spices, but ha[lfe] ye sugar. y^n cover ye pot & let it stand 24 hours. y^n put [in] ye other halfe of ye sugar & a pinte of new milke. stir them [well] together, y^n put them in a bagg y^t is small at one end, [&] put a whalebone on ye top y^t it may hang even. when it [is thorough (?)], bottle it close. it will keep a quarter of a ye[ar].

This recipe for hippocras varies only in minor details from the preceding one. Note the description of *Manica Hippocrates*, mentioned in S 258.

* Written *othes*.

260   TO MAKE MEAD

Take 8 or 9 pound of raysons of ye sun, or els ye best
maligoe, & beat them. & take halfe an ounce of
nutmegg, a quarter of an ounce of cloves, & one penny
worth of cinnamon. beat & mix all these together. If y^e
weather be hot, put in 2 leamons, If not, ye pills of 2. &
put to it 5 or 6 gallons of spring [water]* & 2 quarts of
honey. then stir it [morning & evening (?)] 4 dayes
together. & when it gathers to ye top, then strayne out
halfe ye tubfull, & ye other halfe, culler with turnesell
strayned into it. & perfume it with muske or
ambergreece & halfe a pinte of rosewater. & then bottle
it up. ye bottles you drink soon, fill not too full, but If
you would keep them long, fill them full.

Mead is an alcoholic drink made by fermenting honey and water.
Back through all the ancient forms, we finally get to Sanskrit *mādhu*,
meaning sweet. The first mention in English is in *Beowulf* (the
eight-century work that survives only in a manuscript of around
1000) as *medo (OED)*.

    Raysons of ye sun are those dried on the stem in the sun;
maligoe are raisins from Malaga. *Turnesell*, or turnsole, is a violet
dye (S 188).

    Clearly, one does not "stir it 4 dayes together." I supplied
"morning & evening," as it agrees in spirit with other recipes, but
it is speculation.

261   TO MAKE MEAD

Take a quart of honey & 7 quarts of water; of bay,
rosemary, & hyssope, of each a sprigg. mix them
together & boyle them halfe an houre, & then let it
stand till it be clear. then put it up in a pot with a tap,
& set new yeast on it, & let it worke untill it be clear,
then bottle it up & let it be two moneths ould before

* Supplied.

To
Mrs Curtis
There

Cowslip Wine

To every eight gallons of water put 16 pounds
of Sugar stir it well in yͤ water and boyl them
together halfe an hour Skym it very clean and let it
stand til it bee no more than blood warm then pour
it on eight pecks of Cowslips and cover it close
Next morning put to it 14 spoonfulls of good ale yest
and squeze in yͤ juice of 16 Lemmons and yͤ peels
of 8 let it stand in a vessel a month, then bottle it
itshus will keep a year when you bottle it
put into every bottle a lump of loaf Sugar
some put in but one peck of Cowslips to 3 gallons
a peck and halfe of flowers will make it very
very strong to 3 gallons of water

you drink it. it may be drunk before, but ye keeping it
soe long makes it brisker.

Mead is discussed in S 260. For *bay,* see S 319.

COWSLIP WINE*

To every eight gallons of Water, put 16 pound of Sugar.
Mix it well in ye watter amd boyl them together halfe
an hour. Skym it very clean and let it stand til it bee no
more than bloud warm. then pour it on eight pecks of
Cowslips, and cover it close. Next morning put to it 14
spoonfulls of good ale yest and squeset† in ye juice of 16
Lemmons and ye peels of 8. let it stand in a vessel a
month, then bottle it. this will keep a year when you
bottle it. put into every bottle a lump of loaf Sugar.
Some put in but one peck of Cowslips to 3 gallons. a
peck and halfe of flowers will make it very very strong
to 3 gallons of water.

This recipe for cowslip wine was pasted in *A Booke of Sweetmeats*
at some later time, perhaps even by the museum. It is written in
an entirely different hand from that of our scribe. On the back of
the paper, in yet another hand, is written:

To

M^{rs}. Custis

These

Neither hand is represented in the scratchings of the inner
pages (see page 456), nor have I been able to identify them. The
whole aspect of the recipe is infinitely more modern than that of
any in the manuscript proper, not so much in content as in language and in writing style. It is *peels,* not *pills,* for instance, and
every *j* and *i,* as well as *v* and *u,* are systematically differentiated.
I feel that the recipe may have been given to Martha Dandridge
Custis rather than to Frances Parke Custis, but I would be hard
put to give a cogent reason except that it also seems more modern
than any of the recipes of the inner pages; certainly it is tidier and
more literate.

* Pasted in recipe, following S 261.
† Unclear.

The giver of the recipe had trouble with her arithmetic. She started out with the proportion of one peck of flowers for each gallon of water; she ended up by claiming that one half that proportion "will make it very very strong." For cowslips, see S 137.

---

262   TO MAKE METHEGLIN

Take a quart of honey & 6 quarts of wat[er]. let it boyle
ye third part away, & boyle [wth] it 3 races of ginger.
when it is cold, put it [in] a pot which hath a spicket, &
put yeast into [it] & let it stand 3 dayes, then bottle it
up & put into y^r bottles a little leamon & a stick of
cinna[mon] & a few raysons of ye sun. & let it be a
fortnig[ht] befor you drink it.

Metheglin is a spiced or medicated honey drink, lightly fermented, originally peculiar to Wales. The name comes from Welsh *meddyg,* healing, and *llyn,* liquor; *OED* is firm that there is no etymological connection between this word and *mead* despite the tempting analogies.

A *race* is a hand of ginger (S 92). A *spicket* is a spigot; the word survives in dialect in both England and America.

---

263   TO MAKE STEPONY

Put 5 quarts of spring water, boyled, into [an] earthen
pot, & put therein 2 pound of rayson[s] of ye sun,
stonned, 2 leamons, ye one with [y^e] pill & ye other
squeesed but not ye pill (& [y^t] which remains after y^e
leamon be strayned, cast into ye pipkin allsoe),* & one
penny worth of the best sugar, & cover y^r pot very
well. let it stand 4 or 5 dayes, stiring it once or twice A
day, then let it run thorough a thin cloth, [y^n] bottle it
up & put into every bottle a lump of hard sugar as bigg
as a wallnut. stop it up clo[se] & set it in a chamber
window where ye sun comes 5 or 6 dayes. & after that
in a close roome for A fortnight. and then you may
drink [it]. in stead of one penny worth of sugar
prementioned, you must put in halfe a pound.

* Parentheses supplied.

Stepony is a kind of raisin wine. Blount's *Glossographia*, 1656, says that it was "drunk in some places of London in the summer time" (*OED*).

Squeese is a seventeenth-century form of squeeze. The first citation of the word is in Ben Jonson in 1599 (*OED*) and Cotgrave uses it in a definition in 1611 (*squeeze*, in both instances). The word appears rarely in our manuscript and only in what appear to be later recipes; the customary word is *wring*, a word reaching back into Old English.

Note the correction on the amount of sugar. It is hard to say, but a *penny worth* of sugar may have been an ounce.

---

264   TO MAKE NECTOUR

Take 2 pound of raysons of ye sunn* and shread them, & a pound of powder sugar, & 2 leamons sliced, one leamon pill. put these into an earthen pot. take 2 gallons of water & let it boyle halfe an hour, then take it of ye fire, & put it into ye pot, stiring it very well. let it stand 3 or 4 dayes, & stir it twice a day. soe strayne it and bottle it. in a fortnights time, it will be ready to drink.

Nectour, nectar, the drink of the gods or any pleasant drink. This recipe differs little from that for *Stepony*, S 263; I must suppose that the names are largely fanciful.

---

265   TO MAKE SHRUB

Take one quart of brandy & a quart of white wine, & a quart of spring water. mix them together then slice 3 leamons, & put in with a pound of sugar. stir these very well, cover y^r pot close, & let it stand 3 dayes, stiring it every day. then strayne it, & bottle it, & crush ye leamons very well inside it.

Shrub is a drink involving citrus fruit and spirits. The name comes from Arabic *shrub*, drink, and is related to *sharāb* and *sharba* (see S 2) that gave us syrup and sherbet. The first citation *OED* gives for *shrub* is 1747. Since we know that this fair copy of our manu-

* Badly blurred.

script was made by 1706 (see page 457), at the very latest, the word manifestly was in use well before that.

However, I do believe that these last few recipes, beginning with *Stepony*, are among the last additions to this family manuscript. The use of *brandy* is one such indication; it is not supposed to have been current before nearly mid-seventeenth century *(brandwine* came earlier), but we have a remarkable illustration of how the printed word lags decades behind usage. (It is also impossible to comb all the sources, and manuscripts prove to reflect popular usage more quickly and more accurately.) That said, the use of *squeese* (S 263), *shrub*, and *brandy*, mark these last three recipes as "modern" ones.

---

266   TO MAKE PERSENCIA

Take a stone of maligo raysons, pick, wash, & stomp y^m. then boyle 10 gallons of spring water, & put in y^r raysons. let it stand 2 hours, then boyle it. y^n after it hath stood an houre, strayne it into a tub. ye next day, clear it into a runlet, & put to it 4 quarts of new milke from ye cow, y^n shake it well for halfe an houre. y^n put in a leamon or 2, sliced, & ye rinde of one. stop up ye runlet & at 14 days end, bottle it. & put a bit of s[ugar into e]very bottle & a [few] cloves, if you like them.

I can find no trace of *Persencia*. A Persian association has been suggested, an attractive notion and not impossible since Persia was often invoked for its romantic connotations (but one expects pomegranates or rose water), or perhaps simply because Persia was associated with cooling drinks (see *julip*, S 280). (The French made a drink called *persicot*, so named because it was made by macerating peach kernels; while it did indeed cross the Channel, it involves the wrong fruit altogether.)

Maligo raysons are from Malaga; a *runlet* is a cask (S 254). A *stone* is a half of a quarter of a hundred-weight (C 145), so should have been 12 ½ pounds; in practice, it varied wildly. It is now 14 pounds.

---

267   TO MAKE SYDER

Beat & squeese your apples, & let them sta[nd] 4 dayes at ye least to settle. then tun ye liquor up into a clean vessell, but close it not up [till] it hath done working, & then hang A little ha[nd] (?)] bagg full of spices in ye midst of ye vessill. then stop it up very close, & at 6 months end, draw it out, & bottle some of it, & drink ye rest at y^r pleasure.

Syder is a fifteenth- to eighteenth-century form of *cider*, and comes from Old French *sidre (OED)*. Robert traces the word to *sicera*, an ecclesiastical Latin rendition of *chekar*, Hebrew (by way of Greek) for "inebriating beverage," and so used in translating the Bible. It is not clear when the word was first attached to the fermented juice of the apple—apparently rather late—but Normans and other peoples had long been drinking it; the fruit of unimproved trees is good for little else, and cider neither keeps nor travels well, so that whatever name it went under in various regions would tend to not get into learned lexicons. Anne Wilson says that cider making was introduced into England from Normandy around mid-twelfth century, but also has a tantalizing reference: "The Anglo-Saxons had had some knowledge of 'apple wine,' " but she does not elaborate. In any event, " 'Wine of pearmains' [a variety of apple] formed part of a rent paid in Norfolk in 1205," she writes.

It should be noted that *perry* was made from pears in the same way in the same regions and was nearly as popular.

---

268   TO MAKE CAPON ALE

Take an old capon with yellow leggs. pu[ll] him & crush ye bones, but keep ye scin whol[e], & then take an ounce of carraway seeds, and an ounce of anny seeds, and two ounces of har[ts] horne, and one handfull of rosemary tops, a piece or 2 of mace, and a leamon pill. sow all these into ye bellie of your capon and chop him into a hot mash, or hot water, and put him into two gallons of strong ale when it is working. after, let it stand two or three dayes, & then drink it. or you may bottle it after it hath stood 4 or 5 dayes, & put a lump of sugar into every bottle [w^ch] will make it drink brisker. this ale is good for any who are in a consumption, & it is restorative for any other weakness.

Capon ale was one of the popular "restorative" drinks of the sixteenth and seventeenth centuries. (See also *cock water*, S 285.)

To *pull* a bird is to pluck or draw it. From ancient cookbooks, it is clear that *pulling* originally referred to the feathers and
drawing to the viscera, but in about 1440, Galfridus in *Promptorium
Parvulorum* defines *pullynge* as *plukkyng of fowle* and again, as *draw-
ynge*. So that *pull, pluck,* and *draw* are hopelessly entangled
historically insofar as fowl are concerned. *Pluck,* for instance, still
refers to those parts of the viscera used as food in England and,
figuratively, as courage, or *guts.* The use of *pull* in these senses
lingered in dialect, but the last citation in *OED* is from Shakespeare,
and it is figurative and can be otherwise explained (" . . . pull his
Plumes," *Henry VI*).

Sow is a sixteenth-century form of *sew. Chop into* means
to put or clap into. Halliwell cites "Chopt up in prison," from
Northumberland. One would hardly chop the bird after taking care
to "keep ye scin whole."

Consumption means tuberculosis of the lungs, but the word
was more often applied to a vaguer, more general "wasting away,"
or debilitation. (This caution applies to other terms as well, most
notably *cancer*, which more often designated an open sore, or
canker, than a malignant tumor.)

---

269   TO MAKE AQUIMIRABELIS

Take gallinggall, quibbibs, licorish, annyseeds, cloves,
nutmegg, cinnamon, mace, & ginger, of each a quarter
of an ounce, small beaten. y^n take halfe an ounce of
each of these: mellilot, flowers and leave, angelico,
cowslips, mayden hayr, margerum, draggons, balme,
mint, hearts tongue, pimpernell, bay leaves, liverwort.
If you like ye taste, take ye flowers of rosemary,
cowslips, bittony, & mary goulds, Jilleflowers, & red
roses, burrage, & buglos (of each eyther green or dry),*
ye quantety of halfe an ounce, or as much & as many of
them as you can get. take of ye Juice of sullendine A
pinte. mix these alltogether, being cut small, & put
them into an earthen pot well glased, & with a close
mouth. allsoe put in your spices, then put in a pottle of

* Parentheses supplied.

ye best white or biscoyn wine, or 3 quarts. let these
things be well mixed together, & stand all night in y^e
pot with ye mouth very close stopt to keep in ye spirits.
in ye morning, put in a pinte of ye best aquavite or
stomack water. soe stir them well & put them into a
rose* water still very close pasted up. but If you would
have it strong, still it in A limbeck or glass stilletory, &
keep a pint of ye best droping by it selfe, & ye smaller
by it selfe, but ye third sort will be [weak (?) ye weak]
you may mix with ye strongest at your pleasu[re]. when
you give any of it, sweeten it with powde[r] of white
sugar candy or loaf sugar, which you please. 4 ounces
of sugar will serve for ye fa[ir (?)] proportion of water.
this must be stilld slow[ly] with a temperate fire, which
must not goe out day nor night, till it is stilld.

Aquimirabelis, properly *Aqua mirabilis*, miraculous water (see S 271
and 272), is the first of a series of composed waters. While they
are made as palatable as possible, they are entirely medicinal. Some
seem to be all-purpose, some are cordial (good for the heart, literally), some are specific to the plague.

Gallinggall, galingale, is the aromatic root of one of two
East Indian plants, true galingale *(Alpina* and *Kaempferia)*, or English galingale, *Cyperus longus*, a sedge. They were all considered
to have similar virtues. The name comes from Arabic *Khaulinjan*,
which comes from Chinese *Ko-liang-kiang*, meaning mild ginger
from Ko *(OED)*. Gerard says: "If it be boiled in wine, and drunke,
it provoketh urine, driveth forth the stone, and bringeth down the
natural sicknesse of women." Johnson, in 1636, says of the *true
Galingale* roots: "They are usefull against the Collicke proceeding
of flatulencies, . . . they conduce to venery, and heate the too cold
reines [kidneys]. To conclude, they are good against all cold
diseases."

Quibbibs, cubebs *(Piper cubeba* or *Cubeba officinalis)* are from
Java. The name comes from Arabic *kabābah* by way of Old French
quibibes (OED). The English knew of them at least as early as the
fourteenth century. Gerard claims that "they are good against the
cold and moist affects of the stomacke, and flatulencies . . . they
heate and comfort the brain. The Indians [of India] use them to
excite venery."

* First written *strong*, but crossed out with *rose* written above.

Mellilot, melilote (probably *Melilotus officinalis),* is a leguminous plant *(OED).* Gerard says that boiled in wine, it "asswageth the paine of the kidnies, bladder and belly, and ripeneth phlegme, and causeth it to be easily cast forth."

Draggons is dragonwort *(Dracunculus vulgaris).* Gerard says: "The distilled water hath vertue against the pestilence or any pestilentiall fever or poyson." But he warns: "The smell of the floures is hurtfull to women newly conceived with child."

It is surely *balm gentle* that is wanted here; see S 296. For *bay,* see S 319.

Hearts tongue, hart's tongue *(Scolopendrium vulgare),* is a fern *(OED).* Gerard says: "Common harts tongue is commended against the laske and bloudy flix."

Pimpernell was called *Pimpinella Saxifrage* by Turner in 1548, which was in line with his time. Gerard, in 1597, correctly classified *Pimpernell* under Anagallus (now *Anagallus arvensis),* but described *Burnet Saxifrage* as a "great kinde of Pimpinell," which made it understandable in popular tradition. So that a small doubt remains as to which was wanted here; let us stay with the pimpernel. This is the scarlet pimpernel of literature, which was thought to be male, a popular error; the flowers of the "female" plant were "of a most perfect blew colour," according to Gerard. Among its virtues, he writes: "It praileth against the infirmities of the liver and kidneys, if the juyce be drunke with wine."

Liverwort (Marchantia polymorpha) is a lichen-like plant. (However, *anemone, Hepatica,* was also called liverwort, for its lobed shape. Although it was used in medicine, I think it is not indicated here, having to do mostly with treating the eyes and sores.) Gerard writes of the first named: "It is singular good against the inflammations of the liver, hot and sharp agues, and tertians that proceed of choler . . . *Dioscorides* teacheth . . . that it is a remedie for them that have the yellow jaundice."

Bittony, betony, is *Stachys betonica.* Gerard claims: "It maketh a man to have a good stomacke and appetite to his meate; it prevaileth against sower belchings . . . It is singular against all pains of the head: it killeth wormes in the belly: [and] helpeth the ague."

Sullendine is celandine *(Chelidonium majus).* Gerard writes: "The root of Celandine boiled with Anise seed in white wine, opens the stoppings of the liver, and cureth the jaundice very safely, as hath been often proved." The legendary virtue of celandine has to do with its use in treatment of the eye; there is the ancient tale of swallows healing the sight of fledglings with the herb, hence the popular name of *swallow-wort.*

Biscoyne was wine from Biscay by name, but in fact came through the port of Bordeaux, and must have been ill-differentiated from *gascoyne* (S 275).

Aquauite, or *Aqua vitae* (often called *aquavity* in the manuscript), was supposed to be the product of the first distillation, but early came to refer to any strong spirits.

Stomack water is spirits that have been medicated with various stomachic elements.

Limbeck is an aphetic form of alembic, from Arabic *al-enbīq,* an apparatus formerly used in distilling. *Stilletory* is an obsolete word for still.

I should note that while distilling is called for in these recipes, simple maceration of spice and herbs in appropriate spirits will work perfectly well in most cases. It may take from 6 to 8 weeks.

---

270 THE UERTUES OF THIS WATER

It is excellent good to clense ye lungs with out any

greevance, beeing wounded or decayd [it] healeth. it

suffereth not ye bloud to be putri[fi]ed, but increaseth

it. it disperseth melancholly & causeth cheerfullness, &

expelleth rhume, & comforteth ye stomake, & causeth a

good disgestion, & good culler. it helpeth ye memory. &

it is good against windiness of ye spleen, & dispelleth

ye palsie & cold humers. it must be usually taken y^e

quantety of 2 spoonfulls every three dayes, but in

summer, one spoonfull at a time will be enough, If it be

distilld in a limbe[ck]. but If it be stilld in an ordinary

still, you make take a greater proportion at A time and

oftener, as your stomak shall require. you may put ye 4

ounces of sugar or sugar candy into your glass bottles,

& let the water distill upon it. or sweeten it as you use

it, whether your fancy shall direct you too.

It is interesting to compare the language of this entry with its preceding companion recipe. A recipe and its virtues were published together in just this way, usually. Yet the language of the virtues is a good deal older than that of the recipe. The reason is simple: the latter was a working prescription that had been gone over by many hands, while the list of virtues was referred to only on occasion and the tendency was to make a fair copy.

Vertues refers to the medicinal characteristics of a substance. *OED* lists *uertue* as a fourteenth-century form.

---

271   TO MAKE AQUIMIRABELIS

Take 2 quarts of sack; one pinte of ye Juice of sellandine; halfe a pinte of ye Juice of mint; mellilot flowers, rosasolis, cardimons, quibbibs, gallinggall, mace, nutmeggs, cloves, and ginger, of each a dram; one handfull of the flowers of Cowslips; and a little saffron. beat these alltogether, exept ye cowslips and saffron, and mix them with ye sack and Juice over night. and distill it leasurely in a cold still, pasteing the sides close, & let it drop upon some white sugar or sugar candy, which you must put into y^r receiving bottle. or swetten it as you use it.

For *Aqua mirabilis,* see S 269.

The name of *nutmeg* (*Myristica fragrans*) comes from Old French *nois mugue,* musky nut. It appears in English by the fourteenth century. The best comes from Mollucca (*OED*). Gerard says: "The Nutmeg is good against freckles in the face, quickneth the sight, strengthens the belly and feeble liver, taketh away the swelling in the spleen, stayeth the laske, breaketh wind, and is good against all cold diseases in the body." Also, "Nutmegs cause a sweet breath, and mend those that stinke, if they be much chewed and holden in the mouth." *Mace* is the dried outer covering of the nutmeg. While Gerard describes it, he ascribes no specific virtues to it so it apparently shared those of nutmeg.

The ultimate source of the name *saffron* (*Crocus sativus*) is Arabic *za'farān.* Saffron was known to the English at least as far back as 1200, when it appeared as *saffran,* most likely a gift of the Crusades. Gerard says: "Common or best knowne Saffron groweth plentifully in Cambridge-shire, Saffron-Waldon, and other places thereabout, as corne in the fields." As to its virtues: "But the moderat use thereof is good for the head, and maketh the sences more quicke and lively, shaketh off heavy and drowsie sleepe, and maketh a man merry. Also Saffron strengtheneth the heart, . . . opens the lungs, and removeth obstructions." And, as Dioscorides taught, "it is also good against a surfet." (See S 302.)

Sellandine is celandine (S 269); the other herbs are treated under their respective names.

Swetten is not an error. *Swette* was a Kentish fifteenth-century form of *sweet*; there are other evidences of this form in our manuscript, one of which was corrected. Actually, the single *e* forms were rather more common than the double *e* until the sixteenth century, particularly in the comparative forms, as *swetter* and *swettest*. The persistence of the single *e* forms may tell us something about the pronunciation. Also, *exept* is a bona fide form. For dram, see S 70.

---

272   TO MAKE AQUIMIRABELIS

Take 6 pintes of good white wine, or else sack, and two pintes of Aquavite or Aquicompesita, and two pintes of the Juice of Sellandine. then take cloves, mace, cardimons,* seeds, ginger, and gallinggal, nutmeggs, quibbibs, and mellilot, of each of these, two drams. beat them well to powder and mingle all these ingredients together, and then still them in A cold still very leasurely. & let not your still or fire goe out, night nor day, till you have done. let it drop on sugar, as above mentioned [or sweeten] it as you use it.

Aquicompesita, properly *aqua composita*, is any compounded or medicated spirits. See *Aqua miribilis*, S 269 and 271.

---

273   TO MAKE AQUECELESTIS

Take of cinnamon 6 ounces; cloves one dram; nutmeggs one dram & a halfe; ginger 2 drams & a halfe; gallinggall one dram & a halfe; quibebs 2 drams; callamus roots one dram. bruise all these & keep them in a paper. then take of bittony & sage flowers, of each one handfull; margerum & penny royall, the like quantety. bruise all these hearbs. then take of the powders of arromaticum rosatum,† 3 drams; diumbr[e],

* There is a comma in the original. Perhaps the scribe intended to write *anny seeds*.
† Written *rosarum*.

diamargariton frigidum, diamascum dulce, of each a dram & halfe. you must put all these into A gallon of ye spirit of wine, or If y^t cannot be compos'd, in[to] white wine & 2 quarts of brandy, & steep them in it 3 dayes & 3 nights. shake them well every day, & then distill it in a limbeck. & when it is distilld, you must hang halfe an ounce of yellow sanders in it with 20 grayns of musk & amber. & when you us[e] it, sweeten it with sugar.

Aquecelestis, properly *aqua celestis* or heavenly water, is one of the compounded waters (see S 269). It appears to be an anti-depressant, or was so considered.

Cloves (*Caryophyllus aromaticus*) are from Molucca. *Cloue* comes from French *clou de girofle,* because of its resemblance to a nail. It is fairly clear how *girofle* came from Greek *caryophyllon* (Robert); what is tantalizing is that Gerard claims that the classical Greeks did not know the spice. He also tells us that in India it was called *Calafur* and that the Mauritanians called it *Charumfel.* The spice seems to have entered both medicine and cookery in England at the time of the Crusades.

Gerard says that it is hot and dry in the third degree, and that "The Portugall women that dwell in the East Indies draw from the Cloves . . . a certaine liquor by distillation, of a most fragrant smell, which comforteth the heart, and is of all Cordialls the most effectuall." He also claims that, "The weight of four drams of the pouder of Cloves taken in milke procureth the act of generation." But should one weigh it on apothecaries' scales where 4 drams is equivalent to ½ ounce (see S 70), or on common scales where 4 drams would equal only ¼ ounce? *Quel drame!*

Gerard says that, "The true *Calamus Aromaticus* [possibly the Sweet-scented Lemon Grass of Malabar] groweth in Arabia, and likewise in Syria." *Acorus calamus,* or *sweet rush,* was the accepted substitute and was used as far back as Dioscorides. "It provoketh urine, helpeth the paine in the side, liver, spleen, and brest; convulsions, gripings, and burstings . . . helpeth much against poison . . . and all infirmities of the bloud," according to Gerard. It was also used to "provoke womens naturall accidents."

Arromaticum rosatum is a powder containing *red Roses* among its some 15 ingredients; it was highly popular and was sold in the apothecary shops. Culpeper gives the prescription in *A Physical Directory,* 1651, and claims that it "strenthens the Brain, Heart, and stomach."

Diumbre, rather *Diambra,* another ancient compound, is based on ambergris (see S 20) as is indicated by its name, and some 16 other ingredients. In the *Directory,* Culpeper claims that it strengthens the brain and "causeth mirth."

Diamargariton frigidum is another ancient compound of some 25 ingredients, among them ivory and the requisite powdered pearl. (*Margariton* means pearl [for medical virtues, see S 308]; *dia* is Greek, meaning composed of or based on, and was early taken over in classical Latin medical language as a combining prefix.) Culpeper gives the formula in the *Directory;* for once, even he is skeptical of its virtues and says that it is much too costly. The ingredients were all regarded as cold, some dangerously so; its primary use was against fevers.

Diamascum dulce, which Culpeper calls *Diamascu dulcus* (surely in error), is another ancient compound powder of over 20 ingredients, including musk, the characterizing ingredient. Culpeper claims that "it wonderfully helps afflictions of the brain, that come without a Feaver . . . [and] sadnesse without a cause."

Yellow sanders is citron sandalwood (*Santalum freycinetianum*). The word, usually in the plural, appears as *Saundres* about 1330 and is directly from Old French *sandre;* its ultimate source is Sanskrit by way of Arabic *çandal.* (See *red sanders,* S 186.) Gerard writes: "*Avicen* [Ibn Sina, the great Arab physician of the early eleventh century] affirmeth it to be good for all passions of the heart, and maketh it glad and merry."

---

274   TO MAKE ROSASOLIS

> Take licorish, 8 ounces; anny seeds & carroway seeds, of each an ounce; raysons stoned & dates, of each 3 ounces; nutmeggs, ginger, cinnamon, & mace, of each halfe an ounce; gallinggall, A quarter of an ounce; quibebs, one dram; figgs, 2 ounces. bruise these & distill them with a gallon of Aquavity, as you doe aquicellesti[s], but when it is distilld, you must culler it with the hearb rosasoliss, or for want of it with alkenet roots.

Rosa solis, the cordial or liqueur, was originally flavored with the herb; it was still popular in the seventeenth century, but lost favor and is now only historical. The correct form for the herb (*Drosera rotundifolia*) was *ros solis,* literally sun dew, a common name, but the *ros* became assimilated to *rosa,* much as happened with rosemary. Gerard says that the distilled water drawn from *Sun-Dew* "is of a glittering yellow colour like gold," and that *Rosa Solis* "strengtheneth and nourisheth the body." He also claims: "Cattell of the female kind are stirred up to lust by eating even of a small quantity [of the herb].

Aquauity was a popular name for *aqua vitae*. (See S 269.)

Alkenet, *Alkanna tinctoria*, formerly *Alkanna spuria*, to distinguish it from Arab *al-hennā* or *al-kanna.* The European alkanet was also called *wilde Buglosse* by Gerard. He reports: "The roots . . . are used to color sirrups, waters, gellies, & such like infections [confections] as Turnsole is. . . . The Gentlewomen of France do paint their faces with these roots, as it is said."

Other herbs and spices are discussed under their respective names. For medicinal waters, see S 269.

---

275   TO MAKE DOCTOR STEEPHENS HIS CORDIALL WATER

Take a gallon of ye best gascoyne wine; then take cloves, ginger, gallinggall, cinnamon, & nutmeggs, graynes, anny seeds, fennell seeds, carraway seeds, of each a dram. then take wilde time, lavender, sage, mints, hysope, red roses, garden time, pellitory of ye wall, & rosemary, of each one handfull. bray the hearbs small, & stamp ye spices alltogether very small & put all into your wine & cover it close for 12 hours, except when you stir it, which must be often. distill it in A limbeck, & keep ye first water by it selfe, it beeing ye strongest. but of ye second sort, you may drink A greater quantety.

As mentioned elsewhere, *cordial* was applied to medicines, food, or beverages that were considered invigorating or comforting to the heart, literally. *Cordial* was being used in the figurative sense at the time, but the physiological sense, now replaced by *cardiac*, was predominant. I discuss the good doctor and the virtues of his cordial water in S 276. For medicinal waters, see S 269.

Gascoyne is a seventeenth-century form of *Gascon*, according to *OED*. (Actually, it appeared a good deal earlier, see S 276, showing once again the pitfalls of taking first citations as necessarily the first.) Boorde, in 1542, wrote that, "The chefe towne of Gascony is Burdiouse." Popularly, Bordeaux wines were included among Gascon wines, in fact were Gascon wines virtually, so that it is difficult to know with certainty what sort of wine is meant.

Graynes are grains of Paradise (*Amomum meleguetta*) from West Africa, hence the popular name, *Ginny graynes* (*OED*). Gerard says: "They comfort and warm the weake cold and feeble stomack, help the ague, and rid the shaking fits, being drunk with Sacke." They were tremendously popular in English medieval cookery but by the time of Elizabeth, one rarely encounters them outside of medicine, and that was declining. They are a warm and aromatic spice, perhaps a bit like cardamum but more pungent.

Of *wilde time* (*Thymus serpyllum*), Gerard says that "boiled in wine and drunke, [it] is good against the wamblings and gripings of the belly, . . . bringeth down the desired sicknesse, . . . stayeth the hicket, . . . helpeth the Lethargie, frensie, and madnesse, and stayeth the vomiting of bloud."

The flowers of *lavender* (*Lavandula vera*), mixed with spices, "and given to drinke in the distilled water thereof, doth help the panting and passion of the heart, prevaileth against giddinesse, turning, or swimming of the braine," according to Gerard. *Lavandula spica*, or French lavender, was considered particularly effective against headache.

Sage (Salvia officinalis) was revered down through the ages for its medicinal virtues. Gerard says: "Sage is singular good for the head and braine; it quickneth the sences and memory, [and] strengthneth the sinews." He reports that Agrippa called it the *Holy-herbe* because it "maketh [women] fruitful [and] it retaineth the birth."

Of *pellitory of the wall* (*Parietaria officinalis*), Gerard writes: "Pellitory of the wall boiled, and the decoction of it drunken, helpeth such as are vexed with an old cough, the gravell and stone, and is good against the difficulties of making water."

---

276   THE VERTUES OF THIS WATER

This water comforts ye vitall spirits, it preserveth ye Joynts, & helpeth inward disseases comeing of cold, it is good against ye shaking of ye palsie, it cureth ye contraction of ye sinews, it helpeth conception in women y^t are barren, it killeth worms in ye body, it comforteth ye stomack, it is good for ye cold dropsie & stone in ye bladder & in ye reynes, it helpeth a stinking breath. and whosoever useth this water sometimes, but

not too often, it preserveth theyr health & causeth them
to look young.

I have noted perhaps two score recipes for *Doctor Steephens Cordial
Water*. The earliest is in Thomas Cogan's *The Haven of Health*, 1584,
and the latest in E. Smith's *The Compleat Housewife*, first American
edition, 1742 (and undoubtedly in later editions). No seventeenth-
century book on *Physicke*, or household medicine, was complete
without it; it was the Bayer's aspirin of its day and its use spanned
two centuries. The difference between Cogan's recipe and that of
our manuscript amounts to this: ours omits oregano and camomile
but substitutes hyssop. *Gascoyne* is spelled the same, as are most
of the ingredients; this is more remarkable than one might think.
The differences in language are trifling; the list of virtues is virtually
identical except that a copyist nodded and wrote "worms in y^e^
body," rather than "in the bellie" (the latter being correct). And
the copyist cut things short and omitted the final and most persuasive virtue: "It preserved Doctor Stevens that he lived 98 yere."
I have not been able to further identify him except that Markham,
in *The English Hus-wife*, 1615, claims to present the recipe as given
to the Archbishop of Canterbury by Stevens "a little before the
death of the said Doctor." It is possible. The language of Markham's version is actually more archaic than that of Cogan's (published, nevertheless, 31 years later), and it contains pennyroyal,
which appears in neither Cogan's recipe nor ours. Quincy, in *Pharmacopoeia Officinalis*, 1720, felt it useful to give the formula, saying
that it was still much prescribed, but that many omitted pennyroyal, thus robbing the medication of a principal ingredient. I am
persuaded that our recipe was copied from Cogan's book, or that
the two came from a common source; such differences as exist are
easily accounted for by successive copyings. (See the two recipes
for *Honey of Roses*, S 73 and 249, for example.)

---

277 TO MAKE ANOTHER OF DOCTOR
STEEPHEN[S] HIS HOT CORDIALL
WATERS

Take rose leavs, one dram; burrage, buglose, & violet,
& rosemary flowers, of each a dram and an halfe;
spiknard, a dram; cinnamon, 2 ounces; ginger, one
ounce; cloves & nutmegg, of each halfe an ounce;
cardomans, one dram; pepper, 3 drams; anny seeds,
carraway seeds, & fennell seeds, of each an ounce;

lignum alloes, halfe a dram; corrall & pearl in fine
powder, of each a dram. bruise these & put them in A
pottle of aquavity & a quart of sack, & use them in
every respect as you doe aquicelestis.

True *spikenard* is *Nardostachys jatamansi*, or *Indian Nard*, from which
an aromatic, balsamic ointment is obtained (*OED*). Johnson says
that it "dries up the defluxions that trouble the belly and intrails,
as also that molest the head and brest." Spike, or French Lavender,
was also commonly called *spikenard*, but it is not listed with the
other flowers, and this arrangement is rather strictly followed.

Pepper, apparently *Piper nigrum*, which is the pungent aromatic peppercorn so familiar to us in the kitchen. It was known
in England from early times and it is thought that the Romans
brought it. One Old English form was *pipor*. Gerard has this to say:
"All Pepper heateth, provoketh urine, digesteth, draweth, disperseth, and clenseth the dimnesse of the sight, as *Dioscorides*
noteth." The best is thought to come from Malabar. (More often,
it is *long pepper* that entered medicinal preparations, but it was
always specified.)

Lignum alloes, or *Lign-aloes*, the East Indian *Agalloch*, genus
Aloe. (The bitter aloe, Pomet tells us, was administered in *Purging
Pills*, never in potions, "by reason of its intense Bitterness.") The
wood of this sweet aloe is commended by Gerard "in dysenteries
and pleurisies; and put also into divers cordiall medicines and
antidotes as a prime ingredient." Several authorities warn that it
was often counterfeited.

For medicinal waters, see S 269; for cordial waters, S 275.
The remaining herbs and spices are treated under their respective
names.

---

278   TO MAKE THE PLAGUE WATER

Take of draggons one pound; of avens, woormwood,
sage, pimpernell, hearb of grace, may weed, muggwort,
sorrell, bittony, egrimony, rosasolis, tormant[il],
scabious, fetherfue, burnet, sellandine, cardus
benedictus, of each a pound; of rosemary, 2 pound; &
ellycomepane roots, halfe a pound, slyced. chop all
these small & put them into a great earthen or brass
pot. & put as much white wine into ye hearbs as will
cover them, & swim an Intch above ye hearbs. let it

stand thus 3 dayes, then distill it in A common still,
and save the first comeing of by it selfe, and the next
by it selfe. but ye last will be very weak, which you
may give a little childe, sweetned with sugar. or mix it
with ye strongest at y^r pleasure.

We have here two prescriptions that were considered especially
efficacious against the plague. Most of these medicinal waters (see
S 269) were thought to ward off pestilence, among other virtues,
but in time of plague, stronger medicine was resorted to. Plague
was an ever present threat in the sixteenth and seventeenth centuries; whether or not the preventive measures accomplished their
ends is something else again, but there was nothing paranoid in
people's preoccupation with these measures. (Herbs not listed here
are discussed elsewhere under their respective names.)

Auens (*Geum urbanum*) or *Wood Avens*, was more popularly
called *Herb Bennet*, which comes from Old French *herbe beneite*,
blessed herb (*OED*). Gerard says: "The decoction of Avens made
in wine is commended against cruditie or rawnesse of the stomacke, [and] paine of the Collicke."

The *hearb of grace* is an obsolete name for *rue* (*Ruta graveolens*). Gerard reports: "Rue or Herb grace provokes urine, [and]
brings downe the sickness. . . . It is a remedy against the inflammation and swelling of the stones, proceeding of long abstinence
from venerie . . . [and] is good against all evill aires, the pestilence
or plague."

Of *may weed* (*Anthemis cotula*), Gerard says that "The
whole plant stinketh . . . May-weed is not used for meat nor
medicine . . . notwithstanding, it is commended against the infirmities of the mother, seeing all stinking things are good against
those diseases."

A popular name for *mugwort* (*Artemisia vulgaris*) was *moth-
erwort*. From Gerard we learn that "*Dioscorides* writeth, That it
bringeth downe the termes, the birth, and the afterbirth."

Of *sorrel* (*Rumex acetosa*), Gerard says: "It cooleth an hot
stomacke, moveth appetite to meat, tempereth the heate of the
liver, and openeth the stoppings thereof." It was also used against
the ague.

Of *tormentil* (*Potentilla tormentilla*), Gerard writes: "The
leaves and roots boiled in wine . . . provoke sweat & by that means
. . . preserve the body from infection in time of pestilence." It is
also "good against choler and melancholy."

"The juice [of *scabious*] beeing drunke procureth sweat,
especially with Treacle; and it speedily consumeth plague sores,

if it be given in time, and forthwith at the beginning . . . It is thought to be forceable against all pestilent fevers." So says Gerard. He also says that, "It is reported that it cureth scabs." *Scabiosa* is not to be confused with *scabwort*; see elecampane (S 91). *Treacle* is not molasses; see S 284.

Featherfew, the popular name for *Pyrethrum parthenium,* is a corruption of *feverfew* (*OED*). Gerard affirms that "it draweth away flegme and melancholy." He also says that it is good for those who have "the turning called *Vertigo,*" and that "it procureth womens sicknes with speed."

Burnet is the popular name for genera *Sanguisorba* and *Poterium*. *OED* cautions that the old herbalists often confused this with *Pimpinella*; Gerard repeats the warning. He tells us that *Sanguisorba* is so named because "it stauncheth bleeding . . . as well inwardly taken, as outwardly applied." Eaten as salad, burnet "is thought to make the heart merry and glad, as also being put into wine." Burnet frequently replaced borage in the tankard (S 88).

Carduus benedictus, the Blessed Thistle, is now classified *Cnicus benedictus*. Gerard informs us that, "The powder of the leaves . . . is very good against the pestilence, if it be received within 24 houres after the taking of the sicknesse. [It] healeth the griping paines of the belly, killeth and expelleth wormes . . . is excellent good against the French disease, and the quartaine ague." Curiously, Gerard insists that it is not a thistle; here, he was in disagreement with both the old herbalists and modern botanists.

---

279   A CORDIALL WATER GOOD AGAINST THE PLAGUE, SURFITS, OR ANY OTHER SICKNESS

Take ye roots of scordium, ellycompane, tormentill, zedary,* of each halfe an ounce; of angelico & gentisin roots, of each a quarter of an ounce; A little handfull of marrygolds, flowers & leavs; halfe an ounce of harts horne; & a litle licorish slyced. then take sellandine, rosemary, red sage, rue, rosasolis, baum, dragons, egrimony, bittony, scabious, wormwood, mugwort, & penny royall, of each one handfull. wash & dry ye hearb[s] in a clean cloth very well, & wash & slit ye roots y^t are to be washed, & ye other scrape. then put

---

* Written *zedany.*

them all into a gallon of sack or white wine, or halfe y^e
one and halfe ye other. soe let them stand in A deep
earthen pot close covered for 2 dayes & 2 nights. then
distill it leasurely, & put into ye glass y^t it runs into,
some white or brown sugar candy; less then halfe a
pound of sugar candy will serve all ye quantety. draw
about a quart at ye first of ye strongest and keep it by it
selfe, & soe ye second and third by themselves. y^e
strongest is for strong persons & ye weakest for
chilldren new borne. it is very good for convultion fits,
giveing this werme.* you must distill it in may or June.
you may mix in ye water for old persons, A little
alkermis & sirrup of clove Jilleflowers to make it more
cordiall, & for women y^t lie in, & for sick per[sons].

A surfeit is an overindulgence. For these medicinal and plague
waters, see S 269, 275, and 278. Herbs not discussed here are to
be found elsewhere under their respective names.

Of *scordium*, or Water-Germander (*Teucrium scordium*),
Gerard says that "it draweth out of the chest thicke flegme and
rotten matter," and that it is given with success to people "that
have the small pocks, measles, or purples, or any other pestilent
sicknesse whatsoever, even the plague it selfe."

Zedoary is an aromatic tuberous root of *Curcuma*, of the
Zingiberaceae. The name comes from Arabic *zedwār* (*OED*). Gerard
claims that it "stops laskes, resolves the Abscesses of the wombe,
staies vomiting, [and] helps the Collicke." Johnson adds that it
"is much used in Antidotes against the plague, and such like con-
tagious diseases."

A popular name for *gentian* (*Gentiana*) was *Felwoort* (*OED*).
Gerard says: "It is excellent good, as *Galen* saith, when there is
need of attenuating, purging, clensing." It was also commended
"for such as are burst, or have fallen from some high place: [and]
for such as have evill livers and bad stomackes."

Alkermes, the Kermes or Scarlet Grain. It is an insect, the
female of *Coccus ilicis*. The word comes from Arabic *al-qirmiz* (*OED*).

* Possibly an error, although one Old English form was *wearm*.

408

280 TO MAKE THE LADY ARMYTAGES CORDYALL WATER

Take sage, sellandine, rosemary, wormwood, rosasolis, muggwort, pimpernell, draggons, scabious, egrimony, baum, sullendine, cardus benedictus, bittony flowers & leaves, centery [tops (?)] & flowers, marrygold flowers & leavs, of each of these a good handfull. then take ye roots of tormentill, Angelico, Elicompane, licorish, very clean scraped, of each halfe an ounce. let all ye hearbs be washd & layd on a clean linnen cloth till they are dry. shread them all together, ye root & all. then put them in a gallon of white wine & let them steep in an earthen pot, well leaded. soe let them remaine close covered 2 dayes & 2 nights, stirring them alltogether every day once. then distill it in an ordinary still (& not a limbeck)* with a gentle fire, reserving A pin[te] of ye first running by it selfe, & a quart of ye second running by it selfe, close stoped with corks & tyed about with a leather. close y^r still well with paste. If y^r still be not large enough, keep two a goeing day & night with a temperat[e] fire, till it be distilled of. of ye first running of thi[s] water, 2 spoonfulls may be given to a man or woma[n], though shee be with childe; & of ye second sort, you may give as much to a weak person; & ye third sort is fit for young chilldren. this is proper to give in any [sirrup (?)] or to mix in Julips, swetned with sugar candy or sugar.

For these medicinal waters, see S 269. Herbs not discussed here can be found elsewhere under their respective names. (The scribe did not notice that *celandine* is listed twice.) "Though shee be with childe," would seem to indicate that physicians of the day were at least as aware of possible harmful effects of medications on the fetus as are those of today.

Centaury is one of two gentianaceous plants of *Centaurium*, whose medical properties of wound healing are said to have

---

* Scribe's parentheses.

been discovered by Chiron the Centaur (*OED*), the mentor of the legendary Greek physician Aesculapius. Gerard tells us that Theophrastus listed *Centauria* among his "*Panaces* or All-heales." *Small Centorie* "helpeth the yellow jaundise, and likewise long and lingering agues: it killeth the wormes in the belley; to be brief, it clenseth, scoureth . . . and doth effectually performe whatsoever biting things can," Gerard says. The nomenclature of *Centaurium* has been in disarray since the sixteenth century; interestingly, Gerard seems to have been correct, but there is no way of knowing which herbalist the writer of this recipe was following. The various plants to which the name was been applied, however, were ascribed medical virtues not unlike these, so all was well.

Iulip or julep, was a drink, often sweetened as a vehicle for medication. The word comes, by way of French *julep*, from Arabic *julāb*, which in turn came from Persian *gul* and *āb*, rose water (*OED*). So that our own Southern mint julep, laced with bourbon, had medicinal beginnings. For *swetned*, see *swetten*, S 271.

Leaded means glazed; it is obsolete in this sense.

---

281 A CORDIALL WATER

Take burrage & buglos flowers, as many as will [fill]* a still, & put thereto as much sack & clare[t] as will wet them well. & to every pinte of water, you must put 2 ounces of white sugar candie & one grayne of ambergreece, finely beaten. ye sugar candy must be put into ye glass bottles & let ye water distill upon it very gently.

Cordial waters are discussed in S 275; also see S 269. The *sugar candy* that is called for so frequently in these recipes is given in S 100.

---

282 TO MAKE THE LORD VERNEYS VSQUEBATH

To a pottle of aquevity, take a pound of raysons of ye sun; & A pritty quantety of licorish, scraped & slyced; 6 dates, & 10 figgs slyced; two ounces of cinnamon, A little bruised. let all these lie in ye Aquavite 10 dayes,

* Supplied.

410

stir it every day 2 or 3 times, and then strayne it &
bottle it for your use.

Vsquebath, or usquebaugh, literally water of life from Irish and
Scottish Gaelic *uisge*, water, and *beatha*, life (*OED*). (*OED* does not
speculate on whether this may have been the Gaelic translation of
aqua vitae.) It is, of course, the word that has given us *whisky*
(Scottish) and *whiskey* (Irish), but that word did not appear until
the eighteenth century, according to *OED*.

As can be seen, this is a medicinal water and has no
relationship whatsoever with any whiskey today. See S 269. Another recipe for *usquebaugh* follows.

---

283   TO MAKE VSQUEBATH

Put in A pound of raysons of ye sun, stoned & slyced,
into a quart of aquavite. & slyce in an ounce of licorish,
& an ounce of cinnamon, 4 dates, as many figgs slyced,
A few carraway seeds bruised; all these must ly in steep
10 dayes, & be stired 3 or 4 times a day. then strayne it
& put it into glasses for y^r use.

---

284   TO MAKE TREACLE WATER

Take one ounce of harts horne shaved, & boyle it in 3
pintes of faire water till it comes to a quart, then let it
stand till it be cold. y^n put to it 6 pintes of white wine
& 3 pintes of red ros[e] water. y^n take halfe a pinte of
ye Juice of green wallnuts; it must be ye Juice of ye husk
of ye wallnut. then take of ye Juice of ye hearb of grace,
baum, & cardus, of each halfe a pinte; a pinte of
rosemary water. for flowers,* take rosemary, sage,
buglos, burage, bittony, marrigolds, & cowslips, of each
2 ounces; of angelico leavs, a quarter of a pound; and
halfe a pound of green citron slyced; one ounce of y^e
roots of Elicompane, tormentill, cyprus, of each an
ounce. slyce ye apothycarys roots, & then take a pound
of ye best old treacle, & a pinte of ordinary treacle.

* Written *frowers*.

A Cordiall water x

Take burrage & buglos flowers as many as
will a still, & put thereto as much sack & clove
as will wet them well, & to euery pinte of water
you must put 2 ounces of white sugar candie
& one grayne of ambergreece finely beeten, y
sugar candy must be put into y glass bottles & let
y water distill upon it uery gently.

To make the Lord verneys
Vsquebath +

282

To a pottle of aquauity take a pound of ray
sens of y sun, & A pritty quantety of licorish
scraped & slyced 6 dates, & 10 figgs slyced two
ounces of cinnamon A litle bruised, Let all
these lie in y Aquauite 10 dayes, stir it euery
day 2 or 3 times, and then strayne it &
botle it for your use.

To make vsquebath +

283

Put in A pound of raysons of y sun stoned &
slyced into a quart of aquauite & slyce in an
ounce of licorish, & an ounce of cinnamon 4 dates
as many figgs slyced, A few carraway seeds bruised, all these must ly in steep 10 dayes & be stired
3 or 4 times a day, then strayne it & put it
into glasses for y use.

infuse all these together, & let it stand 24 hours in an earthen vessill* close covered. then distill it in a close cold still with a gentle fire. it will be neere a weeke in stilling, for If you still it suddenly with a soft fire, you spoyle it. ~~~~~~~~~~~~~~~~~~~~~~~~~~~~~

this water is good to nourish the spirits, & it is good for sounding and fainting fits, for worms, & for bringing out ye small pox, or for any other infection[s]. to be taken 3 spoonfulls at a time, warme, with a little sugar. & in danger, give 4 grayns of beazar stone wth this water. this is effectuall for ye disseases of the s[pleen (?) If] 2 spoonfulls be taken morning & evening. [in time of(?)] contagion, take 3 spoonfulls, & sweat after it.

Treacle, a sovereign remedy, appeared in Old English unchanged from Old French *triacle*, which in turn came from Late Latin *triaca*, antidote for a venomous bite (*OED*). A treacle is alexipharmic, a broad spectrum cure-all. The fact that the various medicinal qualities of the great number of ingredients (up to 30 and more) might cancel each other out, seems not to have arisen. There were a number of treacles of known composition, the origin of which may have reached back into antiquity; the *treacle of Andromachus*, attributed to Nero's physician, may have been Greek, for example. Several cities in Italy produced treacle down through the centuries, with *Venice treacle* (purportedly the formula of Andromachus) having been the most reputed and correspondingly costly. Treacles were electuaries, of the consistency of heavy honey, which was the customary vehicle. *London treacle*, a relative newcomer, was of a far more common sort, compounded of indigenous ingredients such as herbs and roots for the most part. It was, or came to be, concocted with molasses, the byproduct of sugar refining which was becoming cheap as a result of England's expanding sugar colonies. Considering the date, I believe *London treacle* to be what is meant by *ordinary treacle* here; also, this was a medicinal water and the medicated syrup seems far more likely than plain molasses. Ebbing faith in medieval nostrums during the seventeenth century quite likely made the change in designation of *treacle* from the medicinal *London treacle* to what Americans call molasses a gradual and almost unremarked one. For more on *treacle*, see C 205.

* Corrected from *uessell*, or vice versa.

On walnuts, Gerard notes: "The outward green husk of the Nuts hath a notable binding faculty." Also, see S 72. *Cardus* is *Carduus benedictus*, S 278.

Cyprus was a common corruption for sweet cyperus or English galingale, with an early example appearing as *cyprys* for *cyperus* in Harleian MS. 279, about 1430. Its position among the roots, a convention in listing fairly strictly adhered to in prescriptions, even in our manuscript, leaves little doubt. (Cypress roots appear not to have entered medicine.) For English galingale, see S 269.

The apothecary was the licensed seller of certain nonperishable items such as spices, drugs, comfits, and preserves. He also compounded drugs, a meaning that continued some time after the first became obsolete (*OED*).

Sounding means swooning, from sounding in the ear. The *bezoar* stone is discussed in S 304. *Frowers* (in error for flowers) is a sixteenth-century form of *froe*, a cleaving or pruning tool (*OED*). For medicinal waters, see S 269.

---

285   TO MAKE COCK WATER

Take A red cock & pull it alive, and whip it till it be dead allmoste. then cut him in 4 quarters while he is alive, & drayn him well from bloud with A cloth. then take of penny royall, of pimpernell, of broad time, & rosemary, of each one handfull; 2 pound & a quarter of raysons of ye sun, or currans rather, well piked & rubed in a cloth but not washed; a quarter of a pound of dates cut in slyces from ye stones; and as many burrage, buglos, or cowslip flowers, or clove Jilliflowrs, according to ye season of ye year, as you can get, or about halfe A handfull of each. then put ye cock into y^r still, the bone side to ye bottom; next of all ye hearbs; after ye currans, & strow ye dates all about the currans; & cover all over with leaf gold. then into this, you must poure A pottle of sack & let it stand all night in ye still close luted. after, set ye still in goeing, & let it drop into a glass wherein is 4 ounces of white sugar candy finely beaten. when this is stilled, it must be mixed alltogether

in one, & sweeten it more with sugar. it must be stilld
very leasurely. & drink of it 5 or 6 spoonfulls at a time,
morneing and evening, for it is very restorative &
excellently good for A consumption.

Thomas Cogan gives a virtually identical recipe in *The Haven of
Health* that starts: "Take a red cocke, that is not old, dresse him,
& cut him in quarters . . ." In 1584, it no longer seemed necessary
to whip him and cut him while still alive; there are slight changes
in the list of herbs, but the raisins, the currants, the dates, and the
magical gold leaf—laid down in precisely the same way—are all
there. Doctor Cogan's recipe is certainly less barbaric; ours betrays
a remembrance of sacrifice and witchcraft; only the incantations
are lacking. The physician noted that, "Cockrels are verie convenient for a weake stomach." Male birds were all considered more
restorative than hens. As to why *red* cocks are specified in all cock
water recipes (of which there are many), I can only speculate that
it was part of the spell.

To *pull* is to pluck (see S 268). Gerard says that *Great Broad
leaved Time* has the same attributes as garden thyme (S 246). For
the virtues of gold in medicine, see S 70. For *consumption,* see S
268. *Luted* means pasted or sealed.

---

286   TO MAKE A WATER OR DRINK MOSTE
EXCELLENT FOR A CONSUMPTION

Take ye hearb called rossasolis, as much as will fill a
pottle pot. wash it not in noe wise, but put it into A
large vessell with a pottle of aquavity & stop it close for
3 dayes & 3 nights. & on ye 4th day, strayne it thorough
A clean cloth in A glass or pewter Pot. then put therein
a pound of sugar beaten small; & halfe a pound of
licorish dryed & beaten to fine powder; & halfe a
pound of dates, ye stones beeing taken out & cut in
small pieces. y^n mingle all these together, & stop y^e
glass soe close y^t noe ayre get therein. drink of this A
spoonfu[ll] & halfe or 2 spoonfulls, fasting, in Ale, & y^e
like quantety at night when you goe to bed. the party
y^t useth this medicin 3 dayes together, shall finde more
benefit by it then probably they may imagin[e], eyther
for a consumption or any other weakness. this cured

415

one m^r stobs of Westminster when moste of ye doctors in London had given him over for A dying man. this receipt was sent him by an outlandish man, & in 3 days drinking of it, he walkd upon his feet, & in A short time, with ye continuance of it, he was restored to his perfect health. when you gather this rosasolis, pluck it out of ye ground by ye stalk & put it into a glass or pewter pot, & ye leavs will retayne their full vertue, [but if y]ou touch ye leavs with y^r hand, it is reputed [that] they loose much of their vertue.

Medicinal waters are discussed in S 269. This is a version of *rosasolis* (see S 274), but a good deal earlier and more medicinal. For *consumption*, see S 268.

Herb came into Old English directly from Old French as *erbe*; gradually, the initial *h* from the Latin became accepted in English (as in French), but it remained mute in England until the nineteenth century.

Outlandish is used in the literal sense of foreign, not of this land. (It could refer to someone from a remote part of England, but this is unlikely.)

---

287   TO MAKE SURFIT WATER OF POPPIES

Take poppies that grow in wheat when they look very red, ye quantety of a peck pickt very well from ye blacks & seeds. then put them into a glass bottle & put to them one quart of aquavity or brandy. slyce therein 3 large nutmeggs, then put in allsoe one quarter of a pound of raysons of ye sun stoned. put them to y^r flowers, & corke them downe very close, & ty a leather on them, & set them in a window where ye sun cometh, for 10 dayes, shakeing them every day once or twice a day. then strayne them thorough a fine cloth, & put to ye water a quarter of a pound of lofe sugar. then bottle it & stop it close, but before, put to it a little slyced licorish & a few bruised anny seeds, knit up in A laune ragg, & soe keep it for your use.

Surfeit water was a remedy for overindulgence, a common complaint of the day, as of ours, judging by the number of remedies proposed. Medicinal waters are discussed in S 269. Another surfeit water is given in S 288.

These poppies (*Papaver*) would seem to be what Gerard calls "Corn-Rose or wilde Poppy," the flowers of which were "of a beautifull and gallant red colour." Curiously the medicinal virtues listed by him seem to have little to do with countering a surfeit. Other authorities thought differently, however, and as late as the first American edition of *The Art of Cookery*, 1805, Hannah Glasse includes half a peck of poppies in her recipe for *Surfeit-Water*. Perhaps the sedative effect, which I understand to be very mild, was thought to be helpful; in any event, the poppy was usually combined with other ingredients that were considered efficacious in treating headache, sweetening breath, or countering flatulence.

---

288   TO MAKE THE SURFIT WATER

Take a peck of poppy flowers, clip them & cut ye blacks
clean out, & steep them in 3 quarts of Aquavity, then
strayne out y^r poppies & put in 2 quarts of ye best sack,
4 ounces of raysons of ye sun stoned, as much figgs
slyced, 2 ounces of licorish slyced, 20 cloves, 20 cornes
of whole pepper. let all these be put into a bottle &
sweetned wth sugar. put in 2 ounces of annyseeds
bruised, & soe let y^m stand for a moneth, then strayne
it, & bottle it up in glasses, & corke it close, & soe keep
it fo[r your use].

---

289   TO MAKE CINNAMON WATER

Take a gallon of muskadine, malmsey, or sack & put it
in A vessill y^t may be close covered, & put to it into y^e
vessell a pound of bruised cinnamon. let it stand 3
dayes, & every day stir 2 or 3 times. then put it in a
limbeck of glass, stoped fast. set it in a brass pot full of
water, & put hay in ye bottome & about ye sydes. then
make ye pot seeth, & let it distill in to a glass kept as
close as may be. shift ye glass every houre after ye first

time, for ye first will be ye strongest, & ye last will be
very weak.

These medicinal waters are discussed in S 269. There are some
details of the distilling in this recipe that I do not understand. This
is the first of four recipes for cinnamon water.

Cinnamon is the fragrant inner bark of an East Indian tree,
Cinnamomum zeylanicum (*OED*). Gerard says that cinnamon water
"comforteth the weake, cold and feeble stomacke, easeth the
paines and frettings of the guts and entrailes proceeding of cold
causes, it amendeth the evill colour of the face, maketh sweet
breath, and giveth a most pleasant taste unto divers sorts of meates,
and maketh the same not onely more pleasant, but also more
wholesome." It also "bringeth down the menses, [and] prevaileth
against the bitings of venomous beasts." (Also, see S 299.)

Malmsey was a strong sweet wine, originally from Napoli
di Malvasia; Malmsey, current since the fifteenth century, was an
early corruption of the Greek place name. The name came to be
applied to any similar wine.

---

290   TO MAKE CINNAMON WATER

Put 3 quarts of red rose water & one quart of white
wine into a limbeck of glass. y^n bruise 2 pound of
cinnamon & put therein, & let it stand 12 hours in luke
warme water close stopt. then still it in water on a
gentle fire, but it may not be taken out of ye glass
reserve, the first comeing of, for it will be much y^e
better.

---

291   TO MAKE CINNAMON WATER

Take a pound of ye best cinnamon you can get, &
bruise it well. then put it into a gallon of ye best sack &
infuse it 3 dayes and three nights, and then you must
distill it as you doe your Aquecelestis.

Cinnamon is discussed in S 289; *Aquecelestis* in S 273.

292   TO MAKE CINNAMON WATER WITHOUT
DISTILLING IT

Take one quart of brandy, & halfe a dram of oyle of
cinnamon, & a pinte of water, & half[e] a pound of
white sugar. boyle ye water & sugar together, & mix y^e
oyle & sugar together, y^t is with a little of ye sugar
before you put it to ye rest. then mix them alltogether,
& set it by till it be cold. & then bottle it up.

For *oyle of cinnamon*, see S 23; for cinnamon waters, S 289.

293   TO MAKE WALLNUT WATER

Take green wallnuts before they be hard, just as you
preserve them, & bruise them in a stone morter. then
put them in a cold still & still them as you doe
rosewater. take six spoonfulls of this water in a
morning with a little sugar, or at other times. you may
take it as you have occasion. it is good against winde &
other illnesses.

Medicinal waters are treated in S 269; green walnuts in S 72.

294   TO MAKE BLACK CHERRY WATER

Take black cherries & put them in a stone morter &
bruise them, stones & all. then put them in a cold still,
& still them in it as you doe roses. this water is very
good to be taken in convultions & for ye winde.

Gerard claims that black cherries "do strengthen the stomacke, are
wholesomer than the redde Cherries, the which being dried do
stop the laske." And in addition, "The distilled water of Cherries
is good for those that are troubled with heate and inflammations
in their stomackes." For more on cherries, see S 42; for more on
these medicinal waters, see S 275.

295   TO MAKE ANGELICO WATER

Take dry cardus, A handfull; angellico roots, 3 ounces;
mirh, one dram; nutmeggs, halfe an ounce; cinnamon
& ginger, of each 4 ounces; saffr[on], a dram & halfe;
cardimons & quibbibs, gallinggall, & pepper, of each a
quarter of an ounce; mace, 2 drams; graynes, one dram;
lignum Alloes, & spiknard, Jances adoratus, of each one
dram; sage, burrage, buglos, & rosemary flowers, of
each one handfull. bruise all these & steep them in a
gallon of sack 12 hours, then distill them in A limbeck
as you doe ye rest of y^r hot waters.

Angelico is treated in S 68; medicinal waters in S 269. For *graynes*,
see S 275; *Lignum Alloes*, S 277; *Carduus benedictus*, S 278.
   Myrrh is a gum resin obtained from *Commiphora myrrha*
(*Balsamodendron*), or a tincture made of it. It is aromatic and balsamic, that is, healing and soothing. The word comes from Arabic
murr (*OED*). Culpeper, in *Pharmacopoeia Londinensis,* 1654, says:
"*Mirrh,* heats and dries, opens and softens the womb . . . [and]
helps old coughs and hoarseness." This is the myrrh of the Bible;
since it comes from the East, all manner of substitutions were
made, some fradulent.
   Iances adoratus is properly *Juncus odoratus,* now called
schoenanth or camel's hay (*Andropogon schoenangulum*). We learn
from Gerard that "This growes in Africa, Nabathaea, and Arabia,
and is a stranger in these regions. . . . It is given in medicines that
are ministred to cure the paines and griefes of the guts, stomacke,
lungs, liver, and reins, the fulnesse, loathsomenesse, and other
defects of the stomacke."

296   TO MAKE BALME WATER

Take dry baume, 3 ounces; time & penny royall, of each
an ounce; sweet fennell seeds, an ounce; nutmeggs &
ginger, of each a dram; cinnamon, 4 ounces; gallingall,
one ounce; callamu[s], & ciprus, cubbibs & pepper, of
each 2 drams; of caper roots, halfe a dram; of diptamus,

one dram. bruise all these & put them to a pottle of
sack to steep 24 houres, & then dy[s]till it in a limbeck
as you doe y^r other waters. & when you drink it,
sweeten it to [your tas]te.

True Balsam, *Balsam of Mecca*, and the Biblical *Balm of Gilead*, were
all names for the aromatic resin of *Balsamodendron*. *Balsam* appeared
in Old English, but forms of French *baume* very nearly displaced
it for centuries (*OED*). Its sweet smell and comforting and healing
properties are legendary, and *balm* retains these meanings to this
day, largely figuratively. Gerard says that taken with wine, "it
helpeth those that be asthmatick or short winded, . . . amendeth
a stinking breath, and takes away the shaking fits of the quotidian
ague." However, it is surely the herb *balm gentle* (*Melissa officinalis*)
that is wanted here. (Three ounces of the resin would be prodigal.)
Of this, Gerard says that it "driveth away all melancholy and
sadnesse," and that "the Arabians and Mauritanians affirme Balme
to be singular good for the heart."

We again face the problem of *ciprus* (see S 284). Here, the
choice is somewhat more awkward in that *gallingall* is already called
for. However, that properly refers to the exotic ingredient, and I
do believe that it is *English galingale* that is wanted here, and its
pairing with *callamus* supports this. I must note that there was no
punctuation whatsoever in this passage so that it is not beyond
the realm of possibility that *ciprus* be linked to *cubbibs* and pepper,
which would indicate *Cypress nuts*, as Gerard calls them. However,
their medicinal virtues, of a binding nature, are not in harmony
with the prescription, which is of a soothing and cheering disposition.

Caper roots are from *Capparis spinosa*, a bramble-like bush
of Southern Europe. Gerard says: "The barke of the roots of Capers
. . . profiteth much if it be given in drink, to such as have the
sciatica, palsie, or that are bursten or brused. . . . It mightily provokes urine." He cautions against overuse. (For capers, see C 7.)

Diptamus is a medieval Latin form for dittany (*Oreganum
dictamnus*) that never entered English except as *diptani* (*OED*). Gerard says that dittany "bringeth away dead children [and] procureth
the monethly termes. . . . The juyce taken with wine is a remedy
against the stinging of serpents." (The morbid reference has to do
with expelling a still-born baby or fetus.)

For medicinal waters and *cubbibs*, see S 269.

297   TO MAKE WORMWOOD* WATER

Take wormewood, 2 ounces & a halfe; bittony & sage,
of each halfe a handfull; rosemary tops, one handfull;
cinnamon, 3 ounces; & nutmeggs, halfe an ounce;
cloves & mace, halfe a dram of each; ginger, one ounce;
& gallingall, spiknard, & quibbibs, of each a dram &
halfe; of scordium, halfe A handfull. bruise all these &
put them in a bottle of sack & a pinte of aquavite, and
steep them 24 hours, & then distill them as you doe y^e
fore mentioned waters.

All ingredients are treated under their respective names. For medicinal waters, see S 269.

298   THE SEUERALL VERTUES OF SPIRITS

Spirit of roses is for opening ye lungs and healing y^e
ulserations of them, & is good for preventing y^e
infirmeties of them, & to keep ye breasts from
corrupting. to be taken in the morning, fasting, & at 4
in ye afternoon, & last at night, a good spoonfull at a
time.

Entries S 298 through 304 give the virtues of various spirits. Since
no recipes are given, I must suppose that they were normally
bought at the apothecary shop.
For roses, see S 66.

299   SPIRIT OF CINNAMON

This spirit hath bin approved for women in travell, or
after delivory, to take a spoonful at a time. it is good
when ye spirits are opressed with heaviness; it is good
in swiming or fainting fits; it is very good in a flux, if it
be mixt with spirit of mint, of each a like quantety, 2 or
3 spoonfulls [of each at a (?) t]ime.

---

* There is an ink blot following the first *o* that I believe to be a blotted
r; however, *woorm* is entirely possible (see S 278).

Trauell is travail or labor of childbirth. *Swiming* is vertigo. *Flux* is an abnormally copious flowing of blood or excrement from the bowels or other organs of the body. (*Flix* stems from the pronunciation of French *flux*.) It is an early name for dysentery. *Lask* is a looseness of the bowels, or diarrhea (*OED*).

For cinnamon, see S 289; for spirits, see S 298.

---

300   SPIRIT OF CLARY

It [is]* an excellent restorative in any kinde of
weakness, but chiefly of ye back. it is good for those y^t
are in a consumption, & preserveth those that are
incident to it. it comforteth the heart & healeth y^e
ulcerated lungs, & helpeth ye culler. it is a great
strengthener of women after delivory, takeing 2 or 3
spoonfull [morning]* and evening.

Clary is *Salvia sclarea*. Forms of *slarie* (corrupted from the Latin) appear in Old English around 1000; by the fifteenth century, the *s* had been sloughed off and various names such as *clary, clair-ye, clear-eye*, and inevitably, *Oculos Christi* (Christ's eye), were given the plant, in reference to its reputed virtues in treating eye diseases. (There is no etymological justification whatsoever.) *Clary* is occasionally applied to celandine (S 269) because it was thought to have the same medicinal virtues (*OED*). Gerard says: "The leaves of Clarie taken any manner of way, helpeth the weakenesse of the backe . . . The seed poudered and drunke with wine, stirreth up bodily lust." Mixed with honey, it "taketh away the dimnesse of the eies, and cleereth the sight." In light of this last, its best-known virtue and responsible for its popular name, it is curious that it is not mentioned among these virtues. (Helping the weakness of the back is mentioned, however.) So curious, that I give the following explanation as well, although several factors militate against it and I believe that it is the herb that is praised here. (For *consumption*, see S 268.)

   Clary is also a medicinal cordial of wine, spices, and clarified honey. It appears as *clare* (clear) in the thirteenth century (*OED*), unchanged from Old French, thus having an older and more valid claim to the name than does the herb, in a manner of speaking. There are recipes for the medication in both Old French and Middle English sources. Finally, it is made much like *Hippocras*, without the milk, but with honey (see S 258). Various forms of the

* Supplied.

drink continued into the seventeenth century. This *clary* is not a spirit, of course, but the word was often loosely used.

---

301   SPIRIT OF MINT

It is an exceeding comfortable cordiall. it helpeth ye infirmeties of ye stomack, it streng[h]eneth ye retentive facultys, it stayeth vomiting, it comforts ye spirits, & preserves from putrefaction, it expelleth winde, & helps decocktion, If 2 spoonfulls be taken morning and evening.

Decoction refers to digestion, which was considered a form of decoction or cooking. Citations in *OED* in this sense become increasingly figurative and literary from mid-sixteenth century on; the last citation is 1608.

Mint is further discussed in S 140; these spirits in S 298.

---

302   SPIRIT OF SAFFRON

It comforteth ye heart & helpeth its trembling & preventeth malignaties y^t may oppress it, it expells fumes, it openeth ye obstructions of ye spleen, & is excellent against melancholly, by taking a spoonfull in ye morning & at goeing to be[d]. it is good for women in travell, by takeing 2 or [3] spoonfulls at a time, which hath given grea[t] h[elp in] extremety.

Saffron is treated in S 271; spirits in S 298.

---

303   SPIRITS OF ROSEMARY FLOWERS

It is a good remedy for ye infirmetyes of the stomack, suppressing ye vapours assending from thence into ye head, tis good against ye appoplexey* & all dissiness of y^t kinde, it disgests crudities [crudiness]† of ye stomack, & expells winde, beeing taken morning & evening a good spoonfull.

* The letter after *x* could be a *c*.
† This word is crossed out.

Crudities refers to undigested or indigestable matter. In old phys-
iology, it referred to "imperfect concotion of the humours," according to *OED*. There is no etymological relationship between
crudities, which comes from French *crudité* (Latin *crudus*), meaning
raw, and the Old English *crud* or *crudde*, meaning curd, which may
have come from Irish *cruth*. (*Curd*, which appeared in the fifteenth
century, is a metathetic form of the older word. Various forms of
crud lingered in dialect: *cruddle*, for curdle, for example.)

Perhaps *crudities* was a polite term for indigestion and
crudiness, which can best be translated by *cheesiness*, the more popular one. In any event, the scribe saw fit to delete it in favor of
crudities. See Falstaffe's monologue on *Sherris-Sack*, which follows
(*Henry IV*, Part II, act 4, scene 1):

. . . A good Sherris-Sack hath a two-fold operation in it: it ascends me into
the Braine, dryes me there all the foolish, and dull, and cruddie Vapours
which environ it: makes it apprehensive, quicke, forgetive, full of nimble,
fierie, and delectable shapes: which deliver'd o're to the Voyce, the Tongue, which is the Birth, becomes excellent Wit. The second propertie of
your excellent Sherris, is, the warming of the Blood: which before (cold,
and setled) left the Liver white, and pale; which is the Badge of Pusillan-
imitie, and Cowardize: but the Sherris warmes it, and makes it course
from the inwards, to the parts extremes: it illuminateth the Face, which
(as a Beacon) gives warning to all the rest of this little Kingdome (Man)
to Arme: and then the Vitall Commoners, and in-land pettie Spirits, muster
me all to their Captaine, the Heart; who great, and pufft up with his
Retinue, doth any Deed of Courage: and this Valour comes of Sherris. So,
that skill in the Weapon is nothing, without Sacke (for that sets it a-worke:)
and Learning, a meere Hoord of Gold, kept by a Devill, till Sack com-
mences it, and sets it in act, and use.

---

304   SPIRIT OF BEAZOR

Beazor water is an excellent approoved antidote against
all contagions of ye plague, ye purples, small pox, or
measels. for preventing thereof 2 spoonfulls mixt with
cardus or angellico water y^t is stilld cold onely of y^e
hearbs. & for want of these waters, use possit drink,
which is provokeing towards sweat, & will expell y^e
malignaty of mallady, ye patient beeing kept
temperately warme. it is allsoe good in a violent surfet,
or when ye stomack is oppressed with winde, cold,

phleme, or any superfluity. it is good for disgestion, to
be drunk by it selfe. this is good for ye stone in y^e
kidneys by takeing 6 spoonfulls in halfe a pinte of small
beer. it hath given present ease in ye fits by remooveing
it into ye blather, & soon after caus[eth v]oydance.

Bezoar means antidote. The word is from Persian *pād-zhar*, meaning
counter-poison, by way of Arabic *bāzahr*. Specifically, it was, or
became, the *bezoar stone*, a concretion found in the stomach of
certain ruminants, expecially the wild goat of Persia (*OED*). Those
from Persia commanded very high prices; surely there must have
been a great number of less exotic concretions sold as the real
thing. Culpeper, in *Pharmacopoeia Londinensis*, 1654, says that it
"is a notable restorer of nature [and] a great cordial."

But it was the nearly magical properties of countering
poison that induced people to pay princely sums for a bezoar stone.
For several centuries now enlightened people have dismissed those
properties as superstition or outright quackery. But *Science*, the
journal of the American Association for the Advancement of Science, reported in 1979 that the bezoar stone may well have actually
absorbed poison, especially arsenic, just as the ancient physicians
said it did. (This thesis was suggested by the work of the Scripps
Institute of Oceanography in connection with certain marine algae
in tropical waters that are able to harmlessly absorb arsenates,
along with phosphates, while algae in colder waters cannot.) I do
not suggest controlled experiments, but the report does demon-
strate once again that medieval medical practices may have had
sounder foundations than we moderns would like to think.

Purples was the popular name for *purpura*, an eruption of
purplish pustules. *Blather* is a delightful sixteenth-century form of
bladder. The section on virtues of spirits starts with S 298.

---

305   THE VERTUES OF SEUERALL OYLES
         AND HOW TO MAKE THEM

Oyle of roses is good for all inflamations & swellings.
oyle of violets is of ye same nature but something
colder. oyle of Elder flowers is good for a faintness at y^e
stomack, to be anointed therewith. oyle of cowslips is
good for ye brayne to annoynt ye temples. oyle of worm
wood applyed to ye stomac[k] killeth worms. oyle of
rue is good for winde in ye side, & against blasting

which causeth swelling. Oyle of dill is good for any
strayned Joynt.

The section on medicinal oils consists of two entries. I believe that
these oils are intended for external application. *Oyle*, which comes
from Old Norman French *olie*, is a thirteenth- to seventeenth-century form (*OED*). The oil was olive oil.

For *rue*, see *hearb of grace*, S 278. Gerard says that if the
oil of rue "be ministred in clisters [rectal syringes] it expels win-
dinesse, and the torsion or gnawing paines of the guts."

Blasting was a popular name for flatulence. It should be
noted, however, that oil of rue was also said by Gerard to be
efficacious in treating St. Anthony's fire, a common name for er-
ysipelas, and that *blast* was yet another popular name for it, which
survives in dialect (*OED*).

Dill (*Anethum graveolens*) is a fragrant umbelliferous plant,
common in Europe but absent from our manuscript, except for this
mention. Gerard says: "Common oyle, in which Dill is boyled or
sunned . . . doth digest, mitigate paine, procureth sleepe, bringeth
raw and unconcocted humors to perfect digestion, and procureth
bodily lust." Nothing is said of strained joints.

The other plants are treated under their respective names.

---

306   TO MAKE ALL SORTS OF OYLS BOTH
OF HEARBS & FLOWERS

Your hearbs must be gathered [no more than (?)] 24
hours before you use them. & let them be clean pickt &
wiped with a cloth, but they must not be washed. then
take a clean earthen pot, & put in as much oyle as you
will make, & fill ye pot full of ye hear[bs] or flowers as
you would have oyle on, & set ye pot [in] a pan of hot
water, & let it boyle till it have taken out all ye strength
of ye hearbs or flower[s], which it hath done when they
have quite lost thei[r] culler. then wring them out & put
in fresh. this doe 3 times, & it is sufficient. then clear
your oy[le] in a glass (from ye hearbs) which you intend
to kee[p] it in, & put in some of ye hearbs or flowers
where of y[ou made it] & let y^m be new gathered &
dryed in a cloth [as before] mentiond.

I supplied the insert in the first line in the light of usual instructions concerning the importance of freshly gathered herbs and flowers. *Wring* means to press. See S 305 for these medicinal oils and their virtues.

---

307   DOCTOR GASCOYNS CORDIALL
         POWDER

Take seed pearl, red corrall, crabs eyes, white amber, & harts horne, crabbs toes soe far as they are black, of each an equall quantety. beat all into fine powder, then sift them all together, & make this powder into cakes or balls with ye Jelly of harts horne in which some saffron is dissolved, or rather infused. let them dry, & soe keep them for your use. it will last good 20 years. ye quanteties for a man is 10 or 12 greyns, or more, as you see occasion, & for A childe, 7 or 8 greyns is sufficient.

We have here three recipes for what were tremendously popular cordial powders. On examination, it will be found that prescriptions S 307 and 308 are for the same powder from different sources. It is instructive to list the ingredients for the Gascoyn powder as given by Quincy in *Pharmacopoeia Officinalis*, 1720: *pearls, Crabs-Eyes, red Coral, white Amber, burnt Harts-horn, Oriental Bezoar*, the *black Tips of Crabs Claws*, and *Jelly of Vipers*. Quincy notes that the powder was reputed to be alexipharmic (all-purpose anti-toxic) and a "mighty Cordial," but that he had found the entire virtue of this powder, and similar ones, to be "absorbent," an acute observation. He noted that it was still being prescribed, but this in itself indicates a waning.

Information concerning the identity of the doctors to whom various remedies are attributed is often difficult to come by, but they were practicing physicians and their prescriptions are listed in the *pharmacopoeiae* of the day. As for Doctor Gascoyn, he may or may not have been a Gascon; direct French influence in medicine dated from the Conquest, and for centuries, Montpellier was the medical center of Europe so that a French name must have been of considerable advantage in medicine.

Red coral is a hard calcareous substance consisting of the continuous skeleton secreted by marine coelenterate polyps (*OED*). Culpeper, in *Pharmacopoeia Londinensis*, 1654, informs us that "*Red Corral*, is cold, dry, and binding, [and] stops the immoderate flow of the termes, [and] bloody fluxes."

Crabs eyes, it appears, were neither eyes nor from crabs. Samuel Frederick Gray in *A Supplement to the Pharmacopoeia*, 1821, defines the substance as "A concretion found in the stomach of craw-fish, *cancer Astacus*, at the season in which they are about to change their shell." (This then accounts, at least in part, for specifying the sign of Cancer in S 308.) They seem to have been regarded as antacid and absorbent, properties assigned to crabs claws, as well. (For concretions, see *bezoar*, S 304.) Culpeper, at the time of our manuscript (listed above), claims that the powder "breaks the stone, and opens stoppings of the bowels."

White amber was the common name for spermaceti (see S 323). Culpeper says that spermaceti helps "troubles of the stomach and belly . . . [and] is good for woman newly delivered." However, in professional circles at least, it is amber, the fossil resin, that is wanted. Gray speaks of "Amber, Succinum. Carabe. The whitest is preferred for medical use . . ." (A common use was in treating gonorrhoea and leucorrhoea.) Quincy, earlier, also specified white amber, or succinum, here.

Harts horne "resists poyson, and the pestilence," according to Culpeper. (Also, see S 217.)

As for *crabbs toes*, Culpeper says: "Crab-fish, burnt to ashes . . . helps the biting of mad Dogs, and al other venemous beasts." (But see *crabs eyes*, above.) Other ingredients are discussed under their respective names.

I must specifically credit Frank Anderson for saving me from gross error on the question of *crabs eyes* and the *white amber*.

---

308 TO MAKE ye GASCOYN POWDER

Take ye claws of crabbs when ye signe is in cansur, what quantety you will. beat & searse them, & to 5 ounces of this, add 2 ounces of harts horne; & of pearle, & corrall, 2 ounces; white amber, an ounce; a quarter of an ounce of bezar, which is ye right east indian; & as much of ye bone as is found in ye heart of a frogg. beat all into fine powder & searse it, & mingle it together. & make it up into balls with gum dragon, & put in some saffron, & dry it leasurely. this powder is good against small pox, measles, feavors, [and f]its. you may ad to this as much powder of vit[riol as of (?)] Beazar.

Doctor Gascoyn's powder is discussed in S 307.

The sign of cancer rules from about June 21 to July 21. Astrological mysticism often entered into these remedies; here the magic consists of matching the crab with the constellation and its sign. However, over the centuries, there has been a decalibration in the heavens. In this case, there may have been other reasons; see *crabs eyes* in S 307.

The pearl is a nacreous substance found within the shell of certain bivalve molluscs (*OED*). Culpeper, in *Pharmacopoeia Londinensis*, 1654, says: "*Pearls*, are a wonderful strengthener to the heart . . . they restore such as are in consumption, both they and the red corral preserve the body in health and resist fevers." Not surprisingly, the most costly were considered the most efficacious.

For *bezoar*, see S 304.

The bone in the heart of a frog would be cartilagineous tissue. The bone in the heart of a stag is a *sovereign Cordiall*, according to Culpeper, and it also "resists pestilence and poyson." Quincy, in 1719, says that bone of heart was "mention'd by some old writers," but that its virtues were based on "false philsophy" (the theory of signature therapy) and it was now "justly neglected."

Vitriol was one or another of various natural or artificial sulphates of metals, especially sulphate of iron (*OED*). White vitriol was based on zinc, blue on copper, green on iron, and red was calcined green vitriol. (It should be noted that in modern usage, red vitriol is based on cobalt, but well into the eighteenth century, it was a popular term for colcothar, or red copperas. See S 310.) Pomet, in the *Compleat History of Druggs*, 1712, tells us that white vitriol inwardly "cleanses the Stomach from all Impurities, eases the Headach, stops Fluxes, and is good against *Quotidian* and *Tertian* agues." Red vitriol was also used internally "in a Loosness, Bloody Flux [and] Hemorrhages." Vitriol was not listed in the official prescription, so we cannot know which was meant.

---

309   TO MAKE DOCTOR SMITHS CORDIALL POWDER

Take crabbs claws soe far as they are black, in fine powder, 3 ounces; seed pearle, one ounce; red corr[al] in fine powder, crabbs eyes, white amber, harts horne calcin'd, of each an ounce; gallingall, angellico roots, yᵉ scull of a dead man calcin'd, of each halfe an oun[ce]; cocheneale, 2 drams. powder all these finely, & mak[e] a Jelley of 3 ounces of harts horn & 2 cast snakes

skines, in which make y^r powder into balls. & put in,
in ye makeing up, of muske, 3 grayns; ambergree[ce], 6
grayns; & saffron, halfe a dram. of this powder give 10
or 12 grayns to a man, or woman, & 5 to a child.

It will be seen that this cordial powder is not so different from that
of Doctor Gascoyn (S 307 and 308). The bezoar is missing, but we
have a touch of cannibalism to compensate; also, the snake skins
that properly belong in that formula are in this one. Quincy's
observations on the Gascoyn powder are equally apt here.

Culpeper, in *Pharmacopoeia Londinensis*, 1654, explains that
the "scull of a dead man" is that of "a Man that was never buried."
(What he means, of course, is a body that could not be buried in
consecrated soil or that would not be missed: suicides and home-
less paupers.) In *Pharmacopoeia Officinalis*, Quincy ascribes the use
of skull more to "whimsical Philosophy than any other account,"
in that it was considered appropriate to "Distempers of the Head,
chiefly." He did note that "some think it Balsamick." (See S 296.)

Cochineal is the dried bodies of the insect *Coccus cacti*,
chiefly of Mexico. It gives a brilliant scarlet dye and is used in
medicine as an antispasmodic. There was considerable confusion
over its identity and origin; OED cites Florio, who in 1598 defined
it as "a kinde of rich flie or graine comming out of India." It seems
to have been used more or less interchangeably with *alkermes* (S
279).

Cast snake skines (a fourteenth- to sixteenth-century form)
have been used in medicine from time immemorial. They appear
in the pharmacopoeia of the oldest medical work known, written
in cuneiform script on a clay tablet towards the end of the third
millennium B.C., in Sumer.* They appear in the *Papyrus Ebers*, the
ancient Egyptian work (S 70) and continued down through the
ages. *Jelly of Vipers* is called for with some frequency in English
medicine, as late as the 1720 pharmocopoeia formula for *Gascoyn
Powder* (S 307). Culpeper claims that vipers "help the vices of the
Nerves, [and] resist poyson exceedingly."

---

310   TO MAKE RED POWDER MUCH USED

Take 4 ounces of red copperis, one ounce of camphe[r].
put these into a little black pot, ye copris uppermos[t],
boyle it on a fire of charcole very easily† 3 or 4 hours.

* *History Begins at Sumer* by Samuel Kramer, 1959.
† Written *eaesily*.

cover ye cup & put a paper & a leather on it tied, & a weight, or it will fly in ye boyling. after it hath boyled 3 or 4 hours, let ye fire die of it selfe & ye cup stand till it be cold. y^n beat & searse ye powder with 4 ounces of bole armoneck,* & this will make a singuler good water for a fistula, or any sore or wound, & very good for sore eyes. an ounce will make a pott[le] of water. put an ounce of this into a pottle of spring water in a scyllet on ye fire for a quarter of an houre. then take it of to cool, & stir it. y^n put it in a bottle to sett[le]. If [the wound be] deep, use a serringe. If not, dip coten in y^e [liquid and drip it (?)] in ye wound, & lay ye whiteish playster on it.

This powder is used to make a cleansing astringent wash for open sores and wounds and also a plaster to be laid on to draw out inflammation.

Red copperis is colcothar (from Arabic *qolqotār*), the reddish peroxide of iron that remains in the retort after the distillation of sulphuric acid from iron sulphate (*OED*). Another popular name was red vitriol (see S 308). Pomet describes it in the *Compleat History of Druggs*, 1712, saying that while it occurred naturally, it was rare and reserved for use in *Venice Treacle* (see S 284). John Woodall, in *The Surgions Mate*, 1653, says: "This Colkethor is of two . . . kinds, the one is from the feces of Aqua fortis, and the other from copperas."؛ It is astringent and styptic. (Very finely powdered, it is what is better known as jewellers' rouge.)

Camphor is a whitish crystalline volatile substance, still used in pharmacopoeia. According to *OED*, all European forms of the word come directly from Arabic *kāfūr* which in turn had been preceded by Old Persian, Sanskirt, and Malay forms. Culpeper, in *Pharmacopoeia Londinensis*, 1654, says: "*Camphire*, Easeth pains of the head coming of heat [and] takes away inflammation."

Bole armeniac is an astringent reddish earth from Armenia, formerly used as an antidote and styptic (*OED*). Chaucer mentions *bol armoniak*, so that the English may have learned of it at the time of the Crusades.

A *fistula* is a long, narrow suppurating canal of morbid origin in the body (*OED*). *Playster* is plaster.

* Written *almoneck*, possibly in error.

TO MAKE PERFUMES

311   TO MAKE THE COURT PERFUME

Take 3 ounces & halfe of benjamin, & lay it a night in
steep in rosewater, then beat it fine, & take halfe a
pound of damask roses, ye whites beeing taken away.
beat them fine in a stone morter, y^n put ye benjamin to
ye roses & beat them together till it come to paste. then
take it out & mingle it with halfe a quarter of an ounce
of civit, & mould them with an ounce & halfe of sugar,
finely beaten & searsed. then* make them up into little
cakes, & lay a rose leafe on both sydes of them. then
lay them to dry on a board y^t hath noe savor, where
noe winde cometh. some will lay a little gum tragacant
into ye rosewater with ye benjamin.

We now come to the final section of our still room book, comprising
a number of perfumes, air sweeteners, *sweet waters, Pummatums,*
and other cosmetic preparations. As with sugar and the art of
working it—to say nothing of the greater proportion of the medications represented in our manuscript—it was the Arabs who
introduced perfumery and the requisite ingredients to Europe, as
Shakespeare well knew but we have forgotten.

From a fourteenth-century Catalan manuscript, *Libre de
Totes Maners de Confits* (see S 158), I refer to a formula for perfume:
benjuhi (gum benzoin), *ambre* (ambergris), *estorac* (storax), and *siveta*
(civet), all included in one or another of the following recipes. The
first of our recipes claims to present the formula used at court.
Making sure that the board had no contaminating odors is a nice
touch.

Beniamin, benjamin, is gum benzoin, a dry brittle resinous
substance with a fragrant odor, obtained from *Styrax benzoin,* a tree
of Sumatra. The name comes from Arabic *lubān jāwī,* "frankincense
of Jāwā [Sumatra]." (The *lu* was lost, apparently considered an
article.) In English, the name was typically assimilated to a word
that was understood, the proper name, Benjamin (*OED*).

Ciuit, civet, is a yellowish, brownish unctuous substance
with a strong musky smell, obtained from a sac in the anal pouch

* Written *them.*

433

of the civet, specifically the Central African *Viverra civetta*. The name comes from Arabic *zabād* (*OED*).

I remind the reader that rose leaves were petals (see S 66 and 81).

---

312   TO MAKE AN EXCELLENT PERFUME

Take a quarter of a pound of damask rose buds cut clean from ye whites. stamp them small & put to y^m a spoonfull or 2 of damask rose water. soe let them stand close stopt all night. then take an ounce & quarter of benjamin, finely beaten & searced; 20 grayns of civit; & 10 grayns of muske. mingle these with ye roses & beat them well together. then* make them up in little cakes between rose leav[es]. dry them betwixt sheets of paper.

See S 311. Musk is discussed in S 113.

---

313   TO MAKE A UERY SWEET PERFUME

Take 6 penny worth of benjamin, as much storeax, 3 grayns of ambergreece, as much musk, & beat them alltogether very fine in a marble morter. & put to it 6 pennyworth of oyle of rodium. mix all these well with a spoone, then put to y^m as much damask rose water as will make them up into a paste, & then make them up into little cakes as bigg as 3 pence, & dry them betwixt rose leaves. ~~~~~~~~~~~~~~~~~~~~~~~~~~~~~~

when you have a minde to make use of any of these perfuming cakes, lay one or 2 of th[em] on a chafing dish of coles, which must not be to [hot].

Storax is a fragrant gum resin. Wyclif speaks of storax in 1388. *OED* says that it was once taken from the tree *Styrax officinalis* but later pharmaceutical practice used the balsam of the tree *Liquidambar orientale*.

Oyle of rodium is *oleum rhodii* from rhodium or rosewood.

* Written *them*.

434

For these perfumes, see S 311. I have no idea how much either benjamin or oil of rhodium could be had for sixpence, but that was a fair amount of money at the time; the ambergris (S 20) and musk (S 113) must have been a good deal dearer (see S 317).

---

314   TO MAKE A PERFUME TO STAND IN
        A ROOME

Take 2 or 3 quarts of roses buds or ye leaves of damask roses, & put them in a pot with bay salt, 3 or 4 grayns of muske, & as much of ambergreece, 20 or 30 drops of oyle of rodium, a little benjamin & storeax beat together, & 2 or 3 spoonfulls of rosewater. put all these together in a cheyney pot, or any other y^t is handsome, & keep it allwayes close covered. but when you have a minde to have y^r roome sweet, you m[ay take off] ye cover.

Cheyney is china, or porcelain. The word *china* was the Sanskrit word for China (*OED*).

For these perfumes, see the entire section starting with S 311.

---

315   TO MAKE PUMMANDER

Take of ye powder of oversea roses, & benjamin, powder of violets, a little of ye liquid storeax, & east india balsum, muske, civit, & ambergreece, callimus, oyle of orringes, spirit of roses, & spirit of cloves, a nutmegg grated, & oyle of rodium. for ye quanteties of each of these, you may proportion them according to your fancy, or ye quantety of pommander you intend to make. & put in, or leave out, according as you can procure, or like, or dislike ye ingredients. rub y^r moulds wth ye oyle of benjamin. soe mingle all together & make them up.

A *pomander* (from Old French *pome ambre*, golden apple) was a mixture of aromatic substances, usually made into a ball and carried or worn to ward off infection (*OED*).

East India balsam is the resin described in S 296. Oil of oranges could be what came to be known as *neroli* but could have been made by simple infusion, as in S 306. It is interesting to note the preference for dried roses from overseas; they must have been more fragrant. See the perfume section, beginning with S 311.

---

316   TO MAKE MOSS POWDER FOR A SWEET BAGG

Take 2 pound of ye moss of a sweet apple tree, gathered between ye 2 lady dayes, & infuse it in A quart of damask rose water 24 hours, then take it out & dry it in an oven on sive bottoms. then beat it into powder, & put to it one ounce of lignum Alloes, beaten & searced, 2 ounces of orris, a dram of muske, halfe a dram of ambergreece, a quarter of a dram of civit. put all these into a hot morter & beat them together with a hot pestle. y^n sear[ce] them thorough A course hare searce. after, put it into A bagg, & lay it amongst y^r [linens (?)].

Here is a delightful recipe for a sachet. The Lady Days are Annunciation, March 25, and Assumption, August 15. But Gerard says that, "Mosse upon the tree continueth all the yeare long." All the ingredients are treated elsewhere under their respective names. See also S 311.

---

317   TO PERFUME POWDER FOR HAYRE

Into 2 pound of ordinary hayr powder put 4 greyns of musk, & a shillings worth of amber, & a groats worth of oyle of orpinum, which oyl[e] you must put in ye powder, & set it into an oven after bread is drawne. & when you take it out of ye oven againe, put into it ye muske & amber, & then keep it close in a box.

No work on perfumery would be complete without a recipe for powder for *hayre* (a fifteenth-century form). For other perfumes, see S 311 on. The powder and medicated oil are first dried, then laid aside with the musk and ambergris. *Amber* was the original word for ambergris (S 20), and as late as 1671, Milton speaks of an *amber scent*, but I have the impression that it was archaic and largely poetic by then.

Of *orpine (Sedum telephium)*, Gerard says that one of its names is *Live-long*, and that "it taketh away the white morphew: *Galen* saith the black also; which thing it does by reason of the scouring or clensing quality that it hath." (See S 323 for *morphew*.) Apparently it was efficacious in treating scalp conditions, or so thought to be.

I have no idea how much ambergris was to be obtained for a shilling; different recipes (for batches of varying size and purpose) call for amounts ranging from 4 grains to the weight of fourpence (⅛ ounce). I might note that musk and ambergris were often added in like weights. Nor do I know how much a *groats worth* of oil of orpine may have been. (A *groat* is a silver coin that was worth fourpence; it was not issued after 1662.) A *groatsworth* came to have a figurative meaning of very little, but these prices are literal, I believe. (For weights, see S 70.)

I remind the reader that in this manuscript, we have a recipe for *a Pigg of 3 or 4 shillings Price* (C 35), and that a substantial *household loaf* of perhaps nearly 2 pounds was to be had for a penny. (Twelve pence made a shilling.) Also, as discussed in the introductory notes, Wilson tells us that in the time of Elizabeth a pound of sugar sold for about a shilling, a day's wage for a craftsman at the time (see page 11). I am well aware that these figures cannot be calibrated without weights and better dating, but we are given a hint of relative costs of the day and a glimpse of the chasm that separated those who had from those who had not. And an artisan was an aristocrat among those who labored.

---

318   TO MAKE SWEET WATER TO PERFUME
      CLOATHS IN yᵉ FOULDING AFTER
      THEY ARE WASH'D

Take a quart of damask rose water, & put it in a glass with a handfull of lavender flowers, 2 ounces of orris, one dram of muske, yᵉ weight of A pence in ambergreece, & as much civit, 4 drop[s] of oyle of cloves. stop this close & set it in yᵉ sun A fortnight. when you use this water, put A spoonfull of it into halfe a basone of spring water, & put it into a glass, and sprinkle yʳ cloathes therewith in yᵉ foulding. yᵉ dreggs yᵗ are left in the bottom of yᵉ glass when the water is spent, will make as much more If you keep them, & put fresh rose water to them. & then put a spoonfull or 2 [of it in] ye like premention'd quantety of spring wate[r].

Gerard calls the orris-root (genus *Iris*), "whereof sweet waters, sweet pouders, and such like are made," the *Floure de-luce of Florence*. It has a white flower, he says, but it is only the root that is fragrant, a fragance recalling that of violets, according to *OED*.

The apothecary's dram of 60 grains and the weight of fourpence are each equivalent to ⅛ ounce, ordinary weight (see S 70 and 317). This is a very heavy proportion of three costly substances, even if you use the dregs to concoct another batch, as suggested. The other ingredients are discussed elsewhere under their respective names. See other perfumes, beginning S 311.

---

319   TO MAKE SWEETE WATER

Take halfe a bushell of damask roses & put them in an earthen pot which will hold 3 gallons of water, & fill it allmoste full. & put into it 2 handfulls of lavender knops, & set it in ye sun for a fortnight all ye day. & put in allsoe A good handfull of sweet margerum & a good handfull of bayse. & when it hath stood ye fore mentiond time in ye sun, put in 2 ounces of cloves bruised, & soe still it, hanging in it a little bagg wherein there is 2 grayns of muske. If you would perfume a roome with this water, you must heat A fier shovele red hot & poure some of it into it.

Lavender (*Lavandula vera*) was, above all, loved for its scent; for its medicinal properties, see S 275. *OED* questions the popular etymology of *lavanda*, washing. *Knops* are flower buds.

Bayse could refer to either the fruit or the leaves of the Bay Laurel (*Laurus nobilis*). The word comes from Old French *baie* for berry. From the use of the plural, I suspect that it is the berries wanted here. Gerard says: "The berries and leaves of the Bay tree, saith *Galen*, are hot and very dry, and yet the berries more than the leaves. . . . Bay berries are put into Mithridate, Treacle, and such like medicines that are made to refresh such people as are growne sluggish and dull by means of taking opiate medicines, or such as have any venomous or poisonous qualitie in them."

320   TO MAKE BEANE FLOWERE WATER

Take a gallon of may dew goten of wheat when there
hath bin noe rayne. strayn it clear & put therein halfe a
peck of bean flowers, pickt from ye blacks. corke it up
in a strong glass bottle, & let it stand in ye sun all y^e
summer. & in ye winter, take it into ye house, strayne
it, & set it out againe ye next summer, & clear it
severall times. & ye second summer, put therin a
handfull of wilde tansie, femitory, & egrimony. then
clear it & make use of it. it is very good for freckles,
spots in ye face, & sunburn, & to clear ye scinn. If you
set [it in y^e] sun ye third summer, it will be ye better
[than if you use it] ye first.

This *beane flower* must be the fragrant violet-tinted white flower of
Faba vulgaris; OED refers to the "often-mentioned 'fragrance of the
bean-fields.' " Nothing is said of the use of flowers by Gerard, but
he promises that "the meale of Beanes clenseth away the filth of
the skin." The meal of young beans was also fashioned into a
poultice and used to alleviate all manner of inflammation, including chest colds, engorged breasts, bruises, and so on.

Wild tansy (*Potentilla anserina*) is said by Gerard to be good
not only for freckles, pimples, and sunburn, but also for "wounds
of the secret parts, and [it] closeth up all green and fresh wounds."

Femitory is fumitory (*Fumaria officinalis*). Gerard says that
Fumitory "is good for all them that have either scabs or any other
filthe growing on the skinne, and for them also that have the
French disease." Of *egrimony*, rather agrimony (*Agrimonia eupato-
ria*), Gerard says: "The leaves being stamped with old swines
grease, and applied, closes up ulcers that be hardly healed, as
Dioscorides saith."

And if you fain would gather *may dew*, list Hugh Plat in
Delightes for Ladies, 1608: "When there hath fallen no raine the
night before, then with a cleane and large sponge, the next morning, you may gather the same from sweet herbs, grasse or corne
[grain]." In the month of May, to be sure. May dew was regarded
as having varying medicinal and cosmetic properties depending
on the plant from which it was collected. I found nothing on May
dew of wheat, but Gerard notes that, "The oyle of wheat . . .
healeth the chaps, . . . making smooth the hands, face or any other
part of the body."

321   TO MAKE AN EXCELLENT COOLING
       WATER

Take a quarter of a pound of french barley & boyle it in
allmoste a gallon of spring water. shift it in 3 waters till
it be clear. when ye latter water hath boyled ye 4th part
away, clear it from ye barley in a dish, & let it stand till
it be cold. then put into ye water a quarter of a pound
of bitter almonds, blanch'd & beaten very small, & y^e
Juice of 2 or 3 leamons. then strayne it & bottle it, &
put into ye bottles some leamon pill. & when it hath
stood a week, you may use it, shakeing it every day.
this water is good to clear ye scin, & to take away
inflamations of ye face, by washing of it night &
morning.

Gerard quotes Galen, the great Greek physician of antiquity, as
saying that barley has "a certain force to coole and dry," and also
has a little "clensing qualitie . . . [and] taketh away inflammations." The barley is to be reserved for another use; it is the water
that is wanted here.
    Gerard writes: "[Bitter Almonds] also clense and take
away spots and blemishes in the face, and other parts of the body;
they mundifie and make cleane foule eating ulcers." Nor were
sweet almonds without cosmetic virtues: "The oile of Almonds
makes smoothe the hands and face of delicat persons, and clenseth
the skin from all spots, pimples, and lentils." (For almonds, see
S 20.)
    Gerard says that "The distilled water of the whole Limons,
rinde and all, . . . takes away tetter and blemishes of the skin, and
maketh the face faire and smooth." (See S 235.)

322   TO MAKE PUMMATUM

Take halfe a pound of dears suet & as much hoggs lard,
both hot from ye dear & hogg, & lay them in water 10
dayes. shift it twice a day, & then dry [it] in a cloth. &
beat it in ye cloth till it is very sma[ll]. then put it in a
pipkin y^t was never used, with 4 pippins quartered &
stuck full of cloves. & put in a little civit tyed in a cloth.

440

then take A littl[e] quantety of virgins wax, & halfe a
pinte of rose water. put all these in a pipkin, & set it in
water & boyle it a little in ye water. then take it of &
[let it cool & ma]ke it up as you please.

Pomatum comes from Latin *pōmum*, apple; pomade comes from the
same word. Gerard writes: "There is likewise made an ointment
with the pulpe of Apples and Swines grease and Rose water, which
is used to beautifie the face, and to take away the roughnesse of
the skin, which is called in shops *Pomatum*: of the Apples whereof
it is made." So that our *Pummatum* is perfectly classic.

Dears suet is the fat of a deer. *Uirgins wax*, or virgin wax,
originally meant fresh new wax, produced from the first swarm
of bees, but it came to mean simply pure or refined wax.

---

323 TO MAKE MY LADY LUCAS PUMMATUM

Take a pound of sweet fresh suet of a dear or sheep, &
pull of all its scin. & put it in fayre spring water, in
which let it ly 3 days in an earthen pot. shift it with
fresh water twice a day. at 3 dayes end, take it out &
put it into a faire pipkin or scyllet, & set it on a clear
fire, till it be thorough melted but not boyle. then
strayne it thorough a clean cloth, & put into it 1 or 2*
ounces of ye oyle of bitter almonds, & about halfe a
crowns worth of spermaceetie, one shillings worth of
campher, beat up small with an almond. then mingle
all these together in ye fat when it is bloud warme, &
then put it up in pots or make it up into cakes when it
is cold. & soe use it for y^r face or hands. it is good to
take away morfew, freckls, & to clear ye scin. and make
it smooth.

I know not who Lady Lucas was nor when she lived, but she had
a costly *Pummatum* made up for her use. I cannot tell you how
much spermaceti or camphor she got for her money, but for those
two ingredients alone, the cost was 3 shillings and sixpence. This
represented the cost of an entire young pig at the time (S 317). See
S 322 for a more classic pomatum.

* Corrected by the scribe from *3 or 4*.

441

Spermaceti is a fatty substance found in the head of the sperm whale; it was long thought that the substance was the sperm (*OED*). Culpeper, in *Pharmacopoeia Londinensis*, 1654, says that it is "applied outwardly to eating Ulcers; [and] the marks which the small pocks leave behind them." It also helps bruises and "the stretching of the nerves."

Morphew is a leprous or scruffy eruption of the skin (*OED*).

324　　TO OYLE GLOUES

> Take a payre of kidskin gloves, & turne ye wrong side outward, & let them ly 2 dayes in water. y^n wash them in ye white of an egg beaten in water, & dry y^m on y^r hands. y^n rub them well with ye youlk of an egg, & then take about ye bigness of a wallnut of pomatum, halfe an ounce of parmacitie, halfe an ounce of oyle of sweet almonds, a little oyle of rodium, a [ha]lfe penny worth of virgins wax. melt y^m all to[gether & rub (?) y^r] gloves with it.

It is a laborious and expensive way of cleaning kid gloves. *Parmacitie* was a corrupt form of spermaceti that was fairly common, according to *OED*. The other ingredients are listed throughout this last section.

325　　TO KEEPE THE TEETH CLEAN & WHITE
　　　　& TO FASTEN THEM

> Take cuttle fish bone and make it into very fine powder, & rub ye teeth therewith. then wash them after with white wine & planton water, & 3 or 4 drops of spirrit of vittorell* mixt with them & rub them well with a cloth. & it will preserve ye teeth from putrefaction, & keep them fast, white, & clean, & preserve from ye toothach, If it be used every day.

Plantain water is a decoction of the leaves of *Plantago major*. Gerard claims that it is "singular good . . . to wash a sore throat or mouth."

The distilled essence of *vitriol* is sulphuric acid. Pomet, in *A Compleat History of Druggs*, 1712, says that it may be diluted

* The *o* is blotted.

and used in "Diseases of the Gums and cutaneous Distempers." In *A Physical Directory*, 1651, Culpeper warns: "It kills being taken alone . . . it asswageth thirst, [and] allayeth the violent heat in fevers and pestilences." The white wine seems like a better idea, on the whole.

---

326   TO TAKE FORTH STAYNS OUT OF LINNEN

Take of the powder of the white date of A dogg, & let it be the whitest as you can get. and mix it with as much chalk and bay salt. and mix to them allsoe twice as much sope as them all. then sope ye stayn well with this, and rub it well in with your hands, and lay them abroad to whiten. and wet them very often as fast as they dry, & then wash them up with other sope that you commonly use, and the stayns will be take[n] out.

From Pomet's *Compleat History of Druggs*, 1712, we learn that "*Stercus Canis officinalis*, Dogs white Dung," was listed in the pharmacopoeia. "This is said to clense and deterge," he reports. He goes on to say that it was used in both internal and external medicine, "but it seldom appears to any great purpose." Ours is not a medical recipe, to be sure, but it is interesting to note its use as a detergent. (Perhaps dogs were tidier then; however, occasionally one does see very pale, neat oval turds that whiten on drying.)

APPENDICES

Washington Cook Book

Written by Francis Parke Custis
the Mother of Martha Washington's
first husband. She gave it
to her daughter in law, and
Martha W, in turn . . . .
bestowed it upon her adored
granddaughter, Nelly Custis
after her marriage to Lawrence
Lewis ——

The nineteenth-century inscription that perpetuated the myth attributing the manuscript to Frances Parke Custis (see page 456), confounding the historians.

APPENDIX 1

MANUSCRIPT HISTORY

The Washington manuscript is a small volume measuring about 8 by 6¼ inches plainly bound in brown leather, distinguished only by the pretty italic handwriting, now rather faded but still legible. It is in two parts: *A Booke of Cookery*, containing 205 recipes (the numbers run through 206 but one is omitted in error), and *A Booke of Sweetmeats*, containing 326 recipes. In important English houses, these would have been in separate volumes, one for use in the kitchen and the other in the still room, where medicinal waters were distilled and syrups and preserves were made. In lesser houses, or when daughters made their own copies to take with them (as was most likely the case here), the books were often combined, but in a charming fashion: the copying of the books was started at opposite ends of the new volume in such a way as to bring the completed books back to back and upside down in relation to each other, usually separated by blank pages affording space for later entries. This device was used in our manuscript. (It is interesting to note that this custom continued. I have in my possession a delightful American manuscript, signed and dated *S. C. Wightman, May 1826*, which is organized in just this way.)

What we shall call the front of the book starts off with the index of *A Booke of Cookery*, very neatly entered, and is immediately followed by the index for the sweetmeat book (one leaf of which is missing), which in turn is followed by *A Booke of Sweetmeats*. The back of the book, as it were, starts off directly with *A Booke of Cookery*.

While the copying must have taken some time to accomplish, the two books were done from beginning to end as one continuing project by a single scribe. I do not know how to account for it, but the handwriting in the book of sweetmeats is more graceful and easier than that of the cookery book, although both are indubitably by the same hand. Perhaps the most remarkable aspect of the copying is the fact that no recipe was allowed to spill over onto another page, excepting only those whose length re-then take it out, and Let it Cool, and keep it for use.

To boil Green Pease

When they are Shelled puts them into a Long Gally pot,
and set it into a pot of boiling water and cover y[e] Gally-
-pot Well and in a Short time y[u] will find y[e] Pease to
be fine and tender; then put them out into a dish and
Strew some Salt upon them, and put in a good quantity
of butter, and Shake them well between 2 dishes then
put them into a hots dish and Serve them to Table.
If they who are to eat them Love Sparemint, put in
a Sprig into the pot wth them

To wash white Sarsnets

Lay y[m] smooth and Strait on a board Soup y[e] Dirty
places a fittel if there[s] any take a littel hard brush
Soup it well & rub it in water and make a pret[y]
thick ludder y[n] take it and rub it well the right
way of the Sarsnet Sideways of y[e] brush when you
have washed one side well turn and wash tother than Cast
y[r] whoo[?] double into a Clean Scald ing hot leder
as fast as y[u] wash y[m] and Cover it you wash y[m] 3 time
well on y[e] board after y[e] first luder let y[e] others
be Very hot and Cast them in a scald every time then
make a Scald ing hot leder put in some gum Arabeck
which has bin Steept afore in water and a littel smalt
lett y[m] ly double Close Covered an hour then Dip
them all over take y[m] out and fold them to a small
Compas Squees them Smooth in y[r] hands then Soak
y[u] over brimstone Draw y[m] every way in your hands till
they are a littel more then half Dry y[n]
Smooth y[m] with good hot Irons the
Same way y[u] wished y[m] y[e] right
way of the Silk

quired more than an entire page. This indicates that the scribe has to have been copying from another work, line for line. Occasionally, the writing becomes a bit cramped towards the bottom of the page, but is made to fit.

Between the two books there are a number of blank pages, several of which are filled with recipes entered some time after the completion of the main body of the manuscript. These "inner pages" are filled with a jumble of recipes, medicinal lore, laundry hints, and mathematical doodlings, entered by at least seven different hands, some of them little more than hen tracks. One of these recipes (see facsimile, page 458) provided important dating and ownership information (see page 457) but for the most part, these pages are devoid of any real interest except, perhaps, to document the decline of the family.

To better understand the nature of the Washington manuscript and to trace its particular history, it is necessary to examine the tradition of family manuscript books that existed in sixteenth- and seventeenth-century England. Even so serious a researcher as Jane Carson, discussing the Washington manuscript in her excellent *Colonial Virginia Cookery*, 1968, seems not to have been aware of this tradition. She notes that she was "unable to make an intelligent guess about the date of compilation because sources are not cited," and she concludes that the recipes had been copied from a printed English cookbook unknown to her. But the sources are not cited because the recipes had been in the family for generations; the manuscript is a beautiful and classic example of such family recipe books.

Much as I would, I cannot ignore *The Martha Washington Cook Book* by the historian Marie Kimball, 1940, if for no other reason than that only in this sadly mutilated form have Americans had the opportunity of learning of our culinary heritage in this respect. Mrs. Kimball writes almost as if Martha herself had written the book, although she does dutifully repeat the silly legend that Frances Parke Custis had written the book and presented it to Martha (see page 446). "We know that [Washington] was partial to shad, yet no recipe for shad appears in the *Cook Book*," she writes. "The colored cooks were doubtless familiar with it and needed no special directions." Eggs were "ignored" for the same reason, she explains, except for *Buttered eggs* (C 44), which "were a *specialité de la maison*, and were thus duly set down." And she persists in describing the manuscript as being contemporary in language and spirit with *The Art of Cookery* by Hannah Glasse, 1747 (with editions continuing as late as 1843), while our manuscript, a fair copy of an older one, was penned some time during the latter part of the seventeenth century, if not earlier. Perhaps more serious is the mangling of the recipes. She blithely adds flour to the meat recipes and their accompanying sauces, for example, falsifying the recipes, flouting historical accuracy and scholarly discipline, and showing little sensitivity to culinary niceties.

As might be expected, the earliest English cookery manuscripts we know are from the royal household.* *The Forme of Cury* (pronounced *kewry* and meaning cookery) is a collection of recipes compiled by the master cooks to Richard II and is dated about 1390. The cuisine presented is redolent with Saracen fragrances, complete with rose petals, almonds, musk, dates, pomegranates, currants, and Eastern spices. In this display of Arab opulence, *The Forme of Cury* differs little from other thirteenth- and fourteenth-century manuscripts we have from France or Spain, for instance. Nor was France the only path, although we sometimes forget that the royal line of England was French during those centuries. Aside from trade relations, Edward I married Eleanor of Castile, for example, and she may well have brought chefs with her.

In any event, the cuisine of *The Forme of Cury* and the language in which it was couched, a melange of Anglo-French and Middle English of the time of Chaucer, was to have an incalculable influence on the cooking and cookbooks of the English upper classes from then on; the pattern was set.† Eastern aromas lingered as late as the time of our manuscript; the French terms have persisted in English culinary nomenclature to this day, including the terms for the principal meats: beef, mutton, veal, venison, pork. (Interestingly, most barnyard fowl retained their English names in the kitchen but game birds more often than not took French names.)

Surviving fourteenth- and fifteenth-century cookery manuscripts all appear to be from noble households. The recipes of the later ones show certain evolutionary changes from those in *The Forme of Cury*, but most of them are perfectly recognizable and many are virtually unchanged, with many parallel recipes among the various collections. We see how the nobility were emulating the royal and princely households; inevitably, the gentry followed

*In her notes to *A Noble Boke off Cookry*, Mrs. Napier reports the existence of pages of recipes, written in French, from the reign of Edward I (1272-1307). She reprints two of them and lists the titles of several more, all parallel to recipes contained in *A Noble Boke, The Forme of Cury*, and other medieval collections.

†Direct Roman influence on English cookery from the time of the occupation may be largely discounted, and our knowledge of produce, and particularly of cooking methods, up to the Norman Conquest is based on scanty material.

suit, and family recipe manuscripts came to be kept in all houses of any standing.

It is important to understand that in those times, the mistress of the household, even of high station, was expected to be perfectly familiar with all aspects of running it, including cooking. This is not to say that she actually toiled in the kitchen, but it is not without significance that *lady* comes from Old English words meaning *kneader of loaves*. The tradition of family manuscripts then becomes more understandable.

Until some time in the seventeenth century, these manuscripts were usually accretive, as distinguished from collected ones. It was a question of station: the nobility, even the gentry, *had* their recipes, but the wives of rising merchants had to collect them. (Of course, they could buy printed cookbooks, and did, but manuscripts were a way of recording favorite recipes and, in addition, must have had some cachet.) These collected ones, nearly always signed and dated (making them especially valuable to us), were each the work of one woman; the recipes and their language tended to be of her time. She collected them from friends, relatives, even servants, and there was often a good deal of name dropping, involving recipes of My Lady So-and-So and the Countess of Such-and-Such. For that matter, recipes were usually attributed. All cookery manuscripts, by their very nature, reflect changes in taste and the introduction of new products and techniques more swiftly and more accurately than printed books. The collected manuscripts were more individualistic than the tradition-bound family manuscript and so reacted even more quickly to change. Thus, any collected manuscript from the last quarter of the seventeenth century will surely have recipes involving chocolate; chocolate became the rage among the ladies and those who would be. A classic example of this collected manuscript is one kept by Rebecca Price from 1681 to 1740; the recipes for sauces are particularly revealing, as the early ones are still typical seventeenth-century sauces while those entered later call for flour, which did not become popular in English cookery until sometime in the eighteenth century.

The accretive family manuscripts show less individuality, perhaps, but they are interesting in other respects. As noted elsewhere, each daughter copied the recipes. Since she was usually a young girl at the time, she would tend to make a fair copy, but even so, certain modernizations of language and spelling would insinuate themselves, frequently making for anomalies. When she took her copy to her own home, she would quite likely add new recipes of her own. Her daughters, in turn, when they copied the book, would repeat the process. The recipes in these inherited family manuscripts were arranged according to category and indexed. In each copying, the additions of the previous owner were incorporated into the manuscript according to category and so the book would have to be re-indexed as well. Thus, chronological continuity is shattered; one has to date a recipe by internal evidence alone: the language, the products, and the combinations and techniques peculiar to a particular time and place.

These successive copyings and rearrangements of the recipes introduce a certain amount of extraneous material. As long as the manuscript was a working handbook, cooks tended to add their own emendations, as can be seen in recipes C 114 and 115. If our manuscript had once again been copied in the tradition, these would most likely have been copied as part of the recipe proper, with no change of handwriting to give a clue, much as happened in S 1. And then, while copies tended to be fair copies, certain modernizations and changes did insinuate themselves. This is illustrated by the placing of the identical recipes, *To make Honey of Roses* in with the other flower recipes, S 73, and again in the section of syrups, S 249. Either classification can be justified, the error is that it appears twice. What is interesting, is the little changes that took place in successive copyings, each by the same hand. Since our scribe seems to have done no reclassification whatsoever, this has to have occurred at least one generation back. The wonder is that the anomalies are not more numerous than they are. (On the other hand, our scribe charmingly corrects errors of previous scribes in a number of recipes, S 215, for example, or in S 175, where it may have been her own error.)

Family manuscripts that belonged, or had belonged, to an important household display an interesting characteristic peculiar to them. Each succeeding new mistress of the house would bring her own favorite recipes, some of which would be duly entered into the manuscript. Thus, in the Washington manuscript, we find clumps of recipes that show fascinating common traits that differentiate them from the others. There is what I call the *great oatmeale* clump, where not only is cracked oats a frequently called for ingredient, but there linger traces of Northumbrian dialect; in most of the manuscript, such dialectal forms as there are appear to be from the southeast of England, and a number of them seem to be Kentish. There are also recipes that show signs of having come from the hand of one especially fine cook; besides her perceptive directions, she had her little turns of phrase that are quite distinctive. So long as the manuscript stayed in the house, these additions would be self-evident, but in subsequent copyings, the sections would be broken up and dispersed throughout the book in the manner described above. A pity, from our point of view, but it made the book more convenient for the user. Indeed, once you find recipes simply tacked on at the end, out of category, it indicates that the book was no longer being scrupulously kept up in the tradition; the copyist had simply copied the recipes as they came without bothering to reclassify the caboose section. This can be clearly seen in our manuscript. The *Booke of Sweetmeats* is, for the most part, in exemplary order (deviations are the result of error or inattention). In the *Booke of Cookery*, however, all proceeds correctly until we come to C 195, when we find recipes for posset, marrow pie, fritters, pepper cakes, and almond butter, all clearly tacked on by a later contributor and never properly reclassified. (These recipes are by no means the most modern ones; the marrow pie, for example, is one of the older recipes in the manuscript.) In the "inner pages" we find, higgledy-piggledy, various medicinal mixtures, jellies, and laundering information in several untidy hands. The next copying would have called for placing all these recipes in their proper positions and re-indexing them, but the tradition had long since died out. (See facsimile, page 448.)

I do not mean to say that occasional recipes in these accretive family manuscripts were not copied from printed books. Few seventeenth-century works, manuscript or printed, omit *Doctor Steephens Cordiall water* (S 275), for example. And there is the recipe for *A marmalet that was presented to the queene for A new years gift* (S 20), for which I found a virtual twin in a book on preserving published in 1608. Recipes originally taken from books may have lost specifically identifiable characteristics through successive copyings; this may be the case with *Cream with snow* (C 120), where we have tantalizingly evocative language when compared to a recipe in *A Proper Newe Booke of Cokerye*, 1545 (?). But there was no wholesale copying as has been suggested.

Indeed, the flow of recipes was in the other direction. In 1615, Gervase Markham (1568-1637) published *The English Huswife, Contayning, The inward and outward vertues which ought to be in a compleat woman. As, her skill in Physicke, Cookery, Banqueting-stuffe, Distillation, Perfumes, Wooll, Hemp, Flax, Dayries, Brewing, Baking, and all other things belonging to an Houshould.* It seems to have become the most popular cookbook of the seventeenth century, with editions as late as 1683; the work is invaluable to any student of the period. Markham is of particular interest to us because his recipes and language are contemporary with the bulk of our manuscript. He was born four years after Shakespeare, and was also contemporary with John Gerard, the herbalist. Following the title page, there is an extraordinary note: "Thou mayst say (gentle Reader) what hath this man to doe with Hus-wifery, he is now out of his element . . . . I shall desire thee therefore to understand, that this is no collection of his whose name is prefixed to this work, but an approved Manuscript which he happily light on, belonging sometime to an honorable Personage of this kingdome, who was singular amongst those of her ranke for many of the qualities here set forth. This onely he hath done, digested the things of this booke in a good method, placing every thing of the same kinde together, and so make it common for thy delight and profit . . ." It is signed R. I., apparently Roger Jackson, for whom the book was printed. Florence White in *Good Things in England* quotes Markham as identifying the lady as "an Honourable Countess," but neglects to give her source.

This then explains why sixteenth- and seventeenth-century English cookbooks read as if they had been written by women, even though it is almost invariably a man's name that appears on the title page. It also establishes that this cuisine, parallel in so many ways to that of our own manuscript, was that of a titled Elizabethan household.

This custom of pillaging the ladies' family manuscripts started in the sixteenth century when hack writers and publishers discovered the gold mine of recipe books. One of the early signed ones of this type was Thomas Dawson's *The Good Huswifes Jewell*, 1585 (?), and *The Second Part of the Good Hus-wives Jewell, Wherein is to bee found most apt and readiest wayes to distill many wholsome and sweete waters. In which likewise is shewed the best maner in preserving of divers sorts of Fruits, & making of Sirrops*, 1585. At the end of directions for *A pouder peerelesse for wounds*, we read: ". . . next underneath written, and it &c. [Sic] The rest wanteth." I doubt that Dawson even read the manuscript before sending it to the printers, or surely he would have tidied up that touching ending. The book is a treasure trove of culinary lore of the period. A certain number of the recipes in our manuscript are contemporary with the Dawson recipes, meaning that they had been collected for a certain number of decades previously. (Many of our recipes were entered later, to be sure, but the less archaic aspect of the older ones is due to their having been recopied later.) Some of the likenesses to be remarked upon include the archaic and rare usage of *frying* of liquid (C 2), which I have not noticed elsewhere, and of *walme*, which is less rare. More striking is the use of yeast in fish cookery (C 186), which I believe to have been old-fashioned by 1585. There are other old techniques, such as the use of *caudles* and *possets* in the preparation of cakes (S 152) and pies, and the specification of half wine and half ale in a number of dishes. None of the recipes, I might add, are alike enough to have come from the same source, except for the ubiquitous *Doctor Steephens Cordiall Water* (S 275), and even that is by no means identical.

In 1653, there appeared *A Choice Manuall, of Rare and Select Secrets in Physick and Chirurgery: collected and practised by the Right Honourable, the Countesse of Kent, late deceased*, and a companion book *A True Gentlewomans Delight*, by W. Jar, both comprising a single volume. According to A. W. Oxford, the entire work is catalogued by the British Museum under the name of Elizabeth Grey, Countess of Kent, who died in 1651, an attribution that Elizabeth David does not accept for the latter book, a judgment that I find convincing. But the cookery recipes indubitably constitute some unknown gentlewoman's manuscript. What is interesting here is how very modern the cookbook is compared to our manuscript, not only in what must have been editorial excision of "old-fashioned" recipes employing old techniques, but in the language as well. Yet the recipes must have been collected during the early years of the seventeenth century, if not earlier.

And in 1661, Hannah Woolley published *The Ladies Directory*, which appears to be the first English cookbook to bear the name of a woman author.

English home cookery may be the most amply documented of home cuisines. It is not that the manuscript tradition was peculiar to England. French women, for example, kept manuscripts; I have in my possession a handsome example from mid-eighteenth century, or a little earlier, and I know others from other periods. What is unusual about England is that so many of them found their way into print, followed by an extraordinary number of women writers of cookbooks. In France, cookbooks were written by professional male chefs, although illustrious figures occasionally dabbled at it as well; only rarely was any attention paid to home cooking and women writers were virtually unheard of. French women managed nicely without such books, but I would give a great deal to have the wealth of documentation on the home kitchen in France during those centuries that we have for England. We must be grateful to the Dawsons and Markhams; whatever their intentions, they preserved for us bits of the past that might otherwise have been lost and, of course, the books themselves wielded considerable influence. It would have been more honorable and more gracious on their part to have straightforwardly acknowledged their "borrowings," but such rectitude was not the way of cookbook writers then, no more than now.

APPENDIX 2

DATING

An inscription in the Washington manuscript states that it was written and given to Martha by Frances Parke Custis, the mother of Martha's first husband. Now, Martha Dandridge Custis Washington was born June 2, 1731; Frances died March 13, 1714/15*. It is curious that no historian has noted this remarkable discrepancy. Nor did Frances compile the recipes. The present manuscript is a fair copy of a manuscript that represented the accretion of recipes by several generations of an English family of some standing.

The manuscript is prettily written in a legible italic hand. In attempting to date and identify this hand, I sought the opinion of three experts. First is R. E. Alton of St. Edmund Hall, Oxford University, who specializes in historical documents; his opinions will be attributed, but the other two men, both American, prefer not to be named. According to Mr. Alton, the hand is a mature one "with no sign of the uncertainties and experimentation usually associated with handwriting in the early teens." He also said that it could have been written any time in the second half of the seventeenth century, allowing either extremity.

The most significant clue to dating the work is to be found in the inner pages. Disregarding several pages of mathematical doodling, there are eleven pages of recipes, penned in six different hands, most of them untidy, and all "of a seventeenth-century type," according to Alton. Fitting together bits of historical information and internal evidence, I am convinced that they could not have been entered after the death of Frances in 1715. At some time after the main body of the manuscript was completed and after the doodling and some of the recipes of the inner pages had been entered, as well, the manuscript was damaged by fire along what I call the lower edges. The writing on a number of pages skirts the damage, showing that it was done after the accident (page 448).

* Douglas Southall Freeman, *George Washington*, Vol. II, 1948.

456

Among these inner pages is entered what I call the "prescription" (see facsimile, page 458). It is written in a curiously crabbed hand and calls for opium, among other ingredients, and promises to "procure Sleep, & abate all disorders in the humours or Spirits." The dosage is given and I believe the author of the prescription to have been a physician. At the bottom, in yet another hand, is a date: "April the 30: 1706." So far as I have been able to ascertain, this date has not been remarked upon by anyone who has written about the Washington manuscript. Yet, it demonstrates, at the very least, that the main body of the manuscript had been completed by that date; everything about the entry points to it having been entered decades after the completion of the manuscript.

The date was written by Jane Ludwell Parke, the mother of Frances. The autograph material is a four-page letter to Daniel Parke, her husband, and it is headed: "Virginia: July the 12: 1705."* The calligraphic similarities were so striking that I noted them before I was able to place them side by side. Alton, a cautious man, writes: "One date isn't much to go on, but in this cases we have enough for there to be little doubt." The letter is badly mutilated, and the handwriting resembles nothing so much as badly blurred hen tracks.

Jane tells of having the "dying sickness," and her letter is a tragic one. Col. Parke, who was referred to by a contemporary as "a sparkish gentleman" and by others as "a slashing blade,"† deserves a book to himself. Suffice it to say here that he had been in England for several years cultivating the friendship of Marlborough, who chose him to be the bearer of the news of the victory at Blenheim to Queen Anne in 1704.‡ From this he prospered mightily, but he paid no attention whatsoever to his ailing wife, with whom he had left his incorrigible "godson" and his equally incorrigible daughters, Frances and Lucy. Actually, the godson was the issue of one of an inordinate number of liaisons, publicly humiliating his wife and outraging even a society that expected men of his rank to be "slashing blades."

In her letter, Jane entreats her husband to take care of their children because of its "being very hard for a mother to forget her child; and yet as hard to live in the jeopardy I now do, both of body and soul." She reminds him that Frances was "wanting but two months of entering into her 20th year," and that suitable arrangements should be made for her marriage and inheritance

* Virginia Historical Society
† Edward W. Greenfield, *Some New Aspects of the Life of Daniel Parke*, in *Virginia Magazine of History and Biography*, (1946), 54.
‡ Freeman, vol. II.

Take ½ pint of Spirit of Wine put into it 6 drachms
of good Opium 2 drachms of Saffron 2 drachms of
Snakeroot 2½ drachms of Castor set the bottle with
the Spirit & the Ingredients into a vessell with so
much watter in it as may cover the Spirit & in the
ingredients in the bottle keep the watter in a constant
head such as you can hardly dip yor finger it & after it
has thus Infused 24 howers take the bottle out of the watter
pass the liquor warm through a piece of good Linnen.

This you may use in Sack or other wine or balm & other
distilled watters from 20 to 100 or 200 drops in all disorders
of the Spirits pains vomittings faintings & restlesness. to
procure ease or sleep & abate all disorders in the humours
or Spirits

To make this liquor weaker and proper for persons of the
weakest condition and Infants you may put the same quantity
of the formentioned Ingredients in Balm or still watter a
pint you may then make the watter into which you put the
bottle very hot & continue it so for 18 or 20 howers &
after you have taken it out of the vessell with watter strain
it very warm through a piece of good Linnen. This may be
given from ten to 100 Drops in the same distempers as ye former.

March the 30: 1706:

rights. In April 1706 we know that Jane dated a prescription in her recipe book; in September 1708 she died at Green Springs, her brother's home. In the meantime, Frances had married John Custis in August 1705;* Parke had been named Governor of the Leeward Islands as a reward, where he had vast holdings as well as in Virginia, and Custis had been assured that he was marrying the heiress to a large fortune. However, when Parke was assassinated in Antigua in 1710 (not without provocation), it transpired that his property in the Islands had been left to one of his natural children and that Frances had been left with crushing debts and little enough with which to pay them. The litigation went on for decades and Custis spent the rest of his life paying off the debts. His bitterness was little alleviated by the fact that his misfortune was shared to some extent by William Byrd—founder of Richmond, naturalist, and diarist—by reason of his marriage to Lucy, the younger Parke daughter.

These historical details may seem a digression. However, since popular legend has attributed the Washington manuscript to Frances Custis, it behooves us to examine the facts as best we may. Autograph material of women of the day, even of high station, is scarce. I did unearth a legal document, dated 9 January, 1711/12, signed by the sisters Frances Custis and Lucy Byrd, and their respective husbands.† To an amateur, but one long familiar with the handwriting of our manuscript, there is not the slightest trace of similarity between that hand and the hand of Frances, as evidenced by her signature. Just one example: the scores of upper case C's in the manuscript are all top heavy; not one resembles in the least the C with which she signed Custis, where the weight is below the line. On such scanty evidence—both samples were in photostat—one exceptionally cautious expert refused to commit himself to say that Frances had *not* penned the manuscript; however, he refused even more flatly to say that she *had*. (I was unable to submit this signature to Mr. Alton.)

So the autograph material is inconclusive. But there are more persuasive reasons to believe that Frances could not have penned the manuscript. To me, the most compelling is the character of Frances. All sources, including her great-grandson, George Washington Parke Custis, agree that she was arrogant, capricious, and vile-tempered. Her mother, Jane Parke, in her piteous letter to the Colonel, complained that she could do no more for their

---

* *Virginia Magazine of History and Biography* (1912), vol. 20. Freeman, however, says late 1705 or 1706. If the confusion is due to the change from the old calendar to the new, it would be no later than the first quarter of 1706.
† Virginia Historical Society.

daughters, "they being so much of your temper . . . I have so long stood the brunt of that." William Byrd, a mild man, is quoted by Jane Carson as saying that the Custis home at Arlington was " 'not kept very nicely,' the servants the worst he ever saw in his life, the food monotonous, the wine 'very scarce' and of inferior quality." (It must be kept in mind that in spite of the debts, these were among the wealthiest people of Virginia.) It would seem out of character for such a woman to engage in the labor of love and self-discipline that copying the manuscript represents; it is even more unlikely that her mother, broken in health and spirit, would have been able to insist.

Perhaps even more conclusive are the childish scrawls in various parts of the manuscript. Atop recipes C 115, S 19, and S 265, we find the name *Frances* (in the latter instance, upside down) and again on the second page of the scribe's cookery index. And on the blank page facing the beginning of the cookery book, we find the name *Lucy Parke*, signed in a childish hand, tucked in among several other childish signatures. (See facsimile, page 461.) Frances would not have vandalized her own painstaking work, and Lucy was only a couple of years younger than Frances. The only explanation is that the girls amused themselves by being naughty and scribbling in their mother's heirloom cookery book. There are other minor points. If Frances had indeed penned the manuscript, surely she would have taken it when her when she married and in any event, it is unlikely that Jane would have had the prescription entered into a book which belonged to Frances, who was not known for her generous disposition. There is also the question of her age. She seems to have been born in 1687, which would have made her a little young to have acquired a "mature hand" in time to have entirely completed the manuscript by April, 1706.

If Frances was not the scribe of our manuscript, who was? We know that Jane was not, because she entered the date in 1706 in a totally different hand. I looked first to her mother, Lucy Higginson (or Higgins) Ludwell. Lucy, however, was the daughter of a "citizen and painter-stainer."* Our manuscript did not come from the family of an artisan; it has to have originated in an important house with a lavish and abundant larder. (Also, Lucy Higginson had had a daughter some years earlier by a previous marriage who would have inherited such effects.) Lucy died when Jane was little more than an infant; her father married Lady Berkeley, the widow of Governor Berkeley in 1680 (she retained her title), and Jane was raised by that remarkable woman. Lady Berke-

* *Virginia Magazine of History and Biography* (1917), vol. 25.

from

Peter Kemp

Chas Wilbroad

wife Cond Mad[m]

Lucy Parks

Lucy Parks

Lucy

Lucy Parks

ley was born Frances Culpeper, of the "Kentish Culpepers," in 1634. The Culpeper family, with many branches, traced their history back to the time of King John. (Nicolas Culpeper, the physician frequently cited in the medicinal recipes, was a distant cousin, as was Thomas Culpeper, sometime Governor of Virginia.) According to Fairfax Harrison,* "Their heyday was in the times of the Stuarts, since when, as the hard saying is, they 'have gone down in the world.' " The Culpepers were members of the Virgina Company from 1609 on, and so had vast holdings in America. The titled members of the family stayed in England; Thomas Culpeper (not the governor), the father of Frances, emigrated to Virginia in 1649 and while it seems likely that Frances accompanied him, no specific mention of her has been found before 1669, according to Harrison.

Lady Berkeley was famed for her beauty and seems to have been extraordinarily intelligent and forceful as well, in a day when these latter qualities were even less kindly looked upon in women than they are today. When Lord Berkeley died, she promptly married Philip Ludwell, who promptly became Governor of Carolina. Frances died in 1691, or thereabouts. She had no issue and the Berkeley estate went to Jane's brother, Philip Ludwell. It is thus quite likely that Jane inherited the personal effects of Lady Berkeley, including any cookery manuscripts, in accordance with custom. Apparently Jane was fond of her stepmother; she named her first daughter Frances. Her second daughter she named Lucy after her natural mother, whom she must scarcely have remembered.

I believe that the Washington manuscript was penned well before the time of Frances Parke Custis. If it is in the hand of Lady Berkeley, it would most likely have been done in the 1650s. If it was her mother's manuscript, it would have been earlier. I must emphasize that I found not an iota of hard evidence that the manuscript came from the Culpeper family. I was unable, for example, to locate any autograph material for Frances although she is reported to have signed letters and documents. However, the Culpeper family is precisely the sort of family from which this manuscript must have sprung: once high and mighty, but on the decline. In any event, because it is a fair copy of an older manuscript, the question of whose hand penned it, and when, assumes somewhat less importance than might otherwise be the case.

Whatever the original source, the manuscript must have been in the possession of Frances Parke Custis following the death of her mother in 1708. She herself died of smallpox in 1714/15, when her son (who was to marry Martha Dandridge) was not quite

---

* *Virginia Magazine of History and Biography* (1925), vol. 33. Most of the facts concerning the Culpepers are from this source.

four years old; Lucy died the following year of the same disease. Considering the bitterness which John Custis bore his wife*—not unreasonably, it may be said—and the fact that he is said to have given much of the family silver as presents to various women, it is a wonder that the manuscript survived at all. Daniel must have cherished it as a memento of his mother, and it is quite likely he who is responsible for the family myth that Frances Custis wrote it.

I must add that there is no mention whatsoever of the manuscript at any time in any contemporary source that I could find. The contrary would have been surprising, but it means that I had to rely on internal evidence and what I was able to learn of family manuscript traditions.

To recapitulate. Our manuscript did belong to Jane Ludwell Parke (1668?–1708). This is verified by the identification of the date in 1706 written in her hand, further strengthened by the later association with Martha Washington. Since the date appears in the inner pages, the assumption that the manuscript was already completed can hardly be questioned, and this is supported by the childish signatures of Lucy Parke and of Frances in various unauthorized parts of the book. The manuscript was not written by Jane; I propose that it was given to her by her stepmother, Lady Berkeley, most likely by inheritance in 1691, in accordance with custom. Frances Parke Custis (1687–1714/15) must have inherited the manuscript in 1708 on the death of her mother, in accordance with custom. On the death of Frances, we face a void. We can only speculate that it was kept among the personal effects of Frances by John Custis, her husband, for turning over to their children on reaching maturity. There was a daughter, but she died childless several years before Daniel married Martha Dandridge in 1749. From that point on, we may assume that the manuscript was in the keeping of Martha until her granddaughter's marriage to Lawrence Lewis in 1799. This is attested to only by the same inscription that states that Frances Parke Custis wrote and gave the manuscript to Martha. However, in 1892, the Lewis family gave the manuscript, along with other historical material, to the Historical Society of Pennsylvania, where it still reposes.

* John Custis died in 1749. Freeman (vol. II) states that Daniel Custis was required, on pain of losing his inheritance, to have his father's tombstone inscribed:

UNDER THIS MARBLE TOMB LIES THE BODY OF THE HON. JOHN CUSTIS, ESQ., OF THE CITY OF WILLIAMSBURG AND PARISH OF BRUTON. FORMERLY OF HUNGAR'S PARISH ON THE EASTERN SHORE OF VIRGINIA, AND COUNTY OF NORTHAMPTON, AGED 71 YEARS, AND YET LIVED BUT SEVEN YEARS, WHICH WAS THE SPACE OF TIME HE KEPT A BACHELOR'S HOME AT ARLINGTON ON THE EASTERN SHORE OF VIRGINIA. THIS INSCRIPTION PUT ON HIS TOMB BY HIS OWN POSITIVE ORDERS.

TRANSCRIPTION NOTES

The transcription of any writing separated from us in time always poses vexing problems. Ideally, the material should be transcribed and presented to the reader as found; the only question should be the accuracy of the reading. Any tinkering, no matter how conscientiously and skillfully done, begins to substitute the wisdom of the transcriber for that of the original writer, and results in insidious damage to the work akin to that of rearranging archeological evidence. Also, the reader is deprived of some of the beauty and spirit of the language of another day. The problem is, of course, that a seventeenth-century manuscript, particularly one not intended for publication, would seem rather forbidding to many readers who would otherwise be fascinated by the material contained therein.

If it had been feasible to present a facsimile edition in a companion volume, I would have felt free to modernize spellings and make other concessions to easy readability. Such problems as arise for the modern reader are largely visual and have to do with archaic spellings. (Archaic words and allusions, or puzzling shifts of meaning, are easily take care of by glossing.) Even to the uninitiated reader, Chaucer springs to life when read aloud; the language and spelling of the Washington manuscript are, after all, far more accessible to us than that of the fourteenth century. Still, I reluctantly agreed that certain concessions to readability could be made without grave damage to the manuscript.

The most radical concession was to supply punctuation. Such punctuation as existed was erratic, often serving to actually hinder comprehension rather than to serve it. If certain passages seem over punctuated—and they are—it is because of my reluctance to excise any but the most confusing marks made by the hand of the last scribe. Bracketing hundreds of commas and periods to indicate that they had been supplied would have been ludicrous and distracting. I tried to follow seventeenth-century practice on punctuation but that is nearly as capricious as seventeenth-century spelling practices. In no instance did I change from lower to upper case when I deemed it advisable to start a new sentence, and this is in line with nonprofessional manuscript practices of the day. Where any change of meaning or emphasis was made possible by shifting punctuation, I so indicated. In any event, the higgledy-piggledy successions of clauses and qualifying phrases, to say nothing of the long lists of ingredients with varying amounts and instructions, made unnecessarily difficult reading, and this I tried to ease.

The other concessions concern typographical conventions, concessions that are nearly standard today, even in scholarly circles. Recipe titles have been left intact, and the spellings in the manuscript are otherwise rigorously maintained, but I did allow myself to conform to modern practice on the differentiation between *u* and *v*, and *i* and *j*. This differentiation was virtually standard in printing shortly after mid-seventeenth century; our manuscript is conservative in this respect.

The typographical confusion between *u* and *v* dates from Roman times, according to *OED*; usage swung back and forth and, at one time, was the reverse of modern practice. Fascinating traces of this persist in our manuscript; *u* is nearly invariable for both *u* and *v*. *V* rarely appears and when it does, it is meticulously, almost painfully formed, in contrast to the legible but easy *u*. (Interestingly, the *v* most often appears in *violet*, but only in recipe titles; in the recipes themselves, the scribe would revert to the undifferentiated *u*.) In a few instances, as in S 50 and 244, for example, we find *vse* standing for *use*.

The *j* was a relatively late modification of *i* to indicate the letter's consonantal value, which had evolved from the sound of *y* in *yet* to that of *j* in *jelly*. This differentiation became fairly standard in printing well before that between *u* and *v*; it is nearly invariable in Gerard's *Herball*, 1597, for instance, while that between *u* and *v* was inconsistent. (Understandably, this lack of differentiation persisted longest in proper names; in the publication of the *First Folio* in 1623, for instance, the eulogy to Mr. William Shakespeare is signed "Ben: Ionson.") For our scribe (in what certain experts say is the latter half of the seventeenth century), this differentiation had only just begun. It is *Iumbals*, *Ielly*, *Iellyflowers*, and *Iuice* (more rarely *iuice*, but see facsimile S 27). Occasionally, these forms worried our scribe; they had begun to look archaic. In S 216, for example, she makes an elaborate *J* in *Jelly*, very different from her upper-case *I*, which could resemble a *J* out of context. (In S 165, both *Iuice* and *If* occur.) In the jelly recipes that follow, she variously uses *I* and her fancy *J*, occasionally correcting the *I* to *J*.

465

More rarely, she uses *j* for *i*, but in S 159, we have a pristine *jce* for ice.

To some extent, the same historical situation obtained for *i* and *y*, but because the differentiation has never been completed (*y* still serves as a vowel in many words, frequently changing to *i* in other forms), it does not seem so strange to us.

The charming, but slightly confusing long *s*, *ſ*, has also been dropped. I should add that I have tended to observe these typographical conventions in citing earlier sources as well.

The *y* in *y^e*, *y^t*, and so on, is a relic of the runic thorn, signifying *th*. Sometime in the fourteenth century, the *y* and the thorn became confused and *y* came to serve as a symbol for *th* in manuscripts and printing. As *OED* explains, it is now only used jocularly, as in *Ye Olde Shoppe*, but at the time of our manuscript, *y^e* and other quick forms such as *w^{ch}* were as normal as *Mr.* and *Mrs.* are today. With the exception of *y^r* for *your*, the *y* stands for *th* and is so pronounced. Thus, *y^e* is pronounced *the*.

There are other archaic orthographic usages in the manuscript involving the use of stressed and unstressed forms of various prepositions. The scribe invariably uses *thorough* for *through*, for instance, although differentiation was complete by the time of Caxton, the great printer (1421-91); since early in the sixteenth century, *thorough* has served only as adjective, except where it survives in old words: *thoroughfare*, for instance, but *through* street. The inconsistent differentiation between *to* and *too* should cause no difficulty, but *of* is made to serve for both *of* and *off*, and this can be disconcerting. According to *OED*, the emphatic *off* appeared around 1400, and by the time of Shakespeare, differentiation was effectively complete. Also, *then* is made to serve for both *then* and *than*, a practice that did not survive the sixteenth century. They were originally forms of the same word (*OED*).

The quarter century following the publication of *The Authorized Version of the Bible* in 1611 was a time of great change in the English language, particularly in spelling. (Perhaps I should say, rather, of stabilization.) Before that time, spelling had been charmingly capricious; with the spread of the printed word, a tendency to settle into more or less accepted forms developed. In 1615, Markham published *The English Hus-wife*, already an old-fashioned spelling. By 1637, it had become *The English House-wife*, an important step. (*Hous* forms date back to the thirteenth century, coexisting with other forms.) *Contayning* had become *containing* and the *u* and *v* had become almost completely differentiated. (The *i* and *j* are differentiated in the first edition, making it far more modern than our manuscript in this regard.) The language no longer looks archaic; by the 1660 edition, it is very nearly modern.

A number of explanations can be put forth for the fact that our manuscript is more archaic than the 1615 edition; the hominess of the subject, a manuscript may have lagged behind printing and, because of their relative intellectual isolation, women's writing behind that of men. But I believe that the compelling reason is that our scribe, as discussed elsewhere, was copying from a much older master copy and was doing her best to make a fair copy. In a number of cases, spelling is actually corrected by the scribe to a more archaic form.

I want to emphasize that the various forms are not illiterate forms. There are indeed a number of scribal errors, many of which are noted, but most of the spellings are those of recorded forms, current at various times. The use of more than one form in a single paragraph is entirely typical. There are fascinating traces of dialectal forms, which I have noted in some cases. In many cases, variant spellings tell us much about the way a word was pronounced at the time.

A word on my use of brackets. The pages of the manuscript were badly damaged along two edges. All reconstructed portions are carefully bracketed. Where there can be no reasonable doubt about a missing word or a set phrase, I bracket it without comment, using common forms from the manuscript for the most part. Occasionally, I am assisted by the presence of characteristic upper or lower strokes. Any truly speculative reconstruction is commented on. Occasionally, the scribe clearly omits a word or phrase; this is always noted. Obvious errors clearly corrected by the scribe have not been noted unless they seemed significant in some way. Recipe titles, when necessary, are reconstructed from the scribe's own index; it should be noted that there are occasional minor differences between the titles as they appear in the text and in the index.

The scribe occasionally used parentheses in setting off phrases, and I took advantage of this in setting off difficult passages. I always noted it.

BIBLIOGRAPHY

I should like to have listed my sources and reading material by category—cookery, gardening, medicine—but many works resist such classification. Likewise, chronological presentation poses problems involving the date of the material as distinct from the date of publication so that, finally, the books are presented pell-mell. I did, however, establish a separate manuscript category that includes unpublished works as well as those published long after their time; they are arranged by author, title, collector, or subject, as appropriate. Dates in parentheses refer to first editions unavailable to me. Bracketed material refers to information obtained otherwise than from the work itself. I have thought it useful to list modern reprints and facsimile editions that have come to my attention. It is pertinent to note that such works listed under Walter J. Johnson, Norwood, New Jersey, are published in conjunction with Theatrum Orbis Terrarum, Amsterdam.

BASIC REFERENCE WORKS

Battisti, Carlo. *Dizionario Etimologico Italiano*. Florence, 1952.

Bitting, Katherine Golden. *Gastronomic Bibliography*. San Francisco, 1939.

Corominas, Joan. *Breve Diccionario Etimologico de la Lengua Castellana*. Madrid, 1961.

Cotgrave, Randle. *A Dictionarie of the French and English Tongues*. London, 1611. Facsimile: Norwood, N.J.: Walter J. Johnson, 1971; Columbia: University of South Carolina Press, 1950.

Du Cange, Charles du Fresne (1610–1688). *Glossarium Mediae et Infimae Latinitatis*. Paris, 1840–45.

English Dialect Dictionary (EDD), Joseph Wright, ed. Oxford: Henry Frowde, 1898–1908.

Florio, John. *First fruites. Also a perfect induction to the Italian, and English tongues*. London, 1578. Facsimile: Norwood, N.J.: Walter J. Johnson, 1969.

——*Second frutes*. 1591. Facsimile: Norwood, N.J.: Walter J. Johnson, 1969.

——*A world of wordes, or most copious and exact dictionarie in Italian and English.* 1598.

Galfridus (fl. 1440). *Promptorium Parvulorum Siue Clericorum, Lexicon Anglo-Latinum Princeps.* London: Camden Society, 1843–65; London: Early English Text Society, 1908.

Godefroy, Frederic. *Dictionnaire de l'Ancienne Langue Française et de tous ses Dialects du IX au XV Siècle.* Paris, 1881-1902.

Halliwell, James Orchard. *Dictionary of Archaic and Provincial Words.* London, 1889.

Littré, Emile. *Dictionnaire de la Langue Française.* Paris, 1863-77.

Lowenstein, Eleanor. *Bibliography of American Cookbooks, 1742-1860.* Worcester, Mass.: American Antiquarian Society; New York: Corner Book Shop, 1972.

Oxford, Arnold Whitaker. *English Cookery Books to the Year 1850.* London: Oxford University Press, 1913.

Oxford English Dictionary (OED). London: Oxford University Press, 1971.

Palsgrave. Jehan. *Lesclarcissement de la Langue Françoyse.* London, 1530; reprint, Paris, 1852.

Robert, Paul. *Dictionnaire Alphabetique & Analogique de la Langue Française.* Paris: Societé du Nouveau Littré, 1967.

Vicaire, Georges. *Bibliographie Gastronomique.* Paris, 1890.

I have also quoted from *Mr. William Shakespeare Comedies, Histories, & Tragedies.* First Folio of 1623. Facsimile: New Haven: Yale University Press, 1954; and Geoffrey Chaucer, *The Prologue to the Canterbury Tales,* as read by Mark H. Liddell. New York: Macmillan, 1908.

READING LIST

Acton, Eliza. *Modern Cookery for Private Families.* London: Longman, Brown, Green and Longmans (1845), 1855; the latter in facsimile, London: Elek, 1966. Miss Acton was one of the most perceptive of cooks.

——*The Best of Eliza Acton.* Selected and Edited by Elizabeth Ray. London: Longmans, 1968. A smattering of recipes—some truncated—from the 1845 edition; the introduction by Elizabeth David makes it worthwhile.

Anderson, Frank J. *An Illustrated History of the Herbals.* New York: Columbia University Press, 1977. A scholarly introduction to the ancient herbals.

L'Art de Bien Traiter . . . Exactement recherché, & mis en lumière, par L. S. R. Paris, 1674. Facsimile, Luzarches: Daniel Morcrette, 1978.

Audot, Louis-Eustache. *La Cuisinière de la Campagne et de la Ville, par M. L.-E. A[udot].* Paris: Audot (1818); 3d ed., Paris: Audot, 1823.

   La Charcuterie. 1st ed. Paris: Audot, 1818.

   La Pâtissière de la Campagne et de la Ville, Suivie de l'Art de Faire le Pain-d'Epices, les Gaufres et les Oublies. 1st ed. Paris: Audot, 1818.

   L'Art de Conserver et d'Employer les Fruits. 2d ed. Paris: Audot, 1823.

   The four companion books were published separately; some time later, the material was consolidated in a single tome. Curiously, the three latter books are mentioned neither by Vicaire nor Bitting. The figure of 248 pages given by Vicaire for the 1818 edition of *La Cuisinière* corresponds to that of 289 pages in the somewhat expanded third edition.

———*La Cuisinière de la Campagne et de la Ville.* 90th ed. Paris: Audot, 1912. 782 pp.

Beau Chesne, John de and John Baildon. *A Booke Containing Divers Sortes of Hands, as Well the English and French Secretarie.* London, 1602. Facsimile: Norwood, N.J.: Walter J. Johnson, 1977.

Beeton, Isabelle. *Mrs. Beeton's Book of Household Management.* London, 1861. Facsimile: London: Jonathan Cape, 1968. This compendium dominated Victorian and Edwardian cookery, appearing in innumerable versions and editions as late as the 1920s.

———*Mrs. Beeton's International Cookery.* New York: Platt & Peck, n.d. [about 1912]. But it is printed in England and bears no trace of adaptation.

Beverley, Robert. *The History and Present State of Virginia.* London: Richard Parker, 1705. Reprint: Chapel Hill: University of North Carolina, 1947. Beverley was a historian and a perceptive observer. His chapters on the Indians, their way of life, and their cooking, are of particular interest here.

Billinsley, Martin. *The Pens Excellencie or the Secretaries Delight.* London, 1618. Facsimile: Norwood, N.J.: Walter J. Johnson, 1977.

[Bonnefons, Nicolas de]. *Les Délices de la Campagne: Suitte de Jardinier François, Dedié aux Dames Mesnageres.* Paris (1654), 1662. A delightful and important book.

———*Le Jardinier François, Dedié aux Dames Mesnageres.* Paris (1651), 1692. This companion volume contains not only valuable gar-

471

dening and horticultural material but instructions for making all manner of fruit and flower preserves and confections such as *massepains* (marchpane).

Boorde, Andrewe. *Here foloweth A Compendyous Regyment or A Dyetary of Helth made in Montpylior.* London, 1542. Same, second edition, 1562, annotated by F. J. Furnivall. London, Early English Text Society, 1870. A most important work for those who would study Tudor food, customs, and medicine.

Briggs, Richard. *The New Art of Cookery, According to the Present Practice.* Philadelphia: Spotswood, Campbell, and Johnson, 1792. First American edition of an English work of 1788. The earliest recipe including love apples (tomatoes) and the first for ice cream known by me to have been published in the United States are included in this book, although such recipes had long circulated in English editions of Hannah Glasse's work.

Bullock, Helen. *Williamsburg Art of Cookery.* 2d ed. Richmond, Va.: Colonial Williamsburg, 1939. This archly quaint book is of minimal historical interest because most of the recipes are heavily modernized.

Byrd, William. *William Byrd's Natural History of Virginia or the Newly Discovered Eden.* Bern, 1737; in German. Reprint, including an English translation by Richard Croom Beatty and William J. Malloy. Richmond, Va.: Dietz Press, 1940. Byrd was a naturalist, a member of the Royal Society, and founder of the city of Richmond.

Carson, Jane. *Colonial Virginia Cookery.* Williamsburg, Va.: Williamsburg Research Studies, 1968. An invaluable study of the subject.

Carter, Susannah. *The Frugal Housewife, or Complete Woman Cook.* Boston, 1772; New York, 1792; Philadelphia, 1796, 1802, 1803. All are editions of the English work; the last one contains interesting American recipes. The fine plates are by Paul Revere. Reprint of the first edition as *The Frugal Colonial Housewife,* New York: Dolphin, Doubleday, 1976; it is marred by inexplicable editing errors.

Chauncey, Martine. *Le pain d'épice de Dijon.* Paris: Christine Bonneton, 1978.

Child, Lydia Maria. *The American Frugal Housewife. Dedicated to Those Who Are Not Ashamed of Economy.* Boston, 1832. Facsimile: Columbus: Ohio State University Libraries, 1971. The book includes some of the earliest printed recipes for many peculiarly American dishes.

A Closet for Ladies and Gentlewomen, or, The Art of Preserving, Conserving, and Candying With the manner howe to make divers kinds of Syrups: and all kind of banqueting stuffes. Also divers soveraigne Medicines and Salves, for Sundry Diseases. London, 1608. This book and our manuscript contain a number of parallel still room recipes.

Cogan [also Coghan], Thomas. *The Haven of Health: Chiefly gathered for the comfort of Students, and consequently of all those that have a care of their health.* London, 1584. Doctor Cogan gives the earliest recipe that I have found for the sempiternal cordial water of Doctor Stevens.

Cosman, Madeleine Pelner. *Fabulous Feasts, Medieval Cookery and Ceremony.* New York: Braziller, 1976. This lavishly illustrated book, with pages of imposing "archive aids," contrives to present over 100 recipes, many of which are highly questionable, without citing a source or giving one original text. Recipes include baking powder, pineapple *(Ananas)*, and other historical anomalies. Dr. Cosman is a historian.

The Country House-wives Garden, Containing Rules for Hearbs and Seeds of Common Use, with their times and seasons when to set and sow them. Together, With the Husbandry of Bees, published with secrets very necessary for every House-wife. Printed by Anne Griffin, London, 1637. Reprint, Milford, Conn.: Rosetta E. Clarkson, 1940.

La Cuisinière Républicaine. Paris: 1794/95. Facsimile, Luzarches: Daniel Morcrette, 1976. A book of recipes devoted to *pommes de terre* (white potatoes), not to be confused with *Topinambours* (Jerusalem artichokes), often called *pommes de terre* in old works. There was also some confusion in nomenclature with truffles.

Culpeper, Nicholas. *Pharmacopoeia Londinensis.* London, 1654.

——*A Physical Directory.* 3d ed., London, 1651. Culpeper, *Student in Physick and Astrology,* was the great popularizer of medical lore of his time, angering the medical profession by translating pharmaceutical works from the Latin. (See Morellus Petrus.) He may have been a bit of a fraud, but his works reflect the beliefs of the time.

Custis, George Washington Parke. *Recollections and Private Memoirs of Washington, by his Adopted Son.* New York, 1860.

A Dairie Book for Good Huswives. Very profitable and pleasaunt for the making and keeping of white meates [dairy products]. Printed for

Bibliography

Thomas Hacket, London, 1588; Facsimile, Norwood, N.J.: Walter
J. Johnson, 1975.
David, Elizabeth. *English Bread and Yeast Cookery*. London: Allen
Lane, Penguin, 1977; Penguin, 1979; New York: Viking, 1980.
——*Spices, Salt and Aromatics in the English Kitchen: English Cooking,
Ancient and Modern*. Vol. I. Harmondsworth: Penguin, 1970.
——*Summer Cooking*. Harmondsworth: Penguin, 1965. A personal
favorite of mine.
——*Syllabubs and Fruit Fools*. Printed for the author, London, 1969.
From the works of our foremost writer on food, I have chosen
only those dealing primarily with English cooking.
Dawson, Thomas. *The Good Huswifes Jewell. Wherein is to be found
most excellent and rare Devises for conceites in Cookery, found out by
the practise of Thomas Dawson. Whereunto is adjoyned sundry approved receits for many soveraine oyles, and the way to distill many
precious waters, with divers approved medicines for many diseases.*
London, (1585?), 1586, 1596.
——*The Second Part of The Good Hus-wives Jewell. Wherein is to bee
found most apt and readiest wayes to distill many wholsome and sweete
waters. In which likewise is shewed the best maner in preserving of
divers sorts of Fruits, & making of Sirrops. With divers conceits in
Cookerie with the Booke of Carving.* (1585), 1587, 1597. Facsimile,
Part I, 1596, and Part II, 1597, bound together. Norwood, N.J.:
Walter J. Johnson, 1977.
Digby [Digbie in some editions], Kenelme. *The Closet of the Emi-
nently Learned Sir Kenelme Digby, Kt., Opened.* London, 1668, 1669.
Evelyn called him a mountebank but the work, characterized by
an inordinate number of medicinal and cordial waters, is most
interesting.
Pedanius Dioscorides of Anazarbos, The Greek Herbal of A.D. 512. Eng-
lished by John Goodyear. London, 1655; same, edited by Robert
T. Gunter, London: Oxford University Press, 1934.
Dronne, Louis-François. *Traité Historique et Pratique de la Charcuterie
Ancienne et Moderne.* Paris: Lacroix, n.d. [1869].
The Edinburgh New Dispensatory, A new edition edited by William
Lewis. Philadelphia, 1741.
Emerson, Lucy. *The New-England Cookery.* Montpelier, Vt., 1808.
Entire sections of this book are lifted verbatim, errors and all,
from Amelia Simmons.
Emmison, F. G. *Elizabethan Life, Home, Work & Land, From Essex
Wills and Sessions and Manorial Records.* Chelmsford: Essex County

Council; Plymouth, Mass: Pilgrim Society and Plimoth Plantation, 1976.

——*Tudor Food and Pastimes.* London: Ernest Benn, 1964.

——*Tudor Secretary.* Chichester: Phillimore & Co., 1970. (*Tudor Food
and Pastimes* is largely included in this work.) These works are
invaluable for students of the period.

Evelyn, John. *An Account of Bread . . . Entituled, Panificium, or the
several manners of making Bread in France.* London, A Collection
of Letters for the Improvement of Husbandry and Trade, Number 12, January 16, 1682/3 (final digits unclear). The recipes are
actually adapted from *Les Délices de la Campagne* by Bonnefons
(Evelyn had translated his *Le Jardinier François* into English, 1658)
and so represent French practice rather than that of *French bread*
in English cookbooks. The remarks on flour and ovens are illuminating, as: "The whiter the *Flower,* the less goodness in
tast."

——*Acetaria: A Discourse of Sallets.* London, 1699; reprint, Brooklyn,
N.Y.: Brooklyn Botanic Garden, 1937. A charming and enlightening work.

Farmer, Fannie Merritt. *The Boston Cooking-School Cook Book.* Boston:
Little, Brown, 1896, 1914, 1916, 1926, 1965. First edition in facsimile, New York: Crown, 1973. The maiden aunt of home economists who spelled the end of the era of good American cookery.

Favre, Joseph. *Dictionnaire Universel de Cuisine et d'Hygiène Alimen-
taire.* Paris, 1883–1891.

Forster, John. *Englands Happiness Increased, or A Sure and Easie Remedy against all succeeding Dear Years; By A Plantation of the Roots
called* Potatoes, *whereof (with the Addition of Wheat Flower) excellent,
good and wholesome Bread may be made . . . for halfe the Charge as
formerly . . . . Invented and Published for the Good of the Poorer Sort.*
London: 1664. This rare work (brought to my attention by Elizabeth David at press time) is a tract, backed by the Royal Society,
effectively calling on Charles II to sponsor the cultivation of potatoes in England, specified by Forster as "*Irish Potatoes,* being
little different from those of *Virginia.*" (The white potato had
been cultivated in Ireland for some time.) They are carefully
differentiated from sweet potatoes, "those of greatest request,
[which] are the *Spanish Potatoes.*" In addition to planting instructions, he gives recipes for bread, pastries, and puddings, all involving the use of pureed boiled white potatoes as bulk to eke
out wheat. (See *A Collection of choise receipts,* page 485.) I think

it safe to say that until the closing years of the seventeenth century, perhaps later, recipes calling for sliced potatoes (as in the Countess of Kent's potato pie or the ancient olio pie in C 53, which see) require sweet potatoes; white potatoes were fit for the poor.

Furnivall, F. J., editor. *Early English Meals and Manners: the Boke of Norture of John Russell, the Bokes of Kervynge, Curtasye, and Demeanor, the Babees Book, Urbanitatis, &c.* London: Early English Text Society, 1868.

Gardiner, Richard. *Profitable Instructions for the Manuring, Sowing and Planting of Kitchin Gardens. Very Profitable for the common wealth and greatly for the helpe and comfort of poore people. Gathered by Richard Gardiner of Shrewsberie.* Imprinted at London by Edward Allde for Edward White, 1603. Facsimile, Norwood, N.J.: Walter J. Johnson, 1973.

Gerard, John. *The Herball or General Historie of Plantes. Gathered by John Gerarde of London, Master in Chirurgerie,* London, 1597. Facsimile, Norwood, N.J.: Walter J. Johnson, 1974.

——Same, *Very much Enlarged and Amended by Thomas Johnson, Citizen and Apothecarye of London,* 1636.

[Glasse, Hannah]. *The Art of Cookery, Made Plain and Easy; Which far exceeds any Thing of the Kind ever yet published . . . By a Lady. Printed for the Author,* London, 1747; same, by Mrs. Glasse, London, 1751, 1755, 1765, 1796; same, by Mrs. Glasse, Alexandria, Va., 1805. This was the most popular cookbook in both England and the colonies into the nineteenth century. The Virginia edition has some interesting American recipes.

Glasse, H. *The Complete Confectionery: Or the Whole Art of Confectionery made Plain and Easy.* London, 1762.

Gray, Samuel Frederick. *A Supplement to the Pharmacopoeia.* London, 1821.

Hariot, Thomas. *A Briefe and True Report of the New Found Land in Virginia: of the commodities there found and to be raysed, as well marchantable, as other for victuall, building and other necessarie uses for those that are and shall be the planters there; and of the nature and manners of the naturall inhabitants.* London, 1588. Facsimile, Norwood, N.J.: Walter J. Johnson, 1971.

Harrison, William. *The Description of England.* London, (1577, in Holinshead's Chronicle I). Reprint, F. J. Furnivall, ed. London: New Shakespeare Society, 1877.

Hartley, Dorothy. *Food in England*. London: MacDonald and Janes, 1954, 1975. There is delightful material in this book but do beware of her muddled dating; it has tripped many a "borrower."

Hazlitt, W. Carew. *Faiths and Folklore of the British Isles. A Dictionary of National Beliefs*. London, 1905. Reprint, New York, 1965.

Henisch, Bridget Ann. *Fast and Feast, Food in Medieval Society*. University Park: Pennsylvania State University Press, 1976. A valuable book.

Herman, Judith and Marguerite Shalett Herman. *The Cornucopia. Recipes, Containing Good Reading and Good Cookery from more than 500 years of Recipes, Food Lore, Etc . . .* [1390–1899]. New York: Harper & Row, 1973. The material from English and American sources is well chosen and presented with one small reservation on my part concerning unnecessary modernization of archaic spellings.

Hess, John L. and Karen Hess. *The Taste of America*. New York: Viking, 1977; Penguin, 1977. A polemical and historical sketch of the decline of American food and cookery from colonial times to the junk and "gourmet" food of today.

Hieatt, Constance B. and Sharon Butler. *Pleyn Delit: Medieval Cookery for Modern Cooks*. Toronto: University of Toronto Press, 1976. Original text and working versions are given.

Hutchinson, Peggy. *Peggy Hutchinson's Old English Cookery Book*. London: W. Foulsham, n.d. [about 1935]. The old-fashioned recipes, largely from Northumberland, are highly interesting.

[Countess of Kent, Elizabeth Grey]. *A Choice Manuall, of Rare and Select Secrets in Physick and Chirurgery: collected, and practised by the Right Honourable, the Countesse of Kent, late deceased. As also most Exquisite ways of Preserving, conserving, Candying, &c.*

——*A True Gentlewomans Delight, Wherein is contained all manner of Cookery: Together with Preserving, Conserving, Drying, and Candying. Very necessary for all Ladies and Gentlewomen*. London: W. J. Gent, 1653, 1659. The two companion books are usually bound together although they are quite distinct, and in actual fact, only the first book is attributed to the countess by W. Jar, the author of record. Oxford reports that the books are listed under the name of Elizabeth Grey by the British Museum Library.

Kimball, Marie. *The Martha Washington Cook Book*. New York: Coward-McCann, 1940. (See page 449.)

Kinsley, H. M. *One Hundred Recipes for the Chafing Dish*. New York: Gorham Silversmiths, 1894. Facsimile, New York: Arno, 1973.

Kramer, Samuel Noah. *History Begins at Sumer.* New York: Doubleday Anchor, 1959.

Labarage, Margaret Wade. *A Baronial Household of the Thirteenth Century.* London: Eyre & Spottiswoode, 1965.

Lagriffe, Louis. *Le Livre des Epices, des Condiments, & les Aromates.* Vauvenargues en Provence: Robert Morel, 1968.

Leslie, Eliza. *Directions for Cookery, in Its Various Branches.* Philadelphia: Cary & Hart, 1837, 1843, 1848, 1870. Facsimile of 1848 ed., New York: Arno, 1973. Miss Leslie and Mrs. Randolph are two of our most perceptive American cooks.

Lewis, Edna. *The Taste of Country Cooking.* New York: Knopf, 1976. The lovingly remembered cookery of Freetown, Virginia, founded by freed slaves. The traces of Mrs. Randolph's cookery of 1824 are strong, but the increase in the amounts of sugar called for is striking.

Liger, Louis. *Dictionaire Pratique du Bon Ménager de Campagne et de Ville.* Paris: Ribou, 1715, first edition. An invaluable source.

Lincoln, Mary J. *Mrs. Lincoln's Boston Cook Book. What to do and what not to do in Cooking.* Boston: Little Brown, 1883, 1893, 1926. The original textbook of the Boston Cooking School, antedating Fannie Farmer's book by thirteen years.

Lorwin, Madge. *Dining With Shakespeare.* New York: Atheneum, 1976. A sampling of recipes from the period with text and working versions.

M[arkham], G[ervase]. *The English Hus-wife, Contayning, The inward and outward vertues which ought to be in a compleat woman. As, her skill in Physicke, Cookery, Banqueting-stuffe, Distillation, Perfumes, Wooll, Hemp, Flax, Dayries, Brewing, Baking, and all other things belonging to an Houshould. A Worke very profitable and necessarie, gathered for the generall good of this kingdome.* Printed at London for Roger Jackson, 1615. *(Second book of Countrey Contentments.)* Facsimile, Norwood, N.J.: Walter J. Johnson, 1973. Same, various formats and printers, 1623, 1631, 1637, 1660, 1683. It was the most popular cookbook of the seventeenth century and early came to the colonies, perhaps with the Pilgrims in 1620.

Marnette, Monsieur. *The Perfect Cook, Being the most exact directions for the making all kind of Pastes, with the perfect teaching how to Raise, Season, and make all Sorts of Pies, Pasties, and Florentines, etc.* London: Nath. Brooks, 1656.

[Massialot]. *L'Escole Parfaite des Officiers de Bouche, contenant Le Vray Maistre-d'Hostel, Le Grant Escuyer Tranchant, Le Sommelier Royal,*

478

Bibliography

Le Confiturier Royal, Le Cuisinier Royal, et Le Pâtissier Royal. Paris: Ribou, 1676.

May, Robert. *The Accomplisht Cook, Or the Art and Mystery of Cookery . . . Expert and ready wayes for the Dressing of all sorts of Flesh, Fowl, and Fish; the Raising of Pastes; the best Directions for all manner of Kickshaws, and the most Poinant Sauces; with the Tearms of Carving and Sewing.* London: Nath. Brooke, 1660, 1671, 1678. An important book by a professional cook.

[Menon]. *La Cuisinière Bourgeoise.* (Paris: 1746); Bruxelles: 1754. It is the only eighteenth-century culinary work of importance directed to women cooks. (See *La Cuisinière Républicaine* and Parmentier.) It became highly popular and editions continued until mid-nineteenth century, gradually being displaced by Audot.

Morel, Ambroise. *Histoire Illustreé de la Boulangerie en France.* Paris: Syndicat Patronal de la Boulangerie de Paris et de la Seine, 1924.

Moryson, Fynes. *An Itinerary.* London, 1617.

Muffet [Moufet, etc.], Thomas. *Healths Improvement or Rules Comprising and Discovering the Nature, Method and Manner of Preparing All Sorts of Food Used in This Nation, corrected and enlarged by Christopher Bennett, Doctor in Physics.* London, 1655.

[Murrell, John]. *A New Booke of Cookerie, Wherein is set forth the newest and most commendable Fashion for Dressing or Sowcing, eythere Flesh, Fish, or Fowle . . . Set forth by the observation of a Traveller. I. M.* London: John Browne, 1615. Facsimile, Norwood, N.J.: Walter J. Johnson, 1972.

——*Murrels Two Books of Cookerie and Carving. The fourth time printed with new Additions.* London: John Marriot, 1631.

Neckam, A. *De Utensilibus.* In *A Volume of Vocabularies,* Thomas Wright, ed. London, 1857.

Nola, Maese Ruperto de. *Libro de Guisados, Manjares & Potajes.* Logroño, 1529. Reprinted, Madrid–Palma de Mallorca, 1969.

Oxford Book of Food Plants (S. G. Harrison, G. B. Masefield, Michael Wallis, and B. E. Nicholson). London: Oxford University Press, 1969.

The Oxford Sausage; or, Select Poetical Pieces, written by the most Celebrated Wits of the University of Oxford. With designs by Thomas Bewick. London, 1764. (See recipe C 25.)

Parkinson, John. *Paradisus in Sole, Paradisus Terrestris, or, A Garden of Flowers, with a Kitchen Garden and an Orchard.* London, 1629. Facsimile, Norwood, N.J.: Walter J. Johnson, 1975.

Parmentier, Antoine Augustin. *Aux Bonnes Ménagères des Villes et des Campagnes sur la Meilleure Manière de Faire Leur Pain.* Paris, 1777. A curiously little known work (mentioned by neither Vicaire nor Bitting) by the author of the great classic on bread.

[Partridge, John]. *The Treasurie of Commodious Conceites, and Hidden Secrets, Commonly Called the Good Huswives Closet of provision for the health of her˙houshold.* London, 1573.

Petrus, Morellus. *The Expert Doctors Dispensatory.* Nicholas Culpeper, trans. London, 1657.

Plat, H[ugh]. *Delightes for Ladies, To adorne their Persons, Tables, Closets, and Distillatories; with Beauties, Banquets, Perfume, & Waters. Reade, Practice, & Censure.* London, [1600 ?], 1602, 1608, 1623. Reprint of 1627 edition, Herrin, Ill.: Trovillion, 1939.

——*Divers Chimicall Conclusions Concerning the Art of Distillation. With Many rare practises and uses thereof, according to the Authors own experience.* London, 1594.

Platina [Bartolomeo Sacchi di Piadena], *Platine en françoys tresutile et necessaire pour le corps humain qui traicte de honeste volupte* . . . Lyon, 1505 (first French edition). . . . *Le Grand Cuisinier de B. Platine de Cremonne . . . Traduit de Latin en François par M. Desdier Christol M. à Montepellier* . . . Paris, 1586. The earliest edition of *Platina de honesta voluptate* is from about 1474, according to Vicaire, and bears the approval of the *Presbyterum Cardinalem.* All French editions were "copiously augmented" by Desdier and other doctors in the spirit of the School of Salerno as continued at Montpellier, so that while they are not entirely faithful to Platina, the work exerted tremendous influence in France and illuminates many aspects of French—and English—attitudes towards diet in the sixteenth century. The actual recipes are most interesting and represent a salutary break with medieval excess.

Pliny the Elder, *Historia Naturalis, Commonly called, The Natural Historie of Plinius Secundus* [d. 79 A.D.]. Translated by Philemon Holland, London, 1601. . . . *Historia Naturalis*, with English translation by H. Rackam [on facing pages]. Harvard University Press, Cambridge, 1938-62.

Pomet, Pierre. *A Compleat History of Druggs, Done into English.* London, 1712.

Porter, M. E. *Mrs. Porter's New Southern Cookery Book.* Philadelphia: John E. Potter, 1871. Facsimile, New York: Arno, 1973.

A Proper Newe Booke of Cokerye. A reprint edited by Catherine

Bibliography

Frances Frere, Cambridge, England, 1913. The book was originally published in 1545, according to Oxford.

The Queens Closet Opened. Incomparable Secrets in Physick Chirurgery, Preserving and Candying, and Cookery; as they were presented to the Queen . . . Transcribed from the true Copies of her Majesties own Receipt Books, by W. M., one of her late servants. London: Nathaniel Brook, 1655, 1671, 1696, 1713. The work consists of three books: *The Pearle of Practice, A Queens Delight,* and *The Compleat Cook,* the latter often separately published. This was an influential work.

Quincy, John. *Lexicon Physico-Medicum: or, A New Medicinal Dictionary.* London, 1726, 1787. . . . *Pharmacopoeia Officinalis & Extemporanea: or, A compleat English Dispensatory.* London: 1718, 1719, 1720.

Raffald, Elizabeth. *The Experienced English Housekeeper.* London, (1769), 1789.

Randolph, Mary. *The Virginia Housewife: or Methodical Cook.* Washington, D.C.: Davis & Force, 1824; Baltimore, 1831, 1836 (copyright 1828); Philadelphia, 1860; the latter in facsimile, Richmond, Va.: Avenel and the Valentine Museum, (about 1970). Mrs. Randolph died in 1828, so it would appear that her son took the 1828 edition, changed the date of the author's preface (otherwise identical to that of the 1824 edition), and presented it as an 1831 edition. As compared to the 1824 edition, there are only a few new recipes and minor changes in arrangement; succeeding editions differ from the 1831 edition only on the title page. The work is our finest American cookbook and was pillaged by later Southern writers.

The Herbal of Rufinus [fl. 1190]. Edited by Lynn Thorndike. Chicago: University of Chicago Press, 1946.

Salaman, Redcliffe. *History and Social Influence of the Potato.* Cambridge: Cambridge University Press, 1949.

Salmon, William. *The Family Dictionary; Or, Household Companion.* London, 1696, 1705. This compendium first appeared in 1695 signed by J. H.

Sass, Lorna. *To the King's Taste, Richard II's Book of Feasts and recipes adapted for modern cooking* [from *The Forme of Cury*]. New York: Metropolitan Museum of Art, 1975.

——*To the Queen's Taste, Elizabethan feasts and recipes adapted for modern cooking.* New York: Metropolitan Museum of Art, 1976. We learn here that "veal was a meat which never appeared on medieval English menus," a statement made more absurd by the inclusion of recipes for veal in her medieval book published only the year before.

Serjeantson, M. S. *The Vocabulary of Cookery in the Fifteenth Century,* in *Essays and Studies by Members of the English Association,* Vol. XXIII, collected by S. C. Roberts. Clarendon Press, Oxford, 1938.

Simmons, Amelia. *American Cookery, or the art of dressing viands, fish, poultry and vegetables, and the best modes of making pastes, puffs, pies, tarts, puddings, custards and preserves, and all kinds of cakes, from the imperial plumb to plain cake. Adapted to this country, and all grades of life. By Amelia Simmons, an American orphan.* Hartford: Hudson & Goodwin, 1796. Facsimile, New York: Oxford University Press, 1958. Albany: Charles R. & George Webster, 1796, 2d ed. This seems to be the earliest cookbook of American authorship to be published. The facsimile is of the American Antiquarian Society copy and lists the errata as corrected by the author.

S[mith], E[liza ?]. *The Compleat Housewife; or, Accomplish'd Gentlewoman's Companion: being a Collection of upwards of Five Hundred of the most approved Receipts in Cookery, Pastry, Confectionary, Preserving, Pickles, Cakes, Creams, Jellies, Made Wines, Cordials . . . fit either for private families, or such publick-spirited gentlewomen as would be beneficent to their poor Neighbors.* London, (1727).

Smith, E. Same. Williamsburg, Va.: William Parks, 1742. This, the first cookbook known to have been published in the colonies, harks back to the seventeenth century.

Thomson, Gladys Scott. *Life in a Noble Household, 1641–1700.* London: Jonathan Cape, 1937.

Le Thresor de Santé, Ou Mesnage de la Vie Humaine. Lyon, 1607.

Trease, G. E. *The Spicers and Apothecaries of the Royal Household in the Reigns of Henry III, Edward I and II.* Nottingham: Nottingham Medieval Studies, 1959.

Turner, Wylliam [also William]. *A New Herball.* London, 1551–62.

——*The Names of Herbes in Greke, Latin, Englishe, Duche, Frenche with the Commone Names Herbaries and Apotecaries Use.* London, 1548; reprint, edited by James Britten, London: English Dialect Society, 1881. This is an extremely useful edition because the names are correlated with nineteenth-century scientific names.

[Tusser, Thomas]. *A Hundreth Good Pointes of Husbandrie.* London, 1557. Facsimile, Norwood, N.J.: Walter J. Johnson, 1973. A delightful and illuminating work in doggerel that appeared in succeeding editions.

Bibliography

Tyree, Marion Cabell. *Housekeeping in Old Virginia.* Louisville: John P. Morton, 1879. Facsimile, Louisville: Favorite Recipes Press, 1965.

W., A. *A Booke of Cookrye, Very necessary for all such as delight therin, Gathered by A. W., And now newlye enlarged, with the serving in of the Table, With the Proper Sauces to each of them convenient.* London: Edward Allde, 1591. Facsimile, Norwood, N.J.: Walter J. Johnson, 1976.

White, Florence. *Good Things in England.* London: Jonathan Cape, 1932, 1968. A useful collection of contributed regional recipes.

Wilson, C. Anne. *Food and Drink in Britain, From the Stone Age to Recent Times.* London: Constable, 1973; Harmondsworth: Penguin, 1976. An invaluable reference.

Wood, William. *New Englands Prospect. A true, lively, and experimentall description of that part of America, commonly called New England.* London, 1634. Facsimile, Norwood, N.J.: Walter J. Johnson, 1968.

Woolley, Hannah. *The Gentlewomans Companion.* London, 1673, 1682. Much of the book is concerned with morals and manners, but the recipes are interesting.

——*The Queen-like Closet or Rich Cabinet.* London, 1670.

Worde, Wynkyn de. *The Boke of Kervynge.* London, 1508. Facsimile, Norwood, N.J.: Walter J. Johnson, 1971. De Worde was the printer, associate of and successor to Caxton; the work is surely much older. (See Furnivall.) The printing, even in facsimile, is of extraordinary beauty.

MANUSCRIPT SOURCES

Apicius. *Les Dix Livres d'Apicius.* Translated and annotated by Bertrand Guégan. Paris: René Bonnel, 1933. Guégan's voluminous and scholarly notes are invaluable.

Apicius: The Roman Cookery Book. Translated from the Latin by Barbara Flower and Elisabeth Rosenbaum. London: Harrap, 1958. Apicius died about A.D. 30, so that this is the earliest extant cookbook in the Western world. The work that we know, however, is not classical, as it was compiled in perhaps the fourth century, drawing on a number of Greek and Roman sources of various periods, and is preserved in several manuscripts, the earliest of which is from the ninth century. Its direct influence on English cookery from the time of the Roman occupation may thus be largely discounted. This Latin-English pony version is

Bibliography

especially useful in conjunction with the Guégan work. (The Vehling translation cannot be recommended.)

Antiquitatis Culinariae; or Curious Tracts Relating to the Culinary Affairs of the Old English. Rev. Richard Warner, ed. London, 1791. This work contains chiefly a reconstructed *Forme of Cury* and the Arundel MS.

Arab documents

Arberry, A. J. *A Baghdad Cookery Book.* Translation of a work by Muhammad al-Hasan ibn Muhammad ibn al-Karīm al-Kātib al-Baghdādī, 623/1226, found by Dr. Daoud Celebi in 1934. *Islamic Culture, Hyderabad Quarterly Review,* January and April 1939.

Rodinson, Maxime. *Recherches sur les Documents Arabes Relatifs à la Cuisine.* Paris: *Revue des Etudes Islamiques,* nos. 17 & 18, 1949–50. Several manuscripts are discussed, including the one given above; the approach here is more historical.

Santamaria, Fernando de la Granja. *La Cocina Arabigandaluza Segun un Manuscrito Inedito.* Madrid: Facultad de Filosofia y Letras, 1960.

Arcana Fairfaxiana Manuscripta, A manuscript volume [in facsimile] *of apothecaries' lore and housewifery . . . used, and partly written by the Fairfax Family.* Introduction by George Weddell, Newcastle-on-Tyne, 1890. The early recipes, in an italic hand not so different from that in our own manuscript, are from before 1610; various hands continue through the seventeenth century.

Avery, Susanna (fl. 1688). *A plain plantain: country wines, dishes, & herbal cures from a 17th century household M.S. receipt book.* Russell George Alexander, ed. Ditchling, Sussex, St. Dominic's Press, 1922.

Blencowe. *Receipt Book of Mrs. Ann Blencowe, A.D., 1694.* Introduction by George Saintsbury. London: Adelphi, Guy Chapman, 1925.

A booke of Confictionary is plainelie and perfittlie Set downe for Preserveinge dryinge or Candyinge of any sortes of plomes or of frutes whatsoever and for makinge of all sortes of dryd pastes or any other kind of Sugar woorkes beloning to ye Arte of a confectionary of Comfitte maker as ye Recetes in ye Booke followinge will derecte you. Manuscript in the possession of Elizabeth David. The recipes, entered in several hands, very nearly span the seventeenth century, I would say.

Lady Castlehill's Receipt Book: A Selection of Eighteenth-Century Scottish Fare. Hamish Whyte, ed. Glasgow: Moldendinar, 1976. It is to be noted that the fare is that of upper-class England of the same period.

Circa instans. A pharmaceutical work, our chief legacy from the School of Salerno, in two manuscripts: A, about A.D. 1190, and B, about 1200 to 1225, the two oldest extant copies (independently copied from earlier lost versions after the sacking of Salerno), both in the possession of the New York Botanical Garden Library. I hasten to add that it is Frank J. Anderson who is responsible for the information gleaned from that source for my work. He is preparing an annotated translation of the *Circa instans.*

A Collection of choise receipts . . . In two parts, each with index, (London ?), 1680. New York Academy of Medicine Library. The manuscript is in one hand, an italic script of exceptional quality for a family document, and is in every way a superb example of the collected recipe manuscript as distinguished from the accretive type (see page 451). Of the 390 recipes in Part I, perhaps 250 are culinary, most of them attributed, a number to I. H. (or J. H.), whom I take to be the collector. The date occurs well into Part II, which is medicinal in content. This collection is strikingly modern in comparison to the Washington manuscript, in language, in spelling, and above all in the actual culinary recipes. (Home medicine had changed less.) The medieval traces have all but disappeared; there are five recipes involving chocolate; and there is an early recipe for *Potatoe Bread,* which can only refer to white potatoes as five pounds are called for. (By this time, white potatoes were being cultivated in England; see page 86 and Forster, page 475.)

A Collection of Ordinances and Regulations for the Government of the Royal Household, Made in Divers Reigns, from King Edward iii to King William and Queen Mary. Also Receipts in Ancient Cookery [the Arundel MS., copied from an earlier work in about 1400]. London: Society of Antiquaries, 1790.

[Cookbook]. English, n.d. [seventeenth century]. New York Academy of Medicine Library.

Fettiplace, The Ladie Elynor: her Book. A manuscript dated 1604, in the possession of Hilary Spurling, who has published perhaps a score of the recipes in various articles in English journals. The entire manuscript deserves to be published.

Forme of Cury, The: A Roll of Ancient Cookery, compiled, about A.D. 1390 by the Master-Cooks of King Richard II . . . A Manuscript of the

Editor, *of the same Age [1381] and Subject is subjoined*. Samuel Pegge, ed. London, 1780. *Forme of Cury* (pronounced *kewry*) may be translated as method of cookery. The two documents are regarded as the earliest extant culinary works in English.

Jean Gemel (variously Joan Gembol, etc.), cookery manuscript, n.d. [I assign a date of mid-seventeenth century]. New York Academy of Medicine Library.

Harleian MSS. 279 and 4016, with excerpts from Ashmole MS. 1439, Laud MS. 553, and Douce MS. 55. In *Two Fifteenth-Century Cookery-Books*, Thomas Austin, ed. London: 1888, Early English Text Society, Oxford University Press, reprinted 1964. A scholarly transcription, with glossing, of inestimable value.

Husbandry and *Sòyle for an Orchard, Two Manuals of Gardening from English Manuscript Notebooks of the Seventeenth Century in the Library of Rachel McMasters Miller* Hunt. Pittsburgh: privately printed [by Yale University Press], 1952.

Thomas Jefferson's Garden Book, 1766–1824, Annotated by Edwin Morris Betts. Philadelphia: American Philosophical Society, 1944. No student of American food can afford to be without Jefferson's meticulously kept garden journal.

Liber Albus, The White Book of the City of London. Compiled 1419 by John Carpenter, Common Clerk, and Richard Whittington, Mayor. Translated from the original Latin and Anglo-Norman by Henry Thomas Riley. London, 1861.

Liber cure cocorum, copied and edited from Sloane MS. 1986 [about 1430] by Richard Morris. Philological Society, London, Asher, Berlin, 1862. This culinary work is couched in Northumberland dialect doggerel.

Libre de Sent Soví (archaic Catalan of uncertain meaning). A manuscript cookbook of the early fourteenth century with introduction and annotations (all in Catalan) by Rudolf Grewe. Barcelona: Editorial Barcino, 1979. It should be noted that Catalonian medieval cuisine was perhaps the most highly regarded in Europe; as late as 1474, this admiration is echoed in *Platina de honesta voluptate*.

Libre de Totes Maneres de Confits (Catalan, loosely meaning complete book of confectionery methods). Transcribed in Catalan and annotated in Spanish by Luis Faraudo de Saint-German. *Boletin de Buenas Letras de Barcelona*, Vol. XIX, 1947. The manuscript was last copied in the fifteenth century; the alternative methods of

Bibliography

honey and sugar for many of the recipes suggests an earlier date. Even so, it is an early example of a confectionery book.

Lucayos Cook Book, The: Being an Original Manuscript, 300 years old, never published. Found in the Bahamas. Kept . . . from A.D. *1660 to 1690 by a Noble Family of Elizabethan England.* Nassau, Bahamas, and Morrisburg, Ontario: Old Author's Farm, 1959. As noted (page 200) in the text, documentation is scanty, but the text rings true.

Manners and Household Expenses of England in the Thirteenth and Fifteenth Centuries. Household roll of Eleanor, Countess of Leicester, 1265; The expenses of Sir John Howard, 1462–1469. Roxburghe Club, London, 1841.

Mather, Cotton. *The Angel of Bethesda* [completed 1724], Gordon W. Jones, ed. American Antiquarian Society, Worcester, Mass., and Barre Publishers, Barre, Mass., 1972. The work, never published in its day, is thought to have been the only important medical treatise of colonial times. Mather was a zealot and his very name evokes dark pages of our history. He was, however, perhaps the first American member of the Royal Society and he fervently preached innoculation against smallpox at a time when it was considered the work of the devil. And I cite this moving observation from this work: "The poor Potters, and Plumbers, and Painters who are poisoned with Mineral Fumes; and the People, whose work is much about Quicksilver [mercury]; What shall be done for these, that they may not find their *Death* in their way of *Living?* Proper and early *Antidotes* must be thought upon." (Emphasis in original.) Such progress as we have made in this regard seems to have been in devising ever new ways of finding *Death* in our way of *Living.*

Le Ménagier de Paris . . . composé vers 1393, par un bourgeois parisien. Introduction and notes by Jérôme Pichon. Paris, n. d. [1846]; reprint, Luzarches, Daniel Morcrette, n. d. [about 1970]. The classic that illuminates so many details of daily life in medieval Paris concerning morality, shopping, cooking, and running of a bourgeois household.

A Noble Boke off Cookry FFor A Prynce Houssolde. Reprinted verbatim from a rare MS. in the Holkham Collection, edited by Mrs. Alexander Napier. London, 1882. The manuscript was copied about 1467 although the language indicates an earlier origin.

Northumberland Household Book. The Regulations and Establishment of the Household of Henry Algernon Percy . . . begun 1512. London, 1770.

Penn Family Recipes, Cooking Recipes of Wm. Penn's Wife, Gulielma. Evelyn Abraham Benson, ed. York, Pa.: George Shumway, 1966. A most interesting collection of English seventeenth-century recipes.

Price, Rebecca. Cookery manuscript kept from 1681 to 1740. Published as The Compleat Cook, compiled by Madeleine Masson. London: Routledge & Kegan Paul, 1974.

Randolph, Martha Jefferson. Cookery manuscript in the keeping of the Alderman Library, University of Virginia. It contains Jefferson family recipes going back to Monticello, some attributed to LeMaire, Jefferson's maître d'hôtel, and some as late as 1876. It thus spans nearly a century of the cooking of a prominent Virginia family; the decline over the years is striking.

[Recipes for foods and medicines.] English, seventeenth century (erroneously listed as eighteenth). MS. 186, New York Academy of Medicine Library.

Robertson, Christine, in possession of a family recipe manuscript in several hands, with occasional dates placing it in the eighteenth century and a bit beyond. A number of recipes are attributed to people of the various colleges at Oxford. Mrs. Robertson graciously allowed me to copy large parts of the manuscript.

Tirel, Guillaume, dit Taillevent . . . 1326–95 [chef to Charles V and Charles VI]. Le Viandier. Introduction and notes by Jérôme Pichon and Georges Vicaire. Paris, 1892; reprint: Luzarches: Daniel Morcrette, n.d. [about 1970]. The work consists of a transcription of what was then the oldest extant manuscript (in La Bibliothèque Nationale, about 1375), as well as parts of later manuscripts and a printed edition of about 1490. (Viand means meat in the medieval sense of food so that viandier means cook.)

Also, Un manuscrit valaisan du "Viandier" attribué à Taillevent, by Paul Aebischer in Vallesia, vol. 8, 1953, wherein he gives the text of a manuscript of about 1300 or earlier, patently the prototype of the Viandier penned a century later by Tirel. Clearly, he had simply made his own copy of an already classic work, modernizing the language slightly and inserting a few of his own favorite recipes but retaining the original order and titles. The incident is highly instructive to those who would study the history of cuisine.

Tyrell, The Lady: her book. Dated 1647. A book of cookery recipes compiled between 1647 and c.1677. MS. 558, Guildhall Library, London. Several hands are represented, and the work may be compared to the "inner pages" of our own manuscript with regard to both penmanship and content; the quality is not high.

Wightman, S.C. Cookery manuscript. New England, most likely Connecticut. Dated May 1824. In author's possession.

INDEX

491

Index

Index

503

Index

515